The Pawn Study Composer's Manual

Mikhail Zinar

New edition updated and edited by Sergei Tkachenko

The Pawn Study Composer's Manual
Author: Mikhail Zinar
New edition updated and edited by Sergei Tkachenko

Chess Editor: Anastasia Travkina
Translated from the Russian by Alexei Zakharov
Typesetting by Andrei Elkov
Front cover by Julia Ryzhova
© LLC Elk and Ruby Publishing House, 2022. All rights reserved
Second edition and first English edition
First edition published in Ukraine in 1990

Follow us on Twitter: @ilan_ruby
www.elkandruby.com
ISBN 978-5-6047848-1-5 (paperback); 978-5-6047848-4-6 (hardback)

CONTENTS

Foreword by the Editor

The idea of publishing a new, English edition of this book came up a few years before the death of the brilliant Ukrainian pawn studies expert and my close friend Mikhail Afanasievich Zinar (1950–2021). More than thirty years have passed since publication of the first edition of his book, titled in Russian *Harmony of the Pawn Study*, which enjoyed a print run of 100,000 copies. Much progress has been made in pawn endgame studies in the interim: new examples for the themes and chapters of the book have appeared. It would have been a shame had these new findings not been used in the updated work. New studies and examples (over 140 in total) are marked with ** after the position number.

Also, during that time, the so-called "logical study" arrived on the scene, which has since become the most popular genre of modern study composition. Therefore, I've added a new sub-chapter on the "logic" of pawn studies.

Additionally, Mikhail Afanasievich discovered a new idea in 2016 – the "Eilazyan branch", involving the particular features of a king double threat. Another sub-chapter for the new book was born!

Naturally, the dispassionate computer found various inaccuracies in the positions from the first edition: duals, side solutions, and even unsolvable positions. These defects had to be corrected where possible in the new work. In a few cases, I chose to retain studies that were instructive to the reader even when we found an irreparable flaw. Thus you will encounter a phenomenon that may surprise you: even prize winners of major composition tournaments of the past have proved cooked with the appearance of powerful computers.

Some structural changes were also made to the new edition, to align it with the expectations of the readership in the 2020s. Equally, all my changes have been integrated into the text unless otherwise indicated, as the intention is to provide the reader with an up-to-date, smoothly read manual. Therefore, unless otherwise indicated, references to "I" can normally be taken to come from Mikhail Zinar's pen except in this foreword and with reference to the studies that I added.

Mikhail Afanasievich was very enthusiastic about the idea of publishing a new edition of his book, first suggesting that we work on it together. However, I was busy with one of my historical works at the time and had to decline the Master's tempting offer.

We only returned to this subject several months before Zinar's death, delineating the areas of responsibility for the co-authors. Sadly, though, my friend left this world on 4th February 2021 after his lungs gave way (he was an inveterate smoker), and so I had to finish this work alone. You can read his fascinating life story in my book *Mikhail Zinar's Difficult Pawn Endings* published by Elk and Ruby in 2018, which contains 100 of his best studies.

The reader might ask why the name of chess composer Vladimir Mikhailovich Archakov (1938–2005) was included as a co-author in the 1990 edition but has disappeared from the cover of the current version. In my article "Kings of Chess Infantry" on the Chesspro website, I described the history of the publication of the first edition. The entirety of this book was written by Zinar. But how could he publish the precious work in conditions of collapse of the Soviet economy and, with it, of book publishing in general and chess book publishing in particular? Archakov, who had good connections with a publishing house, acted as the fixer back then. That cost Zinar his sole authorship, which is why I didn't transfer the name of Vladimir Archakov to the new edition's front cover...

And, of course, little did Mikhail expect his book to be updated in conditions of war, with my city being regularly bombed, which considerably slowed progress!

Sergei Tkachenko,
Odesa, Ukraine,
November 2022

Introduction

Congratulations on buying this book! It means that you maybe want to learn how to become a pawn studies composer! There is a long road ahead, and you need to start at the beginning. Once you grasp the concept of harmony of the pawn study you will have made substantial progress along your composition journey. So, let us first break down the concept's substance.

Harmony can be defined as the optimal balance of parts within a whole; a sufficient (but not excessive) number of components of an object or process that are required to ensure its successful existence.

Let's also think about why we refer to endgame studies as "compositions". The structural relationships between the parts of an object determine what we call a composition (especially in the various forms of creative art). Ideally, such a composition should be harmonious, in other words it is consistent with its intended criteria, and therefore aesthetic and beautiful. And being an art form, endgame studies naturally have specific features of compositions.

The requirements for harmonious composition naturally apply to the art of chess as well, but with some distinct differences. With a painting, for instance, we are looking at the result of the work, whereas in chess we are looking at the process – or, to be exact, at its external execution through some logical sequence of moves given a set balance of forces in the initial position.

During the battle between two opponents that unfolds on the chess board, the structure of play and its individual elements cannot be fully predetermined from the outset. Chess composition, on the other hand, uses the rules and patterns of the game (and sometimes others!), but is constructed by the author (or authors) in such a way that a sequence of only moves by both sides (this is what constitutes the composition's harmony) leads to the only possible predetermined or required result.

To better understand what chess composition is, what its main forms are and what harmony of the pawn study means, we now need to digress slightly and take a brief look at the history of chess.

Chess composition first emerged as a separate form of chess creativity at the turn of the 8th–9th century. What is known as a *mansuba* (plural – *mansubat*) first appeared during that period. Mansuba can be translated from Arabic as something that was erected, founded, or built. This term already established a divide between the nascent art of chess composition and chess play per se. Nevertheless, composed positions were tightly linked with practical play. They featured an excessive number of pieces and pawns and had an easy solution – the majority of mansubat can be compared to rather weak actual game fragments. Still, the mansubat not only served as training material for over-the-board play but also sowed the first seeds of chess composition aesthetics.

With time, chess composition got divided into orthodox composition (fully compliant with the rules of the game), unorthodox, fairy problems and special kinds. The required components of an orthodox composition are checkmate of the king as the goal, a board with pieces and pawns as material, and rules of chess as the means. The main tendency in modern chess composition has been the development of orthodox composition.

There are two kinds of chess composition: problems and studies.

A chess problem is a constructed position on the board where one side (usually white) checkmates the other side (black) in a certain number of moves. Therefore, the number of pieces and relative strength of the sides are not the defining features of problems. Black may only have a lone king, and white may still control his entire army – yet this is not what determines white's success. The main goal is to find some hidden way to checkmate the enemy king in a set number of moves.

An endgame study is also a constructed position, but, unlike a problem, it's more closely related to over-the-board endgames. It's white to move at the start of studies (unless it's specified that black is to move), but the goal of a study is not to give checkmate in a certain number of moves. Rather, it is simply to achieve a win (or a decisive advantage) or a draw. The number of moves (unlike in problems) is not specified. The starting position is subject to strict requirements – it must resemble as far as possible a position that could occur in an actual game.

However, an endgame study is *not* simply a position from a real endgame. In a game position, the possible end result can only be determined after analysis,

which is sometimes very difficult and painstaking. In a study, on the other hand, the result which is meant to occur when both sides make their best moves is already known.

It's much harder to solve a study than a problem. To find the solution, one needs to possess both a certain knowledge of theory and creative intuition. Compared with analysis of actual game positions, however, it's easier to solve a study, because the chances of both opponents are often unclear in games, whereas in studies white has a mathematically precise, only way to win or draw, which is unavoidable no matter what black attempts. In addition, an only winning move in an over-the-board game may be quite simple to find, whereas the key move of a study is always original, ingenious, involving subtle, hard-to-find moves and nuances.

Moreover, it's not necessary to use all the remaining pieces to achieve a win in an actual game; in an endgame study, however, *all* pieces on the board must be directly or indirectly involved in the solution. Any chess idea should be expressed in an artistic form and subject to formal requirements. What are these requirements?

Legality of the initial position

The initial position of the study must be reachable from the initial position of a real chess game. An example of an illegal position: white pawns on a2, a3 and b2 – it cannot be reached from the initial position.

Solvability

The goal of the study should be reached in all possible lines. If the goal cannot be reached in at least one of the lines, the whole study is unsolvable. An example of unsolvability: if we put the black king on c1 in **Study 1** of chapter I where white is supposed to play and win.

After 1.♔f7 ♔d2! 2.♔e6 ♔e3! 3.♔d5 ♔f4! 4.♔c6 ♔e5 5.♔b7 ♔d6 6.♔xa7 ♔c7, there's a draw. White failed to reach the goal — the position is unwinnable.

Uniqueness of the solution

The goal should be achieved in exactly one way. If there's another way, then the study has a side solution. For instance, if we remove the black e6 pawn in **Study 82**, also where white is supposed to play and win.

In addition to the author's solution, white can simply play 1.♔d3 ♔b3 2.g5, and the pawn promotes with check.

If the study fails to meet any of the above requirements, it has no right to exist.

In addition to the formal requirements, there are also some artistic requirements, but we shall discuss them later, after reading the main part of the book. First, let's study some special terms. Some of these terms are not used in this book, but you may encounter them elsewhere in your studies adventures.

Analytical study — a type of study where analytical elements prevail over artistic ones. Analytical studies are very close to endgames from real games. Therefore, such studies are often categorized as endgames that still comply with the requirement of the uniqueness of the solution.

Author's solution — the solution of the study that was intended by the author.

Blocked pawn — a pawn that is stopped by the opponent's pawn or piece standing immediately before it.

Dual — a partial side solution, i.e. a way to solve the study that begins after the first move in a way different from the author's solution. There may be acceptable or unacceptable duals in endgame studies, even though there's no consensus on that. Duals are allowed in non-thematic side-lines.

Epaulette mate — a position where a king gets checkmated on the edge of the board, with two of his own pieces (most often rooks) symmetrically taking away the escape squares on both sides. These pieces are called "epaulettes".

Flawed study — a position where the author's idea was found to be incorrect in some way: a side solution, unsolvability, illegal position, duals in thematic (idea) lines. Sometimes called a "cooked" study.

Harmonious piece play — the coordinated action of pieces that were logically positioned to convey the author's idea.

Idea of the study — the author's intention expressed in the composition's content. Ideas are divided into elementary and difficult ones. They may be borrowed from actual games, especially in study composition.

Ideal mate (stalemate) — see **Model mate (stalemate)**

Introductory play — the sequence of moves in a study that immediately precedes the implementation of the author's idea; it masks the main idea to make the study harder to solve. Nevertheless, introductory play should be organically linked to the main idea of the study.

Maneuver — one or more moves by one or more pieces of the same color to reach a concrete goal.

Mating finale — the final position of pieces and pawns on the board after a checkmating move.

Mating zone — chessboard squares around the checkmated king. A mating zone consists of four squares in the corner, of six squares on the edge of the board, and of nine squares otherwise.

Mirror mate (stalemate) — the final position of a study where all squares of the mating/stalemating zone are free of pieces and pawns of both players.

Model mate (stalemate) — a mating (or stalemating) position which is both economical and pure. All white pieces are involved in creating this mating/stalemating position, except for the king and the pawns due to their low mobility (the principle of economy). In addition, no square of the mating position is accessible to the black king for exactly one reason: which is either that the square is attacked by one (and only one) white piece, or because it is occupied by a black piece (the principle of purity). If absolutely all pieces and pawns on the board are involved in a model mate/stalemate then it is called an ideal mate/stalemate.

Naturalness of the initial position — one of the main aesthetic requirements for a chess composition; it follows the principle that the initial position should resemble an ending of an actual game as much as possible. This requirement is particularly strict for endgame studies. Only one set of pieces and pawns should be used in the initial position.

Parallel synthesis — branching of the solution into two or more separate continuations from the first or any subsequent moves; essentially, two or more studies blended into a single composition.

Point (or sometimes the French word *pointe* is used, meaning pinnacle) — the most hard-to-find, subtle or hidden move in a maneuver or combination. The term "key move", which is more appropriate for problems, is sometimes used as well.

Predecessor — a previously published study that is similar in idea, scheme and construction to a newly-published one.

Retrograde analysis (retroanalysis) — a special kind of chess composition. Retroanalysis is based on the restoration (full or partial) of a hypothetical game by identifying the previous moves of both sides; it is done to prove the legality of the starting position of the study or to determine the right to move, to castle or to capture a pawn en passant on the first move of the solution, etc.

Scheme — a position of the main pieces and pawns that allows the expression of the author's idea. The scheme still lacks many pieces and pawns that will be required later, to perfect the study. These additional pieces and pawns play auxiliary roles: they deprive the black king of free squares or liquidate various flaws (duals, side solutions, unsolvability), etc.

Serial synthesis — serial implementation of two ideas: during the first play (combination), white prepares the ground for the subsequent play. This transition from one play to another is characterized by an organic connection between them.

Side solution — achieving the goal set for a study in a thematic (idea) line beginning at any move in a way that is different from the author's intended solution.

Synthesis idea — a blend of several tactical ideas, maneuvers or tricks in the same study.

Task — a composition where the theme (idea) is expressed in the maximum possible amount of variations.

Technique — a purposeful move in a position that can be significant on its own or as part of a maneuver.

Threat — "a series of moves made only by white pieces (and, obviously, black's forced replies to checks) that lead to achievement of the goal." (L. Isaev.) The threat can be **forced** (a check is given), **active** (if black makes some indifferent move, white threatens to checkmate him on the next move), **passive** (using zugzwang) or **quiet** (disguised or hidden, when it will only be carried out after two or more moves).

In a study, there can also be further kinds of threats: to win a piece, to promote a pawn, etc.

Variation — repetition of the main idea of the study with a different material balance or piece position.

Winning a tempo — a tactical trick in a study that is implemented by performing certain maneuvers to weaken the opponent's position.

Zugzwang (German: forced to move) — a position on the chessboard where one side lacks any useful moves. Any move that is made leads to a drastic worsening of the position. There are no checks or threats in zugzwang. The idea of zugzwang is often used in endgame studies as a standalone theme.

If both sides lack useful moves, such a situation is called **mutual zugzwang**.

To avoid drowning in the ocean of studies, we only look at pawn studies in this work, and we only review the main study ideas, i.e. several themes. In pawn studies, where there are no other, more mobile pieces, the composer's intention is easier to perceive and evaluate, and the ideas sound loud and clear.

By thoroughly studying the material offered, understanding "what is good and what is not" and getting some useful advice, a beginning chess composer will be able to direct their creative energy towards the area of chess composition they like the most.

Moreover, since pawn endgame studies have much in common with over-the-board endgames, a thorough analysis of endgame studies will help you to improve your endgame play, which will surely improve your tournament results.

And so, dear friends, take only the kings and pawns out of your chess sets, and have a pleasant journey on the beautiful, albeit difficult, road to becoming a pawn study composer!

Chapter I

BASIC TACTICS OF PAWN STUDIES

Both in over-the-board play and chess composition, the times when chess fans were enraptured by the mere fact of sacrifices of pieces, especially the queen, have long passed. You cannot surprise anyone with that.

However, it's easy to spoil a good idea by tacking some crude, obvious sacrifices onto it. Subtle, disguised piece maneuvers, on the other hand, are valued much higher. The game plan is extremely important. An individual move in the winning line might seem unassuming, but when you remember the entire solution, you are amazed by the unusual path that allowed us to reach the goal.

In pawn studies, the main tactical role belongs to the kings, their maneuvers and techniques. The role of pawns, however, is very different. Due to the peculiarities of their movement – only forward – they lack the capacity to perform maneuvers. That said, they have three techniques at their disposal: sacrifice, loss of a tempo and underpromotion.

The king maneuvers can be divided into **specific** – used by composers to express certain ideas – and **universal**, which can be used to work on many different ideas.

The list of universal techniques includes:

Double threat – the king approaches two targets at once;

Shouldering – the king gets closer to its goal while stopping the opposing king from getting closer;

Triangulation – the king gives up the right to move with a maneuver on nearby squares in a zugzwang position;

Zugzwang sidestepping – the king approaches the target by sidestepping a zugzwang position;

Roundabout way – the king approaches the target by a longer trajectory than the shortest possible one to stop the opponent from strengthening his position;

Feint – a preliminary maneuver with a subsequent return to the initial (or a neighboring) square to provoke a weakness in the opponent's camp.

The first four of these six techniques are very well-studied and turned from study tricks into learning material a long time ago. The roundabout way and the feint, even though they have been used for a long time, have had no theoretical description and have not been studied deeply. They can still be considered study techniques. Other study techniques include specific maneuvers, which we shall cover later. They are the **Reti double threat** – a special case of double threat; the **Reti – Sarychevs feint** – a special case of feint; **luring** ("**attracting**" or "**decoying**") **into check**, the **anti-check retreat** and the **Grigoriev anti-check feint**. These techniques are only used in queening races.

Let's look at the universal maneuvers first.

1.1. Simplest maneuvers

This list includes **double threat, shouldering, triangulation** and **zugzwang sidestepping**.

The **double threat** occurs often and has already lost its aesthetic value. We will see this technique used repeatedly.

Shouldering is also a simple maneuver. For instance, it's hard to find a text book that doesn't feature **Study 1**.

No. 1. I. Maizelis, 1921

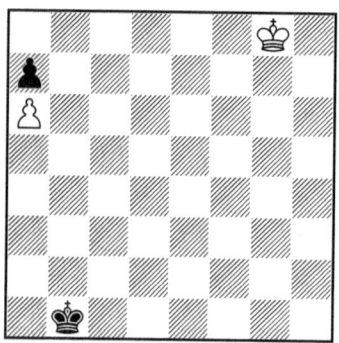

White to play and win

1.♔f7! ♚c2 2.♔e6! ♚d3

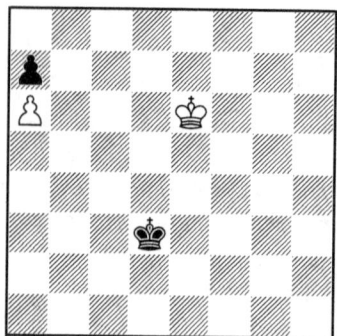

3.♔d5! By moving towards the a7 pawn in a polygonal line, the king used a "power move" to stop his opponent.

3...♚e3 4.♔c6 ♚d4 5.♔b7 ♚c5 6.♔xa7 ♚c6 7.♔b8, and wins.

This maneuver looks even more spectacular in **Study 2**. To push away the opponent's king, white moves towards f6 in a roundabout way, losing a tempo in the process.

No. 2. M. Zinar
64 – Shakhmatnoe Obozrenie, 1985

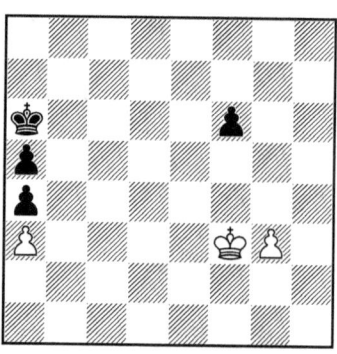

White to play and win

1.♔e4! ♚b5 2.♔d5! The direct attack on the pawn doesn't achieve anything: 2.♔f5? ♚c4 3.♔xf6 ♚b3 4.g4 ♚xa3 5.g5 ♚b4! 6.g6 a3 7.g7 a2 8.g8=♕ a1=♕+, and it's now white who has to scramble for a draw.

2...♚b6. If 2...f5, then 3.♔d4!, still pushing the king away.

3.♔e6! ♚c5 4.♔xf6 ♚c4

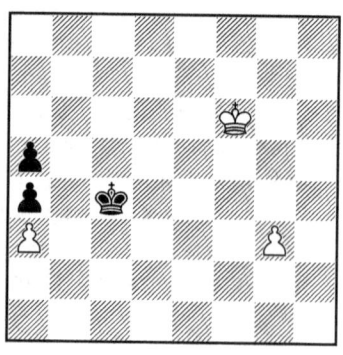

5.♔e5! That's why white didn't hurry with g3-g4: this move led to a draw in the "queen vs. a2 and a5 pawns" endgame. White loses tempi again!

5...♔b3 6.♔d4 ♔xa3 7.♔c3 ♔a2 8.♔c2 a3 9.g4 a4 10.g5 ♔a1 11.g6 a2 12.g7 a3 and white wins.

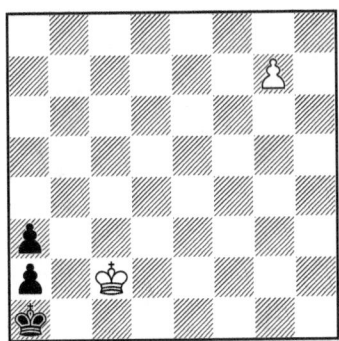

White has two winning lines here:

The fastest way to checkmate is 13.♔b3 ♔b1 14.g8=♕ a1=♕ 15.♕g1#;

Alternatively: 13.♔d2 ♔b2 14.g8=♕ a1=♕ 15.♕g7+ ♔b1 16.♕g6+ ♔a2 17.♕e6+ ♔b2 18.♕e5+ ♔a2 19.♕d5+ ♔b2 20.♕b5+ ♔a2 21.♕c4+ ♔b2 22.♕c2#! with an epaulette mate.

In theory, white could have promoted the pawn to a queen as early as on move 8 (see the false try – note the more usual term in studies is simply "try", but we prefer to call such a line a "false try" for clarity), but it required several more moves for white to win!

It might seem that the theme of shouldering has exhausted itself. But this is wrong! In this miniature **Study 3** (just four pieces!), white skillfully blocks the opponent by... moving away from the pawn!

No. 3**. J. Faucher
Chess Life & Review, 2004

White to play and win

1.♔c3!! Backing off from the pawn! Several false tries: 1.♔c4? ♔a3! 2.f4 ♔b2! 3.♔d5 ♔c3 4.♔e6 ♔d4 5.♔f6 ♔e4; 1.♔d4? ♔b3 2.f4 ♔c2! 3.♔e5 ♔d3 4.♔f6 ♔e4 and 1.f4? ♔b3! 2.♔d4 ♔c2 3.♔e5 ♔d3, with a draw in each case.

1...♔b5. Or 1...♔a3 2.f4 ♔a2 3.♔d4 ♔b3 4.♔e5 ♔c4 5.♔f6 etc.

2.♔d4! And now, full speed ahead!
2...♔c6 3.♔e5 ♔c5

4.f4! But not the hasty 4.♔f6? ♔d4! 5.♔xg6 ♔e3, and the white pawn falls.

4...♔c4 5.♔f6 ♔d5 6.♔xg6. White wins.

And here's how this idea was integrated with some subtle introductory play in the extensive **Study 4**.

No. 4**. V. Barsky
64 – Shakhmatnoe Obozrenie, 2009

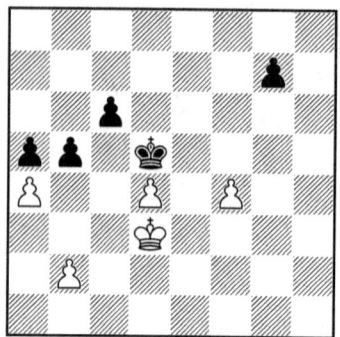

White to play and win

1.b4! There's no success without a breakthrough!

1...axb4 (1...bxa4 2.bxa5 a3 3.♔c2! c5 4.a6!) **2.a5 ♔d6.** 2...c5 loses quickly to 3.a6 c4+ 4.♔e3 ♔c6 5.d5+ ♔b6 6.d6 b3 7.d7 ♔c7 8.a7 etc.

3.♔c2 ♔c7 4.♔b3 ♔b7 5.♔xb4 ♔a7! 5...♔a6 6.f5 ♔b7 7.d5 ♔c7 (7...cxd5 8.♔xb5 d4 9.♔c4 ♔a6 10.♔xd4 ♔xa5 11.♔e5) 8.♔c5 cxd5 9.♔xd5 ♔b7 10.♔c5 ♔a6 11.♔b4 doesn't help, the mutual zugzwang is in white's favor.

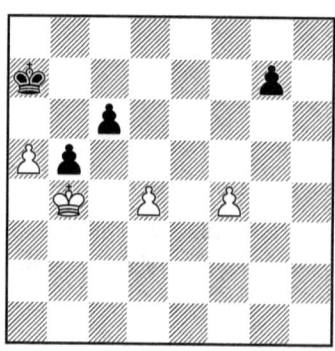

6.d5!! A false try: 6.f5? ♔a6 7.♔c5 ♔xa5 8.♔xc6 b4 9.d5 b3 10.d6 b2 11.d7 b1=♕ 12.d8=♕+ ♔a4 13.♕a8+ ♔b3 14.♕b7+ ♔a2 15.♕xb1+ ♔xb1 16.♔d5 ♔c2 17.♔e6 ♔d3 18.♔f7 ♔e4 19.♔xg7 ♔xf5, just in time!

6...cxd5 (6...♔b7 7.d6) **7.♔xb5 d4 8.♔c4 ♔a6 9.♔xd4 ♔xa5.**

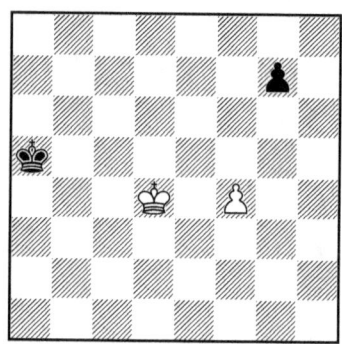

Now a raid for the pawn misses the win: 10.♔e5? ♔b5 11.♔e6 ♔c5 12.♔f7 ♔d5 13.♔xg7 ♔e4 or 10.♔c5? ♔a4!! 11.f5 ♔b3 12.♔d6 ♔c3 13.♔e6 ♔d4 14.♔f7 ♔e5, draw.

Therefore, white should shoulder the black king: **10.♔c4!! ♔a4.** Neither 10...♔b6 11.♔d5 ♔c7 12.♔e6 ♔c6 13.f5 nor 10...g6 11.♔d5 ♔b5 12.♔e5 helps.

11.f5! ♔a3 12.♔d5! Now it is time!

12...♔b4 13.♔e6 ♔c4 14.♔f7 ♔d4 15.♔xg7. White wins. Interestingly, this study grew out of an analysis of the ending of the game Listengarten – Chepukaitis (Baku 1957).

Let's look at another miniature, **Study 5**. The four pieces perform a small show: "How to Avoid the Opponent's Shouldering"!

No. 5**. M. Zinar
Topko JC, 2015
Special prize

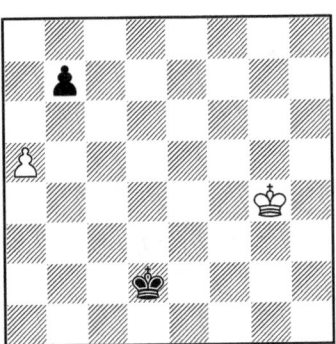

White to play and draw

No. 6**. P. Arestov
Zadachi i Etyudy, 2019
1st honorable mention

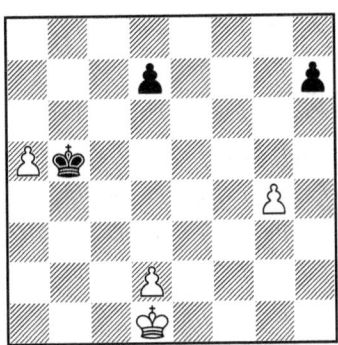

White to play and win

The top breakthrough leads to disaster: 1.♔f5? ♔c3! 2.♔e5 ♔b4 etc. The bottom breakthrough is equally bad: 1.♔f3? ♔d3! (the first shouldering!) 2.♔f2 ♔c4 3.a6 bxa6 4.♔e2 ♔c3 5.♔d1 ♔b2! (and the second!), and the white king will not reach the coveted corner.

Therefore, the middle way is correct: **1.♔f4! ♔c3.** After 1...♔d3, the top breakthrough becomes possible: 2.♔e5! ♔c4 3.♔d6 ♔b5 4.♔c7 etc.

2.♔e3! ♔b4 3.a6! bxa6 4.♔d2 ♔b3 5.♔c1! And now it's the white king who deprives its opponent of the key b2 square. Draw.

And here's another modern spectacle where the white king keeps its counterparty from closing the distance.

The short way towards the black h7 pawn brings no joy: 1.♔e2? ♔xa5 2.♔e3 ♔b4! 3.♔f4 ♔c4 4.♔g5 ♔d3 5.♔h6 ♔e4 6.♔xh7 ♔f4, and the white passer falls.

It's necessary to shoulder the king: **1.♔c2!! ♔xa5 2.♔c3!** 2.♔d3? ♔b4 3.♔d4 ♔b3 4.♔d5 ♔c2 is good for black, with a draw.

2...♔b5 3.♔d4 ♔c6 4.♔e5 d6+ 5.♔f6 ♔d5

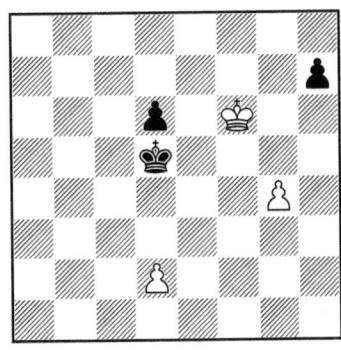

6.d3!! The way to the pawn is blocked: 6.♔g7? ♔e5 7.♔xh7 ♔f4. Also, 6.g5? ♔e4 7.d3+ ♔f4 8.d4 d5 9.♔e6 ♔xg5 10.♔xd5 h5 is no better: the pawns promote at the same time.

6...♚d4 7.g5 ♚e3 (7...♚xd3 8.♚g7 d5 9.♚xh7 d4 10.g6) **8.d4! ♚e4! 9.d5! ♚f4 10.♚e6! ♚xg5 11.♚xd6,** and the d-pawn promotes. White wins. A subtle miniature!

Shouldering looks most spectacular in conjunction with other themes and ideas. **Study 7** is great evidence for that.

No. 7**. P. Arestov
Artistic King and Pawns tourney, 2017
Prize

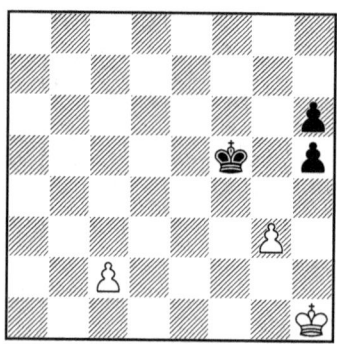

White to play and win

1.♚h2!! Not 1.♚g2? h4! 2.gxh4 ♚g4 3.c4 h5 (or 3...♚f4 4.♚h3 h5 5.♚g2 ♚g4 6.♚f2 ♚f4) 4.♚f2 ♚f4 5.♚e2 ♚e4 6.♚d2 ♚d4 with a series of drawn oppositions in mutual zugzwang.

1...h4! 2.gxh4 ♚g4 3.c4! (3.♚g2? ♚xh4) **3...♚f4!** Or 3...h5 4.♚g2 ♚f4 5.♚f2 ♚g4 6.♚e3 ♚xh4 7.♚f4 ♚h3 8.c5 h4 9.c6, and wins.

4.♚g2! Mutual zugzwang! A thematic false try: 4.♚h3? h5! 5.c5 ♚e5 6.♚g3 ♚d5 7.♚f4 ♚xc5 8.♚g5 ♚d6! 9.♚xh5 ♚e7! 10.♚g6 ♚f8 11.h5 ♚g8,

and the black king sneaks into the saving corner.

4...♚e4! (4...h5 5.♚f2! ♚e4 6.♚g3! ♚f5 7.♚f3 ♚e5 8.♚e3)

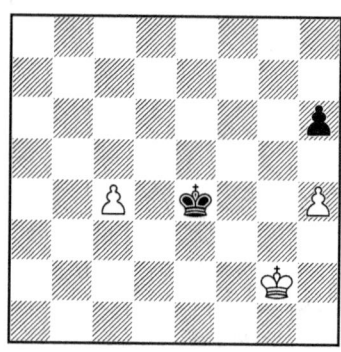

5.♚h3!! Another feint to the right! After 5.♚g3? h5!, white is in zugzwang! 6.c5 ♚d5 7.♚f4 ♚xc5 8.♚g5 ♚d6! 9.♚xh5 ♚e7! with the familiar draw. 5.♚f2? is also bad: 5...♚d4! 6.♚f3 ♚xc4 7.♚g4 ♚d5, draw.

5...h5 (5...♚d4 6.♚g4) **6.♚g3!** Another zugzwang that's good for white!

6...♚e5 (6...♚f5 7.♚f3 ♚e5 8.♚e3) **7.♚f3 ♚d4 8.♚f4 ♚xc4 9.♚g5 ♚d5 10.♚xh5 ♚e6 11.♚g6!** In contrast to the false try, white now manages to shoulder the black king!

11...♚e7 12.♚g7! Another tackle!

12...♚e6 13.h5 ♚f5 14.h6. White wins.

One of the most difficult areas of chess theory is **corresponding squares**. It's an entire field of science! Research on that subject was published in the book by Grandmaster Yuri Averbakh *Shakhmatnye Okonchaniya* (*Chess Endgames*), Moscow, Fizkultura i Sport, 1983, chapter 10.

In the foreword to his book, Averbakh wrote, "The tenth chapter, devoted to the theory of corresponding squares, was written by chess composer M. A. Zinar, a great expert on pawn endgames. Otherwise, this chapter would have looked obsolete."

In this book, we try to explain the theory of corresponding squares in the simplest way possible.

Positions with mutual zugzwang often occur in pawn endgames. If there are two or more of these positions, the neighboring squares may also lead to a zugzwang, or, as it's said in chess, they may be "corresponding" squares. Corresponding zones, therefore, may cover huge swaths of the board, which makes maneuvering extremely difficult. To make it easier, there are certain rules for finding the "corresponding systems".

Every system has its own "markings" (corresponding squares are marked with the same numbers) and its own features. One can seize the corresponding square and then, maneuvering in such a way as to put one's king onto the "number" that's occupied by the opponent or not available to him, get closer to the main zugzwang positions and make a breakthrough in one area of the board.

But we will take a look at a few studies with corresponding squares later. Meanwhile, we now look at simple cases of zugzwang, where there's only a single mutual zugzwang position, as shown in the examples below.

There's a mutual zugzwang in **Position 8**, and so white needs to give up the turn to move to black. Here's how it's done.

No. 8. B. Horwitz, 1879

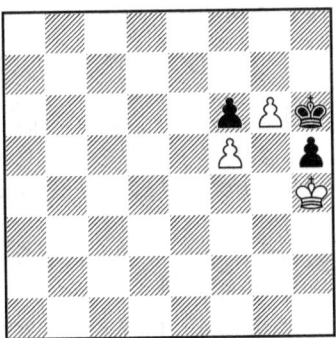

White to play and win

1.♔g3(h3) ♔g7 2.♔h3(g3) ♔h6 3.♔h4, winning a pawn and then the game, after the white king moves to the center. This technique is called **triangulation**.

To be precise, note that the German chess player Bernhard Horwitz never composed such a study. **Position 8** occurs in a proof line of one of his compositions.

A curious incident happened in a game between two well-known players who apparently didn't know the principles of triangulation **(Position 9)**.

No. 9**. L. Yudasin – V. Osnos
Leningrad 1987

Here's how this moment was described by GM Adrian Mikhalchishin in his article "Typical Errors" (*64 – Shakhmatnoe Obozrenie*, No. 6, 2007):

"Yudasin played **1.♔f2** and offered a draw, saying that this was a well-known position featured in text books, and that it was drawn!

The experienced master [playing black] was shocked by his own 'lack of knowledge' and immediately agreed to a draw. However, it is known that after **1...♔e4 2.♔e2 f4 3.♔f2 f3 4.♔f1,** black wins with a king triangulation – e5-f5-e4. It turns out that not everyone knows that!"

The triangulation technique by itself has little artistic value. But it meshes extremely well with other ideas. In **Study 10,** the tempo loss with triangulation is preceded by a spectacular pawn breakthrough. The subsequent post-triangulation play is interesting as well.

No. 10**. V. Kovalenko
64 – Shakhmatnoe Obozrenie, 2003
5th honorable mention

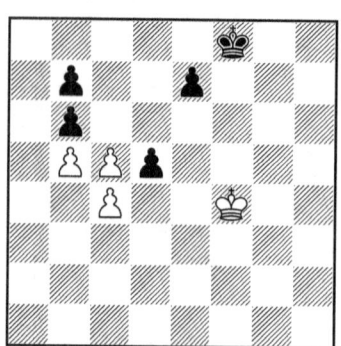

White to play and win

Full speed ahead: **1.c6! bxc6 2.c5! ♔e8!** (2...cxb5 3.cxb6; 2...bxc5 3.b6) **3.cxb6 ♔d7 4.b7! ♔c7 5.bxc6 d4!**

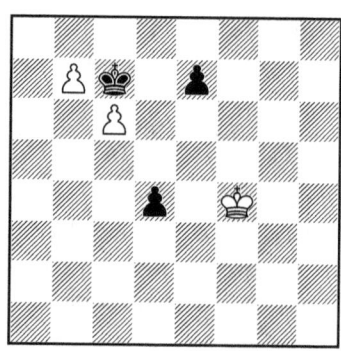

6.♔f3!! A thematic false try: 6.♔e4? e5 (mutual zugzwang) 7.♔d3 ♔b8 8.♔c4 ♔c7 9.♔b5 d3 10.♔a6 d2 11.♔a7 d1=♕ 12.b8=♕+ ♔xc6 13.♕b6+ ♔d7! with equality.

6...e6 7.♔f4! e5+ 8.♔e4! White has given up the right to move to his opponent, putting him in zugzwang.

8...♔b8 9.♔d3! Around is the only way! The shortcut to d6 is lethal: 9.♔d5? d3 10.♔d6 d2, and it's black who wins.

9...♔c7 10.♔c4 ♔b8 11.♔b5! ♔a7. Or 11...d3 12.♔b6 d2 13.c7#.

12.♔c5 d3

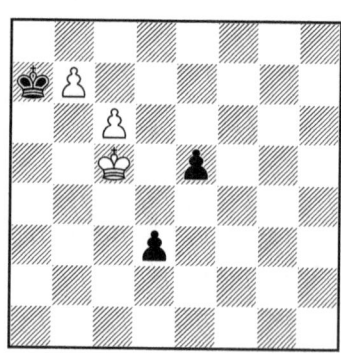

13.♔d6! The white monarch has broken through to d6 in a roundabout way, pushing its counterpart to a7.

13...d2 (13...♔b8 14.♔d7 d2 15.c7+) **14.♔c7! d1=♕ 15.b8=♕+.** White wins.

That said, triangulation can still emerge as the main theme of the study, if this technique is performed several times. A large number of triangulations is shown in **Study 11.**

No. 11**. M. Zinar
A. Beliavsky — 80 JC, 2015
Special honorable mention

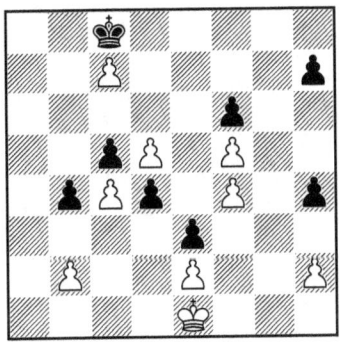

White to play and win

After **1.d6,** the play branches:

A) **1...b3 2.h3! ♔d7 3.♔f1 ♔c8 4.♔g1! ♔d7 5.♔g2 ♔c8 6.♔f3 ♔d7**

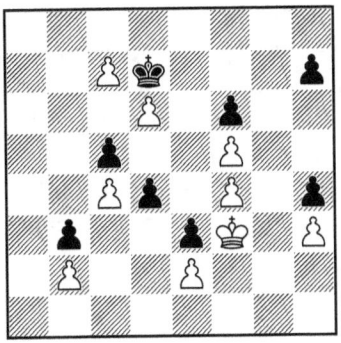

7.♔e4. The first basic stance!

7...h6 8.♔f3! The king returns to the first rank, losing a tempo thanks to triangulation. **8...♔c8 9.♔g2 ♔d7 10.♔f1(g1) ♔c8 11.♔g1(f1) ♔d7 12.♔g2 ♔c8 13.♔f3 ♔d7**

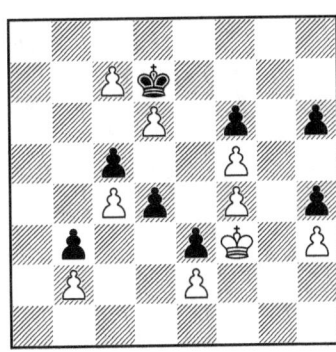

14.♔e4! The second opposition!

14...h5 15.♔f3! ♔c8 16.♔g2 ♔d7 17.♔f1(g1) ♔c8 18.♔g1(f1) ♔d7 19.♔g2 ♔c8 20.♔f3 ♔d7

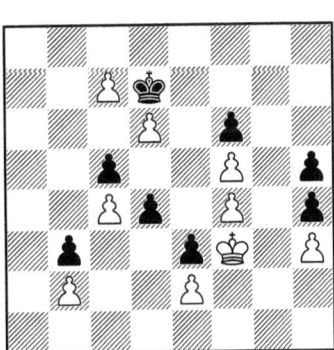

21.♔e4! And the third! Black has no more pawn tempi and is forced to move his king due to zugzwang.

21...♔c8 22.♔d5 ♔d7 (22...d3 23.♔c6 d2 24.d7# or 22...♔b7 23.♔e6 d3 24.♔d7) **23.♔xc5 d3 24.♔b6 d2 25.♔b7 d1=♕ 26.c8=♕+** with a mate next move;

B) **1...h3 2.b3! ♔d7 3.♔d1 ♔c8
4.♔c1 ♔d7 5.♔c2 ♔c8 6.♔d3 ♔d7**

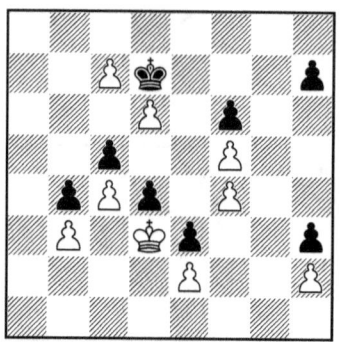

7.♔e4! One!

7...h6 8.♔d3! But not 8.♔d5? d3
9.♔xc5 dxe2 10.♔b6 e1=♕ 11.♔b7
♕h1+, curtains.

**8...♔c8 9.♔c2 ♔d7 10.♔c1(d1)
♔c8 11.♔d1(c1) ♔d7 12.♔c2 ♔c8
13.♔d3 ♔d7**

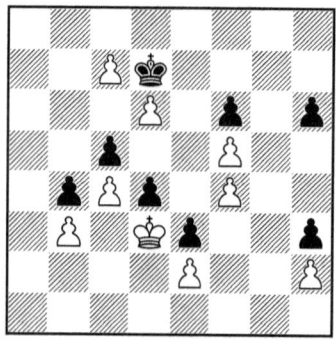

14.♔e4! Two!

**14...h5 15.♔d3 ♔c8 16.♔c2 ♔d7
17.♔c1(d1) ♔c8 18.♔d1(c1) ♔d7
19.♔c2 ♔c8 20.♔d3 ♔d7**

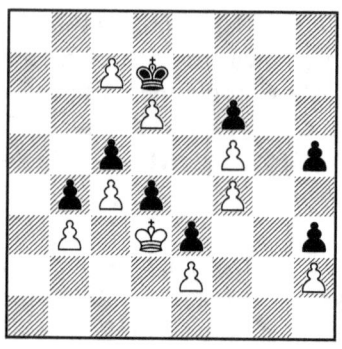

21.♔e4! Three!

**21...h4 22.♔d3 ♔c8 23.♔c2 ♔d7
24.♔c1(d1) ♔c8 25.♔d1(c1) ♔d7
26.♔c2 ♔c8 27.♔d3 ♔d7**

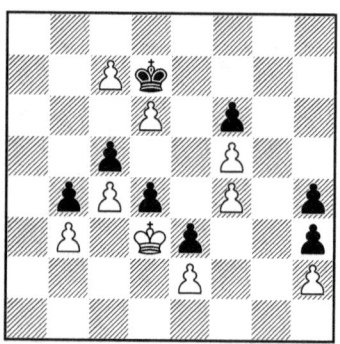

28.♔e4! Four!

**28...♔c8 29.♔d5 ♔d7 30.♔xc5
d3 31.♔b6 dxe2 32.♔b7 e1=♕
33.c8=♕+.** White wins.

White continuously loses tempi with
triangulations, and this trick is shown in
two parallel lines. Such serial/parallel
synthesis had never occurred before.
A strict critic might point out that the
white king has a choice of move order
when it performs triangulations. Yes —
alas, these are organic duals inherent in
studies with so many repeat maneuvers.

There are duals in **Study 12** as well,
which stretches for 77 moves! The

black pawns lose all the tempi in the meantime. And the reason for their plight is that the white king performs six triangulations.

No. 12**. M. Zinar
Victory competition, 2020
Special honorable mention

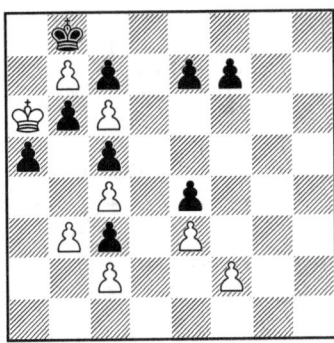

White to play and win

The white king cannot move to the kingside to get rid of the black pawns because black will break through on the queenside. How can he win then? With triangulation!

1.♔b5! ♔a7 2.♔a4 ♔b8 3.♔a3 ♔a7 4.♔a2 ♔b8

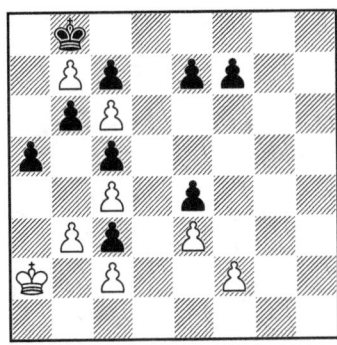

5.♔a1. Here and later, there are some organic duals: 5.♔b1 ♔a7 6.♔a1 ♔b8 7.♔a2 etc.

5...♔a7 6.♔b1 ♔b8 7.♔a2! Not 7.♔c1? ♔a7 8.♔d1 ♔b8 9.♔e2 ♔a7 10.f3? exf3+ 11.♔xf3 b5 12.cxb5 c4 13.♔e2 f5 14.bxc4 e5 15.♔d3 a4, and black wins.

7...♔a7 8.♔a3 ♔b8 9.♔a4 ♔a7 10.♔b5 ♔b8

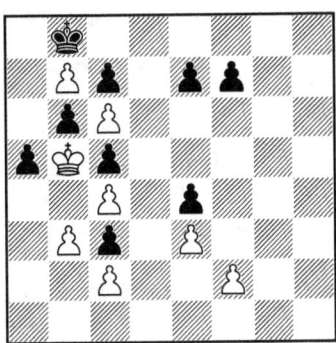

11.♔a6! The initial position repeats, but now it's black to move.

And now, white slowly devours the tempi of the black infantry...

11...e6 12.♔b5! ♔a7 13.♔a4 ♔b8 14.♔a3 ♔a7 15.♔a2 ♔b8 16.♔b1 ♔a7 17.♔a1 ♔b8 18.♔a2 ♔a7 19.♔a3 ♔b8 20.♔a4 ♔a7

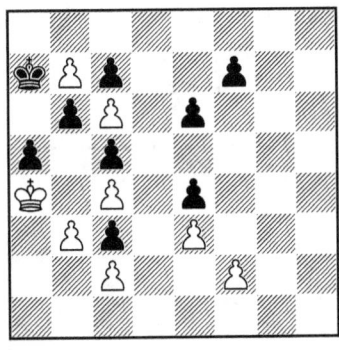

21.♔b5 ♔b8 22.♔a6 e5 23.♔b5 ♔a7 24.♔a4 ♔b8 25.♔a3 ♔a7 26.♔a2 ♔b8 27.♔b1 ♔a7 28.♔a1 ♔b8 29.♔a2 ♔a7 30.♔a3 ♔b8

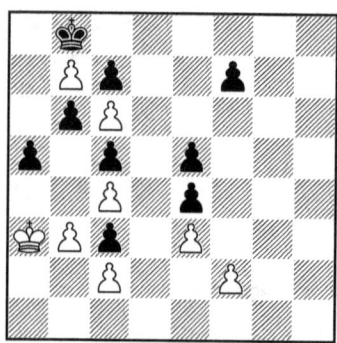

31.♔a4 ♚a7 32.♔b5 ♚b8 33.♔a6 f6 34.♔b5 ♚a7 35.♔a4 ♚b8 36.♔a3 ♚a7 37.♔a2 ♚b8 38.♔b1 ♚a7 39.♔a1 ♚b8 40.♔a2 ♚a7

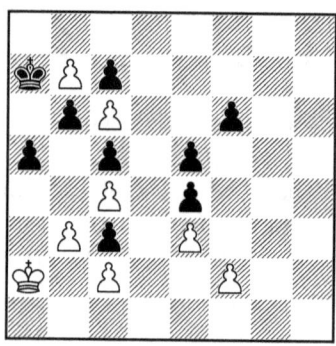

41.♔a3 ♚b8 42.♔a4 ♚a7 43.♔b5 ♚b8 44.♔a6 f5 45.♔b5 ♚a7 46.♔a4 ♚b8 47.♔a3 ♚a7 48.♔a2 ♚b8 49.♔b1 ♚a7 50.♔a1 ♚b8

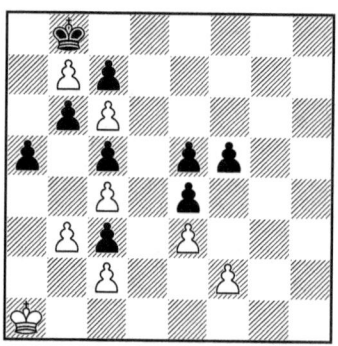

51.♔a2 ♚a7 52.♔a3 ♚b8 53.♔a4 ♚a7 54.♔b5 ♚b8 55.♔a6 f4 56.♔b5 ♚a7 57.♔a4 ♚b8 58.♔a3 ♚a7 59.♔a2 ♚b8 60.♔b1 ♚a7

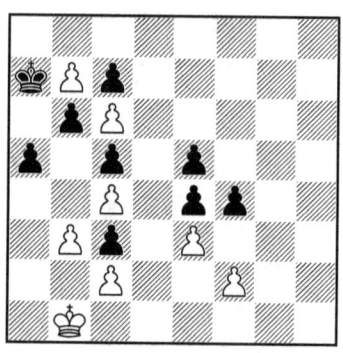

61.♔a1 ♚b8 62.♔a2 ♚a7 63.♔a3 ♚b8 64.♔a4 ♚a7 65.♔b5 ♚b8 66.♔a6 f3 67.♔b5 ♚a7 68.♔a4 ♚b8 69.♔a3 ♚a7 70.♔a2 ♚b8

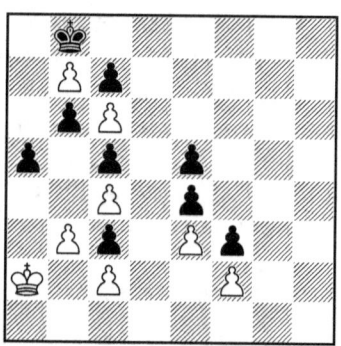

71.♔b1 ♚a7 72.♔a1 ♚b8 73.♔a2 ♚a7 74.♔a3 ♚b8 75.♔a4 ♚a7 76.♔b5 ♚b8 77.♔a6! Black has no more pawn tempi! White wins.

Nevertheless, it's even possible to avoid duals! Ten precise triangulations of the king (a record, as of today!) are presented in **Study 13**.

No. 13**. M. Zinar
V. Tarasiuk — 50 JC, 2018
Special prize

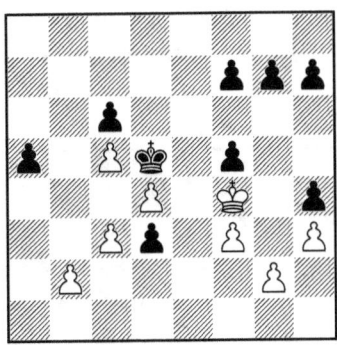

White to play and win

First of all, the black kingside pawns have to be neutralized...

1.♔e3 ♔c4 2.♔d2 a4

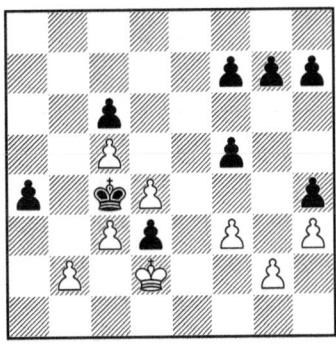

3.♔c1! White even loses after 3.♔e3? a3! 4.bxa3 ♔xc3 etc. 3.♔d1? doesn't win either: 3...♔b3 (the simplest) 4.d5 ♔xb2 5.dxc6 a3 6.c7 a2 7.c8=♕ a1=♕+ 8.♔d2 ♕c1+ with perpetual check.

3...♔d5. And now 3...♔b3 doesn't help: 4.d5 d2+ 5.♔xd2 ♔xb2 6.dxc6 a3 7.c7 a2 8.c8=♕, curtains.

4.♔d1 ♔c4 5.♔d2 f6 6.♔c1! ♔d5 7.♔d1 ♔c4 8.♔d2 f4

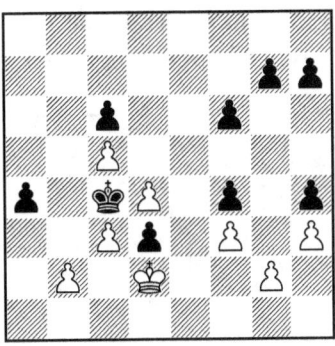

9.♔c1! ♔d5 10.♔d1 ♔c4 11.♔d2 f5 12.♔c1! ♔d5 13.♔d1 ♔c4 14.♔d2 g6 15.♔c1! ♔d5 16.♔d1 ♔c4 17.♔d2 g5 18.♔c1! ♔d5 19.♔d1 ♔c4 20.♔d2 g4

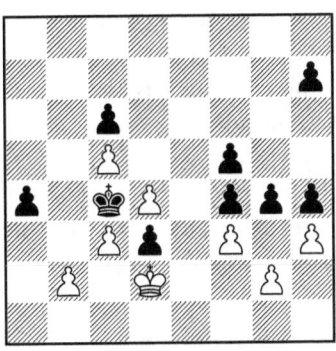

21.♔c1! ♔d5 22.♔d1 ♔c4 23.♔d2 g3 24.♔c1! ♔d5 25.♔d1 ♔c4 26.♔d2 h6 27.♔c1! ♔d5 28.♔d1 ♔c4 29.♔d2 h5 30.♔c1 ♔d5 31.♔d1 ♔c4 32.♔d2! The last repetition! Black is out of waiting moves...

32...♔d5 33.♔xd3. White wins. A fascinating mechanism!

However, triangulation does not always work. In such cases, white has other ideas, for instance, **sidestepping**.

The sidestepping technique is well illustrated by **Study 14**.

No. 14. M. Zinar
Krymskaya Pravda, 1984

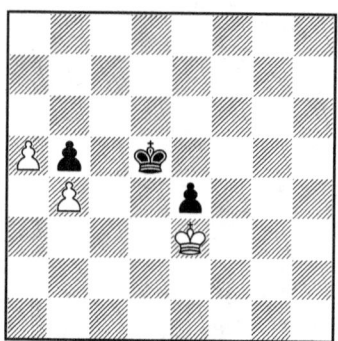

White to play and win

It's impossible to give up the right to move with triangulation: we maneuver on the d2 and e2 squares, but the black king moves to c6 or d6. Attacking the pawn from f4 can help, but you should keep in mind that in the position with white ♔g3 and black ♚d5, the white king cannot get to the fourth rank due to ♚d5–d4. Only zugzwang sidestepping does the trick.

1.♔f2 ♚c6 2.♔g2! ♚d6 3.♔h3! ♚c6 4.♔g4! ♚d5 5.♔g3! ♚c6 6.♔f4 ♚d5 7.♔e3! with a win. White spent seven moves to finally give up the right to move!

Note that the moves 1.♔e2 and 1.♔d2 could also be played at the beginning. However, these moves only serve to prolong the game artificially, as only the author's king maneuver leads to a win. The route in the solution is the shortest way to victory.

A similar sidestep of the zugzwang position is performed in the classic **Study 15**, but here, the play is irreversible. In other words, if the white king gets to e4

first, and then the black king moves to e6, it's a draw.

No. 15. N. Grigoriev
La Strategie, 1936
5th honorable mention
(corrected)

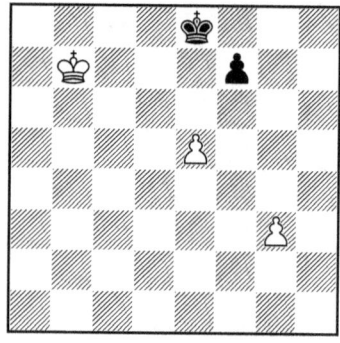

White to play and win

1.♔c6 ♚e7 2.♔d5 ♚d7 3.♔d4 ♚e7

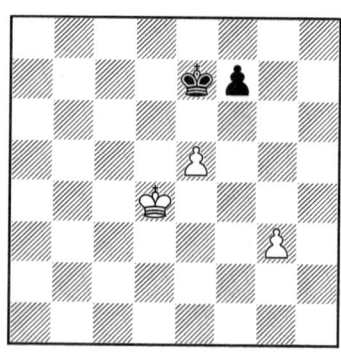

4.♔e3! ♚d7 5.♔f4 ♚e6 6.♔e4 ♚d7 7.♔f5 ♚e7 8.g4 ♚e8 9.♔f6 ♚f8 10.g5 ♚e8 11.♔g7 ♚e7 12.♔g8 ♚e8 13.e6! with a win.

Zugzwang (and, subsequently, the sidestep maneuver) unexpectedly appears in **Study 16**.

No. 16. N. Grigoriev
64, 1931

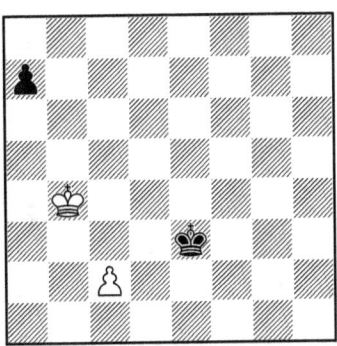

White to play and win

1.c4 ♔d4 2.c5 ♔e5! Another continuation is also interesting: 2...a5+ 3.♔b5 a4 4.c6 a3 5.c7 a2 6.c8=♕ a1=♕ 7.♕h8+ with a win.

3.♔a5! ♔e6 4.♔a6! ♔d5 5.♔b5! Black is in zugzwang, and white wins.

There can follow **5...♔e5** (or 5...♔e6 6.♔c6, and at the end of the line the black king gets checked by the newborn white queen) **6.♔c6 a5 7.♔b7(b6, d7) a4 8.c6 a3 9.c7 a2 10.c8=♕ a1=♕ 11.♕h8+**, curtains.

We have examined some instructive positions that are still artistically valuable even in our times, because good knowledge of them will allow you to understand endgame studies better and will make composing easier.

Additionally, when these techniques are woven into the study's canvas, they add a "game-like" character to any study, eliminating the "schematic" character of some ideas. This is especially true for the "roundabout way" and "feint" techniques, which haven't reached the status of "textbook ideas" yet.

1.2. Roundabout way

No. 17. F. Cassidy
The Chess Monthly, 1884

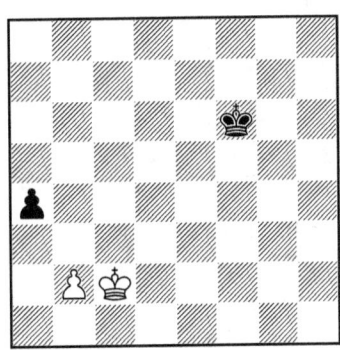

White to play and win

1.♔b1! An amazing move! The king chooses the longest possible way towards the pawn. However, 1.♔c3? is met with 1...a3!, and black is safe.

1...a3! 2.b3! But not 2.b4? ♔e7 3.♔a2 ♔d6 4.♔xa3 ♔c6 5.♔a4 ♔b6!, with a draw.

2...♔e7 3.♔a2 ♔d6 4.♔xa3 ♔c6 5.♔a4! The continuation 5.♔b4? missed the win – 5...♔b6! etc.

5...♔b6 6.♔b4!, and the opposition is achieved. In this case, the roundabout way was chosen because white was concerned about a4-a3.

It was previously believed that the authorship of this study belonged to F. Dedrle, who ostensibly published his discovery in 1921. This study was actually composed by F. Cassidy back in 1884, and Dedrle only skillfully added one brilliant move to the already-known idea! Here's his version:

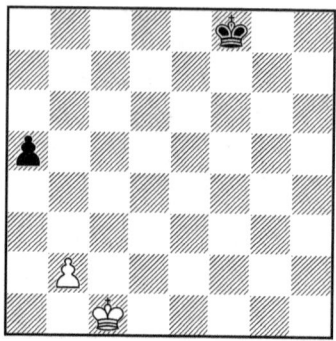

1.♔c2!! a4! 2.♔b1! etc.

In 1927, Alexei Troitsky added an exchange introduction to Dedrle's position, and in 1952, Josef Moravec of Czechoslovakia made a mirror copy of the 1921 position.

In the next study, white is worried about a black king move, rather than a pawn one.

No. 18. M. Zinar
Shakhmaty v SSSR, 1988

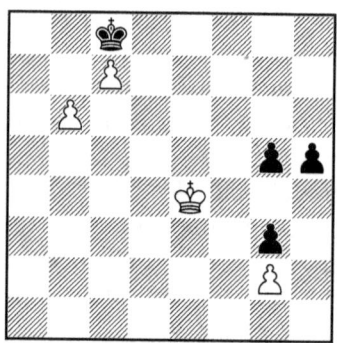

White to play and win

If 1.♔d5?, then 1...♔d7 with a draw. The correct move is **1.♔f5! h4 2.♔e6! h3 3.♔d6 hxg2 4.♔c6 g1=♕ 5.b7#.** White reaches the c6 square in four moves instead of two!

The theme of the roundabout way was expressed well in the following study.

No. 19. M. Zinar
64 – Shakhmatnoe Obozrenie, 1985

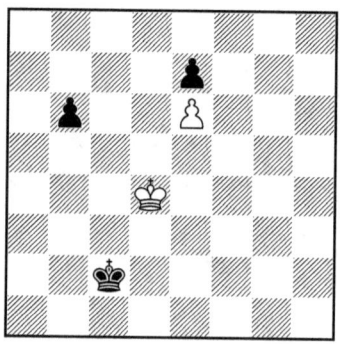

White to play and draw

The straightforward 1.♔d5? loses to 1...b5! 2.♔c5 ♔c3 3.♔xb5 ♔d4, shouldering the white king.

The correct move is **1.♔c4! ♔d2 2.♔b5 ♔d3 3.♔c6! b5 4.♔d7** with a draw.

1.3. Feint

The feint technique appears much more often.

No. 20. M. Zinar
Shakhmaty v SSSR, 1985

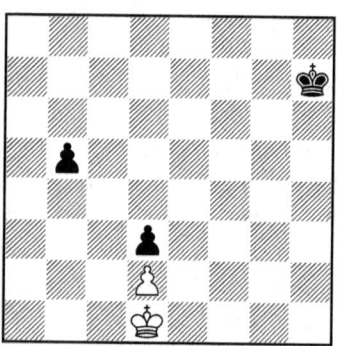

White to play and draw

It's obvious that white should not forget about the b5 pawn. The natural 1.♔c1? is met with the immediate 1...♔g6 2.♔b2 ♔f5 3.♔b3 ♔f4 4.♔c3 ♔e4 5.♔b4 ♔f3, and black wins. Therefore, white should first create threats to the d3 pawn.

1.♔e1! Now 1...♔g6 is bad due to 2.♔f2, and the pawn falls. Black has to weaken his position.

1...b4. Now the attack 2.♔f2? does not work due to 2...b3! But this is exactly what white was counting on: he's going back to the initial square.

2.♔d1!! ♔g6. White has lost two whole tempi! But...

3.♔c1 ♔f5 4.♔b2 ♔e4 5.♔b3 ♔f3 6.♔xb4

And since 6...♔f2? 7.♔c4! ♔e2 8.♔c3! now even loses, black is forced to make a draw with 6...♔e4 (or 6...♔f4).

Without a doubt, the feint technique is aesthetic because of the comeback element.

A feint can consist of several moves as well. Here are some more simple examples to make understanding easier. **Study 21** is similar to the previous one.

No. 21. M. Zinar
Shakhmaty v SSSR, 1986

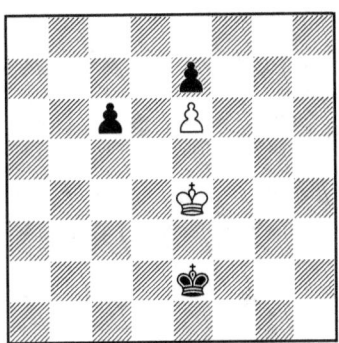

White to play and draw

1.♔d4? loses: 1...♔f3 2.♔c5 ♔e4 3.♔xc6 ♔e5 4.♔c5 (4.♔d7 ♔f6, and wins) 4...♔xe6 5.♔d4 ♔f5 etc.

The correct move is **1.♔f5! c5 2.♔e4!** And now, after the feint, there's shouldering.

2...♔f2 3.♔d5 ♔f3 4.♔xc5 ♔e4 5.♔c4! ♔e5 6.♔d3 ♔xe6 7.♔e4, with a theoretical draw.

No. 22. M. Zinar
Shakhmaty v SSSR, 1985

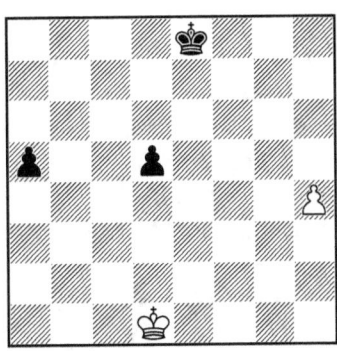

White to play and draw

1.♔c2! ♔f7. The passed d-pawn is more dangerous, but white cannot win it immediately: 2.♔c3? ♔g6 3.♔d4 a4!

4.♔c3 ♔h5 5.♔b4 ♔xh4 6.♔xa4 ♔g4, and the black king has enough time to protect the pawn. Thus, white should first play a feint!

2.♔b3! ♔g6 3.♔a4! d4 4.♔b3! And now back!

4...♔h5 5.♔c4 with a draw.

White puts up a similar fight against black's passed pawns in **Study 23**.

No. 23. M. Zinar
Shakhmaty v SSSR, 1988

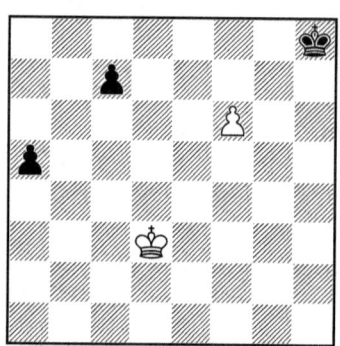

White to play and draw

1.♔c4! A double threat to both the b5 square and, as it turns out later, the b3 square.

1...c6. Now white cannot play 2.♔c5?, since after 2...♔g8 3.♔xc6 a4 4.♔d6 ♔f7, black wins.

2.♔b3! The feint!

2...c5 3.♔c4! a4. The pawns have advanced, but the black king didn't make it to g8 in time.

4.♔xc5! a3 5.♔d6 a2 (5...♔g8 6.♔e7) **6.f7** with a draw.

White's task is more difficult in **Study 24**, but it is still solved with the same technique.

No. 24. M. Zinar
Shakhmaty v SSSR, 1986

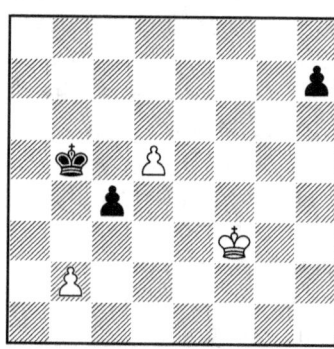

White to play and draw

Black has a dangerous outside passed pawn, and white gaining a draw depends on whether his king has enough time to return to the queenside after capturing it.

In case of 1.♔f4? ♔b6! 2.♔g5 ♔c5! 3.♔h6 ♔xd5 4.♔xh7 ♔d4 5.♔g6 ♔d3 6.♔f5 ♔c2 the white king doesn't make it.

1.♔e4 ♔b6! 2.♔d4! The feint! White threatens 3.♔xc4.

2...h5 3.♔e5! ♔c7. The pawn was forced to move.

4.♔e6! The second feint!

4...♔d8. And the king was pushed away.

5.♔f5! ♔d7 6.♔g5 with a draw.

The white king outplayed the black one on a small section of the board! Just look at the complicated route towards the g5 square: ♔f3–e4–d4–e5–e6–f5–g5! We should point out that in this study, the white king moves to the neighboring squares, and not back to its initial ones, i.e. it loses only one tempo, instead of two like in **Studies 20–23**.

No. 25. M. Zinar
Shakhmaty v SSSR, 1986

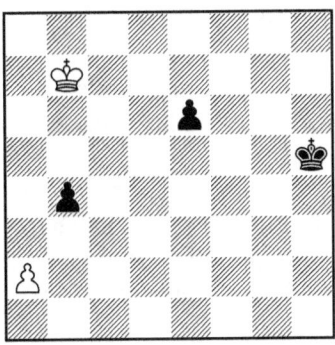

White to play and draw

Another example of returning to the neighboring square...

1.♔c6! ♔g4! Now, the "normal" 2.♔c5? loses: 2...e5 3.♔xb4 e4 etc. White has to feint:

2.♔d6! ♔f5 3.♔c5 e5 4.♔xb4 ♔f4 5.♔c3! ♔f3! 6.♔d2 ♔f2 7.♔d3 ♔f3 8.♔d2, draw.

An interesting example of the king feint is featured in **Study 26**.

No. 26**. I. Agapov
MT Grigoriev – 100, 1997
1st prize

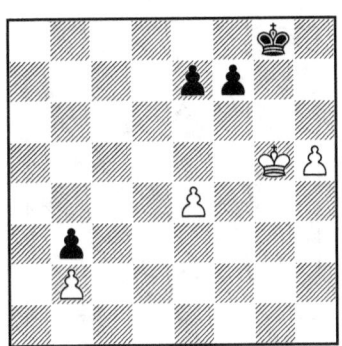

White to play and win

The natural-looking king dash towards the b-pawn is too slow: 1.♔f4? ♔g7 2.♔e3? (2.e5 still saved the draw) 2...♔h6 3.♔d3 ♔xh5 4.♔c3 ♔g4 5.♔xb3 ♔f4 6.♔c4 ♔xe4 7.b4 f5, and white even loses because the black pawn promotes with check.

Pawn thrusts do not help either: 1.e5? ♔g7 2.h6+ ♔h7 or 1.h6? ♔h8! 2.e5 ♔h7, with a draw in both cases.

Eureka: before running towards the pawns, you need to... step back from them!

1.♔h6!! ♔h8! 1...e5 is no better: 2.♔g5 ♔g7 3.♔f5 ♔h6

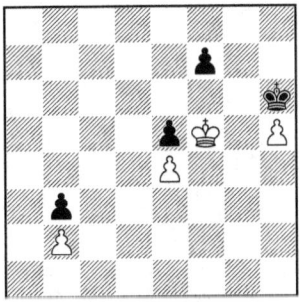

4.♔xe5! (not 4.♔f6? ♔xh5 5.♔xf7 ♔g5 6.♔e6 ♔f4 7.♔d5 ♔e3 8.♔xe5 ♔d3 9.♔d5 ♔c2 10.e5 ♔xb2 11.e6 ♔c2, and the pawns promote simultaneously) 4...♔xh5 (4...♔g5 5.h6 ♔g6 6.h7 ♔xh7 7.♔f6 ♔g8 8.♔e7 ♔g7 9.e5) 5.♔f5 ♔h4 6.e5 ♔g3 7.e6 fxe6+ 8.♔xe6 with a subsequent victory march towards the black pawn.

2.e5 ♔g8 (2...e6 3.♔g5 ♔g7 4.h6+) **3.e6!!**

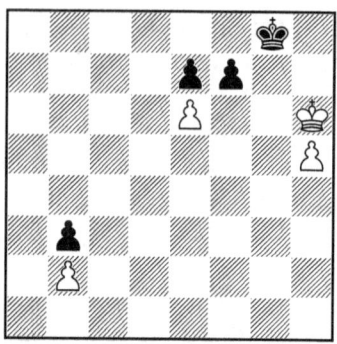

9.♔d6 ♔e4 10.♔c5 ♔d3 11.♔b4 ♔c2 12.♔a3! Mutual zugzwang and a win. A memorable white king voyage from the h-file to the a-file!

In the following subtle miniature, **Study 27**, the white king executes a spectacular feint.

3...fxe6. Or 3...f6 4.♔g6 ♔h8 5.♔f7 f5 6.♔xe7 f4 7.♔f7 f3 8.e7 f2 9.e8=♕+, with a check.

No. 27**. S. Didukh**
Moscow competition, 2018
4th honorable mention

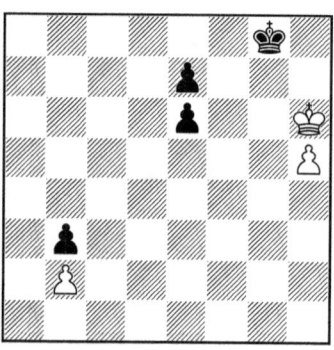

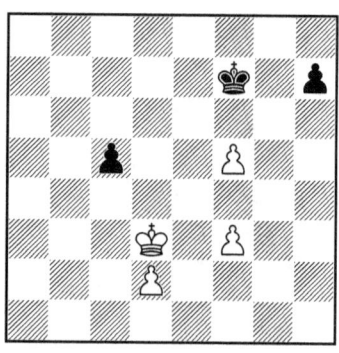

White to play and win

Now that black's pawn structure is shattered, the white king moves back: **4.♔g5! ♔g7 5.♔f4 ♔h6 6.♔e5 ♔xh5 7.♔xe6 ♔g4 8.♔xe7 ♔f5.** And now, nothing stops it from running towards the queenside black pawn!

White's plan is obvious: he needs to support the f5 passed pawn and control the advance of black's rook pawn at the same time...

Therefore, a natural attempt is **1.♔e4? ♔f6 2.♔f4 c4 3.♔e4.**

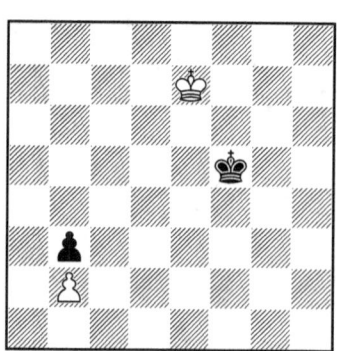

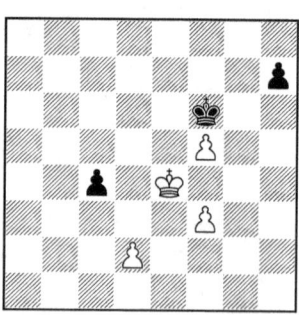

But after **3...h6! 4.♔f4 h5** (mutual zugzwang) **5.♔e4 ♔e7 6.♔e5 ♔f7 7.f6**

(without a check) 7...h4 8.♔f4 ♔xf6 9.♔g4 ♔e5, a draw is unavoidable.

An unexpected feint to the left decides matters: **1.♔c4!! h5!** After 1...♔f6 2.♔xc5 ♔xf5

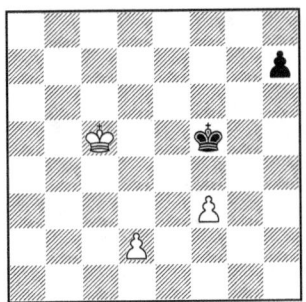

3.♔c4!! (3.♔d4? ♔f4 4.♔d3 ♔xf3, draw) **3...♔f4** (3...h5 4.♔d3) **4.d4 h5 5.♔d3 h4 6.♔e2 ♔g3 7.♔f1 ♔h2 8.d5 h3 9.d6 ♔h1 10.d7 h2 11.♔e2!**, black is doomed.

2.♔d3! And back!

2...c4+ 3.♔e3! With the all-important zugzwang upcoming, white fights for the corresponding squares!

3...♔e7 4.♔e4! (zugzwang) **4...♔f7 5.♔e5!** (another zugzwang!) **5...♔e7**

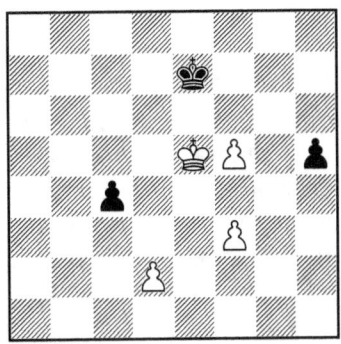

6.f6+! This check is the point of white's entire previous play!

6...♔f7 7.♔f5 h4 8.♔g4 ♔xf6

9.♔xh4 ♔e5 10.♔g3 ♔d4 11.♔f2 ♔d3 12.♔e1! White wins.

In the miniature **Study 28**, the king feint is performed in the currently popular logical genre.

No. 28**. M. Zinar
Cirtdan, 2018
3rd prize

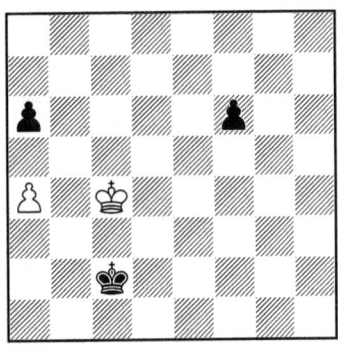

White to play and draw

1.a5! The immediate 1.♔c5? (1.♔b4? f5) is a false try: 1...a5! 2.♔b5 f5 3.♔xa5 f4 4.♔b6 f3 5.a5 f2 6.a6 f1=♛ 7.a7 ♛f3, and black wins.

1...f5 2.♔c5!! The feint in action! After the hasty 2.♔d4? ♔b3 3.♔e5 ♔b4 4.♔xf5 ♔xa5 5.♔e4 ♔b4 6.♔d3 ♔b3 7.♔d2 ♔b2, white cannot save the game.

2...f4. 2...♔b3 does not lead to a win either: 3.♔b6! f4 4.♔xa6 f3 5.♔b7 f2 6.a6 f1=♛ 7.a7 with a draw, because the white king has reached b7.

3.♔d4! And now back!

3...♔b3 4.♔e4 ♔b4 5.♔xf4 ♔xa5 6.♔e3 ♔b4 7.♔d2 ♔b3 8.♔c1. Draw.

We suspect that the theme of the faint is far from being exhausted. Look at a modern miniature on the same theme, **Study 29**.

No. 29**. M. Zinar
FIDE World Cup, 2019
Special honorable mention

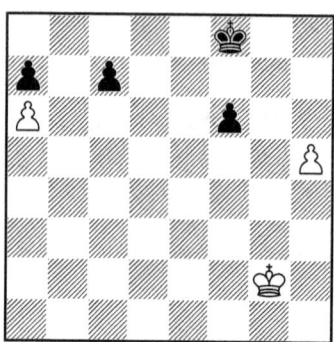

White to play and draw

1.♔f3! Targeting black's queenside! Not 1.♔g3? c5, curtains.

1...♔g7 2.♔e4! The play branches into two lines:

A) **2...♔h7! 3.♔d4!!** Not 3.♔d5? ♔h6! (mutual zugzwang) 4.♔c6 f5 5.♔xc7 f4 6.♔b7 f3 7.♔xa7 f2 8.♔b7 f1=♛, and the h-pawn dooms white.

There might follow 9.a7 ♛b5+ 10.♔c7 ♛a6 11.♔b8 ♛b6+ 12.♔a8 ♔g5 13.h6 ♛c7 14.h7 ♛c8#.

3...♔h6 4.♔d5! Now zugzwang benefits white.

4...c5! (4...♔xh5 5.♔c6 f5 6.♔xc7!) **5.♔xc5 f5**

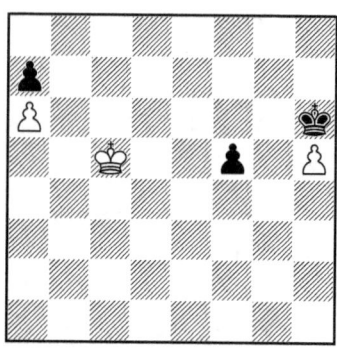

6.♔d5!! A feint to sacrifice the "hostage" pawn!

6...♔xh5 7.♔c6 f4 8.♔b7 f3 9.♔xa7, draw.

B) **2...c6! 3.♔d3!** And here, 3.♔d4? is the wrong way: 3...♔h6! 4.♔c5 f5 5.♔xc6 f4 6.♔b7 f3 7.♔xa7 f2 8.♔b7 f1=♛, and black wins.

3...♔h6 (3...♔h7 4.♔c4 ♔h6 5.♔d4!) **4.♔d4!** But not 4.♔c4? f5! 5.♔c5 f4, and black wins.

4...c5+. Or 4...♔xh5 5.♔c5 f5 6.♔xc6 etc.

5.♔xc5 transposing back to line A) **5...f5 6.♔d5!!** The familiar feint from the first variation.

6...♔xh5 7.♔c6 f4 8.♔b7 etc. with equality.

1.4. Tortoise move

Another universal tactical trick is the loss of tempo with a pawn, or the **"tortoise move"**. This refers to a pawn moving only one square forward from its initial position. This technique is used in zugzwangs, when the king lacks the ability to perform triangulation or sidestepping.

No. 30. N. Grigoriev
Endgame study collection, 1952

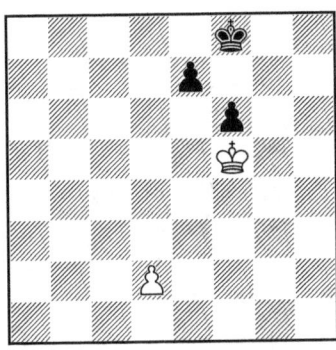

White to play and draw

1.♔e6! ♚e8 2.d3! The key moment!
2...♚d8 3.d4 ♚e8 4.d5 ♚d8 5.d6
exd6 6.♔xd6 or 4...♚f8 5.d6 exd6
6.♔xf6 with a draw.

In **Study 31**, the tortoise move is used
to play for a win. White has an outside
passed pawn, but he needs to disconnect
the d-pawn from the c-pawn. And the
only way to do this is to stalemate the
black king!

No. 31. N. Grigoriev
Endgame study collection, 1952

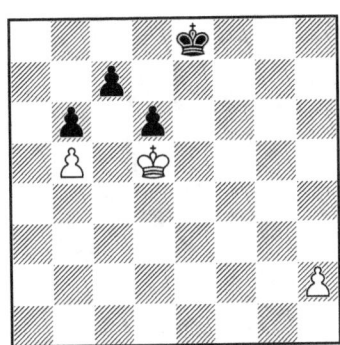

White to play and win

1.♔e6! ♚f8 2.♔f6 ♚g8 3.♔g6 ♚f8

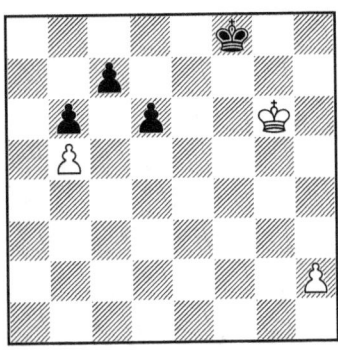

4.h3!! White is aiming far ahead:
his king should be standing on g6 when
black plays d6-d5.
4...♚g8. Interesting play ensues
after 4...♚e8 5.♔f6!! (not 5.h4? ♚e7!
6.h5 ♚f8!, and black gives up the right
to move with triangulation) 5...♚f8 6.h4
♚g8 7.♔g6 ♚f8 8.h5 or 4...♚e7 5.h4
♚e8 6.♔g7! with a win.
**5.h4 ♚f8 6.h5 ♚g8 7.h6 ♚h8 8.h7
d5 9.♔f5** with a win.

The technique of tempo-losing is
used quite often in endgame studies.
It's shown simply and clearly in **Study
32**.

No. 32. F. Richter
Revista de Romana de Sah, 1963

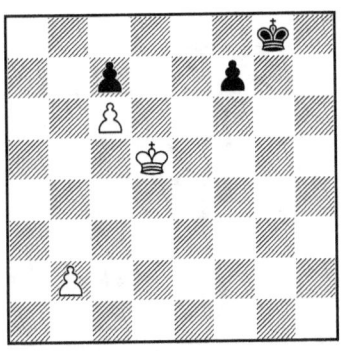

White to play and win

1.♔e5! ♚f8. After 1...♚g7 2.b4 ♚f8 3.♔f6! ♚e8 4.b5 ♚f8 5.b6, white wins easily.

2.♔f6 ♚e8 3.b3! But not 3.b4? ♚f8 4.b5 ♚e8, and black saves the game.

3...♚f8 4.b4 ♚e8 5.b5 ♚f8 6.b6 with a win.

The tempo loss works very well in conjunction with other ideas. For instance, in **Study 33**, the tortoise move is preceded by a queenside break.

No. 33**. V. Kovalenko
Themes 64, 1981

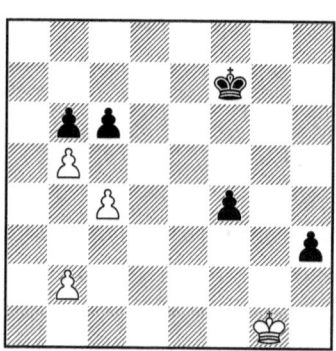

White to play and win

1.c5! ♚e7 2.cxb6 ♚d7 3.b7 ♚c7 4.bxc6 f3

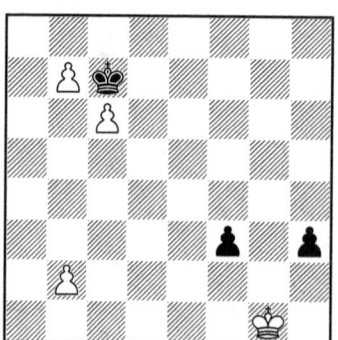

5.b3!! After the sharp 5.b4? ♚b8 6.b5 ♚c7 7.b6+ ♚b8, it's white who is in zugzwang.

5...♚b8 6.b4 ♚c7 7.b5 ♚b8 8.b6! And now black is in zugzwang.

8...f2+ 9.♔xf2 h2 10.c7+! ♚xb7 11.♔g2. White wins.

In **Studies 34** and **35**, the author continued to pursue the topic of a tortoise move that ensures a beneficial zugzwang opposition in the finale.

No. 34**. V. Kovalenko
Shakhmatnaya Kompozitsiya, 2002

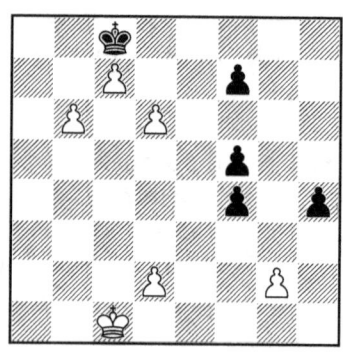

White to play and win

1.♔d1! f3! 2.♔e1 fxg2 3.♔f2 h3 4.♔g1! f4 5.♔f2(h2) f3 6.♔g1 f6! Black loses a tempo.

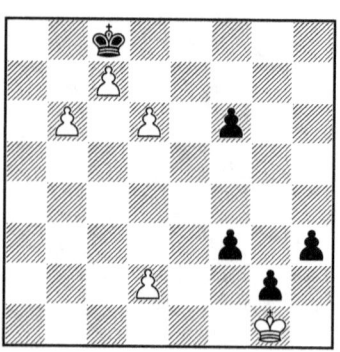

7.d3! White repeats the same trick. After 7.d4? f5 8.d5 f4 9.d7+ ♚xd7 10.c8=♕+ ♚xc8 11.d6 f2+ 12.♚xf2 g1=♕+ 13.♚xg1 f3!, the mutual zugzwang is in black's favor.

7...f5 8.d4 f4 9.d5 f2+ 10.♚xf2 g1=♕+ (10...f3 11.♚g1) 11.♚xg1 f3 12.d7+ ♚xd7 13.c8=♕+ ♚xc8 14.d6! The mutual zugzwang is in white's favor. White wins.

No. 35**. V. Kovalenko
Shakhmatnaya Kompozitsiya, 1998
Special honorable mention

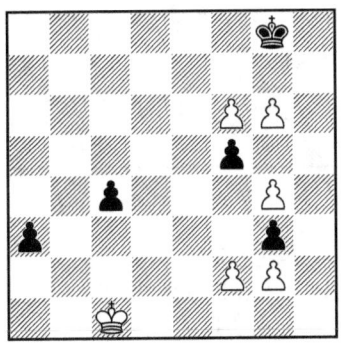

White to play and win

The modest first move leads to two parallel lines with final mutual zugzwang.

1.f3!! A thematic false try: 1.f4? c3 2.♔b1 fxg4 3.f5 ♚f8 4.f7 ♚g7 5.f6+ ♚f8 6.g7+ ♚xf7, and black wins. Or 1.fxg3? c3 2.♔b1 fxg4, which also ends badly.

1...c3 2.♔b1. The play branches into two lines.

A) **2...fxg4 3.f4! ♚f8 4.f7.** But not 4.f5? ♚g8 5.f7+ ♚g7.

4...♚g7 5.f5 ♚f8

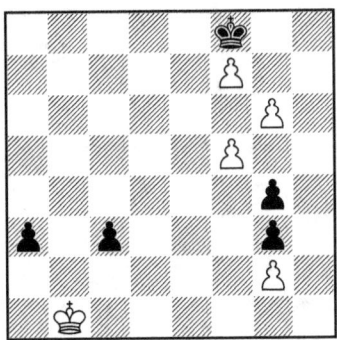

6.f6! Black is in zugzwang.

6...a2+ 7.♔xa2 c2 8.g7+ ♚xf7 9.♔b2. White wins.

B) **2...f4 3.g7! (3.g5? ♚f8 4.g7+ ♚f7) 3...♚f7 4.g5 ♚g8**

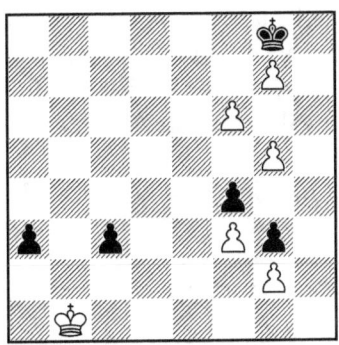

5.g6! Black is in zugzwang.

5...a2+ 6.♔xa2 c2 7.f7+ ♚xg7 8.♔b2. White wins.

As you look at the initial position of **Study 36**, it's hard to believe that white's success hinges on the modest g2 pawn. Nevertheless, it is true!

No. 36**. A. Kuryatnikov, E. Markov
MT Grigoriev – 100, 1997
1ˢᵗ honorable mention

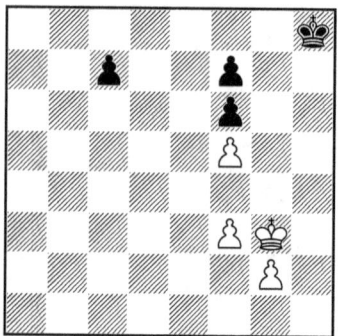

White to play and win

1.f4! The drawing wall cannot be breached after 1.♔f2? ♔g7 2.f4 ♔f8 3.♔e3 ♔e7 4.♔d4 ♔d6 etc.

1...♔g7 2.♔f3 ♔f8. After 2... ♔h6 3.g4!, white erects a fence on the kingside.

3.♔e4 c6 4.♔d4 ♔e7 5.♔c5 (5.g4? ♔d6) **5...♔d7**

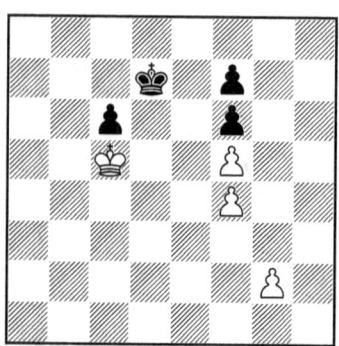

6.g3!! The tortoise move decides! It's not advisable to move the pawn all the way: 6.g4? ♔c7 7.g5 fxg5 8.fxg5 ♔d7 (white is in zugzwang) 9.♔b6 ♔d6, draw.

6...♔c7 7.g4 ♔d7 8.g5 fxg5 9.fxg5. Black is in zugzwang!

9...♔c7 (9...♔e7 10.♔xc6) **10.g6,** and the pawn reaches the promotion square. White wins.

A tortoise move in **Study 37** works as a prelude to a checkmate finale.

No. 37**. I. Aliev
Chess Star, 2015

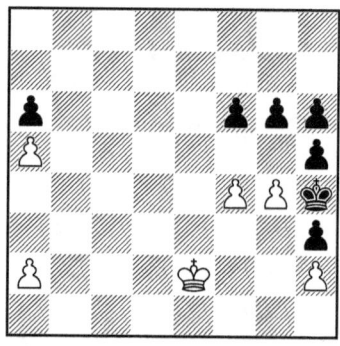

White to play and win

First, sacrifices prepare the mating net: **1.g5! hxg5.** Or 1...fxg5 2.f5 gxf5 3.♔f3 g4+ 4.♔f4 g3 5.hxg3#.

2.f5! gxf5 3.♔f3! f4

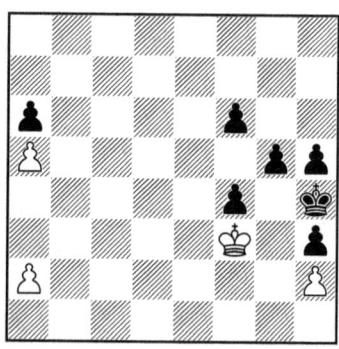

4.a3!! But not 4.a4? f5, and there's no mate.

4...f5 5.a4! Black is in zugzwang and gets checkmated.

5...g4+ 6.♔xf4 g3 7.hxg3#. A classical mate!

A tortoise move is possible even with the minimal amount of pieces. In the miniature **Study 38**, the mating finale is only possible thanks to it!

No. 38**. E. Iriarte
Ajedrez, 1975

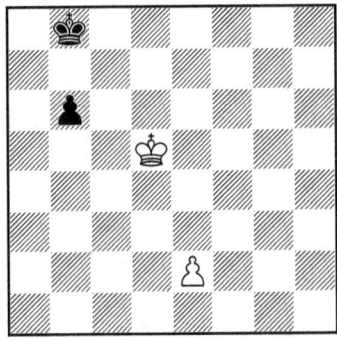

White to play and win

1.♔c6! ♚a7. Black doesn't fare well either after 1...♚c8 2.♔xb6 ♚d7 3.♔c5! ♚e6 4.♔d4!, winning.

2.e3!! The standard tempo loss! After 2.e4? b5! 3.e5 (3.♔xb5 ♚b7! 4.♔c5 ♚c7 5.♔d5 ♚d7 6.♔e5 ♚e7) 3...b4 4.e6 b3 5.e7 b2 6.e8=♕ b1=♕, the draw is obvious.

2...♚a6. Or 2...b5 3.♔xb5 ♚b7 4.♔c5 (or 4.e4 immediately) 4...♚c7 5.♔d5 ♚d7 6.♔e5 ♚e7 7.e4 with a winning opposition.

3.e4 b5 4.e5 b4 5.e6 b3 6.e7 b2 7.e8=♕(♖) b1=♕ 8.♕a8#. The checkmate became possible because the black king moved one square lower!

In **Study 39**, white successfully builds a stalemate construction thanks to a tortoise move. And black also has the same technique in his arsenal!

No. 39**. D. Chmelo and M. Hlinka
Ceskoslovensky Sach, 1992
Commendation

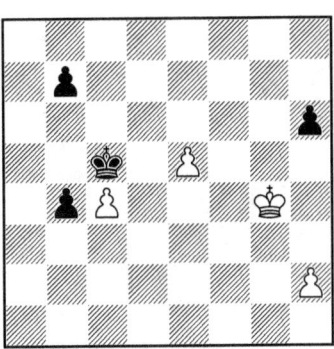

White to play and draw

It's too early to play 1.♔f5?, because after 1...b3 the black pawn promotes with check.

1.e6! ♚d6 2.♔f5! ♚e7. 2...b3 is no better: 3.♔f6! b2 4.e7 b1=♕ 5.e8=♕ ♕f1+ 6.♔g6, and black cannot win.

3.♔e4! Quick, to the black queenside pawns!

3...♚xe6 (3...h5 4.♔d3 h4 5.c5) **4.♔d3! ♚d6 5.♔c2 ♚c6!** (5...♚c5 6.♔b3 h5 7.h4)

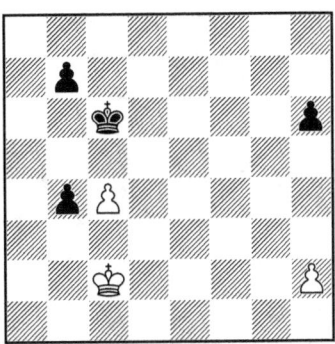

6.♔b3! If white gives up the tempo in return, this leads to disaster: 6.♔b2? ♚b6! 7.♔b3 ♚a5!! 8.h3 h5 9.h4 b6 10.♔b2 ♚a4, and black wins.

6...♔c5 7.h3! A tortoise move by white!

7...h5 8.h4

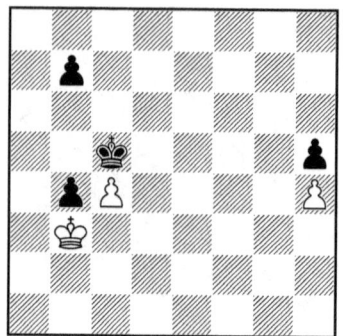

8...b6! And a tortoise move in return! 8...b5 doesn't lead to victory in any case: 9.cxb5 ♔xb5 10.♔b2 ♔c4 11.♔c2 ♔d4 12.♔b3 ♔e4 13.♔xb4 ♔f4 14.♔c3 ♔g4 15.♔d2 ♔xh4 16.♔e1 ♔g3 17.♔f1, draw. **9.♔a4!! ♔xc4** with a classical stalemate.

The loss of tempo can be used in conjunction with other ideas. In **Study 40**, a tortoise move is made to free the white king from prison.

No. 40. I. Bender**
Online competition, 2004
Commendation

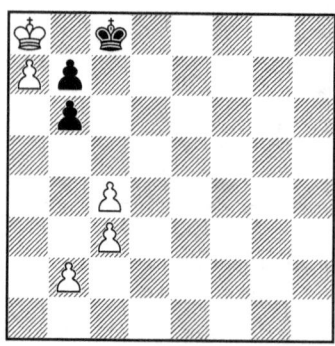

White to play and win

1.b3!! Thematic false try: 1.b4? ♔c7 (mutual zugzwang) 2.b5 ♔c8 3.c5 bxc5 4.c4 (4.b6 c4!) 4...b6, stalemate.

1...♔c7 2.b4! And now it's black who is in zugzwang.

2...♔c8 3.b5! ♔c7 4.c5! bxc5 5.b6+! ♔c8 6.c4! Black is in zugzwang again, and he is forced to let the white king out of the corner. White wins.

In **Study 41**, a tortoise move is used to lure the black king to an unfavorable diagonal.

No. 41. V. Tarasiuk**
MT Grigoriev − 120, 2016
Commendation

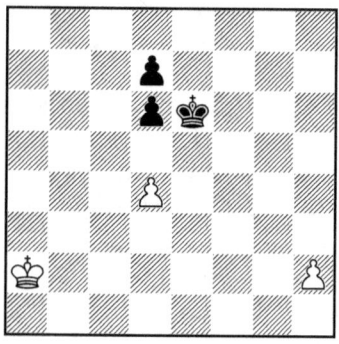

White to play and win

1.♔b3! Not 1.♔b2? ♔f5 2.♔c3 d5 3.♔b4 ♔e4 4.♔c5 d6+ 5.♔xd6 ♔xd4, draw.

1...♔d5 2.♔c3 ♔e4

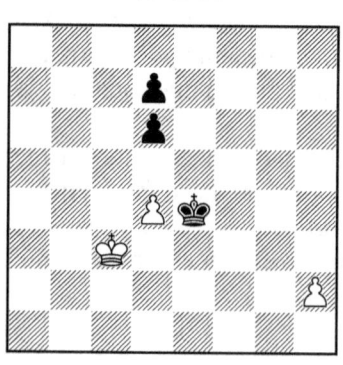

3.h3!! It's not good to send the pawn forward all the way: 3.h4? d5 4.h5 ♚f5 5.♚b4 ♚g5 6.♚c5 ♚xh5 7.♚d6 ♚g6 8.♚xd7 ♚f7 9.♚d6 ♚e8 10.♚xd5 ♚d7 with a drawing opposition.

3...d5 4.h4! Mutual zugzwang.

4...♚f4 5.♚b4 ♚g4 6.♚c5 ♚xh4 7.♚d6! ♚g5 8.♚xd7 ♚f6

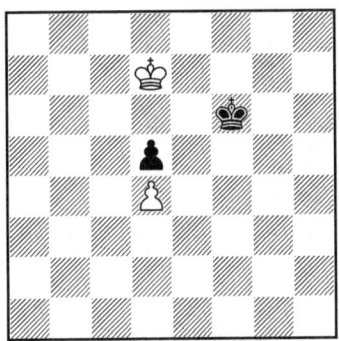

9.♚d6! Shouldering the black king!
9...♚f7 10.♚xd5. White wins.

1.5. Queening the pawn

Not all pawn studies have mating or stalemating finales. Some of them end after queening a pawn. The goal of many studies is to promote the pawn earlier than the opponent, while in drawing studies, the pawns are promoted simultaneously. In these studies, the play aspect comes to the fore, and the value of the composition is determined by the means used to promote the pawn: the tactical tricks employed. Let's look at these techniques.

Breakthrough. The breakthrough technique had been known for a long time. It has occurred many times in real games, often in difficult situations that require precise play. Breakthrough is a sacrifice of one or more pawns

to pave the way forward for a passed pawn. This technique is now common knowledge, and to add artistic value to it, some further subtleties should be introduced.

Study 42 is a classic textbook-type composition, but the nuance found by the author allows us to consider this position an endgame study.

No. 42. T. Kok
De Schaakwereld, 1940

White to play and win

1.♚d2! It's necessary to leave the third rank to execute the breakthrough. If white immediately plays 1.c5? bxc5 2.d5, then black wins after 2...cxb4+. Also, 1.♚b2? ♚f2 2.c5 bxc5 3.d5 cxd5 4.b5 d4 5.b6 d3 is a mistake – black draws.

1...♚f3. It's impossible to prevent the breakthrough: 1...c5 2.dxc5 dxc5 3.bxc5 bxc5 4.♚e3 with a win.

2.c5! dxc5. Or an echo blow: **2...bxc5 3.d5! cxd5 4.b5,** curtains.

3.b5! cxb5 4.d5, winning.

We see the same 3 vs. 3 construction in **Study 43**.

No. 43. M. Zinar
Krymskaya Pravda, 1983

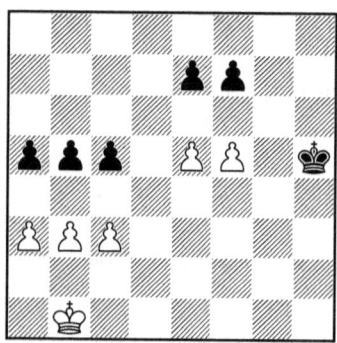

White to play and win

1.b4! cxb4! 2.a4! bxa4 3.c4! The classical breakthrough!

3...♔g5 4.f6! After 4.c5? ♔xf5 or 4.e6? f6! (refusing the "gift"), black wins.

4...exf6 5.e6! Two slowing sacrifices to ensure the breakthrough.

5...fxe6 6.c5 ♔f5 7.c6 with a win.

Slowing sacrifices have been known since 1913. In **Study 44**, repeated sacrifices give a systematic form to the play.

No. 44. A. Troitsky
Deutsche Schachzeitung, 1913
(correction by Mario Garcia)

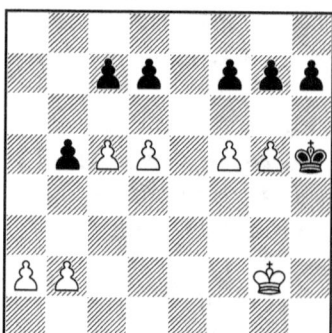

White to play and win

1.g6! After 1.a3? ♔xg5 2.b3, the black king makes it to the square of

the pawn in time through f6−e7−d8.

1...fxg6. If 1...hxg6 2.f6! ♔h6 3.a3!, white wins.

2.f6! gxf6 3.a3 ♔g5 4.b3 ♔f5. The path opens!

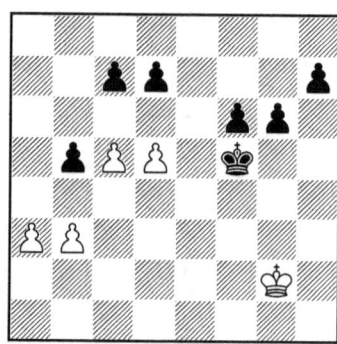

5.a4! Not 5.d6? cxd6 6.a4 bxa4 7.bxa4 ♔e6 8.c6 dxc6 9.a5 ♔d7!

5...bxa4 6.bxa4 ♔e5. And now, echo-sacrifices follow.

7.d6! cxd6 8.c6! dxc6 9.a5 ♔d5 10.a6 with a win.

In **Study 45**, white's pawn breakthrough is complemented by black's counterplay using the Reti maneuver, which we shall discuss a bit later.

No. 45. I. Yarmonov**
Vecherniy Peterburg, 1995
Commendation

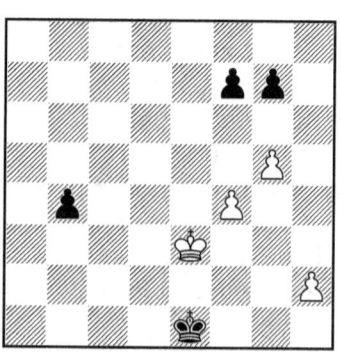

White to play and win

1.f5! Not 1.♔d3? g6! 2.h4 b3 3.h5 gxh5 4.f5 h4, with a draw.

1...♔d1! (1...b3 2.♔d3 g6 3.fxg6 fxg6 4.h4 ♔f2 5.♔c3) **2.♔d3 ♔c1 3.♔c4 ♔c2! 4.♔xb4 ♔d3 5.h4 ♔e4**

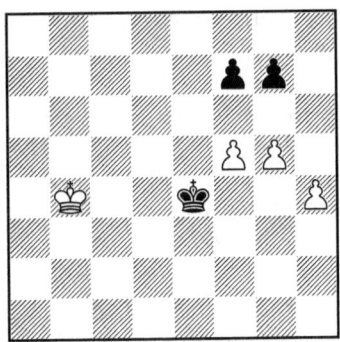

6.f6! gxf6 7.h5 ♔f5 8.g6! fxg6 9.h6 with a rook-pawn excelsior. White wins.

The serial execution of a classical breakthrough is the main line in **Study 46**, where two pawns are racing for the promotion square at once.

No. 46**. V. Dubrovsky**
Shakhmatnaya Kompozitsiya, 1997

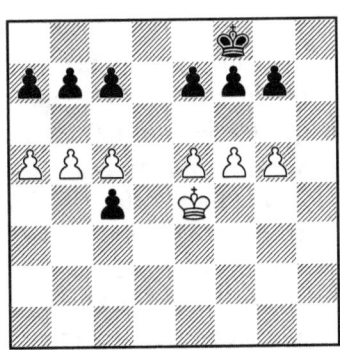

White to play and win

There's no way to win this "conventionally": 1.♔d4? b6 2.axb6 axb6 3.♔xc4 e6 4.fxe6 fxe6, draw.

White is saved by two consecutive breakthrough combinations:

1.b6!! The first blow to the center of black's pawn trio!

1...cxb6! 2.a6! bxa6 3.c6! ♔e8 4.f6! The second blow!

4...exf6!

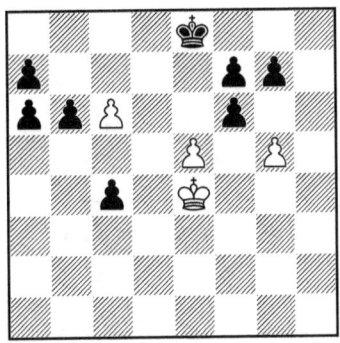

5.g6! fxg6 6.e6! ♔d8 7.♔d5 (7.♔d4 only lengthens the solution) **7...c3 8.♔d6 c2 9.c7+ ♔c8 10.e7.** White wins.

1.6. Reti double threat

No endgame study ever received such great attention as the famous **Study 47**. This study amazes everyone who sees it for the first time. The aphorism "everything ingenious is simple" applies to this unique chess composition as much as to anything else.

Note that it was previously believed that the Czech grandmaster first published this composition in 1922, in the German magazine *Kagan's Neueste Schachnachrichten*. Later, though, it was proven with documents that this study first saw the light of day in the chess column of an obscure newspaper *Ostrauer Morgenzeitung und Handelsblatt* on 4th December 1921.

No. 47. R. Reti
Ostrauer Morgenzeitung und
Handelsblatt, 1921

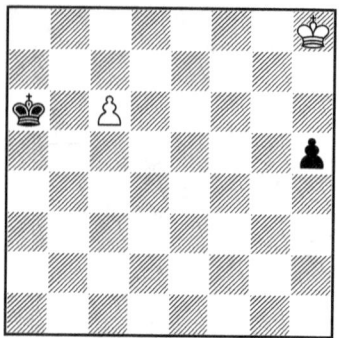

White to play and draw

As you look at the position, it's impossible to believe that the goal is achievable at all. The white pawn cannot promote — it's easily stopped by the black king. The white king cannot make it in time to help his pawn — his black counterparty will take the white pawn three moves earlier. The attempt to capture the black pawn looks even more naive — the white king will need to make three moves in a row to do that!

And yet, the study is solvable. It's necessary (and possible on the chess board!) to get the white king one square closer to *both* white and black pawns, even though they are located in completely different directions. And in this case, the black monarch either allows the white pawn to promote or spends two moves to stop it — exactly the two moves that the white king lacks to catch up with the black pawn.

So, if the king moves in a straight line — 1.♔h7? h4 2.♔h6 h3 etc., this, of course, loses. But it makes an unexpected and paradoxical maneuver:

1.♔g7! The king wants to kill two birds with one stone: to get closer to both its own pawn and the opponent's one.

1...h4 2.♔f6! The approach continues. 2...h3 is met with 3.♔e7(e6) h2 4.c7 ♔b7 5.♔d7, and the pawns promote at the same time.

2...♔b6

3.♔e5!! The key move that made this study so famous!

Now **3...h3 4.♔d6 h2 5.c7 ♔b7 6.♔d7** leads to a draw again, but another continuation changes nothing too:

3...♔xc6 4.♔f4 (or 4.♔e4) **4...h3 5.♔g3 h2 6.♔xh2**, the king catches the pawn on the verge of promotion. Draw.

How did this miracle happen? How did white manage to save the game? This is explained by the unusual geometry of the chess board. We are accustomed to the notion that the shortest way between two points is a straight line. However, on the chess board, the shortest way need not be straight. Here, the king can cover the distance between b8 and b2 in six moves regardless of exactly how it moves — straight ahead or in zigzags.

By choosing the route that looks the strangest, white wins enough time to force the black king to make two extra moves. As a result, the black pawn loses its speed.

We can say that, from the chess king's point of view, the sum of the sides of the right-angled triangle h8-e5-h2 is equal to its hypotenuse! This mathematical theorem can be proved on a chess board.

Reti's idea is one of the most seminal discoveries in chess. The creation of this masterpiece was built on top of the entire history of chess composition, and if Reti hadn't come up with it, a similar study might have been created by another composer. We can draw an analogy with science here: a major breakthrough is often prepared by general progress in the field, but someone gets "lucky" to discover it first.

Reti's four-piece study became a real sensation in the chess world and, of course, drew numerous responses. The geometric idea of the study, which is called the "Reti maneuver" after its discoverer, was later refined and deepened numerous times. However, the purity of form and conciseness of material in the original study is impossible to surpass: there are only two kings and two pawns on the board.

All in all, we can praise the composition for its conciseness, the effect of seeming unsolvability, the freedom of the king's movement, and the three-move double threat, but all that is not what's truly the most important aspect.

We daresay that if the black pawn were on f5, rather than h5, in the initial position (this doesn't change the essence of the study), the composition would have never become so famous. Why? In the author's version, white can pointlessly attack the pawn with 3.♔g5?,

but instead, we move in the opposite direction, 3.♔e5!!, getting further away from the target! The move is correct — we are getting closer to the square of the pawn. But the square is invisible, while the pawn is very real! The main idea of the study is that the king catches up with the pawn in a roundabout way!

As we see, the Reti double threat is a special case of a king double threat, with one target being the square of the opponent's passed pawn. And although we call this one "the Reti maneuver", there can be other kinds of maneuvers, while the essence of this one is a double threat.

The idea that Richard Reti used as the foundation of his immortal study, as any other idea in life, spreads its threads both into the past and into the future. It had a long pedigree and served as a source of inspiration for many copiers and followers. Below, we show various examples that develop and enrich this theme.

We show below a lot of positions that illustrate the peculiar geometry of the chess board. In a number of studies, the Reti maneuver is used in conjunction with other techniques. Some examples from actual games are also shown.

To begin, we return to **Study 1** by Ilya Maizelis.

Further mathematical proof of the chess theorem: the sum of the sides equals the hypotenuse! Here, we have a position where white's goal is to win, rather than make a draw. The a7 pawn is defenseless, and black's only chance is to trap the white king at the edge of the board (after the inevitable ♔xa7) with ♔c7. The shortest way for the white king to reach the a7 pawn comprises 5 moves, and there are 30 ways to cover this distance. However, only one of these ways helps achieve the main goal.

1.♔f7! ♔c2 2.♔e6! ♔c3 3.♔d5! Shouldering – another important maneuver that is often seen in both endgame studies and actual game endings. The black king is pushed back, forced to stay in place and cannot make it to the needed square in time.

3...♔b4 4.♔c6 ♔a5 5.♔b7 ♔b5 6.♔xa7 ♔c6 7.♔b8, and the pawn is promoted.

In fact, this study was actually the ending of the game W. Schlage – C. Ahues (Berlin 1921). White didn't know the subtleties of "chess geometry", and after 3.♔d6? ♔d4 4.♔c6 ♔e5 5.♔b7 ♔d6 6.♔xa7 ♔c7, the game ended in a draw.

No. 48. R. Reti
Kagan's Neueste Schachnachrichten, 1922

White to play and draw

Here, we see a twin of **Study 47**, but this time the goal of stopping the h-pawn has no duals...

1.♔b4! ♔b6. If 1...h4, then 2.♔c5 h3 3.♔d6 h2 4.c7 ♔b7 5.♔d7, draw.

2.♔c4! h4 3.♔d5! and then **3...h3 4.♔d6** with a draw. **3...♔c7** is met with **4.♔e4 h3 5.♔f3 h2 6.♔g2,** again with a draw.

Compared with **Study 47**, the king moves along a polygonal line here, but there's no roundabout way towards the pawn, so this study is not as brilliant.

No. 49. H. Adamson
The Chess Amateur, 1922

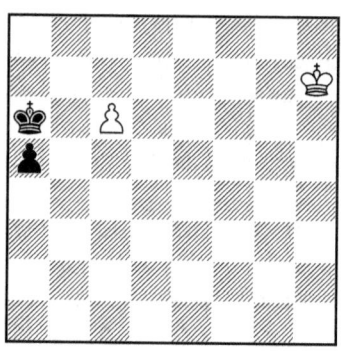

White to play and draw

1.♔g6! ♔b6 2.♔f5! But not 2.♔f6? ♔xc6! 3.♔e5 ♔c5, and black wins.

2...a4 3.♔e5! with a draw. The king moves in a polygonal line to avoid shouldering.

While after **1...a4 2.♔f5 ♔b6 3.♔e5! ♔xc6 4.♔d4,** the white king catches the pawn. Admittedly, in this line white has multiple ways to achieve the draw. Instead of 2.♔f5, white can also save the game with 2.♔f6 a3

3.♔e6(e7). We move the white king to h3 to eliminate the dual in the next study.

No. 50. H. Adamson
The Chess Amateur, 1922
(version, 1990)

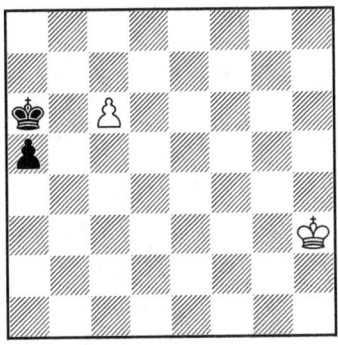

White to play and draw

1.♔g4! a4 2.♔f5! (2.♔f4? a3!) **2...♔b6 3.♔e5! ♔xc6 4.♔d4** − the king also moves along a polygonal line!

There's also a draw after **2...a3 3.♔e6! a2 4.c7 ♔b7 5.♔d7** − this time, the king moves in a straight line!

No. 51. J. Moravec
Ceskoslovensky Sach, 1952

White to play and draw

1.♔g4 b5 2.d4 b4 3.d5! ♔b5

4.d6! If 4.♔f5?, then 4...b3 5.d6 b2 6.d7 b1=♕+, and black wins.

4...♔c6 5.♔f5! The king is at the crossroads!

5...♔xd6 6.♔e4 with a draw. The Reti double threat was further complicated by the anti-check theme, which is achieved with a precise move order.

Or **5...b3 6.♔e6 b2 7.d7**, also with a draw.

No. 52. J. Moravec
Ceskoslovensky Sach, 1952

White to play and draw

In this study, the same goal is achieved with an interesting king maneuver.

1.♔g4! a5 2.♔f5! a4 3.♔g6! Sidestepping the f6 square! The king could get checked there.

3...a3

4.e6! with a draw.

It might seem that by including a new, interesting anti-check maneuver, the author surpassed Richard Reti himself. But no! There's no roundabout way towards the pawn, and the goal looks more achievable. It turns out that by introducing new elements, chess composers lost some other elements, and the losses were much more tangible than the gains.

No. 53. C. De Feijter
Deventer Dagblad, 1939

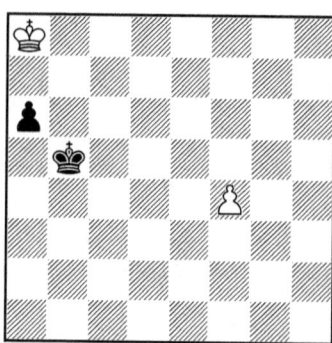

White to play and draw

1.♔b7! a5 2.♔c7! The king moves in parallel to the square of the pawn, but goes further away from the pawn! White plays a feint, forcing the black king to leave the fifth rank.

2...♚c5 3.♔d7! The white king gets closer to its own pawn, but doesn't forget the opponent's pawn either.

3...♚d5 4.♔e7! ♚e4.

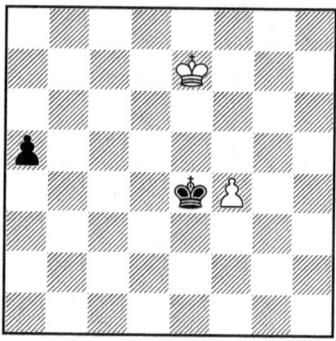

And now, we see a Reti double threat!
5.♔e6! a4. If 5...♚xf4, then 6.♔d5, and the black pawn falls too.

6.f5 a3 7.f6 with a draw.

No. 54. L. Prokes
Sachove Umenie, 1947

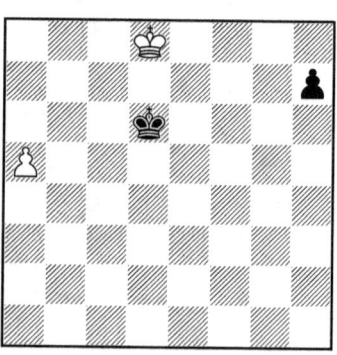

White to play and draw

1.♔c8! This is how the king begins chasing the h-pawn.

1...♚c6 2.♚b8! ♚b5. The feint has been executed, and now the Reti double threat follows:

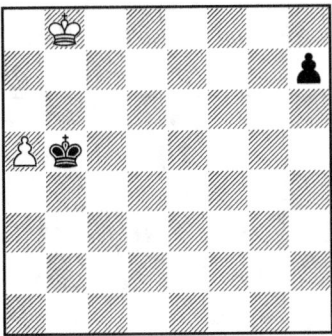

3.♚b7! ♚xa5 4.♚c6 h5 5.♚d5, and white has achieved his goal — the king is in the square of the pawn.

No. 55. E. Pogosyants
Prapor Yunosti, 1976

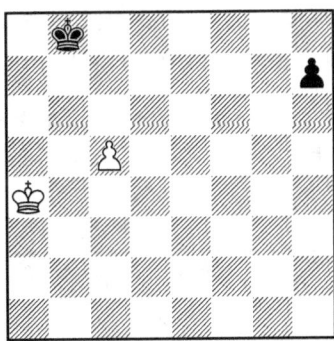

White to play and draw

1.♚b5! h5 2.♚c6! ♚c8. 2...h4 is met with 3.♚d7 h3 4.c6 etc.
3.♚d5!, and the white king is in the square of the pawn.

Conclusion: as a rule, the outcome hinges on a single tempo in these pawn promotion races. One of the available tactical blows in this case, the "Reti double threat" maneuver, allows one to win a lacking tempo.

Of course, such furor caused by the Czechoslovakian grandmaster could not be overlooked by one of the classics of study composition, the Frenchman Henri Rinck. He didn't just create a study that served as the creative reply to the famous Reti study, but even managed to implement a winning idea with the colors reversed.

No. 56. H. Rinck
Schweizerische Schachzeitung, 1922

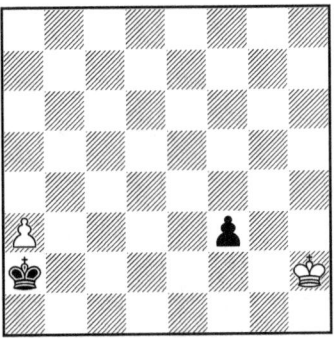

White to play and win

1.a4 ♚b3! The position looks like a Reti study: the king moves diagonally, chasing the white pawn and getting closer to the black one.
2.a5 ♚c3

3.♚g1!! If 3.♚g3?, then 3...♚d4! 4.a6 ♚e3! 5.a7 f2 6.♚g2 ♚e2 with a draw.

3...♔d4! 4.a6 ♔e3 5.♔f1, and wins. The second line: **2...♔c4 3.a6 ♔d3 4.a7 f2 5.a8=♕ f1=♕ 6.♕a6+,** and wins.

And now let's look at Reti maneuver positions with a greater number of pawns.

No. 57. V. Korolkov
All-Union competition, 1950
Commendation

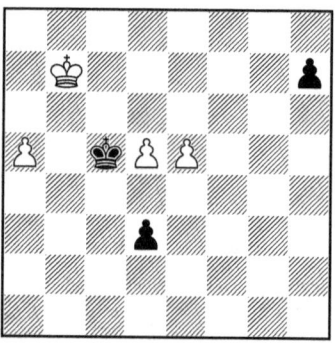

White to play and draw

1.e6! Not 1.a6? d2 2.a7 d1=♕ 3.a8=♕ ♕xd5+ 4.♔a7 ♕xa8+ 5.♔xa8 ♔d5, and black wins.

1...♔d6 2.e7 ♔xe7 3.♔c7 d2 4.d6+ ♔e6 5.d7 d1=♕ 6.d8=♕ ♕xd8+ 7.♔xd8 ♔d6. The introductory play is over. Up until now, both sides have been trying to promote their own pawns, but now they are trying to stop each other's from promoting!

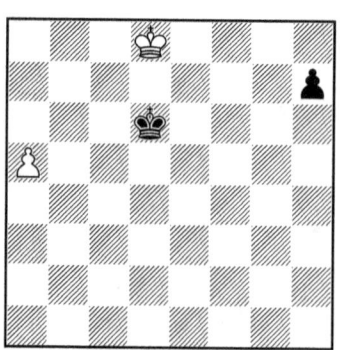

8.♔c8 ♔c6 9.♔b8 ♔b5 10.♔b7 ♔xa5 11.♔c6, draw.

No. 58. T. Gorgiev
Shakhmaty v SSSR, 1967

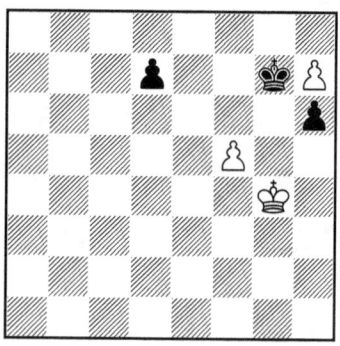

White to play and draw

The material on the board is equal, but while the black pawns advance unopposed, the white pawns are seemingly stuck. And still, white can save the game – white uses the Reti maneuver twice!

1.f6+! ♔xh7 2.♔f5! ♔g8 3.♔g6 d5! 4.♔f5 h5. Or 4...♔f7 5.♔e5 h5 6.♔xd5 h4 7.♔e4 etc.

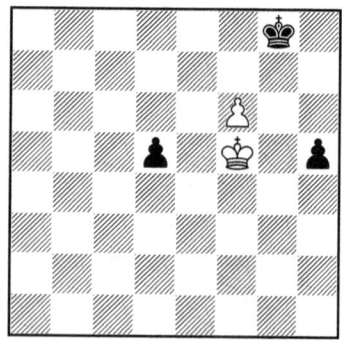

5.♔e6! ♔f8 6.♔xd5 h4 7.♔e4 with a draw.

Chess history has accorded a long and eventful life to Reti's masterpiece. The Czechoslovakian grandmaster's idea didn't just deepen and enrich study composition: it was also occasionally found in over-the-board play, including repeating the study move by move. Here are the most interesting of available examples.

No. 59. C. Schlechter – G. Marco
Vienna 1893

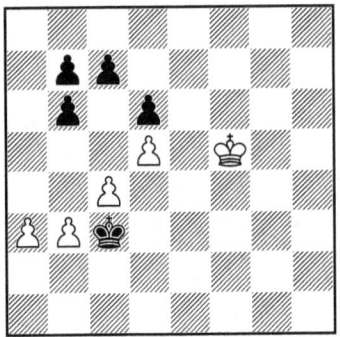

White to move

At first glance, the pawn endgame is completely hopeless for white. But the Austrian grandmaster decided to challenge the "glances" and found an incredible way to save the game.

1.♔e6 ♔xb3 2.♔d7 ♔xc4 3.♔xc7 ♔xd5 4.♔xb6 ♔c4 5.♔xb7 d5

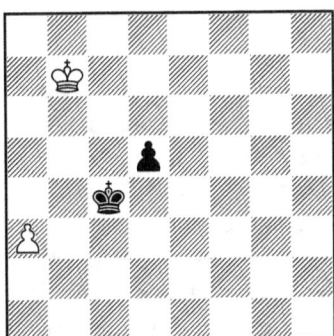

6.a4! ♔b4 7.♔b6!, draw.

Curiously, it was this game that served as a source of inspiration for Richard Reti when he created his evergreen **Study 47.**

Here's what the grandmaster wrote in the chess column of *Ostrauer Morgenzeitung und Handelsblatt* on 4th December 1921: "One can read various accounts on the origins of this peculiar endgame [**Study 47**]. For instance, some say that it occurred in a recent game between some weak unnamed players. In reply, we would like to state that this position was composed by our chess editor, who derived the idea from a simpler position from an unpublished game by Schlechter."

No. 60. Emanuel Lasker – S. Tarrasch
St. Petersburg 1914

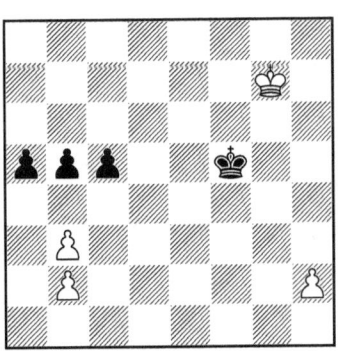

White to move

White's position is of concern: his h-pawn is not dangerous, and black is threatening to create a passed pawn on the other flank.

1.h4! ♔g4 2.♔g6! ♔xh4 3.♔f5.

And now it's black who has to put in some effort to save the game. Here's how it ended:

3...♔g3 4.♔e4 ♔f2 5.♔d5 ♔e3 6.♔xc5 ♔d3 7.♔xb5 ♔c2 8.♔xa5 ♔xb3, draw.

Another example from a game played by leading masters.

No. 61. F. Yates – F. Marshall
Carlsbad 1929

Black to move

1...♔b2! Seemingly supporting the movement of his own pawn...

2.♔xa4 ♔c3! 3.f4 ♔d4, but actually stopping the opponent's passer.

In conclusion, here's an example from less ancient times.

No. 62. B. Gustafsson – J. Bata
Correspondence 1985

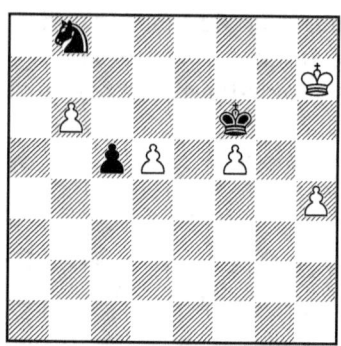

White to move

White resigned here. Black, however, showed that white could have saved the game in a study-like way, using the Reti double threat.

1.♔g8! ♔xf5 2.♔g7!! ♔g4

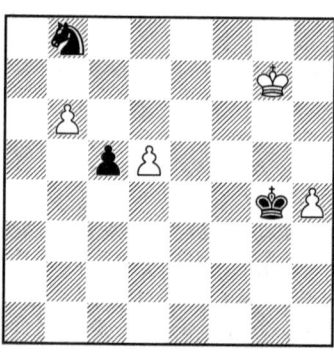

3.♔g6!! ♔xh4 4.♔f5 or **2...c4 3.h5 c3 4.h6** with a draw.

The idea of Richard Reti, born by the imagination of this genius a century ago, continues to bear fruit even in modern times. Moreover, it turns out that Richard Reti's signature maneuver has a much longer history than was previously thought! The researchers of this idea hadn't noticed the interesting **Study 63** before.

No. 63**. B. Horwitz
The Chess Monthly, 1879

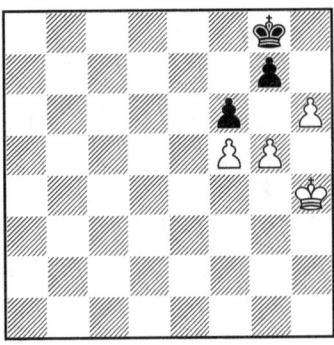

White to play and win

At first glance, it seems that this game should end in a draw. But white finds a subtle maneuver: **1.g6! gxh6.** Obviously, the white king has nothing to do on the kingside: 2.♔h5 ♔g7, and white has to retreat.

Therefore, he should seek happiness on the other flank: **2.♔g3** (the king's route towards the queenside shown here is not the only one possible) **2...♔f8 3.♔f3 ♔e8 4.♔e4 ♔f8 5.♔d5 ♔e7 6.♔c5 ♔e8 7.♔d6 ♔f8.**

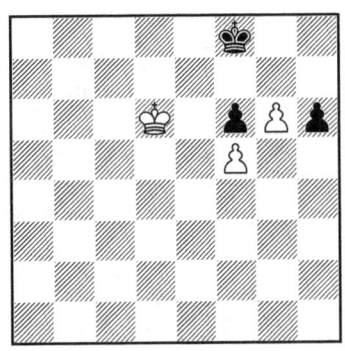

What exactly has white achieved, you might ask? After the obvious 8.♔e6 ♔g7, the white king will again have to retreat ingloriously...

Eureka: **8.♔d7!!**, boldly leaving the square of the h-pawn (in 1928, this trick will gain an official name: the Reti — Sarychevs feint!).

8...♔g8. After 8...h5, white wins with the familiar Reti maneuver, killing two birds with one stone: 9.♔e6! h4 (or 9...♔g7 10.♔d5, catching up with the pawn, as in the main line) 10.♔xf6 h3 11.g7+ ♔g8 12.♔g6 h2 13.f6 h1=♕ 14.f7#!

9.♔e7! ♔g7 10.♔e6! Black is in zugzwang and is forced to move his pawn:

10...h5 11.♔d5

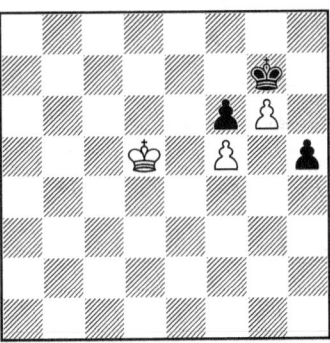

11...h4 (11...♔g8 doesn't save the game either: 12.♔e4 ♔h8 13.♔f4 ♔g8 14.♔g3 ♔g7 15.♔h3! ♔h6 16.♔h4 ♔g7 17.♔xh5, curtains) **12.♔e4 h3 13.♔f3,** catching the runaway pawn. White wins.

It turns out that this maneuver, "chasing two targets", was patented by Bernhard Horwitz 42 years before the publication of Reti's miniature!

Inspired by the mechanism shown in Horwitz's **Study 63**, the author composed task **Study 64** in 2014, with systematic movements and a seven-time repetition of the Reti double threat. A target for future record challengers!

No. 64**. M. Zinar
JC Sochnev – 50, 2014
Special honorable mention

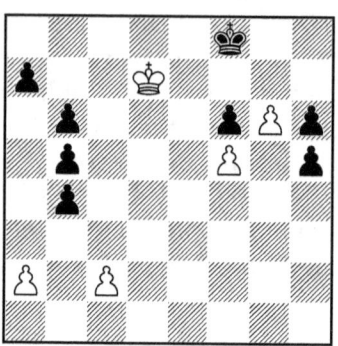

White to play and win

1.♔e6! The first Horwitz-Reti maneuver in action!

1...♔g7. Both here and later, the push 1...h4 doesn't work due to 2.♔xf6 h3 3.g7+ ♔g8 4.♔g6 h2 5.f6 h1=♕ 6.f7#.

2.♔d5 ♔g8 3.♔e4 ♔f8 4.♔f4. Both here and later, the white king play has an organic dual, 4.♔f3.

4...♔g8 5.♔g3 ♔f8 6.♔h4 ♔g8 7.♔xh5 ♔g7 8.♔g4 ♔g8

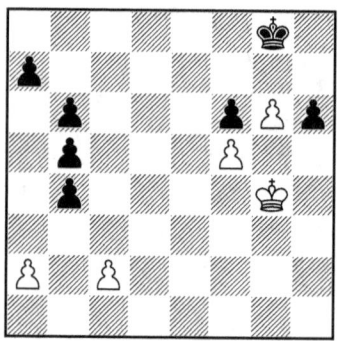

9.♔f4 ♔f8 10.♔e4 ♔e8 11.♔d5 ♔e7 12.♔c6 ♔e8 13.♔d6 ♔f8 14.♔d7! ♔g8. A second performance of the Horwitz-Reti maneuver also

followed after 14...h5 15.♔e6!, but with another pawn.

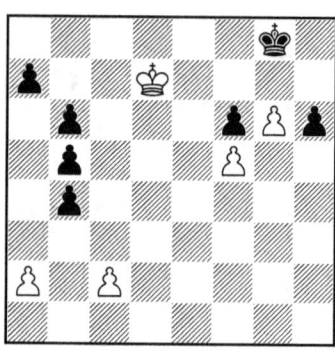

15.♔e7! ♔g7 16.♔e6 a6 17.♔d6 ♔f8 18.♔d7! ♔g8. The third time: 18...h5 19.♔e6! etc.

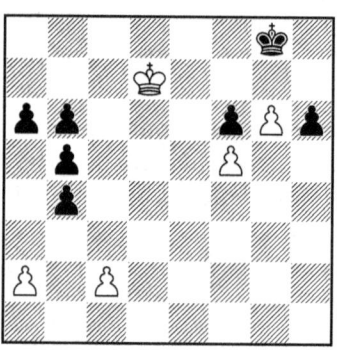

19.♔e7! ♔g7 20.♔e6 a5 21.♔d6 ♔f8 22.♔d7! ♔g8. The fourth: 22...h5 23.♔e6!

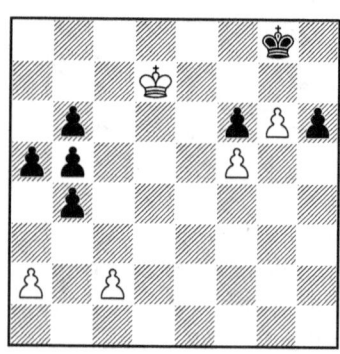

23.♔e7! ♚g7 24.♔e6 a4 25.♔d6 ♚f8 26.♔d7! ♚g8. The fifth: 26...h5 27.♔e6!

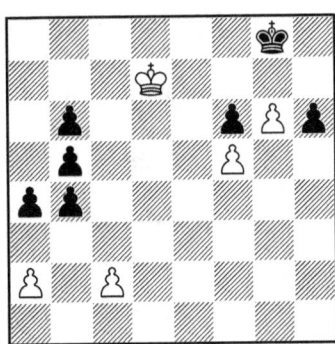

27.♔e7! ♚g7 28.♔e6 a3 29.♔d6 ♚f8 30.♔d7! ♚g8. The sixth: 30...h5 31.♔e6!

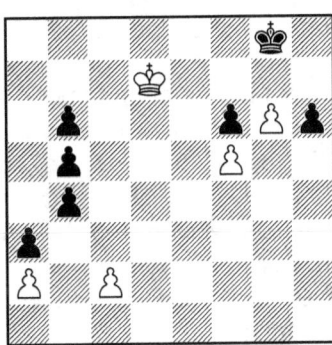

31.♔e7! ♚g7 32.♔e6 b3 33.cxb3 b4 34.♔d6 ♚f8 35.♔d7! ♚g8. The seventh: 35...h5 36.♔e6!

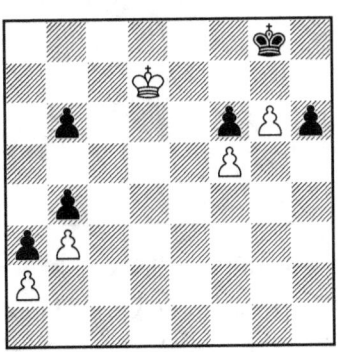

36.♔e7! ♚g7 37.♔e6 h5 38.♔d5 ♚g8 39.♔e4 ♚g7 40.♔f4 ♚g8 41.♔g3 ♚g7

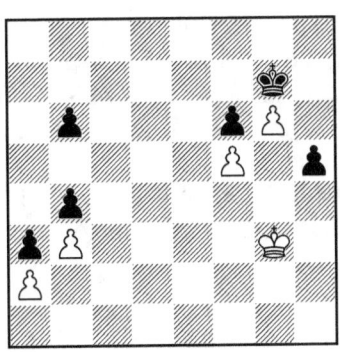

42.♔h3! ♚h6 43.♔h4 b5 44.♔g3 ♚g7 45.♔h3 ♚h6 46.♔h4 ♚g7 47.♔xh5 ♚g8 48.♔g4 ♚f8 49.♔f4 ♚g7 50.♔e4(e3). White wins.

Mikhail Zinar dedicated this study to the big birthday boy — the composition judge and grandmaster Alexei Sochnev, who turned 50 that year (that's why the solution of the study is 50 moves long!).

In the miniature **Study 65**, the Reti maneuver is preceded by an anti-check king retreat to the 8ᵗʰ rank.

No. 65. D. Goldberg and A. Malyshev**
Springaren, 2001

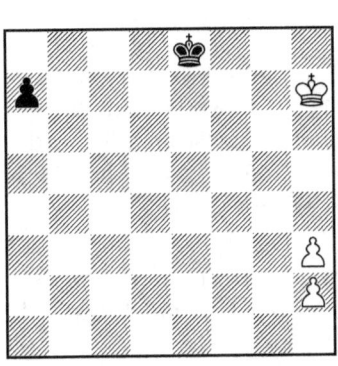

White to play and draw

1.♔g8!! After 1.♔g7? a5! 2.h4 a4 3.h5 a3 4.h6 a2, the black pawn promotes with a check. Nor can white play 1.h4? ♔f7, as the white king gets trapped on the h-file.

1...♔e7! Now the a-pawn push lacks venom: 1...a5 2.h4 a4 3.h5 a3 4.h6 a2 5.h7, and the pawns promote at the same time.

2.h4 ♔f6! 3.h5! ♔g5 4.♔g7! ♔xh5 5.♔f6 a5 6.♔e5, catching up with the pawn. Draw.

Let's look at another spectacular miniature, **Study 66**, a true anthem to this old idea!

No. 66**. O. Pervakov
Shakhmatnoe Obozrenie, 2000
1ˢᵗ prize

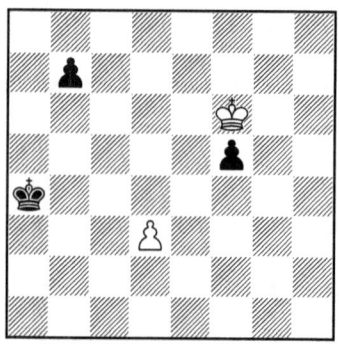

White to play and draw

White cannot save the game without pushing his pawn. But how to execute this plan? The straightforward march 1.d4? f4 2.d5 f3 loses: the black pawn promotes with a check.

If the king immediately captures the f-pawn, then the tempo blow is struck by the other black pawn: 1.♔xf5? b5 2.d4 b4 3.d5 b3 4.d6 b2 5.d7 b1=♛+ (check!)

1.♔e5? is also a mistake: 1...b5 2.d4 b4 3.d5 b3 4.d6 b2 5.d7 b1=♛ 6.d8=♛ ♛e4+! 7.♔f6 (7.♔d6 ♛d4+) 7... ♛h4+, and the white queen falls.

Eureka: **1.♔g5!!** The king moves as far away as possible from the black passed pawn on the b-file! The play now branches:

A) **1...b5 2.d4 b4 3.d5 ♔b5!**

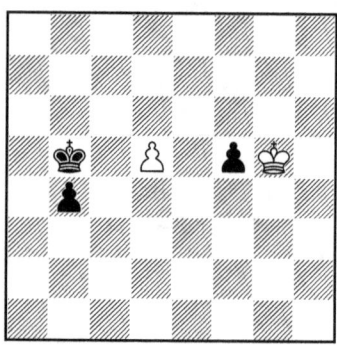

4.d6! White's attempt to perform the Reti trick is skillfully thwarted: 4.♔f6? ♔c5! 5.♔e6 b3 6.d6 b2 7.d7 b1=♛ 8.d8=♛ ♛e4+ 9.♔f7 ♛d5+!, and black wins. **4...♔c6 5.♔xf5! ♔xd6.** Or 5...b3 6.♔e6! b2 7.d7, draw.

6.♔e4 ♔c5 7.♔d3 ♔b5 8.♔c2 ♔a4 9.♔b2. Draw.

B) **1...♔b3 2.♔xf5 ♔c3**

3.♔e5! But not 3.♔e4? b5 4.d4 b4 5.d5 b3 6.d6 b2 7.d7 b1=♛+, and the white monarch is in check again.

3...♔xd3 (3...b5 4.d4) **4.♔d5! ♔c3 5.♔c5.** Draw.

So, how many Reti maneuvers were performed in this masterpiece? The correct answer is three! Two in the actual solution, and another one in the false try!

The Reti maneuver plays a big part in the multi-pawn **Study 67**!

No. 67**. V. Kovalenko
Shakhmatnaya Kompozitsiya, 2004
Commendation

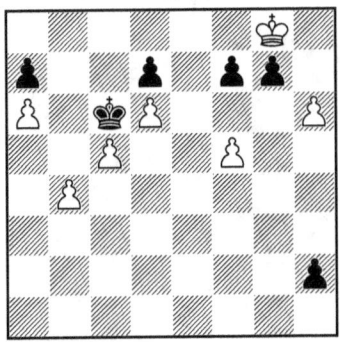

White to play and win

1.h7 h1=♕ 2.h8=♕ ♕xh8+ 3.♔xh8 g5! 3...g6 is toothless: 4.f6 (the simplest) 4...g5 5.♔g7 g4 6.♔xf7 g3 7.♔e8, and the queen endgame is hopeless for black.
4.fxg6. En passant!
4...fxg6

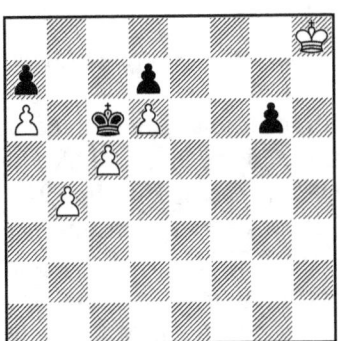

5.♔g7! Chasing the pawn!
5...g5 6.♔f6! g4 7.♔e5! g3 8.♔d4! g2 9.♔c4! g1=♕ 10.b5#. The black pawn reached the promotion square, but checkmate is more important!

Did you notice? The white king walked four squares along the long diagonal — this is a record for the Reti maneuver!

It turns out that this old maneuver can even serve as a foundation for a positional draw study. Here's how the "perpetual Reti maneuver threat" was executed in a modern endgame study.

No. 68**. M. Zinar
JC [Albert] Belyavsky — 80, 2015
Special prize

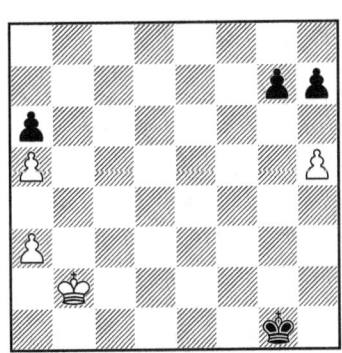

White to play and draw

First of all, we witness a classic march towards the black a6 pawn, keeping an eye on the kingside in the process...
1.♔c3 ♔f2! After 1...g5 2.hxg6 hxg6 3.♔d4 ♔f2 4.♔e5 ♔e3 5.♔f6, the draw is obvious.
2.♔d4! Disaster strikes after 2.♔c4? g5 3.hxg6 hxg6 4.♔c5 g5 5.♔b6 g4 6.♔xa6 g3 7.♔b7 g2 8.a6 g1=♕, and white loses because of his a3 pawn.

2...♔f3 3.♔c5! And now the king can turn towards the queenside! After 3.♔e5? ♔g4, black wins.

3...♔e4! 4.♔b6 ♔d5 5.♔xa6 ♔c6

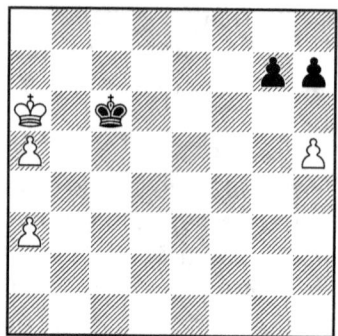

6.♔a7! ♔c7! It turns out that the standard break 6...g5 7.hxg6 hxg6 is met with the saving Reti maneuver: 8.♔b8! ♔b5 9.♔b7! ♔xa5 10.♔c6, entering the square of the black pawn.

7.♔a6! Self-stalemating doesn't work: 7.a4? g5 8.hxg6 hxg6 9.a6 g5 10.♔a8 g4 11.a7 g3 12.a5 g2 13.a6 ♔b6 14.♔b8 g1=♕ 15.a8=♕ ♕g8#.

7...♔c6! Or 7...g5 8.hxg6 hxg6 9.♔b5 g5 10.♔c5 g4 11.♔d4 g3 12.♔e3, draw.

8.♔a7. A positional draw with the perpetual threat of the Reti maneuver!

The Reti maneuver even allows us to construct a stalemating niche. Here's how this idea was executed in **Study 69**.

No. 69**. M. Gawne
British Chess Magazine, 2003

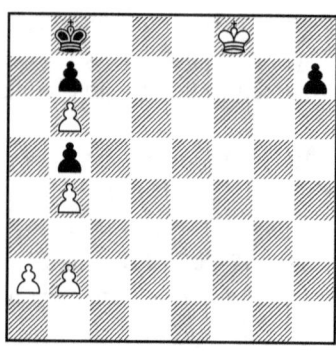

White to play and draw

1.♔e7! h5 2.♔d6 h4 3.♔c5 h3 4.♔xb5 h2

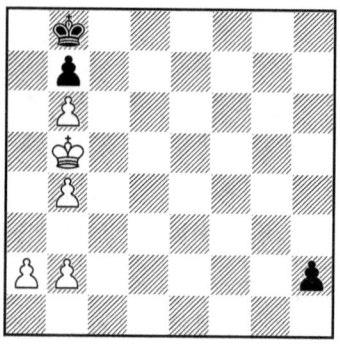

5.♔a5! Not the hasty 5.a4? h1=♕ 6.♔a5 ♕e1, curtains.

5...h1=♕ 6.b5! ♕g2 (6...♕e1+ 7.b4) **7.a4! ♕xb2.** Stalemate.

1.7. Reti — Sarychevs feint

Both of these great maneuvers — the feint and the Reti double threat — appeared in the 1920s. In 1928, they crossed paths for the first time, but in a piece study. Evidently, logic suggested to the composers that if the king can catch up with the pawn using the Reti maneuver, then it can first leave the square. Why? The answer is simple: to hunt for the pawn! Let's see:

No. 70. R. Reti
Deutsch Osterreichische Tageszeitung, 1921

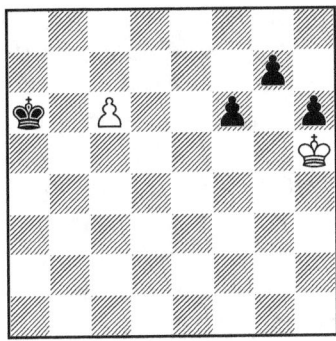

White to play and draw

1.♔g6! h5. Both 1...f5 and 1...♔b6 lead to the same lines, but white is steadfast.

2.♔xg7. Bring it on!

2...h4 3.♔xf6 ♔b6 4.♔e5! Draw.

So, the king *can* leave the square of the pawn! A feint is a preliminary maneuver that causes the opponent to weaken his position. Therefore, a situation might occur when you need to provoke the movement of a passed pawn, and then catch up with it with a Reti maneuver! This is necessary in cases when the pawn cannot be won if it doesn't move. That's how the special case of the feint was born, the Reti – Sarychevs feint.

It was previously thought that **Study 70** was first published in 1928. However, the well-known endgame study database by Harold van der Heijden lists a different date – 1921 (https://www.arves.org/arves/index.

php/en/magazine-eg/harold-van-der-heijden-database-sources). It's no secret that Reti often published his great discoveries in obscure newspapers, and later republished them in other sources, forgetting the place of first publication.

No. 71. A. Sarychev and K. Sarychev
Shakhmatny Listok, 1928
Commendation

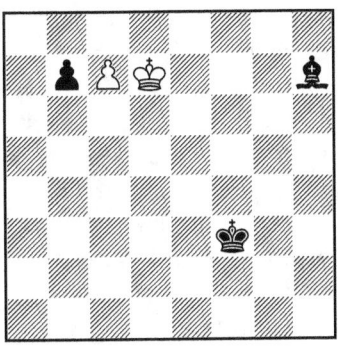

White to play and draw

We quote here the annotations to this study from the book *Etyudy* (*"Endgame Studies"*, Moscow, Fizkultura i Sport, 1961) by A. S. Gurvich, USSR Master of Sports in chess composition.

"The study was first published in *Shakhmatny Listok* in the following form:

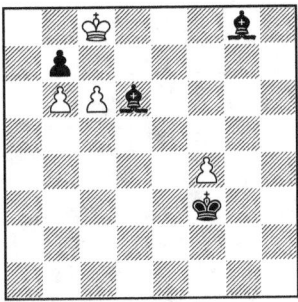

White to play and draw

After 1.♔d7 ♗xf4 2.c7 ♗xc7 3.bxc7 ♗h7, there follows a position that we recommend the readers to study carefully. We discard the introductory play with trades, which, in our opinion, only lowers the aesthetic value of the great Sarychev brothers' study.

[In addition to the purely aesthetic flaw, the study has two side solutions: 1.c7 and 1.♔xb7 ♗d5 2.♔c8 ♗xc6 3.b7.]

White cannot play 1.c8=♕ [in the amended version] because of a check on f5, after which the bishop captures the queen and defends the pawn. Heading to b6 is equally useless due to the same maneuver, 1...♗f5 and 2...♗c8, and then the black king joins the play.

Nor can white play 1.♔e6, because black will reply with any king move to the fourth rank, controlling the f5 square again. White's position seems completely hopeless, and the draw looks like a pipe dream.

But who would have thought that if the black pawn was on b4, rather than b7, then white would have been much closer to his goal, making a draw, than in the initial position?! Who would have thought that when the pawn ran three squares ahead of the white king, it actually became closer and *more* reachable?! Nevertheless, this is true!

If the black pawn stood on b4

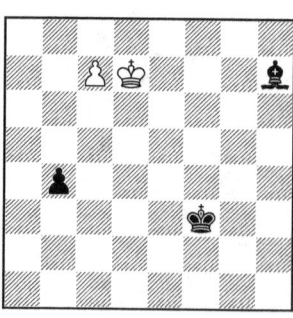

then white would have played the smart 1.♔d6!, getting one step closer to the pawn. Then, after the forced 1...♗f5, he would have attacked the bishop with 2.♔e5, getting one step closer to the pawn, and when the black king steps in to protect the bishop (or the bishop retreats along the c8-h3 diagonal, controlling the promotion square), white wins the third tempo: 3.♔d4!, breaking into the square of the 'unreachable' pawn and forcing a draw. But all that is a very big if...

Nevertheless, back to the main diagram, and the most daring dreams come true in the best endgame studies. So here, to achieve that dream, white makes an incredible move of rare beauty:

1.♔c8!!, blocking his own pawn and getting as far away from the black pawn as possible – it immediately moves two squares ahead:

1...b5. But the white king immediately goes back:

2.♔d7!, and after **2...b4** (white threatened 3.♔c6), the 'big if' suddenly becomes reality:

3.♔d6! ♗f5 4.♔e5 ♗c8 5.♔d4! with a draw.

The first move of this subtle combination is the point, and thus, naturally, it becomes the last one in the explanation of the solution.

We have seen an artistic, spectacular, comprehensive expression of one of the great laws of chess struggle. The king is fighting on two fronts at once, which should seemingly tear it apart. But if the king tries to choose only one front and focus all its efforts there, ignoring the other, it will fail and lose. The only way to achieve success on one of the fronts is to walk on a tightrope, pursuing two goals at once with every step. If you try to catch one rabbit, you fail. But if you try to catch two rabbits at the same time, you will catch one!..

The author of Reti's studies collection, Artur Mandler, correctly claims that none of the numerous imitations of his famous study ever reached its level. This extends even to Reti himself, who later (in 1928) implemented the same idea by adding a black bishop.

However, the Sarychev brothers' study, also published in 1928, concurrently with the new composition of the prominent grandmaster, is, without a doubt, deeper and more spectacular than that composition. It should take its rightful place alongside the famous Reti study as an equally brilliant and distinct creation. This place of honor is secured by the first move alone, which introduces a new, very sharp and contradictory element to a familiar idea.

In Reti's study, as well as in many other variations on this theme, the king immediately moves onto the 'tightrope' and goes after its target; on the other hand, in the Sarychev brothers' study, the king first takes an 'insane' step in the opposite direction, creating a hopeless-looking position where a draw looks impossible."

In the pawn form, the Reti – Sarychevs feint was first expressed in the "sketch" **Study 72.**

No. 72. J. Moravec
Ceskoslovensky Sach, 1952

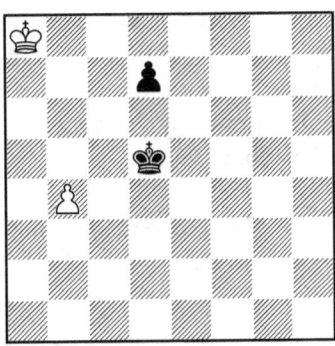

White to play and draw

1.♔b7 ♔c4 Now, 2.♔b6? ♔xb4 gives nothing – white cannot win the pawn. But what if he first performs a feint?

2.♔c7! d5 3.♔c6! Now it's a draw. Still, this is too simple.

No. 73. M. Zinar
Shakhmaty v SSSR, 1984
Special commendation

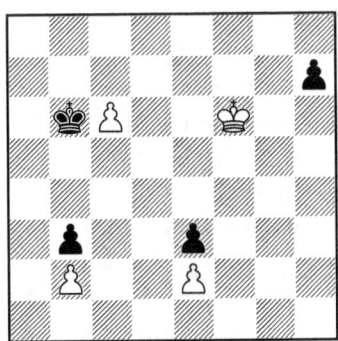

White to play and draw

The Reti – Sarychevs feint is vividly illustrated here. The king is in the square and can capture the pawn, but the banal 1.♔g5? ♔xc6 2.♔h6 ♔d5 3.♔xh7 ♔e5 4.♔h6 ♔f4 loses, while the paradoxical

1.♔g7!! h5 2.♔f6! h4 3.♔e5! leads to a draw.

Pawn studies only rarely win top prizes in composition competitions. **Study 74** is a rare exception. I think that the judge of the annual contest was enraptured by the Reti – Sarychevs feint!

No. 74**. L. Katsnelson
64, 1977
2nd prize

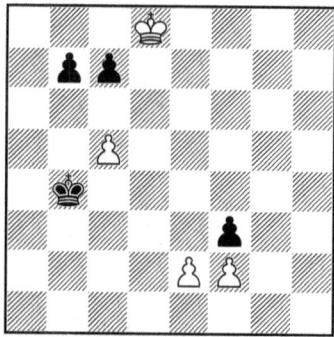

White to play and draw

1.c6! Not 1.exf3? ♔xc5 2.♔e7 ♔d5! 3.f4 ♔e4, curtains.

1...bxc6 2.exf3 ♔c5! 3.♔e7!! A false try: 3.♔d7? (3.f4? ♔d6!) 3...♔d5! 4.f4 c5 5.♔e7 c4! 6.f5 c3 7.f6 c2 8.f7 c1=♛ 9.f8=♛ ♛c5+ 10.♔e8 ♛xf8+ 11.♔xf8 c5, and black wins.

3...♔d4! 4.f4! ♔e4

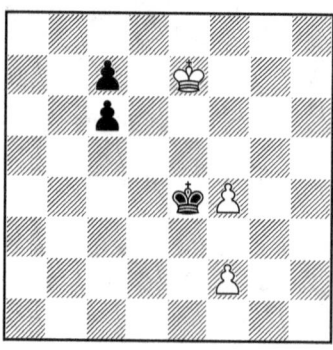

5.♔d7!! The Reti – Sarychevs feint in action! White can't immediately play 5.♔e6? due to 5...♔xf4.

5...c5 6.♔e6! ♔xf4. 6...c4 now doesn't work: 7.f5 c3 8.f6 c2 9.f7 c1=♛ 10.f8=♛ ♛c6+ 11.♔f7!, and black can't trade queens.

7.♔d5, entering the square of the pawn. Draw.

And, of course, the Reti – Sarychevs feint serves as a great addition to other ideas. For instance, in **Study 75**, it's used as a prelude to the mating attack!

No. 75**. V. Kovalenko
64 – Shakhmatnoe Obozrenie, 1990

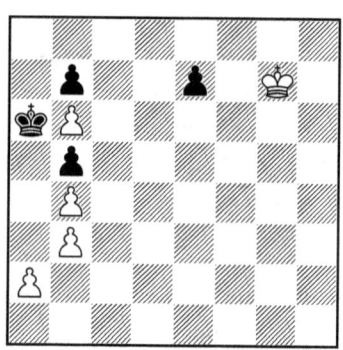

White to play and win

Stopping the black pawn looks like an obvious idea: 1.♔g6? But after 1...♔xb6 2.♔f5 ♔c7 3.♔e6 ♔d8 4.♔d5 ♔d7 5.♔c5 ♔e6! 6.a4 bxa4 7.bxa4 ♔d7! 8.♔b6 ♔c8, black holds confidently.

White wins by leaving the square of the pawn: **1.♔f7!! e5 2.♔e6!** Threatening to re-enter the square!

2...e4 3.♔d5 e3

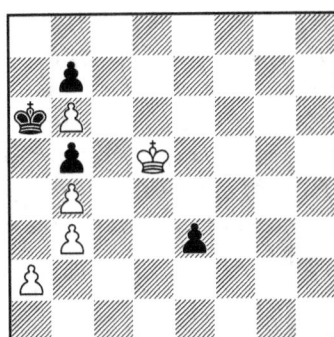

4.♔c5! Changing the target of attack! There's a choice between two mating finales:

4...e2 5.a4 e1=♕ 6.axb5# or **5...bxa4 6.b5+ ♔a5 7.b4#!**

1.8. Luring into check

Another way to win a tempo in a pawn race is to give a check with a pawn or a newly-created queen. The checking and anti-checking techniques have already provided a lot (and, undoubtedly, will give a lot more) of great playful studies with unexpected maneuvers by the kings.

No. 76. O. Duras
Narodni Listy, 1904

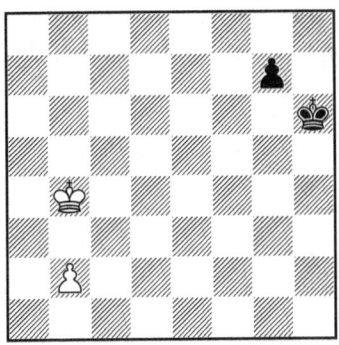

White to play and win

A classical composition!

1.♔c5! A double blow against the resources 1...g5 and 1...♔g6.

1...g5 2.b4 g4 3.♔d4! ♔g5 4.b5! g3

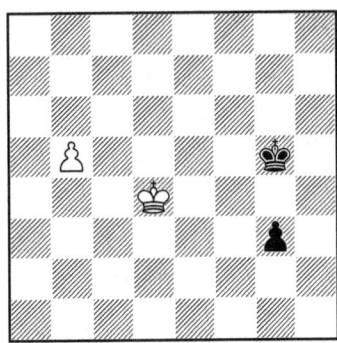

5.♔e3! ♔g4 6.b6 ♔h3 7.b7 g2 8.♔f2! ♔h2 9.b8=♕+.

This most popular checking technique – luring the black king to the second or third rank – can be called the "Duras decoy". The author expressed the idea very clearly.

Note that this study contains another instance of luring into check, but unfortunately it is fraught with duals at the last stage of the solution: **1...♔g6 2.b4! ♔f7** (2...♔f6 3.♔d6!) **3.b5 ♔e7**

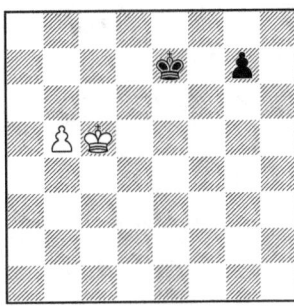

4.♔c6! ♔d8! 5.♔b7 (or 5.♔b6) **5...g5 6.b6 g4 7.♔a8 g3 8.b7 g2 9.b8=♕+** etc..

No. 77. M. Zinar
Shakhmaty v SSSR, 1989

White to play and draw

1.♔a5! ♚c5 2.h4 b4 3.♔a4! ♚c4
4.h5 b3

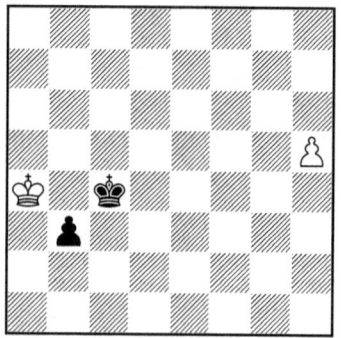

5.♔a3! ♚c3 6.h6 b2 7.h7 b1=♕
8.h8=♕+, draw.

No. 78 C. De Feijter
Deventer Dagblad, 1939

White to play and win

This study looks similar to the Reti maneuver from **Study 53**. Here, however, it's performed by black, and black's destiny in endgame studies is to fail! Such cases are called "anti-Reti". Here, the king gets into check.

1.♔g5! b5 2.♔f4 ♚f2 3.h4 ♚e2
4.♔e4 ♚d2

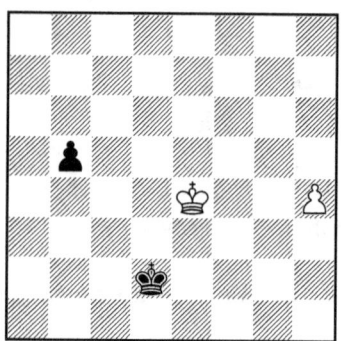

5.♔d4(d5). An unpleasant dual, because after 5.♔d5 a set of completely different ideas emerges. If 5...♚c3, then the king is checked immediately, while if 5...♚d3, then the black queen is lost after a skewering check from h7.

5...♚c2 6.♔c5 ♚c3 7.h5 b4 8.h6 b3 9.h7 b2 10.h8=♕+, and the white rook's pawn promotes while checking the opponent's king.

In **Study 79**, the black king is decoyed into check by subtle play of the white king.

No. 79**. N. Kralin
Moscow championship 2001
1st prize

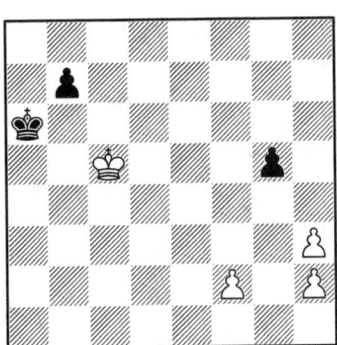

Black to move. White wins

1...b6+! 2.♔d5!! The point! As subsequent events show, the white king should both keep an eye on the b-pawn and prevent the black king from moving to the kingside. So, it's wrong to play 2.♔c4? b5+ 3.♔b4 ♔b6 4.h4 gxh4 5.f4 ♔c6 or 2.♔c6? b5 3.♔c5 ♔a5 4.h4!

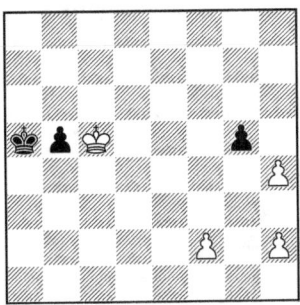

4...b4!! 5.♔c4 ♔a4 6.hxg5 b3 7.♔c3 ♔a3 8.g6 b2 9.g7 b1=♕ 10.g8=♕ ♕b2+ 11.♔d3 ♕xf2, and the queen endgame is drawn. Both 2.♔b4? ♔b7 3.♔b5 ♔c7 4.f3 ♔d6 and 2.♔d4? ♔b7! 3.♔d5 ♔c7! 4.f3 ♔d7 are also bad, and black achieves equality.

2...b5. 2...♔b7 doesn't save him either: 3.♔d6! ♔c8 (3...b5 4.♔c5 b4 5.♔xb4 ♔c6 6.♔c4) 4.♔c6, curtains.

3.h4! (3.♔c5? ♔a5 4.h4 b4!) **3... gxh4**

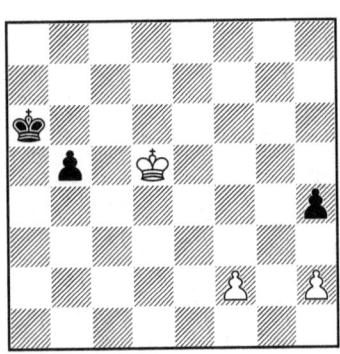

4.♔c5! But not 4.f4? ♔b6 5.f5 ♔c7 6.f6 ♔d7, draw.

4...♔a5 5.f4 b4 6.♔c4 (6.♔d4? ♔b5) **6...♔a4 7.f5 b3 8.♔c3! ♔a3** (8...♔b5 9.f6) **9.f6 b2 10.f7 b1=♕ 11.f8=♕+** (check!) **11...♔a2 12.♕a8#.**

A model mate.

Twin endgame studies are studies that are similar in form (just one piece is moved to a different square or removed from the board altogether), but different in solution. Often, the solution of the first study becomes a false try in the second, and vice versa. We see such a case in **Study 80**. The unifying idea behind both of these positions is luring the black king into check.

No. 80** V. Kovalenko
Problemist Yuga, 1996
Commendation

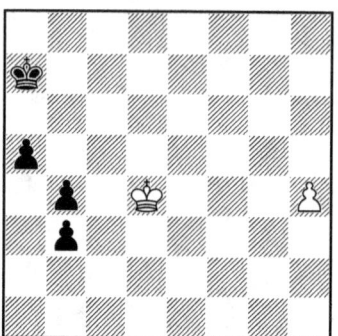

White to play and draw

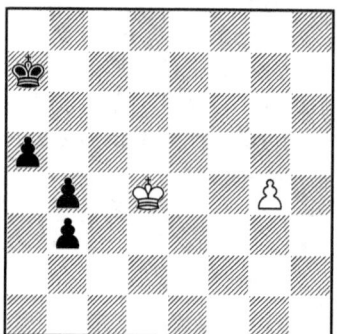

White to play and draw

In the first diagram position, with the white pawn on h4, the decisive line is **1.♔d3 a4 2.♔d2 a3 3.♔c1 b2+**

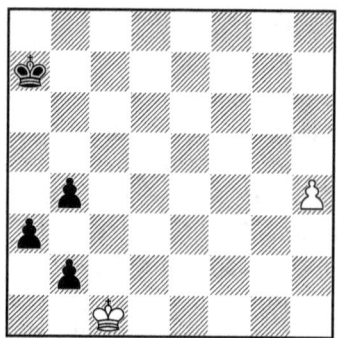

4.♔c2!! False try: 4.♔b1? ♔b6 5.h5 ♔c5 6.h6 ♔c4 7.h7 ♔b3 8.h8=♕ a2#.

4...b3+ 5.♔b1 ♔b6 6.h5 ♔c5 7.h6 ♔c4 8.h7 ♔c3 9.h8=♕+ (check), and there's no checkmate.

If the pawn is moved from h4 to g4 as per the second diagram, then white chooses a different move in the key position: **1.♔d3 a4 2.♔d2 a3 3.♔c1 b2+**

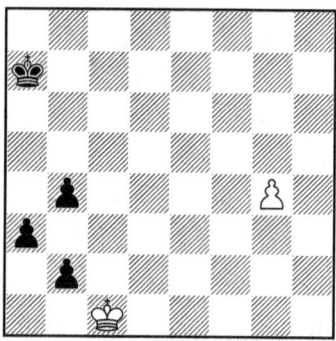

4.♔b1!! Not 4.♔c2? b3+ 5.♔b1 ♔b6 6.g5 ♔c5 7.g6 ♔d4 8.g7 ♔c3 9.g8=♕ a2#. **4...♔b6 5.g5 ♔c5 6.g6 ♔c4 7.g7 ♔b3 8.g8=♕+** (check), and there's no checkmate again.

Luring the king into check is the finishing touch of the two-phase **Study 81**, composed by the seventh world champion.

No. 81**. V. Smyslov
64 – Shakhmatnoe Obozrenie, 2009

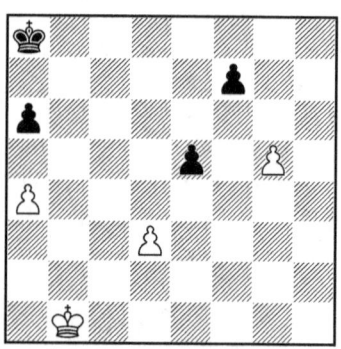

White to play and win

The first phase is the struggle for a beneficial way to achieve opposition.

1.d4! But not the immediate 1.♔c2? ♚b7 2.d4 ♚c6! 3.♔c3 ♚d5 4.dxe5 ♚xe5 5.♔b4 ♚f5, draw.

1...exd4. Or 1...e4 2.♔c2 ♚b7 3.♔d2 ♚c6 4.♔e3 ♚d5 5.a5!, and white wins.

2.♔c2 ♚b7 3.♔d3 ♚c6 4.♔xd4 ♚d6

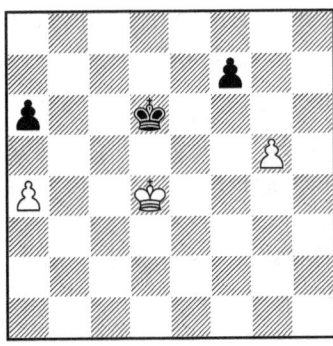

5.a5! Mutual zugzwang.

5...♚e6 (5...♚c6 6.♔e5 ♚b5 7.♔f6) **6.♔c5 ♚f5 7.♔b6 ♚xg5 8.♔xa6 f5.** At first glance, it seems that the pawns reach the promotion squares at the same time...

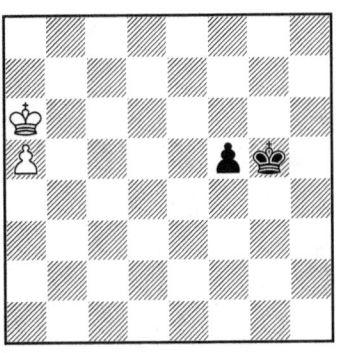

9.♔b5! White still wins by maneuvering his king and luring the opponent's king into check.

9...f4 10.♔c4 f3 11.♔d3 ♚f4 12.a6 ♚g3 13.a7 f2 14.♔e2 ♚g2 15.a8=♕+. White wins.

1.9. Grigoriev anti-check feint

A special case of the feint. Its essence is seen in the following example, despite its artistic flaws.

No. 82. N. Grigoriev
Shakhmaty, 1928

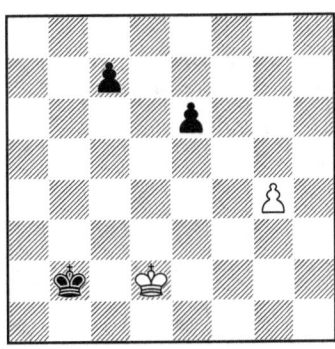

White to play and win

1.♔d3! ♚b3 2.♔d4! ♚b4 3.g5! Black wins after 3.♔e3? ♚c5! 4.g5 ♚d6 5.♔e4 ♚e7 6.♔e5 c5 7.g6 ♚f8 8.♔e4 ♚g7 etc..

3...c5+

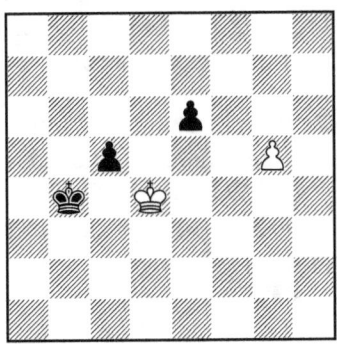

4.♔e3! c4. Unfortunately from the artistic point of view, 4...♔b3 is also possible here.

5.g6, and the white pawn promotes faster. (And here, alas, white can also play 5.♔d2 ♔b3 6.♔c1!, winning. Thus, the most precise continuation is actually 4...♔b3 5.g6 c4 6.g7, etc..)

Therefore, the ♔d3–d4–e3 maneuver was necessary for white to win a tempo. Let's call this pretty maneuver the **Grigoriev anti-check feint**. It's clear from what was stated above why it is a feint. But why "anti-check"?! White was still checked – 3...c5+? Look closer: that check is nothing more than an optical illusion. To confirm this, let's study the next composition.

No. 83. M. Zinar
64 – Shakhmatnoe Obozrenie, 1988

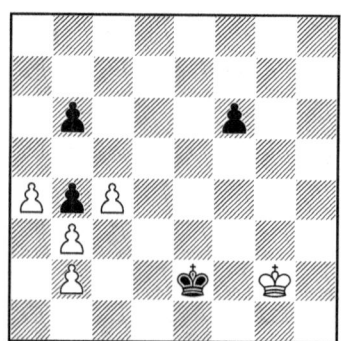

White to play and win

1.♔g3! White should not hurry: after the immediate 1.c5? bxc5 2.a5 f5 3.a6 f4 4.a7 f3+ 5.♔g3 f2, the pawns make it to promotion squares at the same time!

1...♔e3 2.♔g4! ♔e4

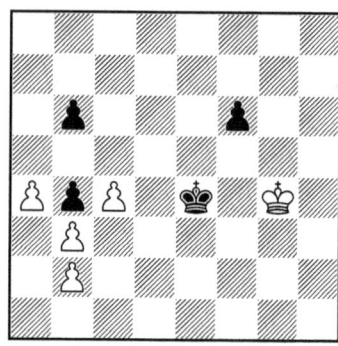

3.♔h3!! In comparison with the previous study, a different move order is seen. Again, 3.c5? is bad due to 3...bxc5 4.♔h3 ♔d4 5.♔g2 c4 with a draw.

3...♔e3. 3...f5 is met with 4.♔g2 f4 5.♔f2 ♔d4 6.♔f3 ♔e5 7.c5 bxc5 8.a5, winning.

4.c5 bxc5 5.a5, and wins. Here, the win is only possible because black couldn't check the white king. In **Study 82**, it's not as clear because of the different move order.

In the next composition, white first performs an anti-check feint and then the Duras decoy, winning two tempi!

No. 84. N. Grigoriev
Izvestia, 1928
(version)

White to play and win

1.♔c3! ♚a3 2.♔c4! ♚a4 3.g4 b5+ 4.♔d3! ♚a3 5.g5 b4 6.g6 b3 7.g7 b2

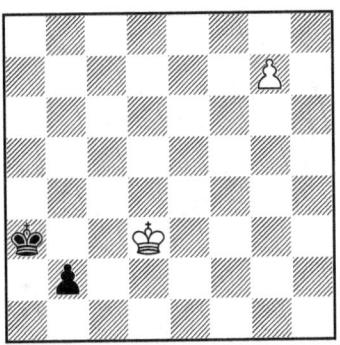

8.♔c2! ♚a2 9.g8=♕+ and wins.

Next up: attraction to the third rank (rather than to the second rank, as in **Study 84**) looks more difficult and spectacular. However, without additional material, the weaker side would manage to save the game. Therefore, the next study features five pawns.

No. 85. M. Zinar
64 – Shakhmatnoe Obozrenie, 1988

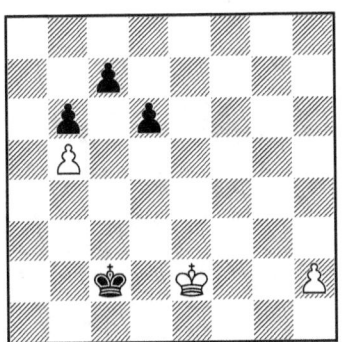

White to play and win

1.♔e3! ♚c3 2.♔e4! ♚c4 3.h4! Not 3.♔f3? ♚d5! 4.♔f4 ♚e6, and the h-pawn is stopped, while the black pawns on the queenside are invincible.

3...d5+ 4.♔f3! ♚b3! If 4...d4, then 5.♔e2! – now stopping the h-pawn is

not dangerous because its black rival, the d-pawn, is not protected by the c-pawn anymore! 5...♚d5 is met with 6.♔d3 ♚e5 7.h5, and wins.

5.h5 d4 6.♔e4 ♚c4! 7.h6 d3

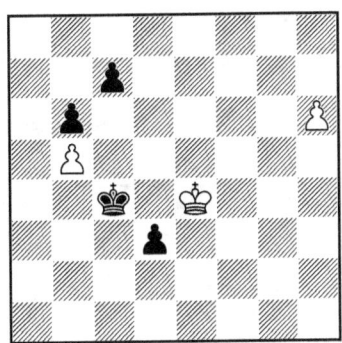

8.♔e3! ♚c3 9.h7 d2 10.h8=♕+, with the Duras decoy.

In addition to the tactical trick used above, there's another popular theme in pawn-promotion studies introduced by Grigoriev. He referred to it as "step by step and strictly in order". In modern parlance, it's called **systematic movement**.

No. 86. N. Grigoriev
64, 1930
2nd prize
(correction by A. Cheron, 1955)

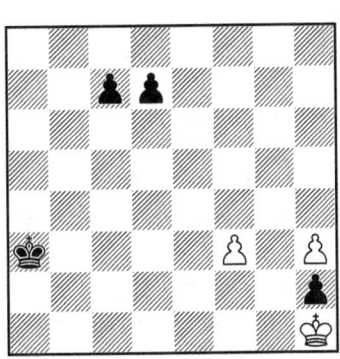

White to play and win

1.f4! To promote the pawn with a check.

1...♔b4 2.h4! Otherwise the black king will enter the square of the h-pawn. The "logical" 2.f5? is bad: 2...♔c5 3.h4 ♔d6 4.h5 ♔e5 5.h6 ♔f6 6.♔xh2 c5 7.♔g3 c4 8.♔f4 c3 9.♔e3 d5 10.♔d3 d4 11.♔c2 ♔f7, and white cannot improve his position.

2...d5. Now the cycle repeats:

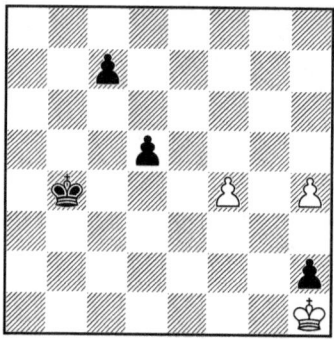

3.f5! ♔c5 4.h5! d4. And again...

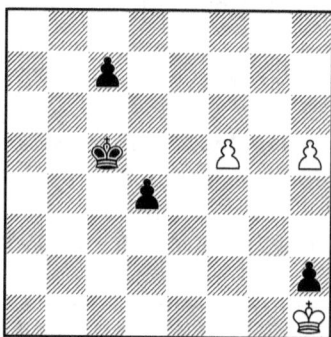

5.f6! ♔d6 6.h6! d3 7.f7! And for the fourth time!

7...♔e7 8.h7! d2 9.f8=♕+! ♔xf8 10.h8=♕+ with a win. A brilliant study!

In **Study 87**, it's necessary to close off the a1-h8 diagonal to promote the pawn. This is achieved by three cycles of implementing the Grigoriev theme.

No. 87. T. Gvardzaladze
64, 1969

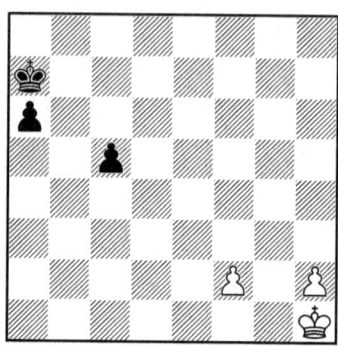

White to play and draw

1.♔g2. White both gets the king away from the first rank to avoid a possible check and stops the c-pawn by threatening to enter its square.

1...a5 2.f4! ♔b6

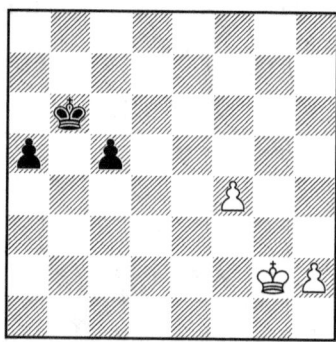

3.h4! Otherwise, the king will enter the square of the pawn. For instance: 3.f5? ♔c6 4.h4 ♔d5 5.h5 ♔e5 6.h6 ♔f6 7.♔f3 a4, curtains.

3...a4 4.f5! ♔c6 5.h5! a3 6.f6! ♔d6 7.h6! a2 8.h7! with a draw, because the diagonal is closed off.

1.10 Anti-check retreat

While the Duras decoy leads the king into check from the promoted queen, the most popular anti-check maneuver in chess composition involves escaping the pawn checks.

The most impressive effect is achieved when the king falls back. From the very first steps in learning chess, we are told that the king should be an active piece in the endgame, but it's different here: the king retreats in cowardly fashion!

No. 88. A. Herbstman
Narodni Listy, 1929
4th prize

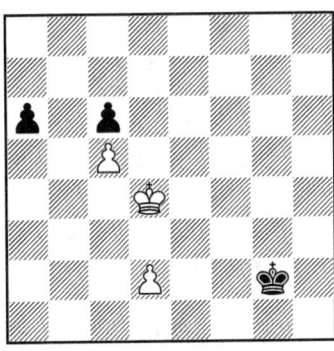

White to play and win

It's necessary to free the way for the d-pawn and push back the king. But after 1.♔e4? a5 2.d4 a4 3.♔d3 a3 4.♔c2 ♔f3 5.d5 cxd5 6.c6 d4 7.c7 d3+, it's a draw.

The correct move is **1.♔e3! a5 2.d4 a4 3.♔d2! a3**

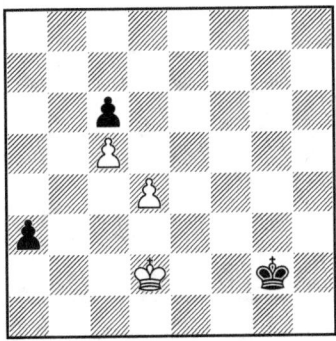

4.♔c1!! ♔f3 5.d5 cxd5 6.c6 d4 7.c7, and black doesn't have time to give a check.

Let's look at **Study 89.** It's clear that after the breakthrough, the king will have to fend off two passed pawns. And so, white immediately moves his king into the square of the black pawn that will soon get to f5.

No. 89. M. Zinar
Pobeda (Feodosia), 1981

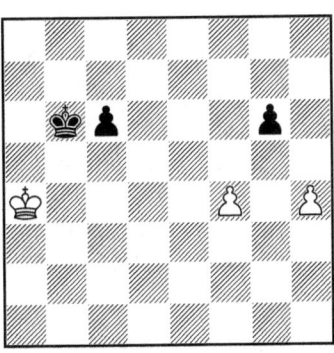

White to play and win

1.♔b3! If now 1...♔c7, then 2.f5 gxf5 3.h5 etc. But black doesn't want to make an extra king move and prefers to further improve the position of his passed pawn.

1...c5! 2.♔c2! A funny situation: the pawn advances, and the king runs away from it!

2...c4!

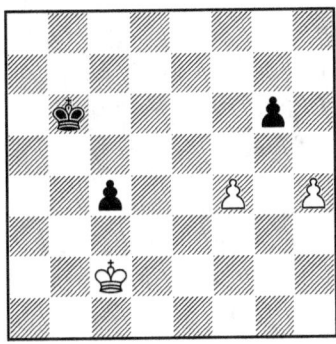

3.♔d1!! After 3.♔d2? ♚c5 4.f5 gxf5
5.h5 f4 6.h6 f3 7.h7 c3+, it's a draw.

3...♚c5. After 3...c3?! 4.♔c2 ♚c5
5.f5 gxf5 6.h5 f4 7.♔xc3, it's curtains!

4.f5! gxf5 5.h5, and wins. Here's
where white's foresight pays off – he
put the king on d1 in advance! The rest
is simple: 5...f4 6.h6 f3 7.h7 f2 8.♔e2!,
curtains.

Examples of the anti-check retreat
theme allow us to see how studies are
composed and how composers develop
their ideas.

In **Study 90**, serial synthesis of the "step
by step and strictly in order" technique
with the anti-check retreat allowed the
author to compose a brilliant study.

No. 90. A. Khachaturov
Shakhmaty v SSSR, 1947

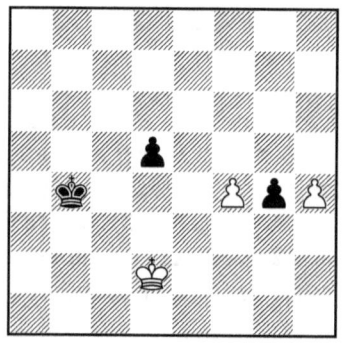

White to play and win

1.f5! Like in the Grigoriev
composition (see **Study 86**), the pawn
wants to promote with a check. The d-
and g-pawns allow white to perform the
anti-check retreat, but right now it's too
premature, because black, wasting no
time on moving the g-pawn, will push
the other pawn, supported by the king.

1...♔c5 2.h5! g3

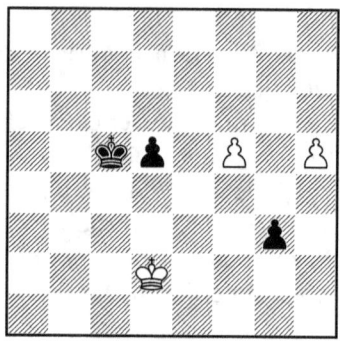

3.♔e1!! d4. In **Study 86**, only
four pieces moved "strictly in order",
while here, all six do! Now the cycle
repeats.

4.f6! ♔d6 5.h6! g2 6.♔f2 d3. And
again!

**7.f7! ♔e7 8.h7 g1=♕+ 9.♔xg1
d2 10.f8=♕+ ♔xf8 11.h8=♕+.**
Systematic movement of six pieces. The
themes are different, but they blend
together very well!

One common way to execute the
idea expressively is to repeat the same
technique several times. The means of
repeating can be different.

No. 91. M. Zinar
Moscow competition, 1985
Commendation

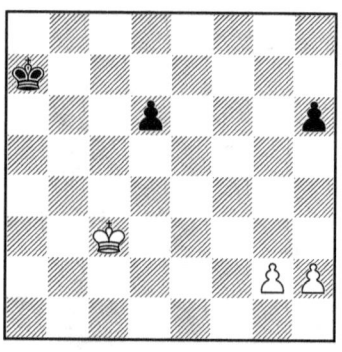

White to play and win

1.g4! ♚b6 2.h4 ♚c5. Transposing into a 1941 V. Mees study.

3.g5 hxg5 4.h5! g4 5.♔d2! g3 6.♔e1! with a known win.

A false try (imitation of the solution): 1.h4? This move has a drawback: the actual solution is easier to find. It is well-known that to create a passed pawn, you should first push the "semi-passer", so you can simply miss 1.h4? Nevertheless, the refutation is beautiful!

1...h5! It's simple to calculate that 2.g4 only leads to a draw here, but why don't we try to prepare a breakthrough, like in **Study 89**?

2.♔d2! d5! The pawn advances towards the king, like in **Study 89**.

3.♔e1. Now white wins after 3... ♚b6 4.g4, but the pawn continues its honorable work:

3....d4!!, with a draw.

But even that is not all! You can achieve an echo-repetition in parallel lines, which also makes the study more expressive.

No. 92. M. Zinar
64 – Shakhmatnoe Obozrenie, 1986

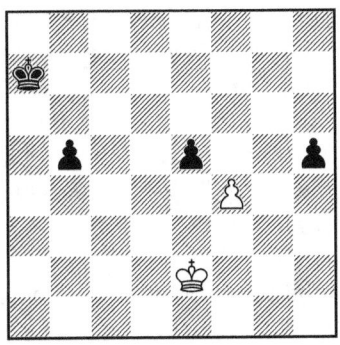

White to play and win

1.f5! b4 2.f6! It's too early to move the king because of 2...h4 with a draw.

2...b3 3.♔d1!, and wins.

Or **1...h4 2.f6 h3 3.♔f1!,** winning as well.

In **Study 93,** a black/white synthesis of the anti-check retreat is performed. Here, it's important that black performs it first, otherwise it looks completely senseless for him.

However, if white is forced to perform the retreat *because* black did it first, this looks impressive!

No. 93. M. Zinar
Moscow competition, 1985
Commendation

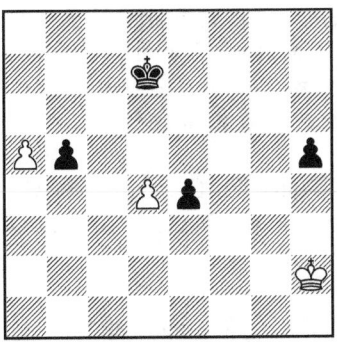

White to play and win

1.a6! ♚c8! 1...♚c7 is simply met with 2.d5 e3 3.♔g2 h4 4.d6+ ♚xd6 5.a7 h3+ 6.♔f1(g3) h2 7.a8=♕ with a win. Now, however, the retreat should be met with a similar maneuver, but first...

2.d5! e3 3.♔g1!!, and wins.

Study 94 features serial synthesis.

No. 94. M. Zinar
64 – Shakhmatnoe Obozrenie, 1986

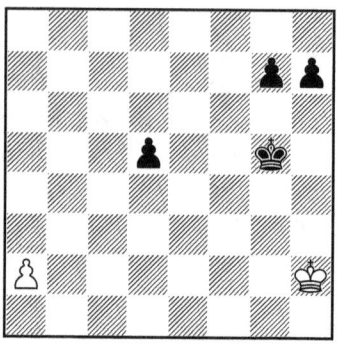

White to play and win

1.a4 d4 2.♔g1!! d3 3.♔f1!! – the second consecutive anti-check retreat, because white is wary of a premature check from the g7 pawn. Two maneuvers in a row, and the aesthetic impression becomes even stronger.

In **Study 95**, the synthesis of similar themes was performed both serially and in parallel!

No. 95. V. Archakov and M. Zinar
Shakhmaty v SSSR, 1986
Special commendation

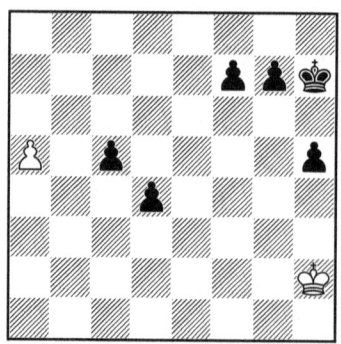

White to play and win

1.♔g1!! A counter-check retreat, out of fear of the h-pawn advance.

1...d3 2.♔f1!!, avoiding the g-pawn, like in the previous study.

Or another line: **1...c4 2.♔f2(f1) c3 3.♔e1!!,** this time avoiding the f-pawn. White cannot play 3.♔e2? f5 4.a6 f4 5.a7 f3+! 6.♔xf3 c2 7.a8=♕ c1=♕ 8.♕e4+ ♔h6 9.♕e6+ g6 and he is out of checks, so black even wins here.

The paradox is that the white king, instead of showing the usual activity in the endgame, "cowardly" retreats to the first rank three times! Obviously, the dual 2.♔f2(f1) is purely academic and does not influence the essence of play.

A curious comment from reader A. Marchenko (Braginovka village, Dnepropetrovsk Oblast) was added to the solution: "Doesn't the philosophy look too deep for such a short solution?"

Our answer: "Here, the anti-check maneuver is performed three times, both in series and in parallel. The material balance also looks attractive: one pawn against five. Let us remember the fact that there must be no unnecessary pieces and pawns in chess composition (unless pawns are used as 'building blocks' for various walls and niches), and therefore, one side cannot possess an advantage too big in a pawn endgame study, otherwise there would be no play and no fight. This study is unique in this regard: black is four pawns up!" (*64 – Shakhmatnoe Obozrenie*, No. 18, 1986.)

It might seem that the theme of the anti-check retreat has been exhausted. But no! Discoveries are still possible!..

No. 96**. I. Aliev
MT Grigoriev – 120, 2016
Commendation

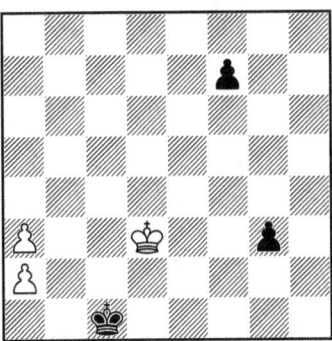

White to play and win

1.♔e2!! False try: 1.♔e3? f5 2.a4 f4+ 3.♔f3 ♔d2 4.a5 g2 5.♔xg2 ♔e2 6.a6 f3+ 7.♔g3 f2, draw.

1...f5 2.a4 f4 3.a5 g2 4.♔f2 f3 5.a6 ♔d2 6.a7 g1=♕+ 7.♔xg1

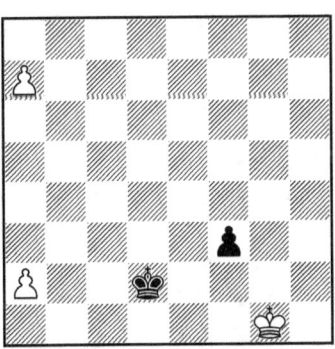

7...♔e1. Or 7...♔e2 8.a8=♕ f2+ 9.♔h2 f1=♕ 10.♕a6+!, with a queen trade and win.

8.a8=♕ (an organic move order change also wins: 8.♔h2) **8...f2+ 9.♔h2 f1=♕ 10.♕h1!** White wins.

"A new position with an anti-check king retreat has been discovered." (M. Zinar, competition judge).

In **Studies 89–96** we introduced techniques of study composition and means of synthesis of similar ideas (serial, parallel, black/white, false tries) as well as ideas that are related but different: "step by step" and the anti-check retreat.

The truly pawn-related idea, promoting the pawn to a queen, still provides ample opportunity for research and discovery. A thorough examination of **Studies 42–96** will help you with this work.

1.11. King double threat (Eilazyan branch)

In the *Problemist Ukrainy* magazine (No. 1, 2016), Mikhail Zinar published a big article called "The Eilazyan Branch", where he described the features of a king double threat in pawn endgame studies:

"As I studied the articles of Eduard Eilazyan [a Ukrainian study composer] on the change of play in endgame studies, I found that one of these changes could be applied to the king double threat in a pawn endgame. Double threat is one of the most popular tactical tricks in pawn studies. As a rule it has little aesthetic value, but in this case it does stand out. I called this special form of the double threat the 'Eilazyan branch', because it looks like a tree branch to me.

The Eilazyan branch is a king double threat played when it is possible to attack both targets separately. Black's refutations in thematic false tries are in turn refuted by white changing the direction of attack."

Here's an outline of the branch:

"A": moves by white that only work towards achieving the first goal; **"a"** is the move that refutes "A".

"B": moves by white that only work towards achieving the second goal; **"b"** is the move that refutes "B".

"C": a double threat by the white king.

Thematic false tries: "A?" is only met with "a!", "B?" is only met with "b!". The solution is "C!"

And now "a" is only met with "B!", and "b" is only met with "A!"

Mikhail Zinar reinforced his theoretical research on the Eilazyan branch with about twenty examples in his article – from simple schemes to full-fledged endgame studies. Here are some of them.

No. 97**. M. Zinar
Problemist Ukrainy, 2016

White to play and draw

First of all, white should avoid shouldering:

1.♔g5! ♔d6 2.♔f4! Not 2.♔f5? ♔d5 3.♔f4 ♔d4, curtains.

2...♔c5! 2...♔d5 is met with 3.♔e3, drawing.

3.♔e4!! The king double threat! Thematic false tries: 3.♔e5? b5! 4.♔e4 ♔b4 and 3.♔e3? ♔b4! 4.♔d4 b5, and black wins in both variations.

3...b5 4.♔d3! ♔b4 5.♔c2 or **3...♔b4 4.♔d5! ♔xb3 5.♔c5 ♔a4 6.♔b6.** Draw. The Eilazyan branch idea is executed here in a horizontal direction.

It later turned out that the position after white's second move had already occurred in a mirrored form in a multi-piece composition (I. Saren, *Helsingin Sanomat*, 1967), after black's fifth move. Indeed, nothing is new under the sun!

And here's a study sketch where the Eilazyan branch is executed in a vertical direction.

No. 98**. M. Zinar
Problemist Ukrainy, 2016

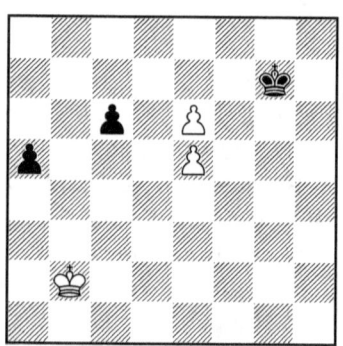

White to play and draw

Thematic false tries: 1.♔a3? c5! 2.♔a4 c4 3.♔a3 ♚f8 4.♔b2 a4 5.♔c3 a3 or 1.♔c3? ♚f8! 2.♔c4 ♚e7 3.♔c5 ♔xe6, curtains.

The correct way is **1.♔b3!! c5 2.♔c4! a4 3.♔xc5 a3 4.♔d6!** But not 4.♔c6? a2 5.e7 a1=♕ 6.e8=♕ ♕a4+, losing the queen.

4...a2 5.e7 or **1...♚f8 2.♔a4! ♚e7 3.♔xa5 ♚xe6 4.♔b6,** with a draw in both cases.

The Eilazyan branch can also be executed diagonally, like in the following sketch, **Study 99.**

No. 99**. M. Zinar
Problemist Ukrainy, 2016

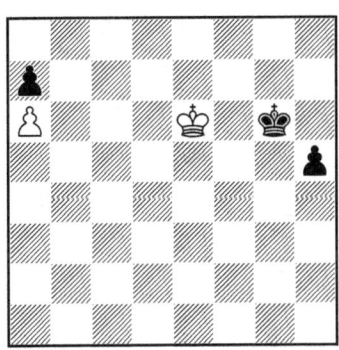

White to play and draw

False tries: 1.♔e5? ♚g5! 2.♔e4 ♚g4 3.♔e3 ♚g3 4.♔e2 ♚g2! or 1.♔d6? h4!, with a tragedy for white.

The decisive move: **1.♔d5! ♚g5 2.♔c6! h4 3.♔b7 h3 4.♔xa7 h2 5.♔b8 h1=♕ 6.a7** or **1...h4 2.♔e4!** with a draw.

Obviously, the Eilazyan branch alone is not enough to compose a study. A synthesis of several ideas is required, like in the next composition.

No. 100**. M. Zinar
Problemist Ukrainy, 2016
Commendation

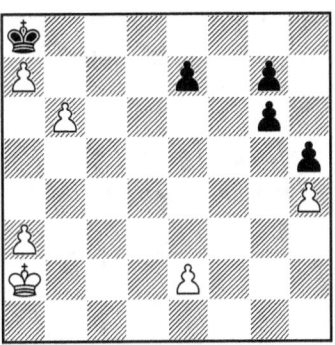

White to play and win

Black is threatening a pawn breakthrough on the kingside. How to stop it? Only with the Reti maneuver!
1.♔b3! g5 2.♔c4! gxh4

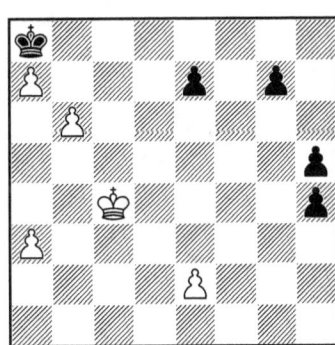

3.♔d5!! Thematic false tries of the Eilazyan branch: 3.♔d4? h3! or 3.♔c5? ♚b7! etc. Next, there are two variations:

A) **3...h3 4.♔c6! h2 5.b7+ ♚xa7 6.♔c7 h1=♕ 7.b8=♕+ ♚a6 8.♕b6#** or

B) **3...♚b7 4.♔e4 h3 5.♔f3 h4 6.♔f2 g5** (6...g6 7.♔g1 g5 8.♔h1 g4 9.♔h2) **7.♔g1 g4 8.♔h2 ♚a8 9.a4! ♚b7 10.a5! ♚a8 11.a6! e6! 12.e3!** After 12.e4? e5, white is in zugzwang.

12...e5 13.e4 g3+ 14.♔xh3, and white has enough time to get his king out of stalemate and win.

In the next composition, the Reti maneuver must be executed at exactly the right moment!

No. 101**. M. Zinar
Problemist Ukrainy, 2016

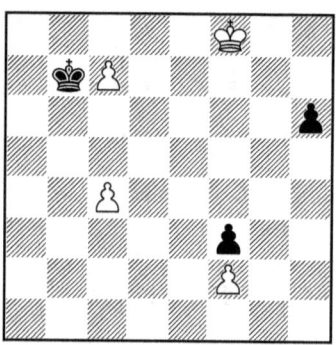

White to play and win

The main plan involving the Reti maneuver does not work immediately: 1.♔e7? ♔xc7 2.♔f6 ♔c6 3.♔g6 ♔c5 4.♔xh6 ♔xc4 5.♔g5 ♔d5 6.♔f4 ♔e6 7.♔xf3 ♔f5 with the drawing opposition.

1.♔f7!! h5. Provoking white to go for the Eilazyan branch with 2.♔f6? h4! or 2.♔e7? ♔xc7, when black wins in both lines.

White wins with a Reti maneuver that starts one rank lower: **2.♔e6!! ♔xc7**. Or 2...h4 3.♔d7!

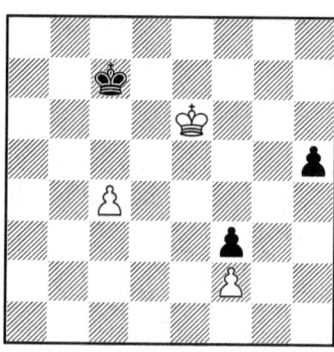

3.♔f5! Not 3.♔d5? ♔b6 4.♔d6 h4 5.c5+ ♔b7 6.♔d7 h3 7.c6+ ♔b6 8.c7 h2 9.c8=♕ h1=♕, and white cannot win.

3...♔c6 4.♔g5! ♔c5 5.♔xh5 ♔xc4 6.♔g4 ♔d5 7.♔xf3 ♔e5 8.♔g4, and black is one tempo short to make the draw. White wins.

Chapter II

STUDY IDEAS

You can solve some studies, such as **Study 47** by Reti, without specialized knowledge: either only black promotes his pawn, or both sides promote their pawns, or only the bare kings remain.

But there's a group of endgame studies that require knowledge of endgame theory, because the entire play is based on the ability (or inability) to reach a certain position. And without theoretical knowledge, it's hard to predict whether this position is won or drawn.

Can such studies be truly considered works of art? The classical legacy says, of course they can! For instance, a lot of brilliant studies are based on the solid foundation of Troitsky's theoretical research into two knights vs. pawn endgames — one of the most complicated areas of endgame theory, which nobody except the author of the analysis could comprehend at the time.

Pawn endgames don't have such complicated theory, but pawn study authors still need to know the subtleties. First of all, they enable you to compose great studies that will look different from others (in a good way) and add an interesting twist to well-known tactical tricks. Secondly, this knowledge will allow you to create studies with different ideas. Thirdly — you will raise your general chess culture.

It's better to classify studies with theoretical ideas according to their final positions. They are called "beacons", because the techniques used to achieve them are common to many ideas: sacrifice, shouldering, corresponding squares, feint, avoiding capture, roundabout way, etc.

At the same time, the final positions themselves are trivial (with rare exceptions), so this group can be classified as "playful" studies without a finale, and therefore evaluated by the sets of tactical tricks used.

2.1. Pawn beacons

This subgroup comprises studies where everything is decided before the queens are involved. In **Study 102**, both sides fight for the key squares of the passed pawn. The solution of the study was original at the time: the pawns — and, therefore, the key squares — move forward by means of sacrifice.

Theory shows that passed pawns have "key" squares, and if the king gets to one of those key squares, it ensures the pawn's promotion. These squares are located two ranks ahead of the passer. The means of the struggle is "opposition" — to achieve the goal, the king should be located two squares away from the opposing king on the same rank.

In **Study 102**, the white pawns are doomed. The key squares of the f7 pawn, which is going to become passed, are located on the fifth rank, and the black king will seize them.

No. 102. H. Mattison
Deutsches Wochenschach, 1918

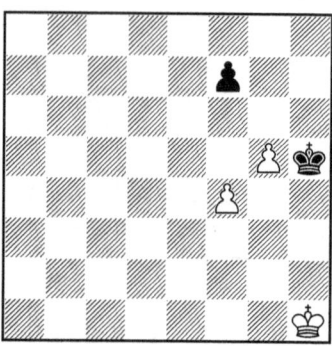

White to play and draw

1.g6! fxg6. Black is forced to capture with the pawn, which moves the key squares one rank lower. But it's too early to celebrate. After 2.♔g2? ♔g4 3.f5 gxf5 4.♔f2 ♔f4, the black king makes it to the key squares in time. While after 2.♔h2? ♔g4 3.f5, it breaks through to the key squares with 3...♔xf5 4.♔g3 ♔g5 5.♔h3 ♔f4 etc.

2.f5! gxf5

3.♔g1! Giving the black king an opportunity to reach the fourth rank.

3...♔g5 4.♔f1! ♔g4 5.♔g2 with a draw.

In **Study 103**, the struggle for opposition is compounded with

avoidance of capture. It's clear that the d3 pawn is the one that decides matters.

No. 103. N. Grigoriev
Shakhmaty, 1923

White to play and win

1.g7 ♔f7 2.♔f5! Because the g5 pawn is more dangerous.

2...♔g8! To meet the natural 3.♔xg5? with 3...e4! 4.dxe4 ♔xg7 and get a draw.

3.♔g4! ♔f7! Sticking to the same tactic.

4.♔xg5! e4. Black expects white to play 5.dxe4. But...

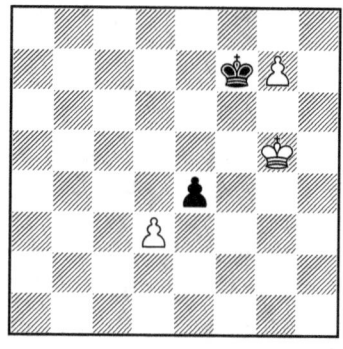

5.♔h6! ♔g8 6.dxe4, and wins.

Rook pawns have their own special features. Their value is diminished because it's enough for the king to seize the corner square or trap the opposing king there to achieve a draw. In most studies on this theme, these nuances come into play.

No. 104. M. Zinar
Pobeda (Feodosia), 1981

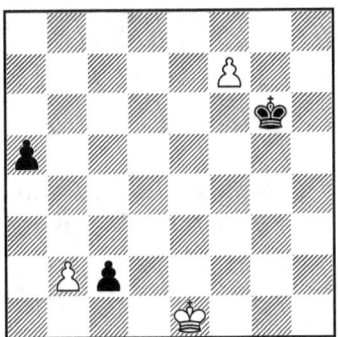

White to play and win

After 1.♔d2? ♔xf7 2.♔xc2 ♔e6 3.♔b3 ♔d5 4.♔a4 ♔c4, it's a draw. First of all, the black king is deflected as far from the main action as possible.

1.f8=♘+! ♔g7. An inventive reply as well, anticipating 2.♘e6+?

2.♔d2! c1=♕+ 3.♔xc1 ♔xf8. And now we have the position from J. Moravec's 1952 study. (As we know, the "patent" actually belongs to Dedrle who first published it in 1921.)

Now, a feint follows: **4.♔c2!! a4.** And we see Dedrle's 1921 study on the board — see **Study 17.** (And this position, as we know, was actually composed by Cassidy back in 1884.)

5.♔b1! etc. A synthesis of simple but beautiful techniques: underpromotion, feint, and roundabout way.

In **Study 105**, several ideas are synthesized serially.

No. 105. N. Grigoriev
Shakhmaty, 1929
5th– 6th honorable mention

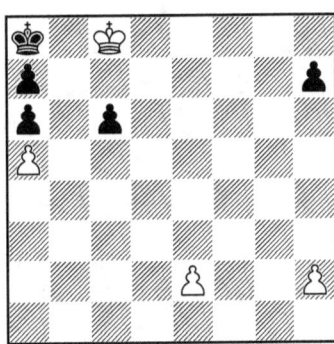

White to play and win

1.e4 c5 2.e5 c4 3.e6 c3 4.e7 c2 5.e8=♘! A rare idea: to force the trade of a promoted piece by interposing against a check.

5...c1=♕+ 6.♘c7+ ♕xc7+ 7.♔xc7 h6! Now it's necessary for white to keep the h2 pawn on the initial square — then, after the trade of the h pawns, the black king won't make it to c7 or c8 in time.

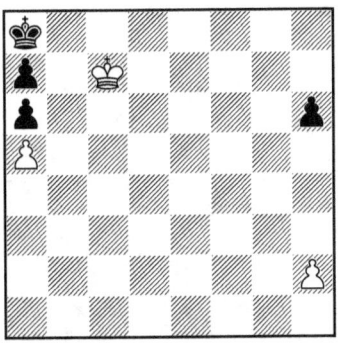

8.♔c8! h5 9.♔c7! h4 10.♔c8! h3 11.♔d7 ♔b8. 11...♔b7 is met with 12.♔d6!, winning.

12.♔e6 ♔c7 13.♔f5 ♔d6 14.♔g4 ♔e5 15.♔xh3 ♔f4

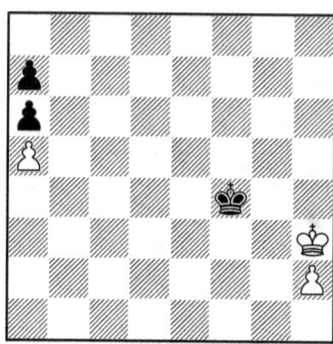

16.♔h4! ♚f5 17.♔g3! ♚g5 18.♔f3 ♚h4 19.♔e4 ♚h3 20.♔d5 ♚xh2 21.♔c6 ♚g3 22.♔b7 with a win.

A Bahr's triangle is depicted on the diagram for **Study 106**, with a rook pawn and an opposing pawn on the neighboring file. If the passed pawn is inside the triangle (as it is on the diagram), and the kings are in a "normal" position (here, ♔f4–♚f6), then black wins regardless of who is to move. If the passed pawn is outside the triangle, it's a draw. If the a+b pawn pair are moved down the board, the passer always wins. Here, white lures the black pawn from the winning zone with a feint.

No. 106. M Zinar
Shakhmaty v SSSR, 1984

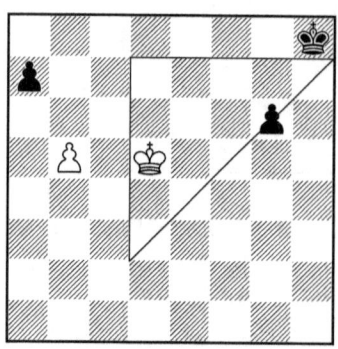

White to play and draw

1.♔c6! g5 2.♔d5! ♚g7 3.♔e4 ♚g6 4.♔f3 ♚f5

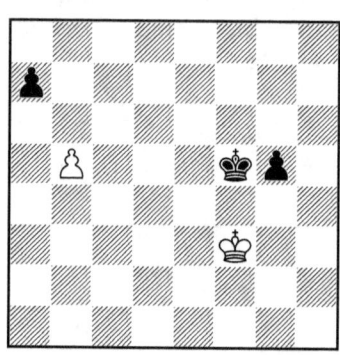

5.♔g3, with a draw – the white king makes it to c1 in time. For instance: 5...♚e5 6.♔g4 ♚d5 7.♔xg5 ♚c5 8.♔f4! ♚xb5 9.♔e3 ♚c4 10.♔d2 ♚b3 11.♔c1 etc.

In **Study 107,** where both opposing pawns are rook pawns, everything boils down to whether the king can make it to the corner in time to hold the pawn. This situation is less favorable for the stronger side in comparison with the study above.

No. 107. M. Zinar
Shakhmatny Bulleten, 1984

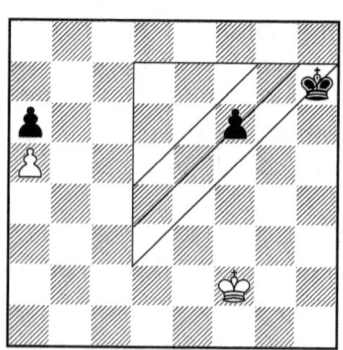

White to play and draw

With the a-pawns as on the diagram (a5–a6), the passed pawn should be inside the middle triangle for black to win (as it currently is) in the event that the kings take up opposition (in this case, on e4 and e6 for the white and black kings, respectively). Then black wins white's rook pawn while white is dealing with the f-pawn. Further, if the pawn pair is moved one rank up (a6–a7), the passed pawn should be inside the small triangle for black to win. Finally, if the pawns are moved one rank down (a4–a5), the passed pawn should be inside the large triangle for black to win. So in our case, the passed pawn is located inside the necessary triangle. White's goal here is hence to drag the black pawn out of the triangle. A feint follows:

1.♔e3! ♚g6 2.♔d4! f5. Otherwise, it's a theoretical draw after 3.♔c5.

3.♔e3! ♚g5 4.♔f3, draw.

2.2. Beacon:
queen versus rook pawn

This group comprises studies with a "queen vs. queen" finale, which often occurs in queen vs. rook pawn endgames. It is known that the queen wins against the rook pawn on the penultimate rank if the king of the stronger side is in the winning zone – the e4-a4-a8-e8 square, but excluding the e4 square itself, as shown on the next diagram.

To make the solution of **Study 108** easier, we need to remember the Bahr triangles. If white pushes his pawn, then the black passed pawn remains in the winning zone. The blend of two theoretical position leads to great complications.

No. 108. M. Zinar
Fizkulturnik Belorussii, 1979
Honorable mention

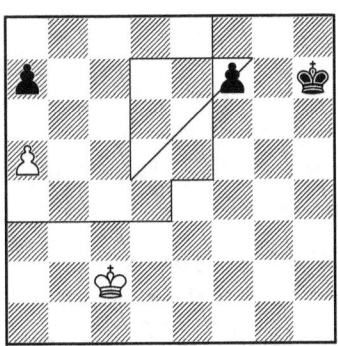

White to play and draw

1.♔d3! ♚g6 2.♔e4!! A hard-to-find double threat! The immediate attack on the pawn, 2.♔c4?, doesn't work due to 2...f5! 3.♔d4 ♚g5 4.♔e3 ♚g4 5.♔f2 a6! 6.♔g2 ♚f4, and black wins. 2.♔d4? ♚g5 3.♔e4 a6 (or 3...♚g4) doesn't work either.

The game move 2.♔e4!! repels both threats. Now the defense 2...♚g5 is met with 3.a6! f5 4.♔f3! with a draw. A principled defense is 2...a6, but then white uses the same feint as in the previous study: 3.♔d4! f5 4.♔e3! with the familiar draw. Therefore, black uses a specific technique applicable only to theoretical studies: entering the zone with the king.

2...♚f6! 3.♔d5! A feint intended to provoke the movement of the passed pawn, but black moves his king into the zone in reply.

3...♚e7!

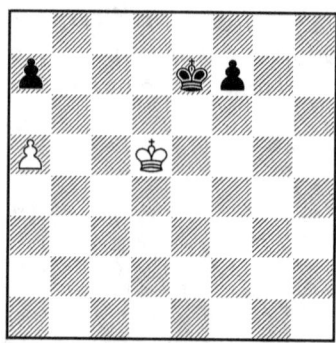

4.♔c6!! f5. The pawn cannot be taken: black is in the zone and wins. For instance: 5.♔b7? f4 6.♔xa7 f3 7.a6 f2 8.♔b7 f1=♛ 9.a7 ♔d7 10.a8=♛ ♛b5+ 11.♔a7 ♔c7, curtains.

Therefore, white plays another feint:

5.♔d5! ♔f6 6.a6!, and now **6...♔g5** is met with **7.♔c6!**, while **6...f4** is followed by **7.♔e4! ♔g5 8.♔f3**, also with equality.

In **Study 109**, the king is in the zone, the pawn is inside the triangle, but it's white to move.

No. 109. M. Zinar
64 – Shakhmatnoe Obozrenie, 1982

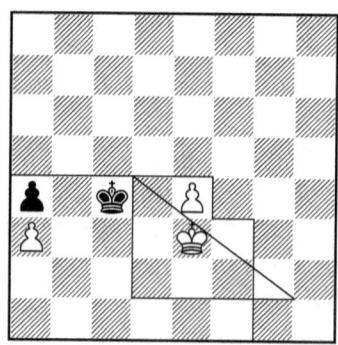

White to play and win

1.e5? is met with 1...♔d5 2.♔f4 ♔e6 with equality. And after 1.♔f4?

black saves the game with 1...♔b3. White needs to give up the right to move:

1.♔e2! ♔d4! 2.♔f3 ♔c4 3.♔e3!, and 3...♔c5 is met with 4.♔d3 (or 4.♔f4). Then after **3...♔b3**

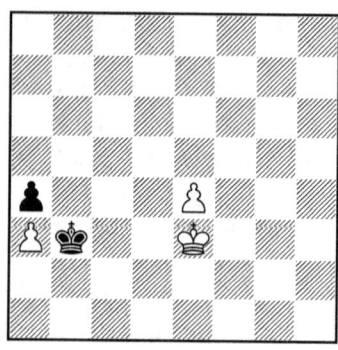

there's a strong reply **4.e5.** (Admittedly, we later found another way to win: 4.♔d3 (or even 4.♔d2) 4...♔xa3 5.e5 ♔b2 (5...♔b4 6.e6 a3 7.♔c2) 6.e6 a3 7.e7 a2 8.e8=♛ a1=♛ 9.♛b5+ ♔c1 10.♛c4+ ♔b2 11.♛b4+ ♔a2 12.♔c2, curtains.)

4...♔xa3 5.e6 ♔b2 6.e7 a3 7.e8=♛ a2 8.♛b5+ with a theoretical win. Thanks to the maneuver ♔e3-e2-f3-e3, black was put in zugzwang.

An important position is the **Polerio beacon**: white – queen anywhere on the 8th rank, ♔d2; black – ♛a1, ♔b3 (b2, b1). If the king is on b3, it's a draw, while if the king is on b1 or b2, white wins.

In **Study 110**, white liquidates the Polerio position with feints.

No. 110. M. Zinar
Shakhmaty v SSSR, 1986

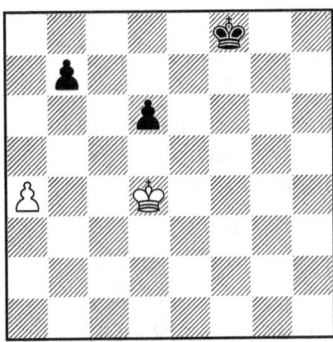

White to play and draw

**1.♔c4! ♚e7 2.♔b5 ♚d7! 3.♔b6!
d5.** Forced, because 3...♚c8 4.a5 ♚b8
5.a6! d5 6.♔c5! leads to a draw.
4.♔c5! Otherwise, white gets
checkmated Polerio-style.
4...♚e6 5.a5! ♚e5 6.♔b6! with
simultaneous pawn promotion.

In **Study 111**, zugzwang is achieved
to avoid an exception from the Polcrio
position rule. White wins using the
tortoise move tactic that we have already
encountered.

No. 111. M. Zinar
Shakhmaty v SSSR, 1987

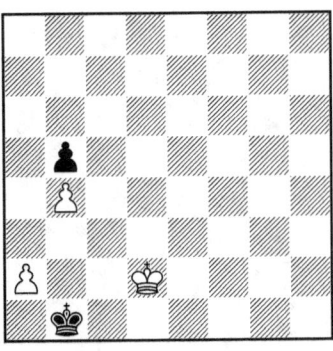

White to play and win

**1.a3! ♚b2 2.a4 bxa4 3.b5 a3 4.b6 a2
5.b7 a1=♕ 6.b8=♕+** with checkmate.

The Polerio beacon may serve as
a theme for a logical study (more on
these later in this book) where white
gets checkmated in the false try. Here's
how this idea was executed in **Study 112**,
with the elegant avoidance of capture.

No. 112**. E. Pallasz
The Problemist, 2012

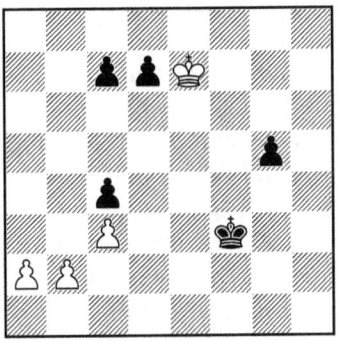

White to play and draw

1.a4! ♚e4 2.♔d8!! Refusing to
capture the pawn with anticipation of
the finale! A logical false try: 2.♔xd7?
♚d5 3.♔xc7 ♚c5 4.♔b7 g4 5.a5 g3

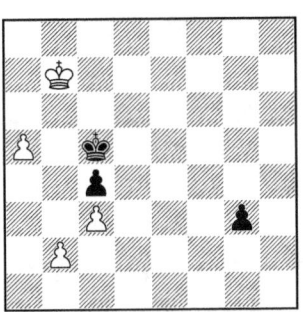

6.a6 g2 7.a7 g1=♕ 8.a8=♕ ♕g7+
9.♔c8 ♕f8+ 10.♔b7 ♕e7+ 11.♔a6
♕d6+ 12.♔b7 ♕d7+ 13.♔b8 ♚b6,
curtains.
2...♚d5 3.♔xc7 ♚c5 4.♔b7 g4 5.a5 g3

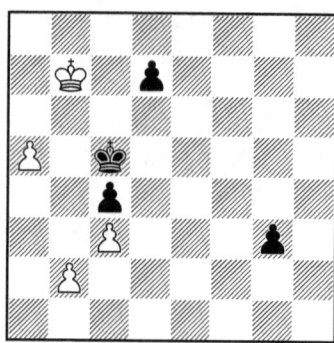

6.a6 g2 7.a7 g1=♕ 8.a8=♕. Draw: the king is shielded by the black pawn.

The **Lolli beacon** is also very important for study composition: white – queen anywhere on the 8th rank, ♔d3; black – ♛a1, ♚b1 (b2, b3). If the black king is on b1, it's a draw, but if it's on b2 or b3, white wins. Of course, there are some exceptions, and, like in the Polerio position, everything still works if the kings are placed symmetrically – if the white king is on c4 instead of d3, and the black king is on b1 or b2.

A specific technique similar to "entering the zone" was used in **Study 113**: lose a tempo to get the Lolli position.

No. 113. Z. Birnov
64, 1930

White to play and win

1.♔e2! 1.f5? squanders the win: 1...a5 2.f6 a4 3.f7 a3 4.f8=♕ a2 5.♕a3+ ♔b1, draw – the white king is outside the zone.

1...a5 2.♔d3! ♔b2 3.f5 a4 4.f6 a3 5.f7 a2 6.f8=♕ a1=♕. And even though black also promotes to a queen, that cannot help him in any way.

7.♕b4+ ♔c1. If 7...♔a2, then 8.♔c2, and wins.

8.♕d2+ ♔b1 9.♕c2#.

White prepares for the future queen endgame in advance in **Study 114**.

No. 114. M. Zinar
Vestnik Pribuzhya (Mykolaiv), 1987

White to play and win

1.a4 b6 2.♔e2! ♔b2 3.♔d3! ♔b3

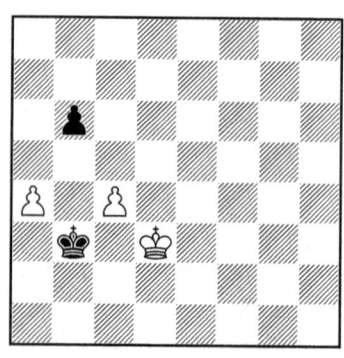

4.a5! bxa5 5.c5 a4 6.c6 a3 7.c7 a2 8.c8=♕ with a Lolli mate.

Unfortunately, white can win here even without knowing the Lolli position: **2.♔e1 ♔b2 3.♔d2 ♔b3 4.a5 bxa5 5.c5 a4 6.♔c1! a3 7.♔b1**, curtains. To correct this study, it's necessary to add another black pawn and move the white king – see **Study 115**.

No. 115**. M. Zinar
Vestnik Pribuzhya (Mykolaiv), 1987
(correction by S. Tkachenko)

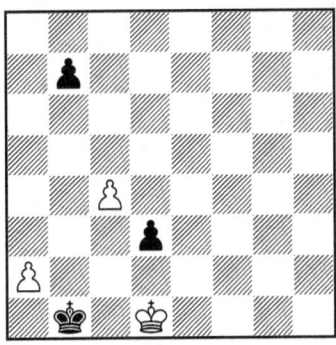

White to play and win

1.a4 b6 2.♔d2! Not the immediate **2.a5?** bxa5 3.c5 a4 4.c6 a3 5.c7 a2 6.c8=♕ a1=♕, and there's no mate on c2 – the black pawn stops the queen.

2...♔b2 3.♔xd3 ♔b3 4.a5 bxa5 5.c5 a4 6.c6 a3 7.c7 a2 8.c8=♕. Now that the black pawn is gone, white wins with a Lolli position.

Study 116 uses the anti-Reti maneuver: black feints to save the game, Reti-style, but white stops just in time, in the Lolli position.

No. 116. J. Moravec
Original source unknown, 1953

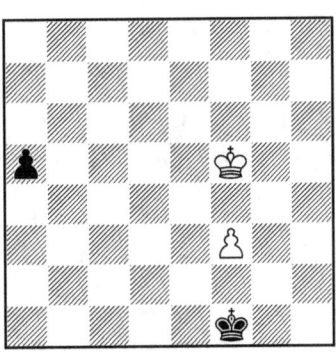

White to play and win

1.♔e4! ♔e2 2.f4 ♔d2! 3.♔d4 ♔c2 4.♔c4 ♔b2

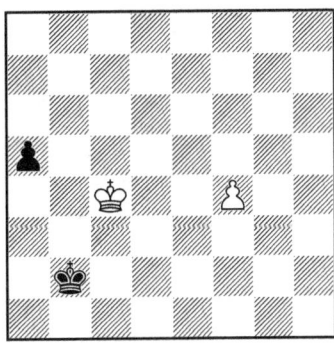

5.f5! But not **5.♔b5?** ♔b3! with a Reti draw.

5...a4 6.f6 with a theoretical win. We analyzed another case of the anti-Reti maneuver in **Study 56**.

If we remove the a4 and a5 pawns in **Study 117**, we reach a Grigoriev study that shared 1st and 2nd place at a thematic competition in *La Strategie* magazine, where the Soviet master achieved an incredible performance: all ten of his pawn studies won a prize or a commendation!

No. 117. A. Botokanov and M. Zinar
Volzhskaya Zarya, 1985
2nd prize

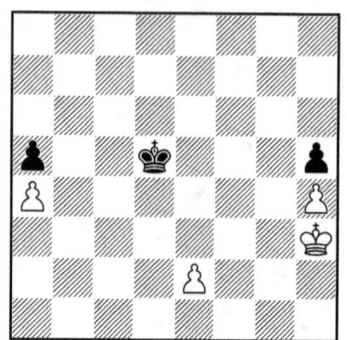

White to play and win

**1.♔g3! ♔e4 2.♔g2! ♔e3 3.♔f1
♔e4 4.♔e1! ♔e3 5.♔d1.** It's obvious
that the a4 and a5 pawns were added to
serve some purpose, let's see!

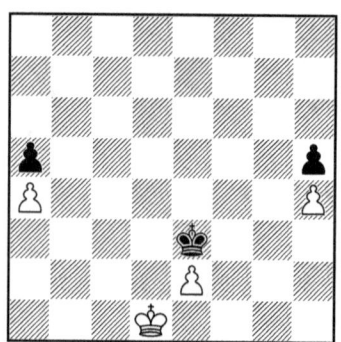

Now, two echo variations occur:
A) **5...♔f4 6.♔d2 ♔g4 7.♔e3 ♔g3
8.♔e4 ♔xh4 9.♔f4! ♔h3 10.e4 ♔g2**

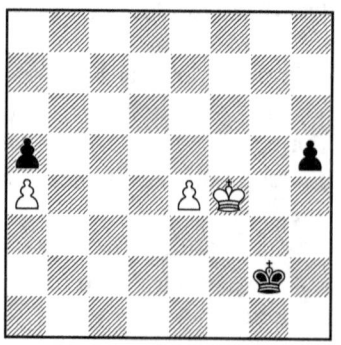

11.e5! (11.♔g5? ♔g3!, draw)
**11...h4 12.e6 h3 13.e7 h2 14.e8=♕
h1=♕ 15.♕e2+ ♔h3 16.♕g4+ ♔h2
17.♕g3#**

B) **5...♔e4 6.♔d2 ♔d4 7.e3+ ♔c4
8.♔c2** (or 8.♔e2) **8...♔b4 9.♔d3!
♔xa4 10.♔c4 ♔a3 11.e4 ♔b2**

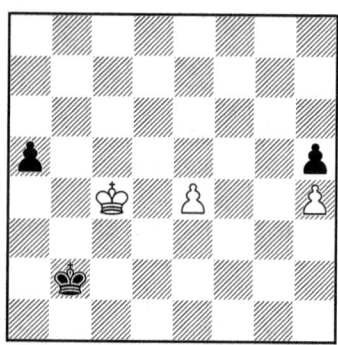

12.e5! (12.♔b5? ♔b3!, draw) **12...
a4 13.e6 a3 14.e7 a2 15.e8=♕ a1=♕
16.♕e2+ ♔c1 17.♕e1+ ♔b2 18.♕d2+
♔a3 19.♕b4+ ♔a2 20.♕b3#,** an echo-
chameleon mate in the opposite corner
of the board.

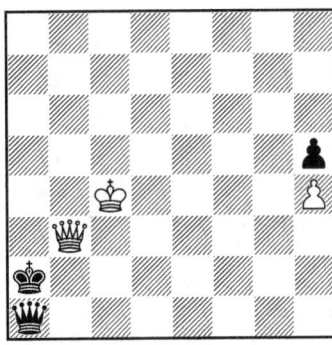

In the next two examples, we see the **"hostage" theme**: the stronger side leaves the opponent's pawn alive and achieves success thanks to that.

No. 118. N. Grigoriev
Molodaya Gvardiya, 1925

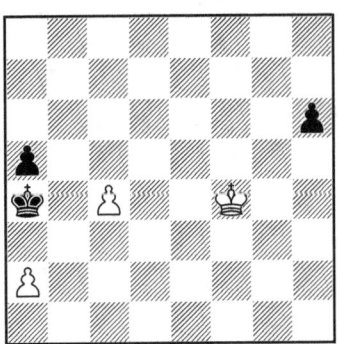

White to play and win

1.a3! h5 2.♔g3! h4+ 3.♔h3! ♔xa3 4.c5

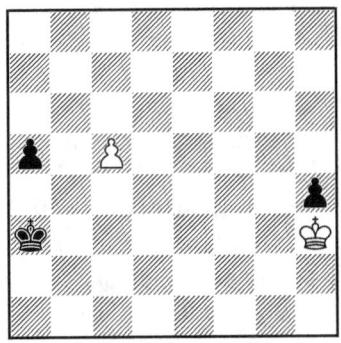

And then, white promotes the pawn, creating a position with white ♕b3 and black ♔a1 with the black pawn on a2:

4...a4 5.c6 ♔b2 6.c7 a3 7.c8=♕ a2 8.♕b7+ ♔c2 9.♕e4+ ♔b2 10.♕b4+ ♔c2 11.♕a3 ♔b1 12.♕b3+ ♔a1

There follows:
13.♔g4! h3 14.♕c2 h2 15.♕c1#.

In **Study 119**, the same checkmate is impossible, but the king makes it to the winning zone in time.

No. 119. V. Archakov and M. Zinar
Ranok (Kyiv), 1986

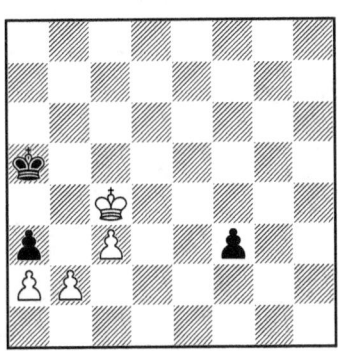

White to play and win

1.b4+ ♔a4 2.♔d3 ♔b5 3.♔e3 ♔c4

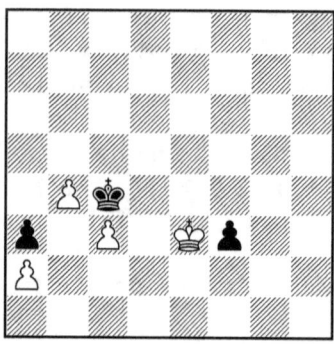

4.♔f2! ♔xc3 5.b5 ♔b2 6.b6 ♔xa2 7.b7 ♔a1 8.b8=♕ a2 9.♔e3! f2 10.♕b5 with a win.

Unfortunately, it later transpired that this study has several side solutions. For instance, white can win as follows: 4.♔xf3 ♔xc3 5.b5 ♔b2 6.b6 ♔xa2 7.b7 ♔a1 8.♔e2 a2 9.♔d3 ♔b2 10.b8=♕+ ♔c1 11.♕b3, curtains.

Interesting play can be achieved in a queen vs. rook pawn endgame if we add... another pawn! The play is built around this pawn in **Study 120**.

No. 120**. M. Zinar
Georgian competition, 2011
Commendation

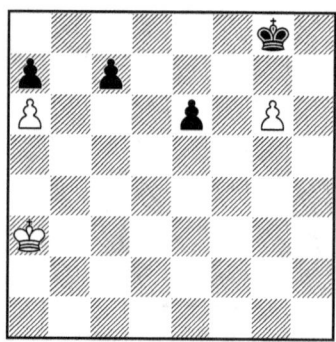

White to play and draw

1.♔b4! e5 2.♔c4!! Not the

"obvious" 2.♔c5? (or 2.♔b5? e4 3.♔c4 c5) 2...c6! 3.♔xc6 (3.g7 e4! 4.♔d4 ♔xg7 5.♔xe4 ♔f6 6.♔d4 ♔e6 7.♔c5 ♔d7 or 3.♔c4? ♔g7 4.♔c5 e4! 5.♔d4 ♔xg6 6.♔xe4 ♔f6) 3...e4 4.♔b7 e3 5.♔xa7 e2 6.♔b7 e1=♕ 7.a7 ♕b4+, and black wins. There might follow 8.♔c7 ♕a5+ 9.♔b7 ♕b5+ 10.♔c7 ♕a6 11.♔b8 ♕b6+ 12.♔a8 ♕c7! 13.g7 ♕c8#.

2...c6

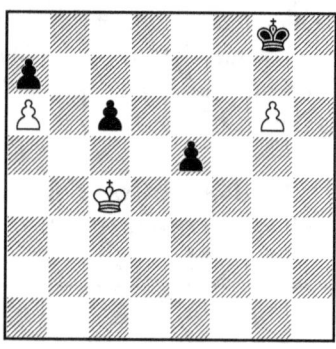

3.♔c5! And now it's black to move!
3...♔g7 (3...♔f8 4.g7+; 3...e4 4.♔d4 ♔g7 5.♔xe4 ♔xg6 6.♔e5) **4.♔xc6 e4 5.♔b7 e3 6.♔xa7 e2 7.♔b7 e1=♕ 8.a7.** Draw, because black lacks a mating tempo.

2.3. Beacon:
queen versus bishop pawn

There are two zones depicted on the initial diagram of **Study 121**, where black is trying to win. If the white king is closer to the drawing corner (a8), then the newly created black queen only wins against the bishop pawn on the penultimate rank if the black king is located in the smaller zone. If the white king is located farther from the corner, then it's enough for the black king to be in the larger zone for him to win.

White lures the black king out of the winning zone with a familiar technique — two feints:

No. 121. M. Zinar
Shakhmatny Bulleten, 1982

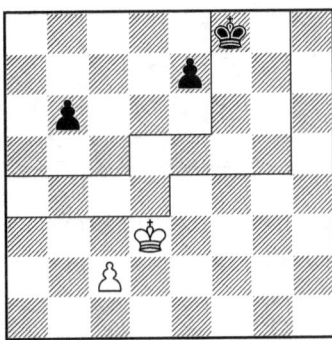

White to play and draw

1.♔c4! ♚e8! Into the zone!
2.♔b5! e5 3.♔c4! ♚e7

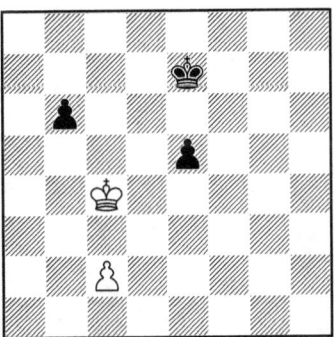

4.♔d5! ♚f6 5.c4! ♚f5 6.♔c6! etc. The rest is simple: 6...e4 7.♔xb6 e3 8.c5 e2 9.c6 e1=♕ 10.c7. Draw.

In **Study 122**, the king is farther away from the drawing corner (a8) than the white pawn. Therefore, a feint follows first.

No. 122. M. Zinar
Shakhmatny Bulleten, 1982

White to play and draw

1.♔f5! ♚h6 2.c5! ♚h5 3.♔e5(f6) with a theoretical draw.

"Extra" pawns play a major role in both rook-pawn and bishop-pawn studies. But success can be achieved only if the "hostage" is unblocked.

No. 123. T. Kok
Residentiebode, 1935

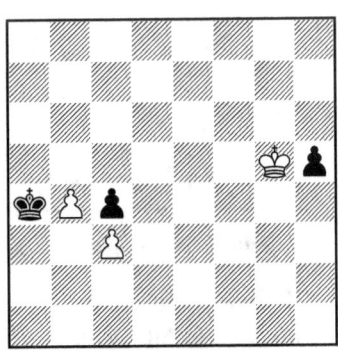

White to play and win

1.♔h4! ♚b5. 1...♚b3 is met with 2.b5 ♚xc3 3.b6 ♚d2 4.b7 c3 5.b8=♕ c2 6.♕b2 ♚d1 7.♕d4+ ♚e2 8.♕c3 ♚d1 9.♕d3+ ♚c1 10.♔g5, winning.
    2.♔xh5! ♚a4

3.♔g4! The king is in the zone!
**3...♔b3 4.b5 ♔xc3 5.b6 ♔d2 6.b7
c3 7.b8=♕ c2 8.♕b2 ♔d1 9.♔f3 c1=♕
10.♕e2#** with a theoretical mate.

In **Study 124**, this technique is blended with the Reti double threat.

No. 124. M. Zinar
Shakhmaty v SSSR, 1982

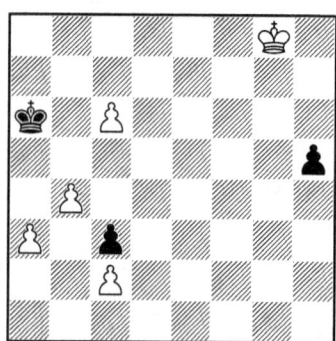

White to play and win

1.♔f7! Giving chase!
1...♔b6 2.♔e6! After 2.b5? h4 3.♔e7
♕c7, it's only a draw. White's second move is also aesthetically pleasing: the king moves away from the black pawn — white blends the Reti maneuver and the roundabout way.

2...♔xc6. If 2...h4, then 3.♔d6, and white wins after a queen trade.

3.♔f5 ♔b5 4.♔g5 ♔a4

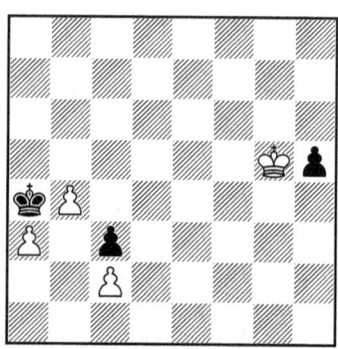

5.♔h4! And zugzwang again: the blocked pawn is not captured immediately!

5...♔b5 6.♔xh5 ♔a4 7.♔g4!, and the king is in the zone. White wins.

In **Study 125**, it's black who is trying to use the hostage technique, so white should be vigilant.

No. 125. M. Zinar
Moscow competition, 1983
2nd prize

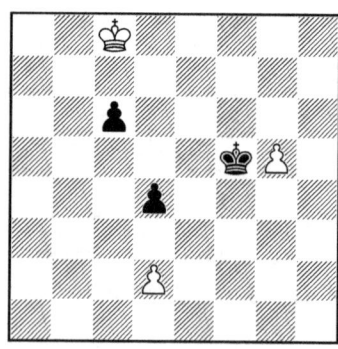

White to play and draw

1.♔b7! But not 1.d3? ♔xg5 2.♔c7
♔f4! or 1.g6? ♔xg6 2.♔b7 c5 3.d3 ♔f6,
and black wins.

1...c5 2.d3 ♔g6! If the white king

were on c7 or d7, black would have simply played 2...c4, and the king would have gotten checked or blocked its own pawn. Now black intends, after 3.♔b6? c4 4.dxc4 d3 5.c5 d2 6.c6 d1=♕ 7.c7 ♕d7 8.♔b7, to unblock the pawn with 8...♔f5! But...

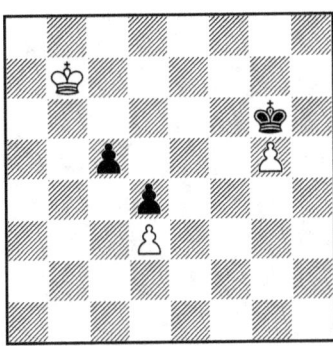

3.♔a7!! ♔f7. If 3...♔xg5, then 4.♔b6! with a draw.

4.g6+! ♔g8 5.g7! ♔xg7 6.♔b6(a6), draw — the black king does not make it into the zone in time.

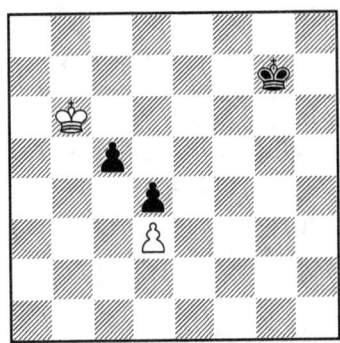

This is clear from the line 6...c4 7.dxc4 d3 8.c5 d2 9.c6 d1=♕ 10.c7 ♕d7 11.♔b7 ♔f6 12.♔b8 etc.

The waiting move 3.♔a7!! is spectacular.

The king's sideways detour in **Study 126** after a series of false tries looks most spectacular.

No. 126**. N. Elkies
Chess Life & Review, 1986

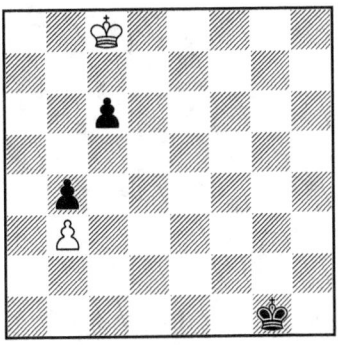

White to play and draw

False try: 1.♔d7? c5 2.♔e6 c4 3.bxc4 b3 4.c5 b2 5.c6 b1=♕ 6.c7 ♕h7!! 7.c8=♕ ♕h3+, with a skewer from the newborn queen.

Other moves are wrong, too: 1.♔c7? c5 2.♔d6 c4 3.bxc4 b3 4.c5 b2 5.c6 b1=♕ 6.c7 ♕f5! or 1.♔b8? c5 2.♔a7 ♔f2 3.♔a6 ♔e3, and white is doomed.

Only the left route works: **1.♔b7!! c5 2.♔a6! c4 3.bxc4 b3 4.c5 b2 5.c6 b1=♕ 6.c7 ♕f5 7.♔b7.** Draw.

In **Study 127**, black also hopes to succeed because of white's "extra" pawn.

No. 127. M. Zinar
JC Kyiv – 1500, 1982
1st–2nd prize

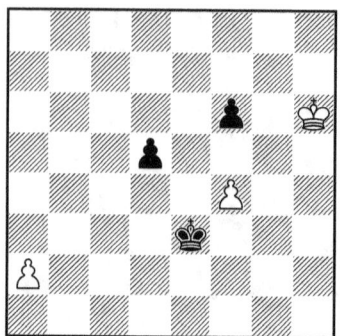

White to play and draw

1.a4 ♚d4 2.♔h5!! But not 2.♔g6?
♚c5! 3.♔xf6 d4, and there's no draw
because of the a-pawn. Or 2.f5? ♚c5!
3.♔h5 d4 4.♔g4 d3 5.♔f3 ♚d4 6.a5
♚c3 7.a6 d2, and the pawn queens with
a check.

2...f5! A principled line occurs after
2...♚c4 3.a5! ♚b5 4.♔g4 ♚xa5 5.♔f5!
♚b4 6.♔xf6 – a small-scale roundabout
way, in which white uses up four moves
instead of two: ♔h6–h5–g4–f5–f6.

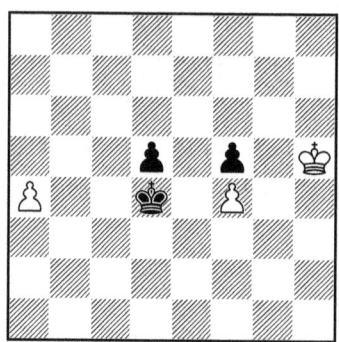

3.♔h4!! The retreat continues. After
the natural 3.♔g5?, black wins: 3...♚c5
4.♔xf5 d4 5.♔e4 ♚c4 6.a5 d3 7.♔e3
♚c3 8.a6 d2 9.a7 d1=♕ 10.a8=♕

♕e1+ 11.♔f3 ♕h1+, winning the
queen via a diagonal skewer. Or 6.f5 d3
7.♔e3 ♚c3 8.f6 d2 9.f7 d1=♕ 10.f8=♕
♕e1+ 11.♔f3 ♕f1+, winning the queen
via a vertical skewer.

3...♚c5 4.♔g3 ♚b4 5.♔f3(f2)
♚xa4 6.♔e3 ♚b5 7.♔d4 ♚c6

8.♔e5! The king has caught up with
the pawn from the other side.

8...♚c5 9.♔xf5 d4 10.♔g6! The
queen is immediately lost after 10.♔e4?
in view of 10....♚c4.

10...d3 11.f5 d2 12.f6 d1=♕ 13.f7
with a theoretical draw.

A rich study: a twofold queen win
in a false try (this alone can constitute
an entire study!), which synthesizes
a number of diverse ideas; getting to
a theoretical position through two
roundabout ways, with the second one
being especially attractive: ♔h6–h5–
h4–g3–f3–e3–d4–e5xf5. So instead
of just two required moves, white spent
eight! Note that in chapter III we briefly
return to this study to discuss a small
flaw.

Study 128 is a variation on the same evergreen theme.

No. 128. M. Zinar
64 – Shakhmatnoe Obozrenie, 1986

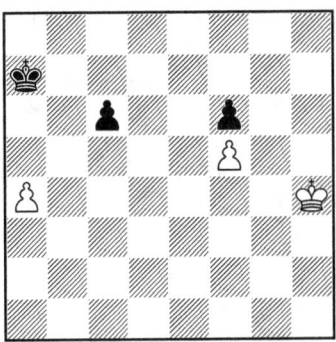

White to play and draw

First, there's a feint: **1.♔h5! c5! 2.♔g4!** White has caused the weakening of the d5 square and now moves towards the f6 pawn in a roundabout way, because the straightforward 2.♔g6? loses due to the a4 pawn.

2...♔a6   3.♔f3(f4)   ♔a5   4.♔c4 ♔b4!

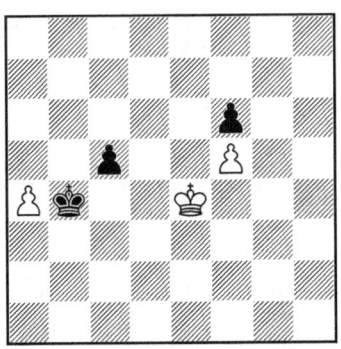

5.a5! But not 5.♔d5? c4 6.a5 c3 7.a6 c2 8.a7 c1=♕ 9.a8=♕ ♕h1+, and black wins.

5...♔xa5   6.♔d5   ♔b5   7.♔e6   c4 8.♔xf6 with a draw.

Two ideas are synthesized very well in **Study 129**. In one variation, the Duras decoy is in play, while in the other, the queen wins against the bishop pawn despite the king being out of the winning zone.

No. 129. N. Grigoriev
La Strategie, 1936
3rd honorable mention

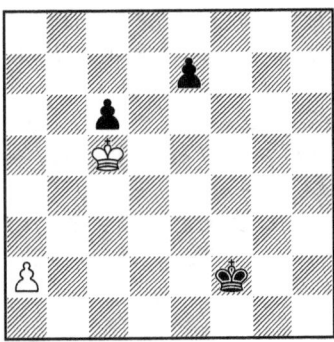

White to play and win

After **1.♔d4!**, there are two continuations with completely dissimilar ideas:

A) **1...c5+ 2.♔xc5 ♔g3! 3.a4! e5 4.a5 e4 5.♔d4! ♔f4 6.a6 e3**

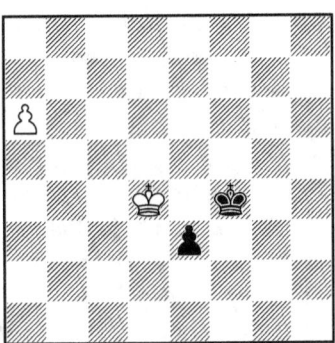

7.♔d3! ♔f3 8.a7 e2 9.a8=♕+, and wins;

B) **1...e5+ 2.♔xe5 ♔e3 3.a4 ♔d3!**

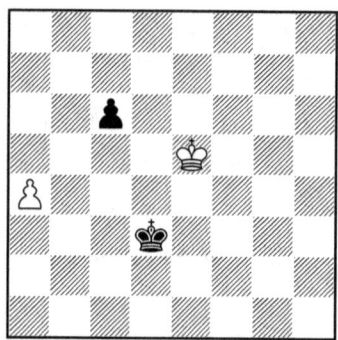

4.a5! c5 5.a6 c4 6.a7 c3 7.a8=♕ c2.
If the black king were on d2, it would
have been a draw. But its position is
poor, which is exploited by white.

**8.♕d5+   ♚e2   9.♕a2!   ♚d1
10.♔d4 c1=♕   11.♔d3,** and wins.
Or **8...♔e3 9.♕g2! c1=♕ 10.♕g5+**
with a win.

Chess composers have also dabbled
with positions with the bishop pawn on
the third (sixth) rank. In such studies,
the win is usually achieved easily, but,
paradoxically, it becomes more difficult
when the king is located farther from the
corner of the board.

Let's assume that while black is
busy trying to promote his passed pawn
in **Study 130**, white will try to put his
king on e7 and get his pawn to f6. The
diagram that depicts the winning zone
shows us that if the black king is in this
zone, it can enter the big winning zone
as well if it has an extra move (see **Study
121**). If the king is outside this zone, the
win is achieved with 1...♕e1+! 2.♔f8
♕b4+!

Conclusion: there are three drawn
positions — if the black king is on c3, e1
or e2, i.e. it's outside the zone *and* stops
the queen from performing the above
maneuver. Depending on your playing

strength you may need to play through
the solution below before you fully grasp
this idea.

No. 130. J. Moravec
Svobodny Slovo, 1950
(reworked by Y. Peipan, 1980)

White to play and draw

1.♔f4! d6! 2.♔g5 ♚c2 3.♔f6! d5.
We have now reached the initial position
of Moravec's 1950 study.

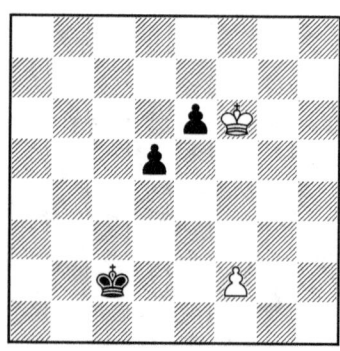

4.♔e5!! The feint that forces the
black king to move to one of the "bad"
squares. After the greedy 4.♔xe6? d4
5.f4 d3 6.f5 d2 7.f6 d1=♕ 8.♔e7 (8.f7
♕d8), black wins with a precise queen
maneuver: 8...♕e1+! 9.♔f8 ♕b4+!
etc.

4...♔c3.   Unfortunately,   the

subsequent solution is not concrete enough: the king moves ♔xe6–e7 and the pawn moves f2–f4–f5–f6 can be made in any order. Such flaws decrease the study's value.

There might follow 5.♔xe6 (or 5.f4) 5...d4 6.f4 d3 7.f5 d2 8.f6 d1=♕ 9.♔e7! ♕e1+ 10.♔f8!, and black cannot stop the pawn's march towards the drawing zone.

White is more creative with his feints in **Study 131**.

No. 131. M. Zinar
Shakhmaty v SSSR, 1986

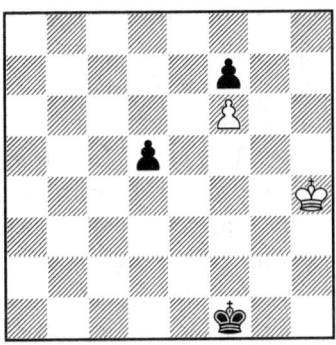

White to play and draw

1.♔g5? loses to 1...d4 2.♔h6 (or 2.♔f4 ♔e2! etc.) 2...d3 3.♔g7 d2 4.♔xf7 d1=♕ 5.♔e7 ♕e1+ 6.♔f8 ♕b4+ etc. Therefore, white first plays a feint:

1.♔g4! Now 1...♔e2 is met with 2.♔g5 (or 2.♔h5), and the black king stops the check from e1. After 1...d4, there's 2.♔f3!, and 1...♔f2 is followed by 2.♔f4!

1...♔g2! To meet 2.♔f4? with the unpleasant 2...♔h3!, and then win with 3.♔e5 ♔g4 4.♔xd5 ♔f5. Therefore, white plays a second feint:

2.♔g5!! d4 3.♔f4! ♔h3 4.♔e4 ♔g4 5.♔xd4 ♔f5 6.♔e3 ♔xf6 7.♔f4, draw.

Study 132 is structurally similar to the previous one; the stronger side manages to overcome the opponent's resistance with precise moves.

No. 132. J. Fritz
Prace, 1951

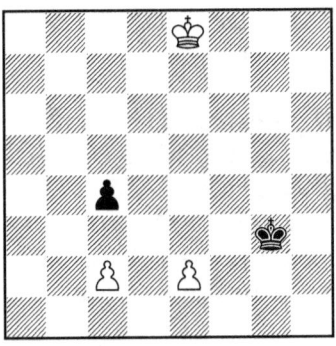

White to play and win

The white king should move closer to the black pawn to combat its advance. 1.♔e7? is clearly poor due to 1...♔f2! 2.e4, and the king blocks the way of its own pawn. 1.♔d7? doesn't work either, because after 1...♔f2! 2.e4 it's a theoretical draw after the black pawn moves to c3.

The correct move is **1.♔f7!!** Choosing the longest way towards the opponent's pawn.

1...c3. 1...♔f2 loses to 2.e4 ♔e3 3.e5! ♔d2 4.e6 ♔xc2 5.e7 c3 6.e8=♕ ♔d2 7.♕d8+! ♔c1 8.♕g5+! etc.

2.♔e6! ♔f2 3.♔d5! ♔xe2 4.♔c4 ♔d2 5.♔b3 with a win.

No. 133. M. Zinar
Themes 64, 1984

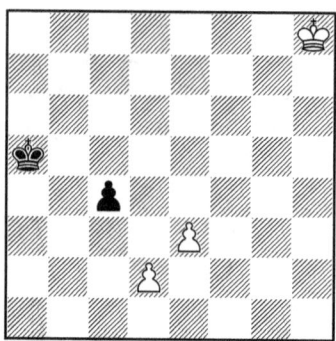

White to play and win

1.e4! ♚b4 **2.e5!** 2.♔g7? is too premature: 2...♚b3 3.e5 ♚c2 4.e6 ♚xd2 5.e7 c3 6.e8=♕ c2, draw.

2...♚c5! 3.♔g7 ♚d5! Or 3... ♚d4 4.e6 ♚d3 5.e7 ♚xd2 6.e8=♕ c3 7.♕d8+! ♚c1 8.♕g5+! with a win for white.

4.♔f6. By using a feint, black has forced the white king to move to a "poor" square. But he missed the fact that the king got closer to the pawn at the same time.

4...♚d4

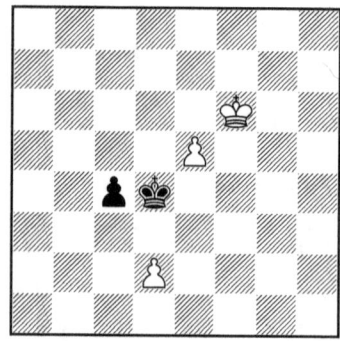

5.♔e6!! ♚d3 6.♔d5 with a win.

No. 134. M. Zinar
Shakhmaty v SSSR, 1981
1ˢᵗ special prize

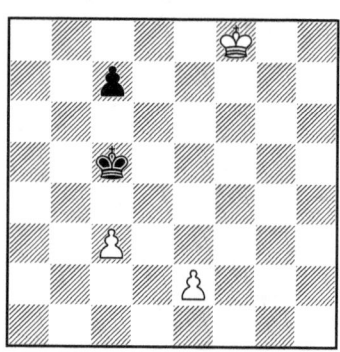

White to play and win

The white king should move closer to the pawns, so that after 1...♚c4 2.e4 c5 white can play 3.e5. 1.♔e7? ♚c4 2.e4 ♚xc3 is bad: the king blocks the path of its own pawn. But the natural 1.♔f7? is also bad due to 1...♚d5!! – an unusual zugzwang is on the board: the kings don't block each other, the pawns can move too, but everything is futile!

For instance, 2.♔f6 (or 2.♔g6 ♚e4 3.♔f6 ♚e3; or 2.e3 ♚e4 with a draw) 2...♚c4! 3.e4 (or 3.♔e5 ♚xc3 4.♔d5 ♚b4, again with a draw) 3...♚xc3 4.e5 c5 5.e6 ♚d2! 6.e7 c4 7.e8=♕ c3 8.♕d8+ ♚c1, and the white king blocks its own queen.

Therefore, **1.♔g7!!** A hard-to find, eccentric move!

1...♚d5!! 2.♔f7!! And now it's black who is in zugzwang. 2...♚c4 is met with 3.e4 ♚xc3 4.e5, winning. While the waiting move 2...c6 is followed by 3.♔e7! ♚c4 4.♔d6 ♚xc3 5.♔c5, which means that the pawn should remain on c7!

2...♚e5 3.♔e7(e8)! ♚d5! 4.♔d7! The move 4.♔d8? ♚c4! 5.e4 ♚xc3! also blocks the queen.

4...♔c4 5.♔c6! If 5.e4? then 5...
♔xc3 6.e5 c5!, and the king serves as a
blocker for its own queen for the third
time!

5...♔xc3 6.♔c5! with a win.

Both the queens and theoretical
calculations stayed off the board, but
they served as the foundation for the
mysterious king moves.

No. 135. A. Botokanov
Shakhmaty v SSSR, 1986
Commendation

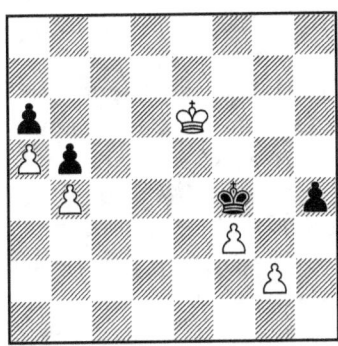

White to play and draw

1.♔f7! It turns out that even in such
a simple position, some deviations from
the norm are possible! The "normal"
1.♔f6? loses here:

1....♔g3 2.♔g5 ♔xg2!

1...♔g3 2.♔g8! That's where the
king was actually heading! Here, the
"normal" 2.♔g7? is also wrong: 2...♔xg2
3.f4 h3 4.f5 h2 5.f6 h1=♕ 6.f7 ♕a1+ and
black wins. 2.f4? is also insufficient: 2...
♔xf4 3.♔g6 ♔g3 4.♔g5 ♔xg2, and
black gets to the queenside faster.

**2...♔xg2 3.f4 h3 4.f5 h2 5.f6 h1=♕
6.f7,** draw.

The king moving to g8 with a
bishop pawn on the board is actually

nothing new. Here, for instance, is the
conclusion of an endgame study by
Vitaly Chekhover:

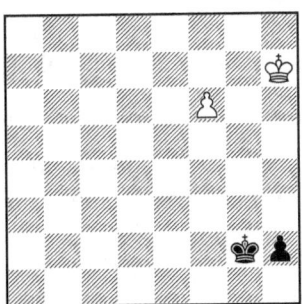

Black to play and draw

1...h1=♕+ 2.♔g8! with a draw.

But in Botokanov's study, the white
king's way to g8 is disguised and begins
from afar. This advance preparation
involves the search for means of fighting
against the opponent's future queen,
whose appearance we always keep in
mind. This circumstance – the "off-
stage" queen, which always looms over
any pawn endgame study – sometimes
forces you to perform unusual king
maneuvers.

The less the creative "beacon" that
leads to a win or to a draw is studied, the
more the "mined" square is disguised
and the more the study looks impressive.
In **Studies 102–135,** you have seen a lot
of interesting and instructive examples,
but, in our opinion, the systematic
development of theoretical ideas is only
beginning.

As you work on theoretical
"beacons", you need to remember
that study composition has a practical
dimension as well – in particular, the
development of endgame theory!

2.4. Winning a pawn

This section covers studies whose goal is to win a pawn. Interestingly, studies with the idea of winning a pawn comprise more than half of all pawn endgame studies!

The reason is simple: a pawn study is more similar to an actual game ending than any other type of study. Studies with an anti-theme are also included here: the purportedly active side prevents the opponent from winning a pawn, and the game ends in a draw.

We only examine a small portion of pawn-winning studies – ones where this idea is blended with other themes.

2.4.1. Zugzwang theme

These studies usually contain a lot of calculations but only a few brilliancies. To make them more artistically pleasing, one has to search for additional subtleties. One of these is the avoidance of capture.

In **Study 136**, the beginning of the solution is obvious.

No. 136. N. Grigoriev
Shakhmaty v SSSR, 1938

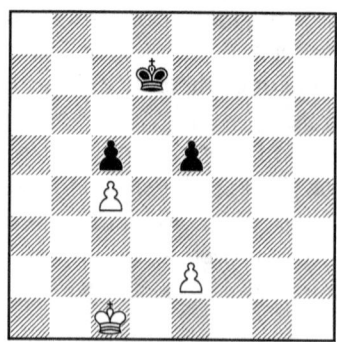

White to play and win

1.♔d2 ♔e6 2.♔e3 ♔f5 3.♔f3 e4+

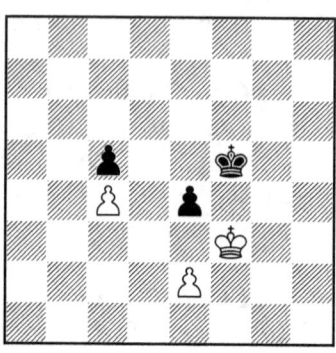

4.♔g3! If now 4...♔g5, then after 5.e3! ♔f5 6.♔h4 ♔f6 7.♔g4 ♔e5 8.♔g5, white wins.

4...e3! Looks like desperation...

5.♔f3 ♔f6! That's the point! After 6.♔xe3?, there's 6...♔e5!, and white is in zugzwang: 7.♔d3 ♔f5 8.e3 ♔e5 9.♔e2 ♔f5 10.♔f3 ♔e5 11.e4 ♔d4 12.♔f4 ♔xc4 13.e5 ♔b3! with a theoretical draw.

6.♔f4! ♔e6 7.♔e4! ♔d6! 8.♔f5!, and, declining to take the e-pawn, white wins the black c-pawn.

The same idea is executed in **Study 137**, but the solution is sort of turned ninety degrees.

No. 137. N. Grigoriev
Izvestia, 1929

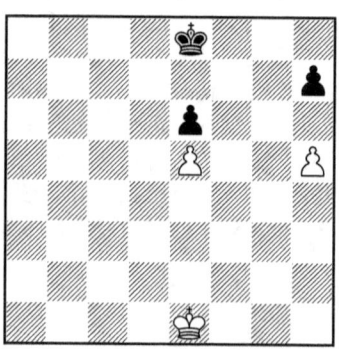

White to play and draw

1.♔f2!! Not 1.h6? ♔f7 or 1.♔e2?
♔d7 2.♔d3 ♔c6 3.♔d4 ♔b5 4.h6
♔b4 5.♔d3 ♔c5 6.♔e4 ♔c4 7.♔e3
♔d5 8.♔f4 ♔d4 9.♔g4! – and then,
similarly to the previous study, 9...♔e4!
10.♔h4 ♔f4! 11.♔h5 ♔f5! 12.♔h4
♔g6!, winning the h-pawn.

1...♔d7. White saves the game in
a curious way after the waiting move
1...♔e7 2.♔f3!, also waiting. But not
2.♔g3? h6! and the black king has
enough time to go around the pawns
from the left, or 2.♔e3? ♔d7! and the
king can't get to the rook file.

2.h6! Outpacing black!

2...♔c6. 2...♔e7 is met with 3.♔e3
♔f7 4.♔d4 ♔g6 5.♔c5 ♔g5 6.♔d6
♔f5 7.♔e7 ♔xe5 8.♔f7 ♔d6 9.♔g7,
draw.

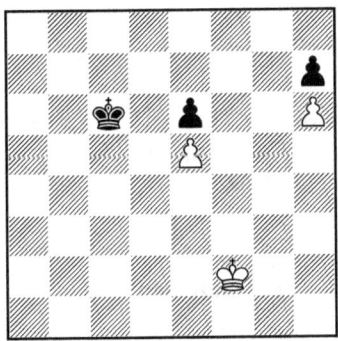

**3.♔g3! ♔d5 4.♔h4! ♔d4! 5.♔h5!
♔e4! 6.♔g4! ♔xe5 7.♔g5 ♔d6 8.♔f6**,
draw.

Nikolai Grigoriev's discovery
led to some creative responses. The
introduction in **Study 138** is quite
unexpected.

No. 138. S. Zhigis
Shakhmatny Listok, 1929

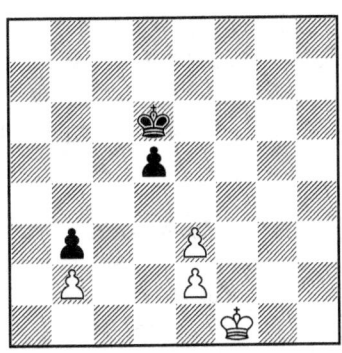

White to play and win

1.♔g2! As becomes clear later,
1.♔f2? is weaker.

1...♔e6! If 1...♔e5, then 2.♔f3
♔f5 3.e4+ dxe4+ 4.♔g3 ♔g5 5.e3,
and then like in the false try of the study
above.

2.e4!! Not 2.♔g3? ♔f5! 3.♔f3 ♔e5
4.e4 d4! 5.e3 d3! with a draw.

2...dxe4 3.♔h3! Again, not 3.♔g3?
♔f5 4.c3 ♔g5 with a draw.

3...♔e5! 3...♔f5 is met with 4.e3,
winning.

4.♔g4. 4.e3? ♔d5! is too early –
black even wins.

**4...♔d5 5.♔f5 ♔d4 6.♔f4 ♔d5
7.e3 ♔c5!**

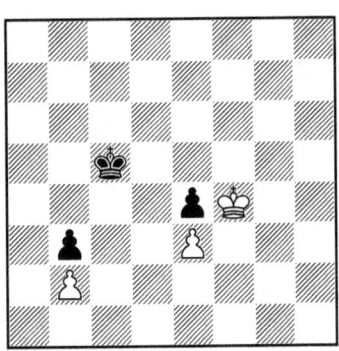

8.♔e5!, and then like in the false try of the previous study, starting from move 10.

8...♚b5 9.♔d5! ♚b4 10.♔d4! ♚b5 11.♔c3! ♚a4 12.♔c4. White wins.

Study 139 doesn't resemble **Study 137** at first.

No. 139. M. Zinar
Themes 64, 1978
4th prize

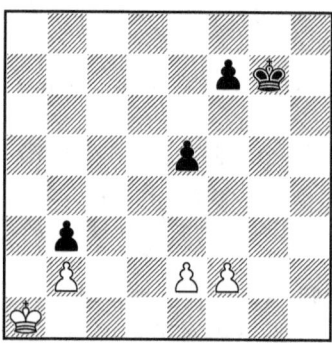

White to play and win

1.♔b1 e4! Otherwise, white will simply capture the b3 pawn.

2.♔c1! Not 2.e3?, because the black king gets into the "breach" – the f3 square.

2...e3! Black disrupts the white pawns!

3.fxe3. 3.f3? loses for white.

3...♚f6 4.♔d2! ♚e5

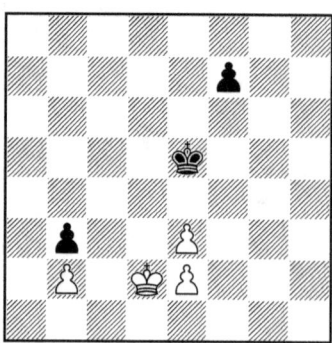

5.♔d3! But not 5.♔e1? ♚e4 6.♔f2 f5 with a draw.

5...f5. Otherwise, white will play 6.e4 and win.

6.♔c3! ♚e4 7.♔d2! ♚d5 8.♔e1. The white king has forced black to play f7–f5 and now returns to the back ranks.

8...♚e5 9.♔f1! ♚d5 10.♔g2! ♚e4 11.♔f2 ♚d5 12.♔f3 ♚e5

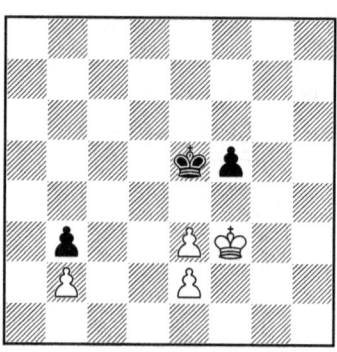

13.e4! White wins by returning the pawn.

13...fxe4+ 14.♔g4 ♚d5 15.♔f5!, and wins like in the study above, beginning from move 5.

The same theme was spectacularly expressed in **Study 140**.

No. 140. M. Zinar
Krymskaya Pravda, 1975

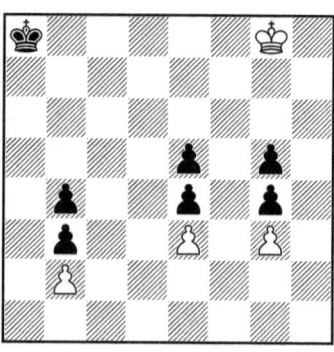

White to play and win

Since the f4 square is attacked twice, the opposition extends from the a-file to the f-file. Yet the main point is not the opposition, but rather the paradoxical way to win, highlighted by multiple capture avoidances. Black has twice as many pawns, but the opposing king is in his camp.

1.♔g7! ♚a7! 2.♔g6! ♚b6! Black has to give up the opposition to save the g5 pawn.

3.♔f6! Not 3.♔xg5? ♚c5 4.♔f5 ♚d5, draw.

3...♚b5 4.♔f5! Not 4.♔xe5? ♚c5!, and the black king gets to d3.

4...♚c6!

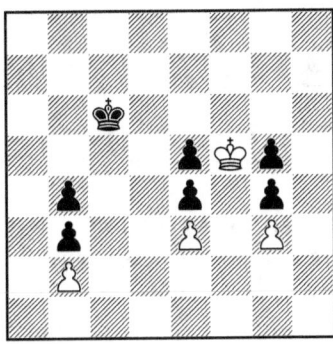

5.♔e6!! A fantastic move! The king attacks four (!) pawns at once, but every one of them is taboo! Both 5.♔xg4? ♚d5 6.♔f5 g4 and 5.♔xe4? ♚d6 6.♔f5 ♚d5 lead to a draw

5...♚b6 6.♔d6! ♚b5 7.♔d5! ♚b6

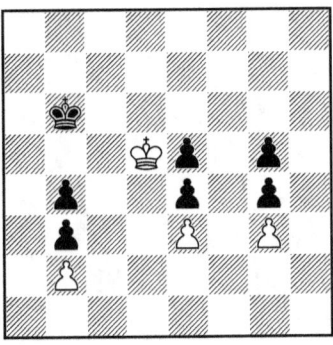

8.♔xe4! The king has danced around the pawns for five moves and finally found a victim!

8...♚c5 9.♔xe5 ♚c4 10.♔e4! ♚c5 11.♔f5 ♚c4 12.e4 with a win. A true anthem to capture avoidance!

Most ideas can be expressed through systematic movement, and almost all ideas are improved by it. Here are some examples where the goal is achieved through repeating maneuvers.

No. 141. M. Zinar
Shakhmaty v SSSR, 1985

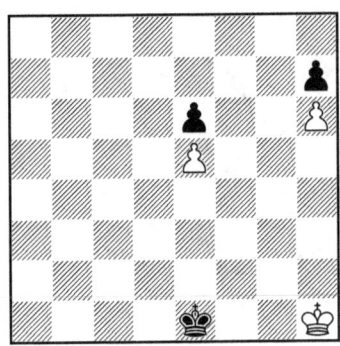

White to play and draw

1.♔g1! ♚d2! 2.♔h2! ♚e2 3.♔g2! ♚d3 4.♔h3! ♚e3

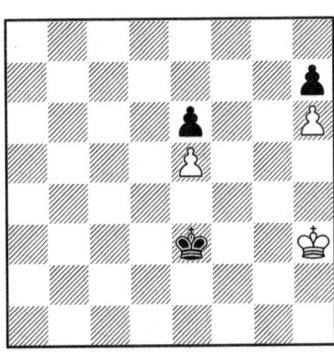

5.♔g3! ♚d4! 6.♔h4! ♚d5 7.♔h5! ♚e4 8.♔g4!, draw.

In **Studies 137–141**, we have basically seen improvements of a single key position found by Nikolai Grigoriev. Now, let's study other examples that illustrate systematic movement.

In **Study 142**, the e4 and f6 squares represent a mutual zugzwang position – as do f4-g6 and g4-h6, accordingly. Both sides fight over these positions!

No. 142. M. Zinar
Revista de Romana de Sah, 1980
2nd honorable mention

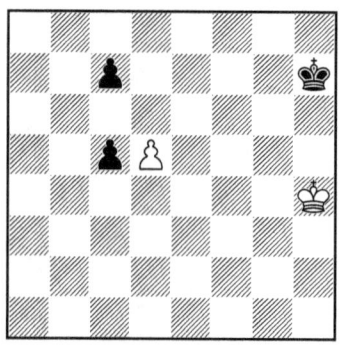

White to play and draw

1.♔g3! The attempt to get an advantageous version of mutual zugzwang is instructive: 1.♔g4? ♔h6! 2.♔f5 ♔g7 3.♔e5 ♔f7! 4.♔f5 ♔e7 5.♔e5 ♔d7, and black wins.

1...♔h6! 2.♔g4! ♔g7 3.♔f3! ♔g6 4.♔f4! ♔f7

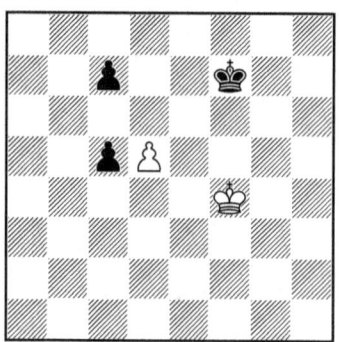

5.♔e3! ♔f6 6.♔e4! ♔e7 7.♔d3! ♔d7 8.♔c3!, draw.

The first composer to show such a "king dance" was Grigoriev.

No. 143. N. Grigoriev
Shakhmaty v SSSR, 1937
1st prize

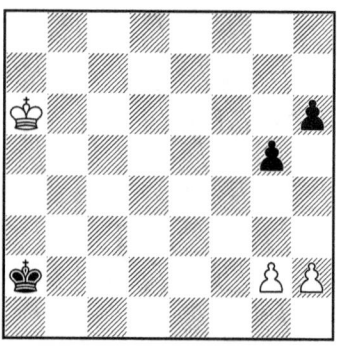

White to play and win

1.g4! The black pawns are fixed, and now the king maneuvers begin.

1...♔a3! 2.♔a5! And now, the corresponding squares for the mutual zugzwang position ♔f5–♔f3 have spread across the entire length of the board.

2...♔b2 3.♔b6! ♔b3! 4.♔b5! ♔c2 5.♔c6! ♔c3! 6.♔c5! ♔d2! 7.♔d6! ♔d3! 8.♔d5! ♔e2! 9.♔e6! ♔e3! 10.♔e5! ♔f2!

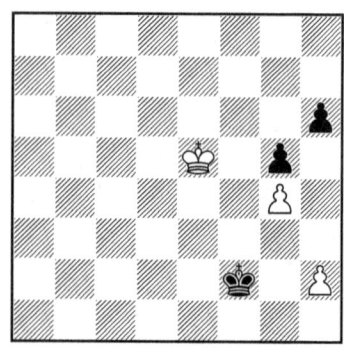

11.♔f6! ♚f3 12.♔f5! ♚g2 13.♔g6 ♚h3! 14.♔h5!, with the last zugzwang. White wins.

In the first part of **Study 144**, white executes an anti-stalemate idea. In the second, there's systematic movement, like in Grigoriev's study, but with a different pawn position.

No. 144. M. Zinar
Na Smenu (Sverdlovsk), 1988
1ˢᵗ special honorable mention

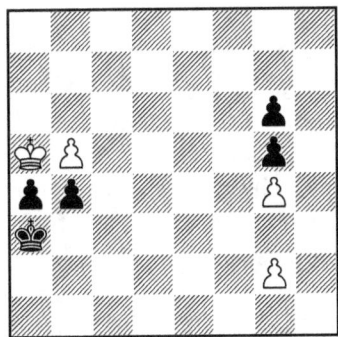

White to play and win
(actually unsolvable)

1.b6 b3 2.b7 b2 3.b8=♖! It's stalemate after promotion to a queen: 3.b8=♕? b1=♕ 4.♕xb1.
3...♚a2 4.♔xa4 b1=♕ 5.♖xb1 ♚xb1 6.♔b5! ♚c2 7.♔c6! ♚c3

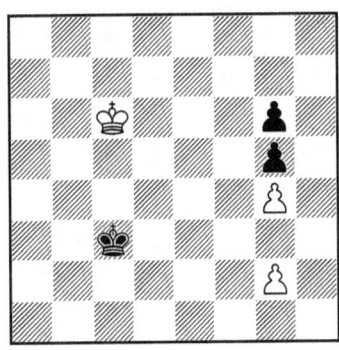

8.♔c5! And here too, the corresponding squares for the main zugzwang position, ♔e5–♚e3, are spread all along the third and fifth ranks to the left.

8...♚d2 9.♔d6! ♚d3 10.♔d5! ♚e2 11.♔e6! ♚e3 12.♔e5! ♚f2 13.♔f6 ♚g3 14.♔xg5 with a win.

Study 145 is one of the most original pawn studies. Black has a protected passed pawn. By using his right to move, white tries to separate it.

No. 145. A. Maksimovskikh
Shakhmatnaya Moskva, 1970

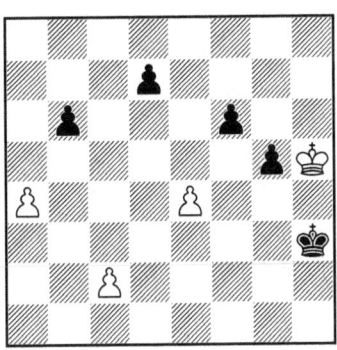

White to play and draw
(actually unsolvable)

1.e5! What's so unusual about this move?
1...fxe5 2.♔xg5 ♚g3 3.♔f5! d6 4.c4!

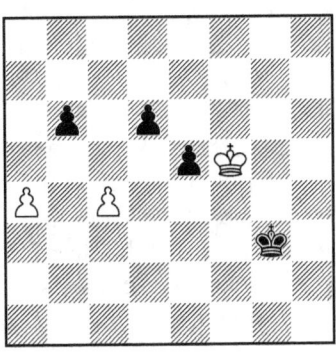

4...♔f3. A familiar situation. What if we repeat it again?

5.c5! dxc5 6.♔xe5 ♔e3 7.♔d5 ♔d3. A paradox! The same situation again!

8.a5! bxa5 9.♔xc5, with a draw. Original systematic movement!

Unfortunately, this interesting endgame study hadn't withstood the test of time. Black wins with the subtle 4...♔f2!! 5.c5 bxc5! 6.a5 c4 7.♔e4 d5+ 8.♔xe5 c3 9.a6 c2 10.a7 c1=♕ 11.a8=♕ ♕e3+ 12.♔f5 d4, gradually converting his extra pawn.

The theme of the Grigoriev zugzwang was treated artistically in the next two studies.

No. 146. N. Grigoriev
Original source unknown, 1937

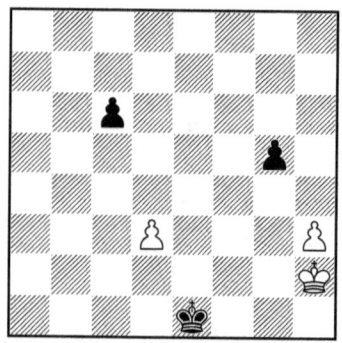

White to play and draw

1.♔g3 c5. If 1...♔e2, then 2.d4! It turns out that exactly where the pawn falls *is* important! Now, after 2...♔e3 3.♔g4 ♔xd4 4.♔xg5 c5 5.h4 c4 6.h5 c3 7.h6 c2 8.h7 c1=♕+ 9.♔g6, there's a rare theoretical position on the board, where the black king stops the queen from getting to the a1-h8 diagonal, and therefore it's a draw, even though the king is only on g6.

2.♔f3! ♔f1! The black king has reached the same distance between the two pawns.

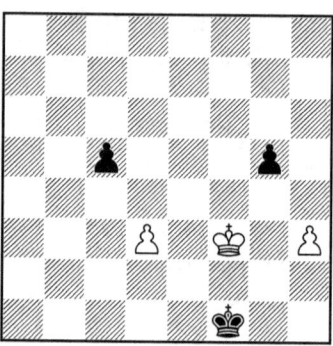

3.♔e4! And the white king too!

3...♔f2! 3...♔g2 4.♔f5, with a draw; or 3...♔e2 4.♔d5!, again with a draw.

4.♔e5! The kings are moving so prettily — which pawn to capture?

4...♔f3! 5.♔e6! ♔f4! 6.♔e7! ♔f3! 7.♔e6!, positional draw!

This masterpiece by the king of pawn studies isn't as famous as it deserves to be!

In the next, similar situation, white wins.

No. 147. N. Grigoriev
Izvestia, 1929

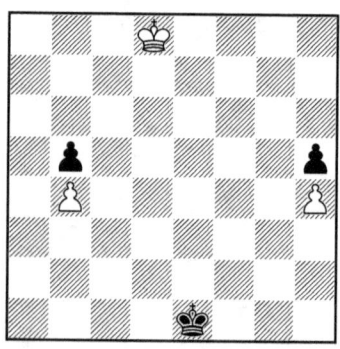

White to play and win

1.♔e7! ♚e2 2.♔e6! ♚e3 3.♔e5! ♚e2 4.♔e4! ♚e1 5.♔e3!, and **5...♚d1** is met with **6.♔d4!** and the inevitable **7.♔c5**, white wins.

Or the echo play: **5...♚f1 6.♔f4! ♚e2 7.♔g5!**, white wins.

2.4.2. The "mined" square

We have already seen similar studies in the section devoted to theoretical "beacons". This theme gives additional color to winning-a-pawn studies.

No. 148. M. Zinar
Shakhmaty v SSSR, 1987

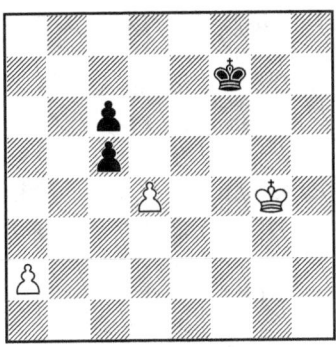

White to play and win

1.a4 ♚e6 2.a5. 2.♔f4? cxd4! loses, while 2.dxc5? ♚d5! only draws.

2...c4! Not 2...♚d6 3.a6 ♚c7 4.dxc5, and white wins.

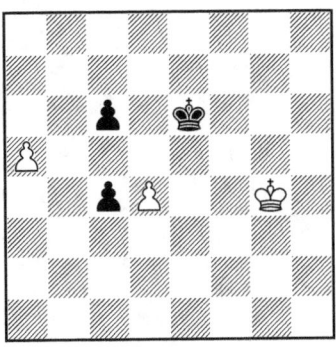

3.♔f3!! The point!

3...♚d6! 4.♔e2! 4.♔f4? c3 draws. Meanwhile, white feared moving to the e3 square! It looks innocuous enough, but it's actually mined: 4.♔e3? c5! — and now 5.a6 is met with the break 5...cxd4+! with a draw. If not for that check, cxd4 wouldn't have worked.

4...♚c7 5.♔d2 ♚d6. A new trap!

6.♔c2! And the c3 square is also mined.

6...c5 7.a6! with a win.

The play in **Study 149** is even subtler.

No. 149. V. Archakov and M. Zinar
Nauka i Suspilstvo (Kyiv), 1986

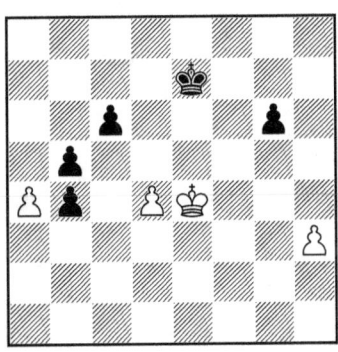

White to play and win

1.a5! b3! Not 1...♚d6 2.♔d3 ♚c7 3.♔c2 ♚b7 4.♔b3! ♚a6 5.♔xb4 g5 6.♔c5 ♚xa5 7.♔xc6: white promotes the pawn with check, then trades the queens and wins.

2.♔d3 ♚d6! Getting ready for the break we have seen in the previous study. Here, white cannot play 3.♔c3? c5 4.a6 cxd4+. The waiting moves 3.h4? b4 4.♔d2 ♚c7 even lead to black's victory.

3.♔d2! g5!

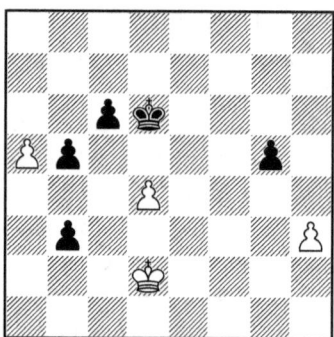

4.♔c1!! The paths you have to take to get to the pawn!

4...♚c7 5.♔b2 ♚b7 6.♔xb3 with a win similar to the one in the annotation to the first move.

The check problem is solved in an original way in the next two studies.

No. 150. N. Grigoriev
Izvestia, 1931

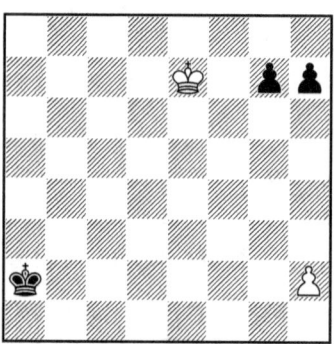

White to play and win

The critical moment comes after **1.h4! h5!** What can white do? After the logical and natural 1.♔f7?, the break 1...g5! follows. And if the king goes around through d6 and e5, then the black king has enough time to come to help.

2.♔f8!! Feint!

2...g6 3.♔e7!! The return is very impressive! White threatens 4.♔f6.

3...g5 4.hxg5, and the pawn promotes with a check. Incredible!

No. 151. M. Zinar
Rybak Primorya, 1982
1st honorable mention

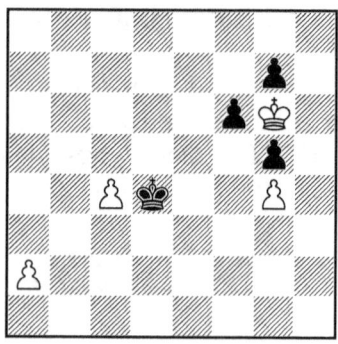

White to play and win

Here, 1.♔xg7? is also met with the 1...f5 break, drawing.

Therefore, **1.c5 ♚d5!** Black has noticed the "mine"! You may think that there's no win at all: the king has no moves, and 2.a4? is met with 2...♚c6 3.a5 ♚b5, drawing. Yet...

2.a3!! A tortoise move!

2...♚c6 3.a4! ♚d5. Or 3...♚c7 4.a5 ♚b7 5.♔f5 ♚c6 6.a6 with a win.

4.a5! ♚xc5. After 4...♚c6 5.a6 ♚c7 6.a7, the king gets checked on the eighth rank.

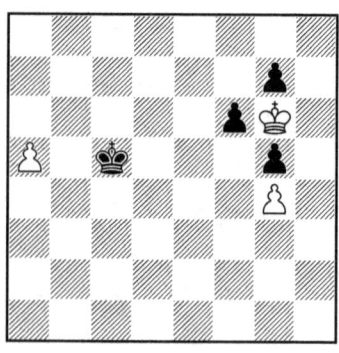

5.♔xg7! f5 6.gxf5 g4 7.f6 g3 8.f7 g2 9.f8=♕+, and white wins.

The mined squares can be sidestepped in various directions. That's how this idea is expressed in **Study 152**, together with other plans.

No. 152**. J. Mikitovics
Problemist Ukrainy, 2008
Honorable mention

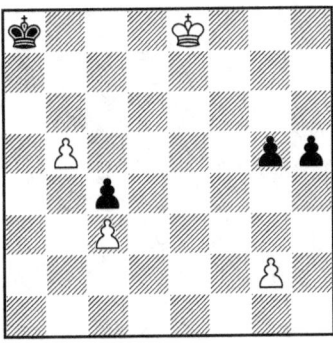

White to play and draw

The black kingside pawns are supposed to tear up white's position. But the Reti maneuver comes to the rescue!
1.♔d7! ♔b7 (otherwise **2.♔c7**) **2.♔e6! g4 3.♔f5 ♔b6 4.♔g5 ♔xb5 5.♔xh5,** and there are two branches.
A) **5...g3 6.♔g4(h4) ♔a4 7.♔xg3 ♔b3**

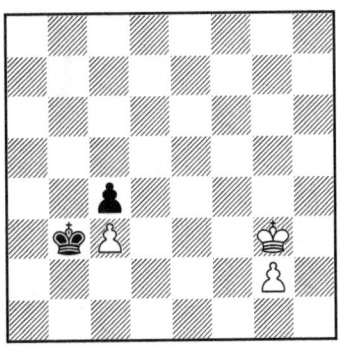

8.♔f2! Sidestepping the "mines" on f3 and f4 from below! Not 8.♔f3 ♔xc3 9.g4 ♔d3 10.g5 c3 11.g6 c2 12.g7 c1=♕ 13.g8=♕ ♕f1+ or 8.♔f4 ♔xc3 9.g4 ♔d4 10.g5 c3. The move 8.♔h2 ♔xc3 9.g4 ♔d4! doesn't work either, and nor does 8.♔h4 ♔xc3 9.g4 ♔d4 10.g5 c3 11.g6 c2 12.g7 c1=♕ 13.g8=♕ ♕h1+ 14.♔g3 ♕g1+, skewering the queen.
B) **5...♔a4 6.♔xg4 ♔b3**

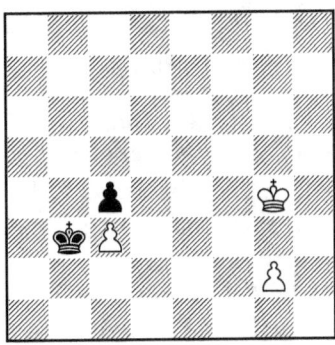

7.♔f5! Sidestepping the "mines" from above! Not 7.♔h5? ♔xc3 8.g4 ♔d4! 9.g5 ♔e5 10.g6 ♔f6 11.♔h6 c3 12.g7 c2 13.g8=♕ c1=♕+, and the white king is lured into check.

From Mikhail Zinar's judge's report: "The Reti + mines combination has occurred in several of my studies. But here the author sidesteps them from both below and above."

2.4.3. Anti-stalemate theme

In this theme, white has to avoid a stalemate trap before winning the pawn.

No. 153. V. Chekhover
Chasovoi Rodiny, 1956

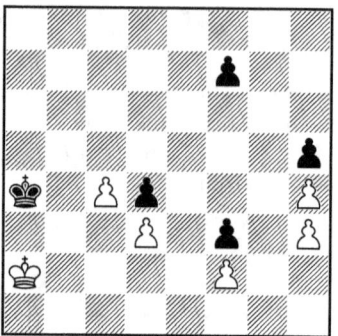

White to play and win

1.♔b2(b1). But not 1.c5? ♔b5 2.♔b3 ♔xc5 3.♔a4 ♔d5 4.♔b5 ♔e5 5.♔c5 f5 6.♔c4 ♔f4 7.♔xd4. White has won a pawn, but there's a stalemate on the board.

1...♔b4 2.♔c2(c1) **♔a4 3.♔d2**(d1) **♔b4 4.♔e1! ♔a4 5.♔f1 ♔b4 6.♔g1** f5 (otherwise the white king breaks through into the enemy camp) **7.♔h2 f4.**

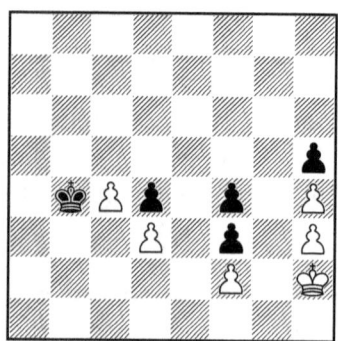

And now back!

8.♔g1 ♔a4 9.♔f1 ♔b4 10.♔e1 ♔a4 11.♔d1(d2) **♔b4 12.♔c2**(c1) **♔a4 13.c5! ♔b5 14.♔b3 ♔xc5 15.♔a4** with a win.

Study 154 is massive, with a whole complex of ideas. I don't claim any brilliant individual moves, but to appreciate and understand such studies, you need to look at them as a whole — at the sum of moves and the winning strategy!

No. 154. M. Zinar
Shakhmaty v SSSR, 1977
Special prize

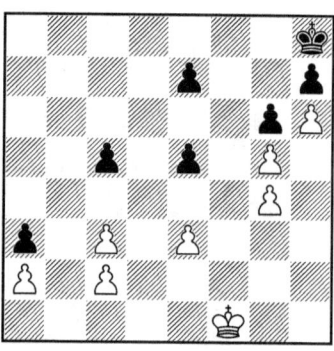

White to play and win

1.♔e2! Precision is required! After 1.c4? ♔g8! 2.♔e2 ♔f7 3.♔d3 ♔e6 black prevents the white king from entering his camp. Or 1.♔e1? c4! 2.♔f2 e4 3.♔g3 e5 — a fortress.

1...e4! 2.c4! ♔g8 3.♔d2 ♔f7 4.♔c3 ♔e6 5.♔b3 ♔d6

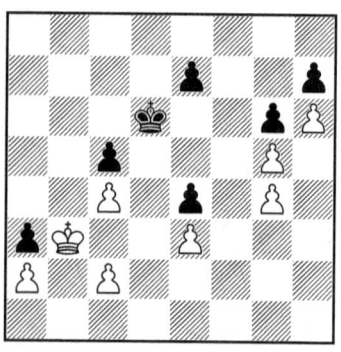

6.♔a4! But not 6.♔xa3? ♚c6 7.♔a4 ♚b6 with a draw. Knowing the previous example, it's easy to see the stalemate trap created by black. White, however, chooses another way!

6...♚c6 7.♔a5 ♚c7 8.♔b5 ♚d6 9.♔b6 e6 10.♔b5 ♚e5!

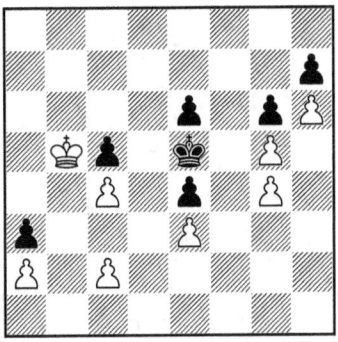

11.♔a5(a6). Of course, not 11.♔xc5?, stalemate. The second capture avoidance!

11...♚d6 12.♔b6 ♚e5! 13.♔b7! ♚d6 14.♔c8 ♚e5! 15.♔d8! ♚d6 16.♔e8 ♚e5! 17.♔f7 ♚d6

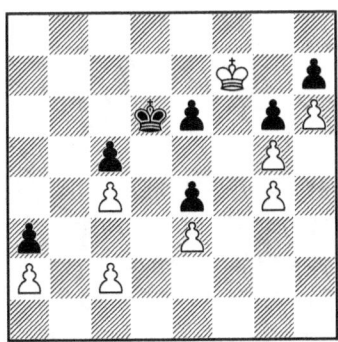

18.♔f6! Not 18.♔g7? ♚e7 19.♔xh7 ♚f7 20.c3 e5 21.♔h8 ♚f8 22.h7 ♚f7, stalemate. The third capture avoidance!

18...♚d7 19.♔e5 ♚e7 20.♔xe4. Finally, there's a pawn that *can* be captured!

20...♚d6

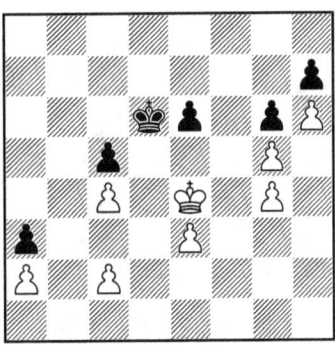

21.♔f4! Not the immediate 21.♔d3? ♚e5 22.♔d2 ♚e4 23.♔e2 e5 24.♔f2, the second stalemate! Nor can white play 21.c3? instead of 21.♔f4! – the pawn should stay on c2, as we shall see later.

21...e5+! 22.♔e4 ♚e6 23.♔d3 ♚d6 24.♔c3 ♚c6.

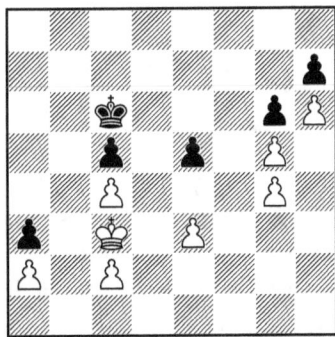

Let's stop and look around: the king has taken a real "round-the-world" trip! Now, the king has returned to its own camp, but it's not enough — from the c3 square, where it stood 20 (!) moves ago, it now embarks on a new journey!

25.♔b3 ♚b6 26.♔xa3 ♚a5 27.♔b3 e4 28.♔a3! Shouldering his counterparty.

28...♚b6 29.♔b2! ♚a5

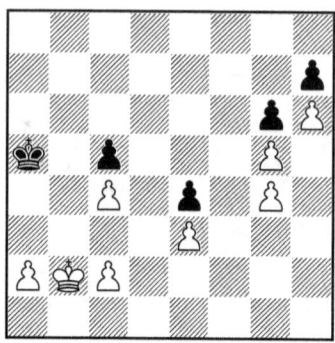

30.♔b3! ♚a6 31.♔c3 ♚a5 32.♔d2 ♚b4 33.♔e2(e1) ♚a3. After 33...♚xc4, the quickest win is 34.♔d2 ♚b4 35.a3+ ♚xa3 36.♔c3 etc.

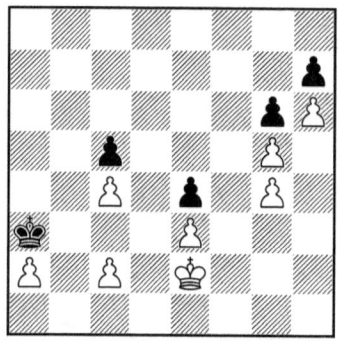

34.♔f2! ♚xa2 35.♔g3 ♚b2 36.♔f4 ♚xc2 37.♔xe4 ♚c3 38.♔d5, winning. If white had played c2-c3 at any point, the game would have ended in a draw.

An extremely long story about two industrious kings! They put in a colossal amount of work!

2.4.4. The snare

Study composers have developed two schemes to snare the enemy king: squeezed between pawns from where it cannot stop a passed pawn, or at the edge of the board.

No. 155. H. Haantola
Tyovaen Shakki, 1935
Commendation

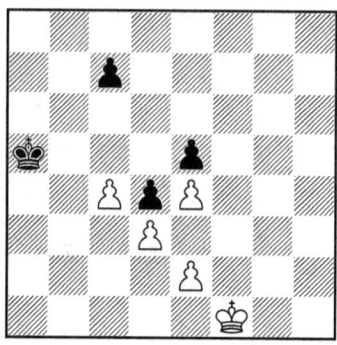

White to play and win

1.e3! dxe3 2.d4! exd4. A breakthrough with the sacrifice of two pawns.
3.e5 ♚b6 4.e6 ♚c6

5.c5! — the king is deprived of mobility, because if it moves, it will leave the square of the pawn.

The rest is simple: **5...d3 6.♔e1,** curtains.

The c5 pawn can be replaced with the e5 pawn, as in the next example. This scheme has been known for a long time and is well-developed. Studies that feature this scheme usually have one of two flaws: either the way to trap the king is too simple, or the subsequent play is too primitive. And while the ways of limiting the king have become more diverse, like in this and the next example, subsequent play has gained little with time: white either finishes play by trapping the king, or the king fights against three connected passed pawns, which makes the play unremarkable.

No. 156. N. Grigoriev
Sbornik Etyudov, 1952

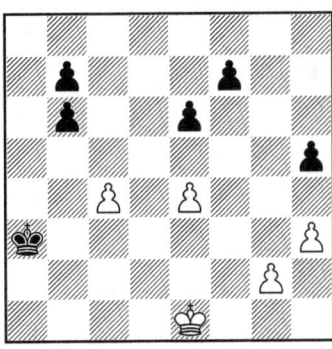

White to play and win

1.e5! Preparing a break and closing off the a3-f8 diagonal at the same time. The black king is now forced to chase after the pawn through a narrow window on f6.

1...♔b4 2.h4! A typical technique for preparing the break.

2...♔xc4 3.g4 ♔d5 4.gxh5 ♔xe5 5.h6 ♔f6

6.h5. The king is snared. The rest is simple.

6...b5 7.♔d2 b4 8.♔c2 e5 9.♔b3 e4 10.♔xb4 b5 11.♔c3 etc.

No. 157. V. Machal and V. Hadac
L. Prokes memorial, 1967
3rd honorable mention

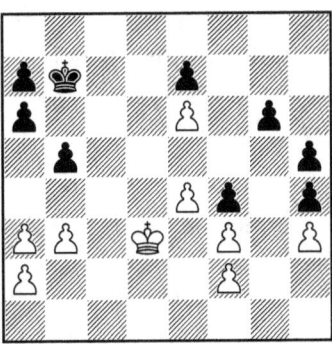

White to play and win

One of the few examples where the authors used the entire set of pawns! In this case, this was necessary to snare both kings *and* execute a black/white repetition in the subsequent play. The authors probably decided: if we get creative, then we get creative until the bitter end... and fight to the last pawn!

1.e5 g5 2.♔e4 g4 3.fxg4 hxg4 4.hxg4 h3 5.♔f3.

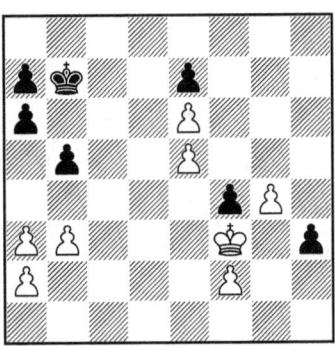

One "snare" has sprung.

5...♚c6 6.g5 ♚d5 7.g6 ♚xe6. And the other has too!

8.b4 a5 9.a4! The black/white synthesis continues! 9.bxa5? a6 10.a4 b4!, and it's now black who wins.

9...bxa4 10.bxa5 a3 11.a6, and black is in zugzwang.

The white king takes an active part in the next scheme, which involves snaring the black king on the edge of the board. Thus, while in the first case the play boils down to the king's struggle against the pawns, and ideas can be further developed in that direction, here, when both kings are out of action, the possibilities are much less diverse. Therefore, the main strength of such studies is the introductory play, before snaring the king.

The technique used in **Study 158** is especially beautiful in this regard: the idea is underscored by repetition of both the queen sacrifice and the subsequent king maneuver.

No. 158. V. Kovalenko
New Statesman, 1975
Commendation
(correction)

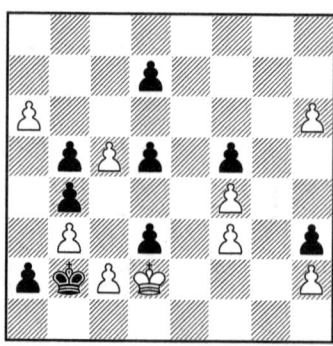

White to play and win

1.h7 dxc2 2.h8=♕+ ♚b1 3.♕a1+! The first sacrifice!

3...♚xa1 4.♚c1! Not 4.♚xc2? – the king gets checked by the d-pawn too early.

4...d4 5.a7 d3 6.a8=♕ d2+

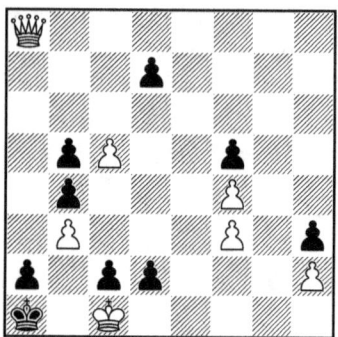

7.♚xc2! But not 7.♚xd2? ♚b1! 8.♕xa2+ ♚xa2 9.♚xc2 ♚a3, and black wins.

7...d1=♕+ 8.♚xd1 ♚b2! Not 8...♚b1 9.c6! dxc6 10.♕xc6 a1=♕ 11.♕c2#.

9.♕h8+ ♚b1 10.♕a1+! And the second sacrifice!

10...♚xa1 11.♚c1! with a win. The technical pawns spoil the study a bit.

Later, the double queen sacrifice was adorned by an interesting mutual zugzwang. That's how the collective **Study 159** came about.

No. 159**. M. Zinar and V. Kovalenko
Kudesnik, 2012

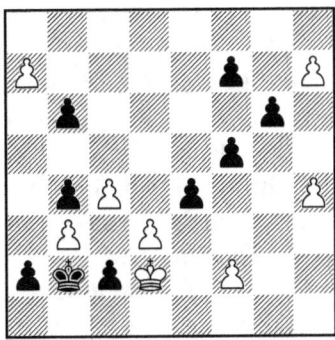

White to play and win

**1.h8=♕+ ♚b1 2.♕a1+! ♚xa1
3.♚c1 exd3 4.a8=♕ d2+**

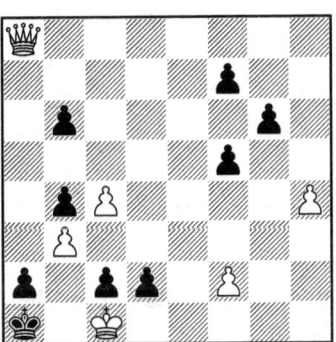

5.♚xd2! Not 5.♚xc2? d1=♕+
6.♚xd1 ♚b1, draw.
**5...♚b2! 6.♕h8+ ♚b1 7.♕a1+!
♚xa1**

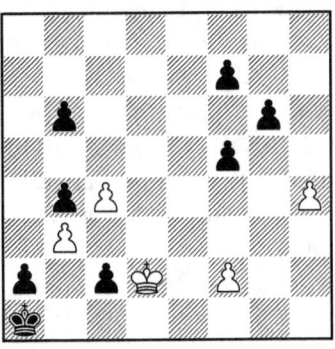

8.♚c1! Thematic false try: 8.♚xc2?
f4! 9.f3 f6! (mutual zugzwang) 10.♚c1
g5 11.h5 g4 12.h6 gxf3 13.h7 f2 14.h8=♕
f1=♕+, and now black wins.
8...f6! 9.♚xc2 f4

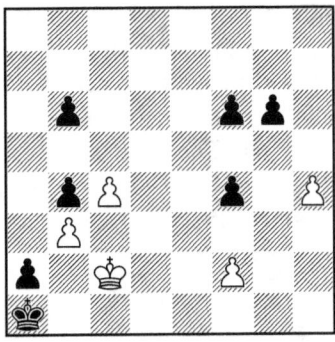

10.f3! And now it's black who is in
zugzwang.
**10...g5 11.h5 g4 12.h6 gxf3 13.h7 f2
14.h8=♕ (♗) f1=♕ 15.♕xf6#.**

In the next study, the theme of
capture avoidance to avoid the king being
snared is brilliantly composed! We quote
the annotations from the book *Sovetsky
Shakhmatny Etyud* (*Soviet Chess Study*),
Moscow, Fizkultura i Sport, 1955.

No. 160. M. Liburkin
Yerevan Chess Club competition, 1950
2nd prize

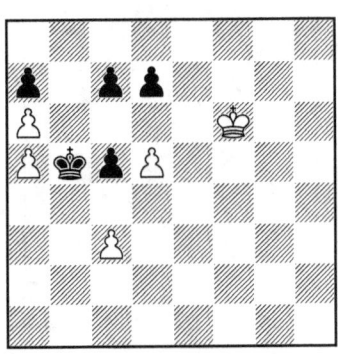

White to play and win

Pawn studies are rare guests in the diverse studies composing career of Mark Liburkin. Even though material is equal, it might seem that black has a small positional advantage – his king is closer to the unprotected opposing pawns than the white one, and white cannot even dream of winning. Because of that, the method used by white to achieve victory looks all the more spectacular.

1.♔e7! c4! The best defense. If 1...♔c4, then 2.♔xd7 ♔xd5 (2...♔xc3 3.♔xc7 and 4.d6)

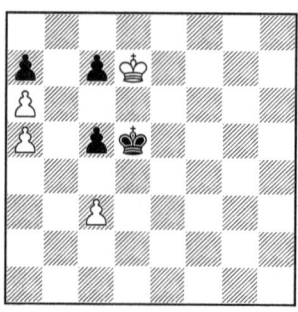

3.♔c8! (3.♔xc7? misses the win: 3...c4 4.♔b7 ♔d6 5.♔xa7 ♔c7, trapping the opponent's king) 3...♔c6 4.♔b8 ♔d7 5.♔xa7 ♔c8 6.c4! or 1...d6 2.♔d7 ♔c4 3.♔xc7 ♔xc3 4.♔b7 c4 5.♔xa7 ♔d3

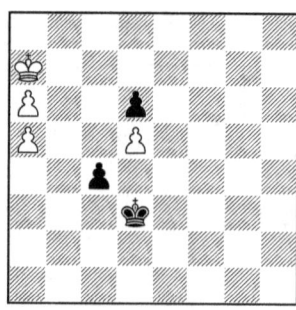

6.♔b8 c3 7.a7 c2 8.a8=♕ c1=♕ 9.a6 ♕g5 10.♕c6 ♕d8+ 11.♔b7, and wins.

2.♔d8!! The first surprise! White cannot play 2.♔xd7? due to 2...♔c5 3.♔c8 (3.♔xc7 ♔xd5 4.♔b7 ♔d6 etc.) 3...c6! 4.♔b7 cxd5 5.♔xa7 d4 6.cxd4+ ♔xd4 7.♔b6 c3 with a draw.

2...c5 3.♔c8!! One surprise after another! The white king continues to sidestep the black pawns, which will later limit the mobility of their own king. If 3.♔xc7?, then 3...♔xd5 4.♔b7 ♔d6 5.♔xa7 ♔c7 with a draw.

3...c6! Offering a trade that should make black's situation a lot easier.

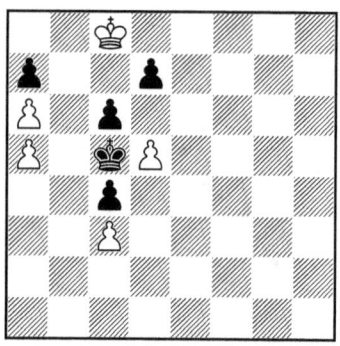

4.d6! White's peacefulness is unlimited! He sees his future allies in the black pawns.

4...♔xd6   5.♔b8! Extreme caution: 5.♔b7? c5!, and white is in zugzwang.

5...c5 6.♔b7! And now black is in zugzwang: 6...♔d5 7.♔xa7. His own pawn, presciently spared by white, stops him from maintaining control over the c7 square. After the black king moves away, white captures the a7 pawn and promotes his own a-pawn unhindered. The idea of capture avoidance is demonstrated in a very convincing and vivid form.

The history of creating this composition is interesting. To begin, the following endgame study won first prize at a major competition:

No. 161. A. Gulyaev
All-Union Physical Education and Sports Central Committee competition, 1948
1st prize

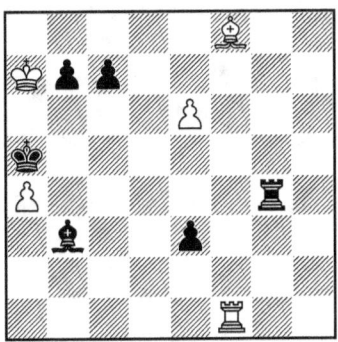

White to play and win

1.e7 ♖e4. Black can't play either 1...♗xa4 or 1...e2, because after 2.♖f5+, the white pawn promotes. **2.♖f4!** White's advantage lies in the fact that the black rook is inextricably tied to the e-file, where it has only three squares available. White should play energetically, without losing even a single tempo, because otherwise black will extricate himself by pushing the e3 pawn. At first glance, 2.♖f5+? looks very strong: the defense 2...♔xa4? is met with the pin 3.♖f4!; and if 2...b5, then 3.♖xb5+ ♔xa4 4.♖b4+! with an interesting double rook sacrifice by white.

However, black plays 2...c5! 3.♖xc5+ ♔xa4, and now white cannot win after either 4.♖c8 ♗f7 or 4.♖f5 (threatening 5.♖f4!) 4...♗f7! (but not 4...e2 5.♖f4! e1=♕ 6.e8=♕+! or 4...♖e6 5.♖f6 ♖e5 6.♖f4+ ♗c4 7.♖xc4+ ♔b3 8.♖c8 with a win) 5.♖xf7 ♔b3!

6.♗h6 e2 7.♗d2 b5! 8.♔b6 b4 9.♔c5 e1=♕ 10.♗xe1 ♖xe1 or 6.♖f4 ♖e6 7.♖b4+ ♔a2 8.♖a4+ ♔b3 9.♖a3+ ♔b2, and white's attacking resources are exhausted.

2...♖e6. Of course, not 2...♖e5 due to 3.♖f5!, and wins. Now the black rook has closed off the way to f7 for the bishop, and the check on f5 becomes possible.

3.♖f5+! ♔xa4 4.♖f6! Forcing the black rook to move to the fifth rank. Not 4...♖e4 5.♖f4!

4...♖e5 5.♖f4+ ♗c4! Black sacrifices the bishop to free his king.

6.♖xc4+ ♔b3. 6...♔b5 is met with 7.♖c5+! – a new double rook sacrifice by white.

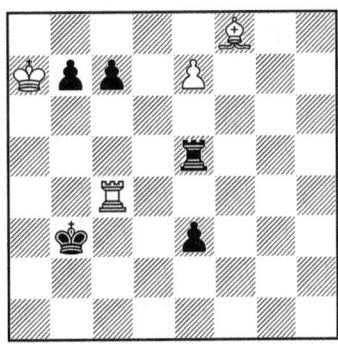

7.♖c3+! Not 7.♖b4+? ♔c2 8.♖b2+ ♔c1! 9.♖e2 ♔d1, and the black king makes it to d1 in time. Having captured the bishop, white gets a winning position by implementing one of the following plans:

1) the black king is lured onto the same rank or diagonal as the black rook, and then the latter is pinned or deflected from guarding the e8 square;

2) the white rook is moved to the d-file with tempo, after which ♖d8 wins;

3) the black king is lured to a5, the black passer is blocked by the rook, and, thanks to that, the white king can get to its pawn faster than the black king can get to e1;

4) the black king is forced onto b1, the black passer is blocked on e2 by the rook, and then white wins with a king maneuver because the black king cannot step onto c1. The rest is now obvious.

If **7...♔a4**, then **8.♖a3+! ♔b5 9.♖d3!** (threatening 10.♖d5+) **9...c6 10.♖d8 e2 11.e8=♕ e1=♕ 12.♖d5+!**, and wins.

Or **7...♔a2** is met with **8.♖c2+.** 8.♖a3+? ♔b1 9.♖a1+ ♔c2 10.♖a2+ ♔c1 is not enough — black makes a draw. Now play branches into two lines.

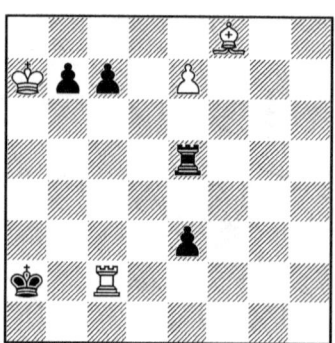

After **8...♔b1**, white plays **9.♖e2!**, and if **9...♔c1**, then **10.♖xe3! ♖xe3 11.♗h6,** and wins.

Black can try to activate his queenside pawns, for instance, 9...c5;

then 10.♔xb7 c4 11.♔c7 c3 12.♔d6 c2 (or 12...♖xe7 13.♖e1+! and 14.♗xe7, or 12...♖e4 13.♔d5 etc.) 13.♔xe5 c1=♕ 14.e8=♕ ♕c3+ 15.♔f4, and wins.

Also, if **8...♔b3**, then **9.♖b2+! ♔c4 10.♖b4+! ♔d3 11.♖d4+!** and **12.♖d8.**

Instead of 9...♔c4, black can move in another direction: 9...♔a4

10.♖b4+ ♔a5 11.♖b1 e2 12.♖e1 ♔a4 13.♔xb7 ♔b3 14.♔xc7 ♔c2 15.♔d7 ♔d2 16.e8=♕ ♖xe8 17.♗b4+, and wins.

The white rook is sacrificed on twelve different squares scattered all around the board, with very diverse motivations for these sacrifices.

In his critical article "Three Studies" (*Shakhmaty v SSSR*, No. 4, 1949), world champion Mikhail Botvinnik wrote, "But how could the white king get to a7? Only through c8 and b8, but this is pure fantasy!"

Therefore, Mikhail Moiseevich composed his own version of the study — in his opinion, it better suited the tastes of over-the-board players.

However, Liburkin demonstrated in **Study 160** that despite Botvinnik's affirmation, it was possible for the white king to capture the black a7-pawn without taking the pawns on c7 and d7.

No. 162. M. Botvinnik
Shakhmaty v SSSR, 1949
(derived from A. Gulyaev)

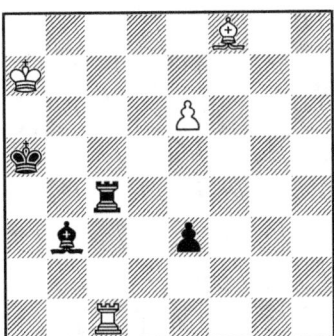

White to play and win

1.e7 ♖e4. 1...♖xc1 is met with 2.e8=♕ ♖c7+ 3.♔b8 ♖c3 4.♕e5+ etc.

2.♖c5+ ♔a4. After 2...♔b4, there's 3.♖e5 ♖xe5 4.e8=♕+ with a win.

3.♖f5!! Taking control over the f7 square.

3...e2. Here, 3...♗f7 doesn't help due to 4.♖xf7 ♔b3 5.♖f4 (or 5.♗h6 e2 6.♗d2) 5...♖e6 6.♖b4+ and 7.♖b8 or 3...♖e6 4.♖f6! ♖e5 5.♖f4+ ♗c4 6.♖xc4+ ♔b3 7.♖c3+ ♔a2 8.♖c8 etc.

4.♖f4! e1=♕ 5.e8=♕+, and wins.

No. 163. F. Prokop
Sach, 1943
4th prize

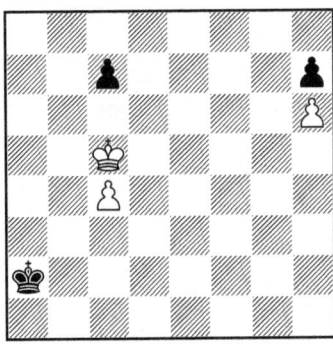

White to play and win

1.♔b4! The first shouldering!

1...♔b2 2.c5 ♔c2 3.♔c4! c6 4.♔d4 ♔b3 5.♔e5 ♔c4. We have reached the initial position of J. Hasek's 1928 study.

6.♔f6 ♔d5!

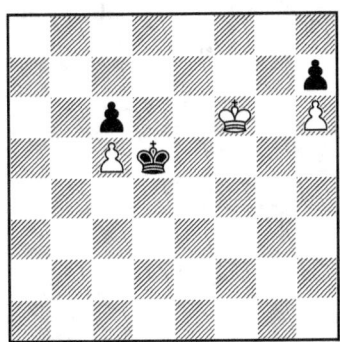

7.♔f7! White wins with triangulation.

7...♔e5 8.♔e7! ♔d5 9.♔f6!, and the second shouldering — white wins.

In **Study 164**, white reaches Hasek's position by using the anti-stalemate promotion. Another two-phase study.

No. 164. M. Zinar
Seletsky memorial, 1987
Commendation

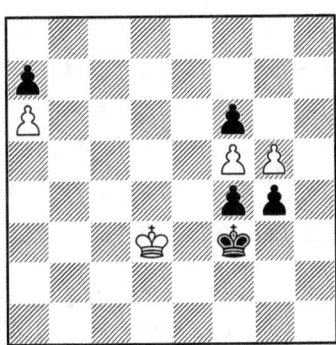

White to play and win

1.g6 g3 2.g7 g2! 3.g8=♖! ♔f2 4.♔e4 g1=♕ 5.♖xg1 ♔xg1 6.♔xf4

♔f2!, and we have reached the position after the third move of the previous study but on the other side of the board.

In **Study 165**, the finale is the same, but in parallel synthesis.

No. 165. N. Grigoriev
Shakhmaty v SSSR, 1938

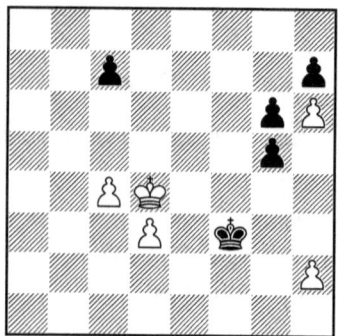

White to play and win

1.♔e5 ♔g2 2.♔f6 g4 3.♔g5!, and now the play branches into two:

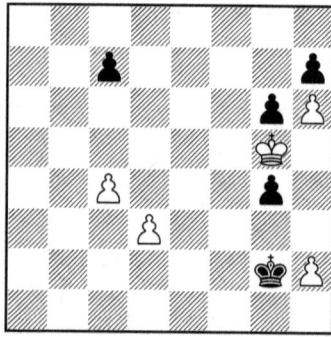

A) **3...♔xh2 4.♔xg4 c5! 5.♔f4! ♔h3! 6.d4 cxd4 7.c5 g5+ 8.♔e4 g4 9.c6,** and the pawn promotes with check. This is a well-known variation with the pawn promotion and check theme. The second variation, however, remained in

obscurity until 1985, when it was first published:

B) **3...g3 4.hxg3 ♔xg3 5.d4 ♔f3 6.d5 ♔e4 7.♔f6 g5! 8.♔xg5 ♔e5 9.c5! ♔xd5 10.♔f6,** and we have reached the Hasek study mentioned in **Study 163**. As a reminder, the win is achieved by giving up the right to move with triangulation.

10...c6 11.♔f7! ♔e5 12.♔e7! ♔d5 13.♔f6! etc.

Study 166 is a rare case where there's no clear and obvious theme, and the pawn is won in an interesting and original way. The introduction is however instructive.

No. 166. N. Grigoriev
64, 1930
1ˢᵗ honorable mention

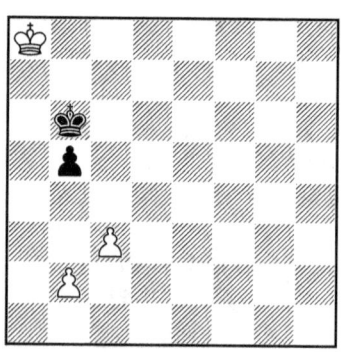

White to play and win

1.b3! After the rash 1.b4? ♔a6!, white cannot get out of the drawing opposition: 2.♔b8 ♔b6 3.♔c8 ♔c6 etc. Or 1.♔b8? b4! with equality.

1...♔a5 2.♔b8! But not 2.♔b7? b4! 3.c4, stalemate.

2...b4 3.c4 ♔b6! 4.♔c8 ♔c6 5.♔d8 ♔d6 6.♔e8 ♔e6 7.♔f8 ♔f6 8.♔g8 ♔g6

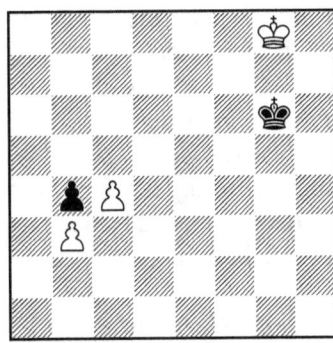

9.♔h8! ♚f6! 10.♔h7 ♚f7 11.♔h6 ♚f6 12.♔h5 ♚f5 13.♔h4 ♚f4

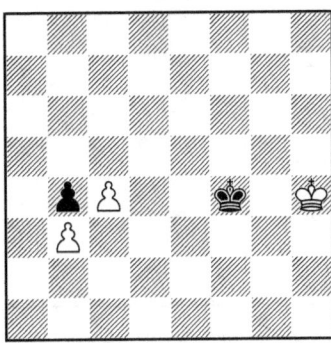

14.♔h3! ♚f5 15.♔g3 ♚g5 16.♔f3 ♚f5 17.♔e3 ♚e5 18.♔d3 with a win. The kings have walked along a fascinating route, drawing three sides of a rectangle.

Obviously, there is still much to be found in the idea of winning a pawn. But true discoveries can only be made by blending this idea with other concepts, themes, forms, maneuvers, etc.. For example, systematic movement, echo variations, capture avoidance, anti-check techniques, stalemate and anti-stalemate ideas – in other words, everything we have seen in **Studies 136–166**.

2.5. Checkmate

Unlike pawn-winning or pawn-promoting studies, the studies in this section have a clear and obvious finale. Unfortunately, the mating patterns are not numerous and not particularly beautiful.

2.5.1. Pawn checkmate

A pawn can give checkmate in any area of the board, except, of course, from its initial square. But the most important point here is that the checkmate should be preceded by interesting and fascinating play.

Study 167 is very old, but it has next to no play. The pawn checkmate is given with the king stuck on the rook file.

No. 167. R. Brown
The Chess Player's Chronicle, 1841

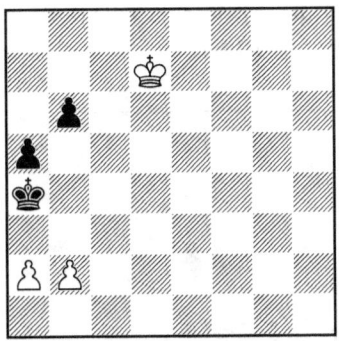

White to play and win

1.♔c6 b5 2.♔c5 b4 3.♔c4 b3 4.axb3#.

167 years later, Brown's idea was embellished by a subtle introduction!

No. 168**. S. Didukh
Problemist Ukrainy, 2008
3ʳᵈ–4ᵗʰ prize

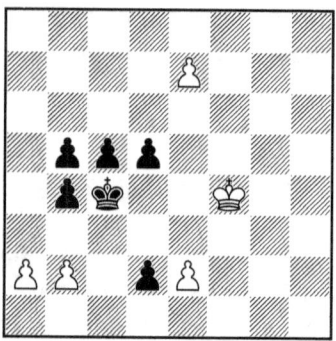

White to play and win

1.e8=♘! b3! Not 1...d1=♕ 2.♘d6+
♚d4 3.♘f5+ ♚c4 4.♘e3+ ♚d4
5.♘xd1, and the knight has traveled
from the 8ᵗʰ rank to the 1ˢᵗ! Nor 1...♚d4
2.♘g7 c4 3.♘e6#.

2.a3 d1=♘! Not 2...b4 3.♘d6+!
♚d4 4.axb4 d1=♘ 5.b5 ♘xb2 6.b6
♘d3+ 7.exd3 b2 8.♘b5+ ♚xd3 9.♘a3,
curtains.

3.♘d6+ ♚d4 4.♘f5+ ♚c4 5.♘e3+
♘xe3 6.♚xe3 b4

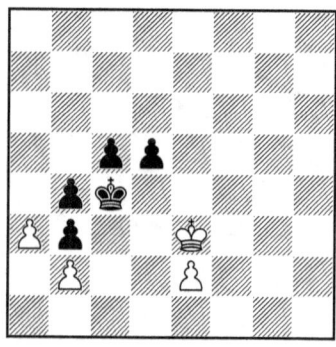

7.a4! d4+ 8.♚e4 d3 9.exd3#!

In 1985, the *Shakhmaty v SSSR*
editors held a pawn endgame study

competition to mark the 90ᵗʰ anniversary
of the birth of the founder of this
genre of chess composition, Nikolai
Dmitrievich Grigoriev. The results of
that competition served as convincing
proof that the resources of pawn studies
are inexhaustible! **Study 169** was the
winner of that competition.

No. 169. A. Kazantsev
N. Grigoriev memorial, 1986
1ˢᵗ prize

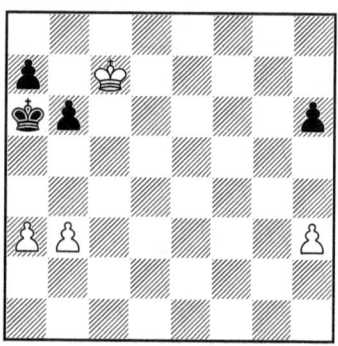

White to play and win

Incredible miracles happen in this
simple and mundane-looking position!
1.♚c6! ♚a5 2.♚b7! a6 3.♚c6!
Not 3.h4? ♚b5 4.a4+ ♚a5 5.♚c6 b5
6.axb5 axb5 7.♚c5 h5, and white is in
zugzwang.
3...b5 4.♚c5 h5 5.h4 b4 6.axb4#.

But that's not all! Were the kingside
pawns blocked, black would have
met 2.♚b7 with 2...b5!, and there's a
stalemate after 3.♚xa7 b4 4.a4. Maybe
black should try and use this opportunity?
The second branch thus begins:
1...h5 2.b4! h4. After 2...b5, white
wins with 3.♚d5 ♚b6 4.h4 a6 5.♚e4
♚c6 6.♚e5 etc.
3.a4! b5 4.axb5#. Fantastic – a pawn
echo-chameleon checkmate! A great

achievement by one of the veterans of Soviet study composition!

No. 170. A. Kazantsev
N. Grigoriev memorial, 1986
1st honorable mention

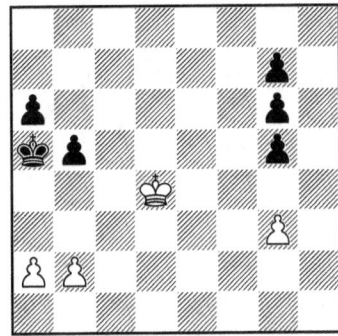

A) diagram;
B) move the g6 pawn to g4
White to play and win

The natural-looking 1.g4? only leads to a draw after 1...♔b4 2.♔d5 a5 3.♔d4 a4 etc. Therefore, **1.♔c5! g4.** Not 1...♔a4, which loses in two ways after 2.♔b6 a5 3.g4 ♔b4 4.a3+ ♔a4 5.♔c5 b4, and now white can play both 6.♔c4 bxa3 7.b3# and 6.axb4 axb4 7.♔c4, winning.
2.b3! g5 3.a3! g6 4.a4 bxa4 5.b4#.
The solution of the twin:

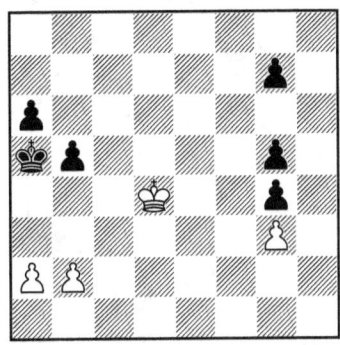

1.♔c5 ♔a4 2.♔b6! a5 3.♔c5 b4 4.♔c4 g6 5.a3 bxa3 6.b3#.

Two echo-chameleon checkmates with a single pawn! Of course, this mating picture is more spectacular than in **Study 169** that won the first prize, but the drawbacks are also apparent.

No. 171. I. Sindler
Svobodno Slovo, 1957

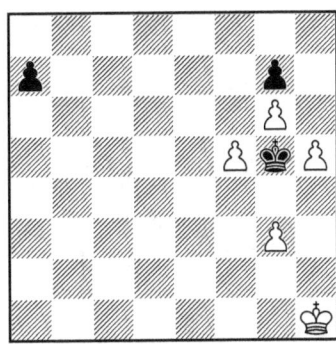

White to play and win

The Reti maneuver, blended with the roundabout way, leads to checkmate.
1.♔g2! a5! 2.♔f3! a4! After 2...♔xf5, there's 3.♔e3, and the pawn is stopped.

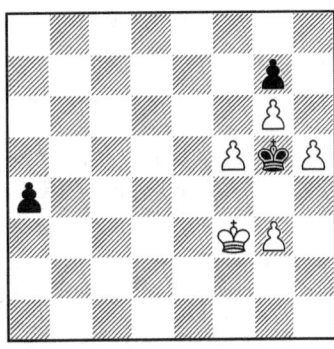

3.h6! ♔xh6 4.♔g4! a3 5.♔h4 a2 6.g4 a1=♕ 7.g5#. The king could have gotten to h4 in three moves, but reached it only in four moves, fearing that the pawns might fall.

No. 172. M. Zinar
Buletin Problemistic, 1978

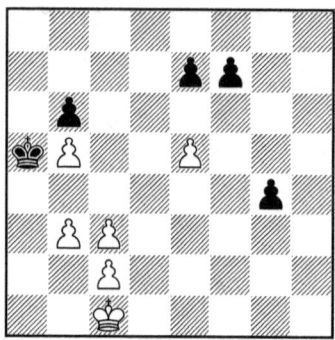

White to play and win

The immediate 1.♔d2? fails: 1...♔xb5 2.♔e3 f5 3.exf6 exf6 4.♔f4 f5 with a draw.

The correct move is **1.c4! g3!**

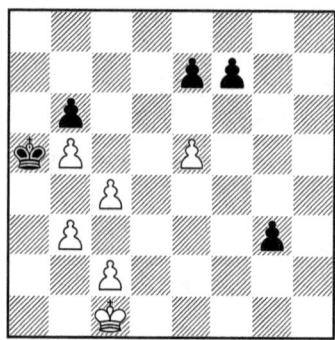

And how to stop the pawn now?

2.♔b2!! Paradoxically — by moving away from it! A feint is used here, albeit executed in an unusual way. It's necessary to lure the black king to c5.

2...♔b4! After 2...g2, there's 3.♔a3 g1=♕ 4.b4#.

3.c3+ ♔c5 4.♔c2!, and 4...g2 is now met with a different pawn checkmate: **5.♔d3 g1=♕ 6.b4#.**

The checkmate finale is slightly spoiled by the long proof line: 4...f6!

5.♔d3 fxe5 6.b4+ (6.♔e2 or 6.♔e3 are also possible) 6...♔d6 7.♔e3 e4

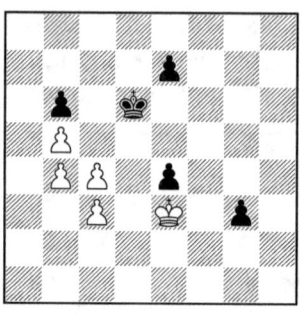

8.♔e2 e6 9.♔e3 e5 10.♔e2 e3 11.♔xe3 e4 12.♔e2 ♔c7 13.c5 ♔b7 14.cxb6 ♔xb6 15.c4 ♔b7 16.c5 ♔c7

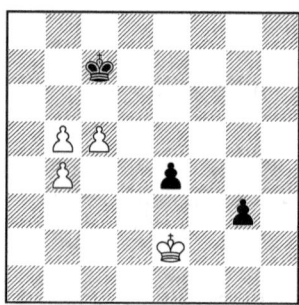

17.b6+! ♔c6 18.b5+ ♔b7 19.♔e3 ♔b8 20.c6 ♔c8 21.b7+ ♔c7

22.b6+ ♔b8 23.♔e2 g2 24.♔f2 e3+ 25.♔xg2 e2 26.c7+ ♔xb7 27.♔f2, curtains.

The theme was further developed in **Study 173**: a third checkmate was added to the feint, and the black pawn is located even farther away!

No. 173. M. Zinar
Shakhmaty v SSSR, 1980
1ˢᵗ special commendation

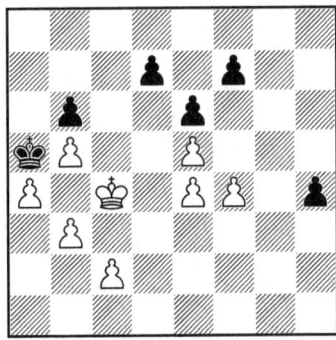

White to play and win

1.♔c3! h3 2.♔b2!! ♔b4. After 2...h2 3.♔a3 h1=♕ 4.b4#, the first checkmate is delivered.

3.c3+ ♔c5 4.♔c2! d5. 4...f5 5.exf5 is weaker. And 4...h2 is met with 5.♔d3 h1=♕ 6.b4# – the second checkmate!

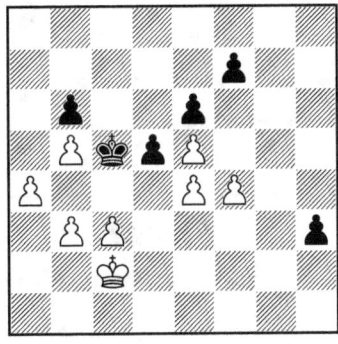

5.♔d3! But not 5.exd5? exd5 6.♔d3 d4!, or 5.exd6 ♔xd6!
5...dxe4+ 6.♔xe4 h2. Or 6...f6

7.♔f3, and the white king is in the square.
7.♔d3! h1=♕ 8.b4+ ♔d5 9.c4# – a third pawn checkmate!

Move the white king to a1 and the black pawn from h4 to h3, and now you will need five moves to catch up with it!

Two decades later, another mating spectacle with the march of a black rook pawn appeared, **Study 174**. In this study, the main emphasis is not on the number of mating finales, but on the play, featuring an original systematic diagonal movement of kings and pawns. The black king moves down and then up the same route.

No. 174**. V. Kovalenko
Springaren, 2002
Commendation

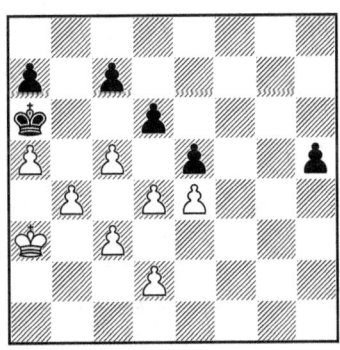

White to play and win

The black king feels rather uncomfortable...
1.c6! ♔b5! (1...h4 2.♔a4 h3 3.b5#) **2.d5! ♔c4!** White threatened 3.♔b3 h3 4.c4+ with checkmate.
3.♔b2! h4. Running away from the trap still doesn't save the game: 3...♔d3 4.b5 h4 5.b6 axb6 6.axb6 h3 7.bxc7 h2 8.c8=♕ with a win.

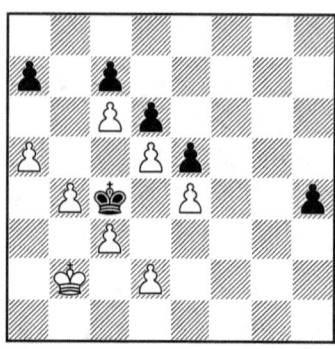

4.♔c2! h3 5.d3+ ♚b5 6.♔b3 h2
7.c4+ ♚a6 8.♔a4 h1=♕ 9.b5#!

In **Study 175**, the black king gets
checkmated on the 8th rank because of
zugzwang.

No. 175. J. Behting
Rigaer Tageblatt, 1894

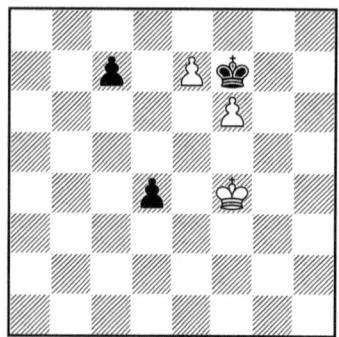

White to play and win

1.♔f3! White is waiting.
1...c6 2.♔f4! c5 3.♔e4! Zugzwang.
3...♚e8 4.♔d5(d3) ♚d7

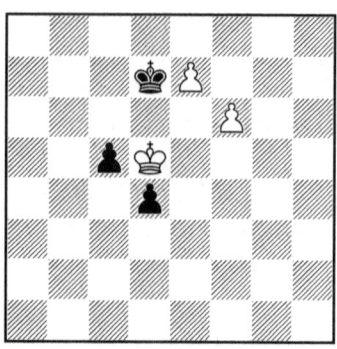

5.♔c4! Another zugzwang!
5...♚e8 6.♔xc5! d3 7.♔d6 d2
8.♔e6 d1=♕ 9.f7#.

J. Behting's study spurred a lot of
creative replies.

In **Study 176**, white first draws
the black king out of the mating
net and then pushes it back in with
zugzwang.

No. 176**. V. Kovalenko
Diagrammes, 1994

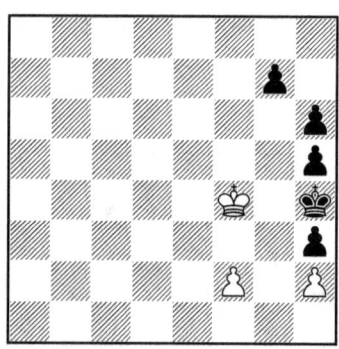

White to play and win

1.♔f5! g5! 2.♔e5! But not 2.♔e4?
♚g4, and white is in zugzwang.
2...♚g4 3.♔e4! Zugzwang in white's
favor.
3...h4 (3...♚h4 4.♔f5 g4 5.♔f4)
4.f3+ ♚h5 5.♔f5! g4 6.fxg4#.

The subtle play in **Study 177**, with a kaleidoscope of ideas, is crowned with a checkmate blow.

No. 177**. A. Kuryatnikov and E. Markov
The Problemist, 1996
Commendation

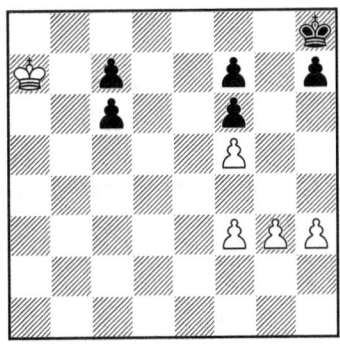

White to play and win

After the black queenside pawns fall, the result of the game should be obvious. Black tries to find stalemating counterplay!..

1.♔a6 ♔g7! 2.♔a5! ♔h6! 2...c5 is toothless: 3.g4 c6 4.♔a4 ♔f8 5.♔b3 ♔e7 6.♔c4 ♔d6 7.f4 h6 8.h4, and black loses.

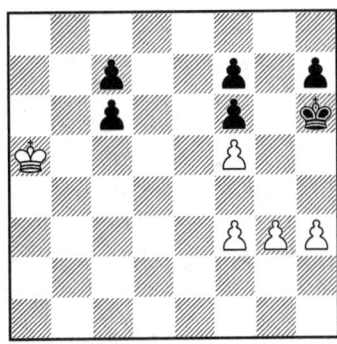

3.h4!! Stopping the black king from reaching g5. The tempting 3.f4? doesn't

work: 3...♔h5 4.♔b4 c5+ 5.♔xc5 h6 6.♔d4 c5+, and white cannot win. The king's raid on the pawns also achieves nothing: 3.♔b4? ♔g5 4.♔c5 ♔xf5 5.♔xc6 ♔e5 6.♔xc7 ♔d4 7.♔d6 ♔e3 8.♔e7 ♔xf3 9.♔xf7 ♔xg3 10.♔xf6 ♔xh3 11.♔g5, with play until the bare kings.

3...♔h5! 3...c5 is hopeless: 4.g4! ♔g7 (4...c6 5.♔a4 ♔g7 6.♔b3 ♔f8 7.♔c4 ♔e7 8.♔xc5 ♔d7 9.f4 ♔c7 10.h5 ♔d7 11.g5) 5.♔b5 ♔f8 6.♔xc5 ♔e7 7.♔c6 ♔d8 8.f4, and white wins.

4.♔b4 c5+! (4...h6 5.♔c4) **5.♔c4!!** Avoidance of capture! After the greedy 5.♔xc5? c6! 6.♔d4 c5+! 7.♔e3 c4 8.♔f2 c3, it's a draw.

5...c6 6.♔xc5! h6 (forced)

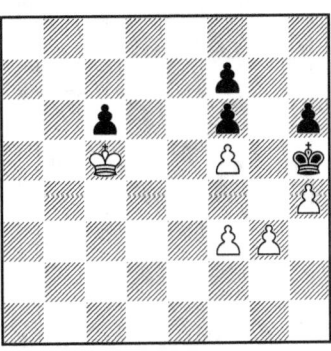

7.♔d4! c5+ 8.♔e3 c4 9.♔f2 c3 10.♔g2 c2 11.♔h3! That's where the white monarch was actually heading!

11...c1=♛ 12.g4#! Impressive route of the white king — from the a-file to the h-file!

Two mating finales in the center of the board and a stalemate in the false try — that's **Study 178**.

No. 178**. V. Kovalenko
JC A. Belyavsky – 70, 2005
Honorable mention

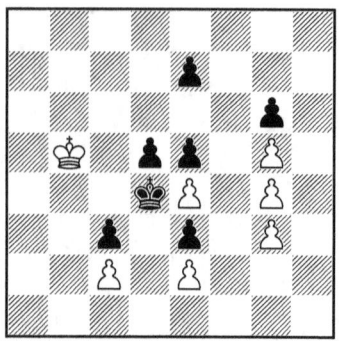

White to play and win

1.♔b4! False try: 1.exd5? ♔xd5
2.♔b4 ♔d4 3.♔b3

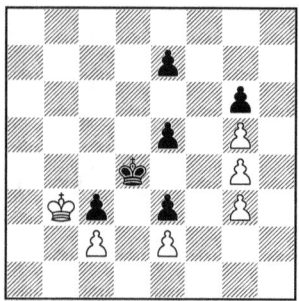

3...e4! 4.♔b4 ♔d5 5.♔xc3 ♔c5
6.♔b3 ♔b5 7.c3 ♔c5 8.c4 e6! 9.♔c3 e5
10.♔b3 ♔d4! 11.♔b4, stalemate.
1...♔xe4. 1...dxe4 doesn't help:
2.♔b3 e6 3.♔b4 ♔d5 4.♔xc3 ♔c5
5.♔b3 ♔b5

6.c4+! ♔c5 7.♔c3 ♔c6 8.♔b4 ♔b6
9.c5+ ♔c6 10.♔c4 ♔c7 11.♔b5 ♔b7
12.c6+ ♔c7 13.♔c5 ♔d8 14.♔d6,
curtains.
2.♔xc3. The play branches:
A) **2...d4+ 3.♔c4 e6 4.♔c5! d3
5.cxd3#;**
B) **2...e6 3.♔b3!** (3.♔b4? ♔d4!) **3...
♔d4 4.♔b4! e4 5.c3+ ♔e5 6.♔c5 d4
7.cxd4#!**

In the finale of **Study 179**, checkmate
in the center of the board is given by a
pawn protected by a queen. A possible
theme for the development of modern
pawn studies?

No. 179**. V. Kovalenko
Moscow championship, 2012
3rd prize

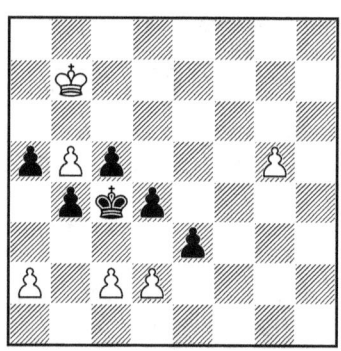

White to play and win

1.dxe3! The natural pawn run is a
false try: 1.g6? e2! (but not 1...exd2? 2.g7
d1=♕ 3.g8=♕+ ♔xb5 4.a4+! bxa3
(4...♔xa4 5.♕b3+ ♔b5 6.c4+ dxc3
7.♕xd1) 5.♕b3#) 2.g7 e1=♕ 3.g8=♕+
♔xb5 4.a4+ ♔xa4 5.♕b3+ ♔b5 6.c4+
dxc3 (en passant!) Draw.
1...dxe3. Or 1...♔d5 2.g6 ♔e6 3.g7
♔f7 4.exd4 cxd4 5.♔c6 a4 6.b6 b3 7.b7
bxc2 8.g8=♕+.

2.g6 e2 3.g7 e1=♕ 4.g8=♕+ ♔xb5.
Black slowly dies after 4...♔c3 5.♕b3+
♔d2 6.b6 ♕e4+ 7.♔a7 ♕xc2 8.♕xc2+
♔xc2 9.b7 etc.

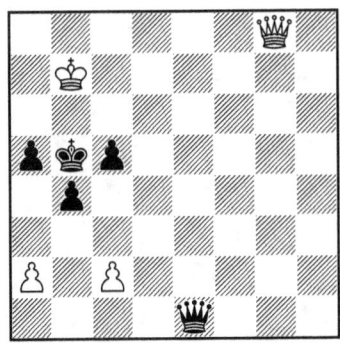

5.a4+! And two checkmate finals:
5...bxa3 6.♕b3+ ♕b4 7.c4# or **5...
♔xa4 6.♕b3+ ♔b5 7.c4#!,** and black
has no en passant capture.

2.5.2. Queen checkmate

Let's start with an examination of
studies with two connected pawns,
similar to Behting's study, and see how
we can reach such a finale by using
all the tactical tricks we have already
mastered.

Imagine that we are holding some
kind of study composition training camp.
For instance, we liked the position from
Study 180, and we decided to create
something on our own, using the ideas
from this study.

No. 180. N. Grigoriev
Shakhist (Kyiv), 1936

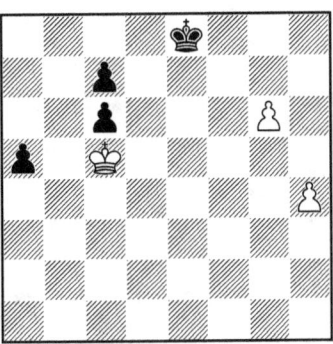

White to play and win

The introductory play is obvious:
1.h5 ♔e7 2.h6 ♔f6 3.h7 ♔g7.

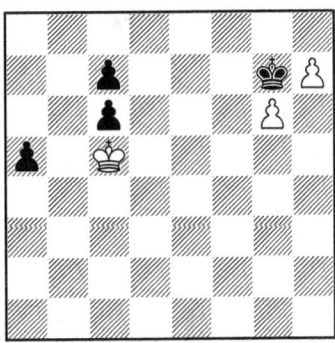

Now the white king is at a crossroads.
Where should it move to? 4.♔xc6? loses
to 4...a4! And what is 4.♔d4? good
for? It turns out that after 4...a4 5.♔e5
a3 6.♔e6 a2 7.h8=♕+ ♔xh8 8.♔f7
a1=♕, there's no 9.g7+. Therefore, the
white king should head for d4 only if the
black king moves to h8.

4.♔c4! Zugzwang.

**4...♔h8 5.♔d4! a4 6.♔e5 a3 7.♔f6
a2**

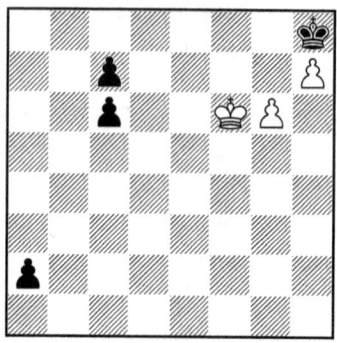

8.g7+! The white pawn makes it to g7 just in time.

8...♚xh7 9.♚f7 a1=♛ 10.g8=♛+ ♚h6 11.♛g6#. But what if something similar was already created earlier? Let's search for older studies.

No. 181. M. Eisenstat
Smena, 1931

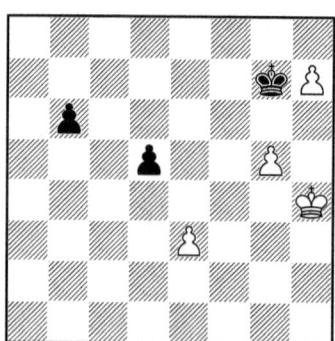

White to play and win

1.g6 b5 2.e4! In the previous study, white made a waiting move. Here, to achieve a checkmate on g6, white closes off the b1-h7 diagonal with a pawn sacrifice.

2...dxe4 3.♚g4! A multi-purpose move: white prevents 3...e3 and gets closer to f7 at the same time.

3...b4 4.♚f5, and it's obvious after that. A year later, Grigoriev added

another pawn to this position, which allowed black to play e4-e3, and the study was much improved.

No. 182. N. Grigoriev
Shakhmaty v SSSR, 1932

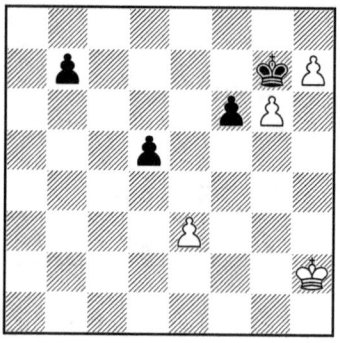

White to play and win

The immediate 1.♚g3? doesn't work: 1...b5 2.♚f3 (or 2.♚f4 b4 3.♚f5 b3 4.♚e6 b2 5.h8=♛+ ♚xh8 6.♚f7 b1=♛ 7.g7+ ♚h7 8.g8=♛+ ♚h6, and g6 is under the control of the black queen; while 2.e4 is now met with 2...b4! 3.exd5 b3 with equality) 2...b4! 3.♚e2 f5 4.♚d3 b3! 5.♚c3

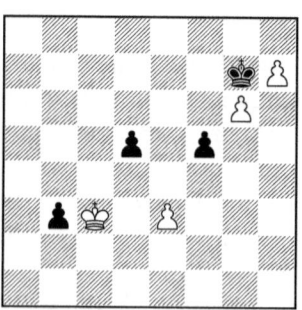

5...d4+! 6.exd4 f4 7.d5 f3 8.d6 f2 9.d7 f1=♛ 10.d8=♛ ♛c1+ 11.♚b4 ♛e1+ 12.♚a4 ♛a1+ 13.♚xb3 ♛b1+, and the white king cannot escape perpetual check.

1.e4! dxe4 2.♚g3! b5 3.♚f4! Another two-pronged move. Now 3...b4 is met with 4.♚f5, mating, because the b1-h7 diagonal is closed.

3...e3! 4.♚xe3, and now there are two branches:

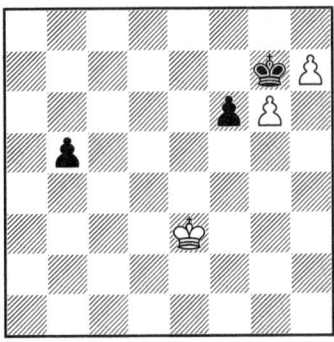

A) **4...b4 5.♚d4!** A double threat to the b4 and f7 squares.

5...f5. The threat to the b4 pawn is repelled, but the diagonal is closed again!

6.♚e5(d5), winning;

B) **4...f5 5.♚f4!** But not 5.♚d4? f4!, opening the diagonal.

5...b4 6.♚e5! – avoiding capture and mating.

No. 183. R. Kauranen
Keskisuomaliannen, 1967

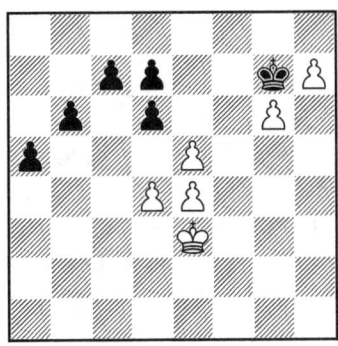

White to play and win

The white king has to break through to the f7 square, but black threatens 1...dxe5.

Therefore, **1.e6! dxe6 2.♚f4! a4 3.d5!** Forcing black to accept another sacrifice. The immediate 3.e5? d5! is no good.

3...exd5 4.e5! Closing the a1-h8 diagonal.

4...dxe5+ 5.♚f5! a3 6.♚e6 – and checkmate is now unavoidable.

No. 184. W. Mees
Tijdschrift v.d. KNSB, 1953
1st–2nd honorable mention

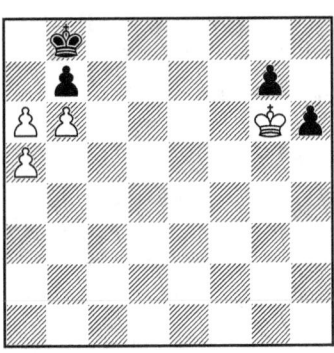

White to play and win

1.a7+ ♚a8. It's easy to calculate that the white king cannot make it to c7 in time to give a mate in two after a5-a6. First, white needs to eliminate the kingside pawns in strict order: the h-pawn first, then the g-pawn second, constantly being on his guard against stalemate. These goals are achieved in a rather original way.

2.♚f5! h5 3.♚e5! h4. White's feint forces a detrimental h-pawn movement. And now the king moves back!

4.♚f4! Not 4.♚d6? h3 5.♚c7 h2 6.a6 h1=♛, and the b7 mating square is protected.

4...g6! 5.♔f3! Zugzwang!
5...g5

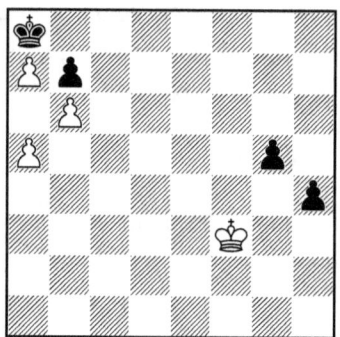

6.♔g4! And white has achieved his goal!

6...h3 7.♔xh3 g4+ 8.♔g2! g3 9.a6! bxa6 10.♔xg3 a5 11.♔f4 a4 12.♔e5, and wins. A complicated route of the white king!

Unfortunately, the composition is blemished by a short side solution: 2.a6! h5 (2...bxa6 3.♔f5) 3.axb7+ ♔xb7 4.♔xh5, curtains. Thankfully, this study can be corrected easily, by a small change as per the following study.

No. 185**. W. Mees
Tijdschrift v.d. KNSB, 1953
1st–2nd honorable mention
(correction)

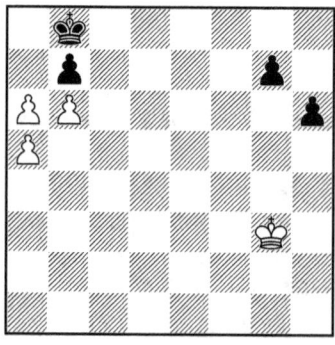

White to play and win

1.a7+ ♔a8 2.♔f4! Not 2.a6? h5! 3.♔f4 h4! 4.♔e4 h3, and now it's white who is forced to fight for equality: 5.axb7+ ♔xb7 6.♔f3 etc.

2...h5 3.♔e5!, transposing to the previous study.

To be fair, we have to say that this opus cannot technically be classified as a mating study. After 3...h4 4.♔f4 g6 5.♔f3 g5 (See the diagram from the previous study.) 6.♔g4 h3 7.♔xh3 g4+ 8.♔g2 g3 9.a6! bxa6 10.♔xg3 a5 11.♔f4 a4 12.♔e5 a3

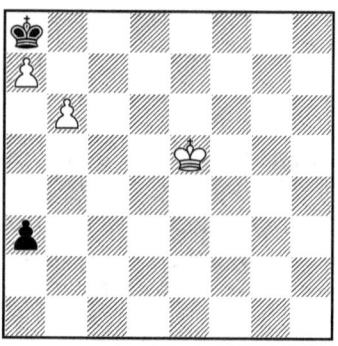

13.♔d6 a2 14.♔c7 a1=♕ 15.b7+ ♔xa7 16.b8=♕+ ♔a6, it's not necessary to give checkmate with 17.♕b6#. White can also win with 17.♕a8+ or 17.♕b7+, and the black queen falls. Therefore, the solution should stop with the promotion of the white pawn.

Many checkmating pawn studies have been composed. So, what new or unusual elements can be added to this theme? In **Study 180**, black got into zugzwang after a waiting move, but there's another technique to achieve zugzwang – triangulation! Enjoy **Study 186**.

No. 186. M. Zinar
Molod Ukrainy, 1987

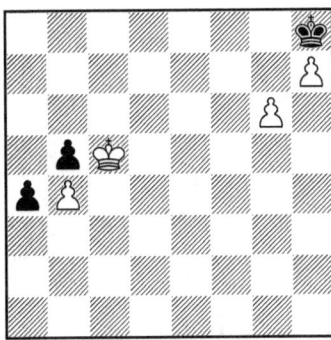

White to play and win

**1.♔d4   ♚g7   2.♔c3(d3)!   ♚h8
3.♔d3(c3)! ♚g7 4.♔d4 ♚h8**

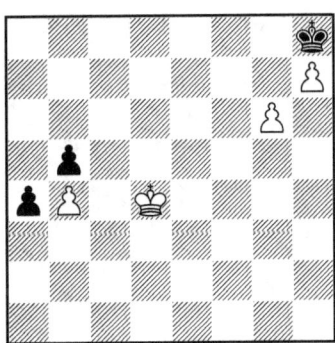

**5.♔e5! a3 6.♔f6 a2 7.g7+ ♚xh7
8.♔f7 a1=♕ 9.g8=♕+ ♚h6 10.♕g6#.**

We know that if the black king is on g7, and a black pawn is on d7, then the white king's path to f7 is one move longer. The outcome hinges on a single tempo and... the Reti maneuver! Enjoy **Study 187**.

No. 187. V. Archakov and M. Zinar
Khliborob Ukrainy

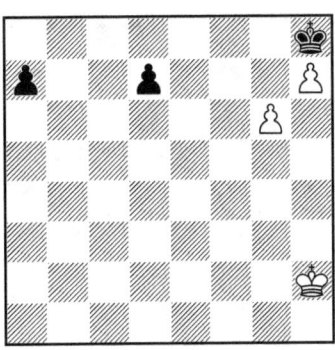

White to play and win

**1.♔g3! a5 2.♔f4! a4 3.♔e5! ♚g7
4.♔d4! d5 5.♔c3!** with a win. Or **3...a3
4.♔f6 a2 5.g7+,** mating.

In **Study 182**, the weakening move in the A line was provoked by the double threat 5.♔d4!, approaching the b-pawn and the f7 square at the same time. But we know that a feint is a more aesthetic way to provoke a weakness. Therefore, enjoy **Study 188**.

No. 188. V. Archakov and M. Zinar
Khliborob Ukrainy

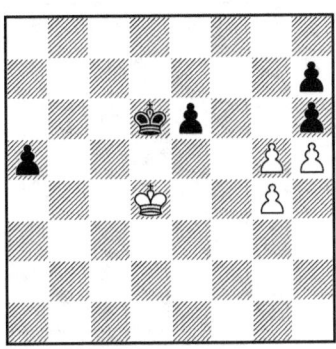

White to play and win

First, a breakthrough: **1.g6! hxg6
2.g5! ♚e7 3.gxh6 ♚f7 4.h7 ♚g7 5.hxg6**

a4. And now a feint to close off the a1–h8 diagonal:

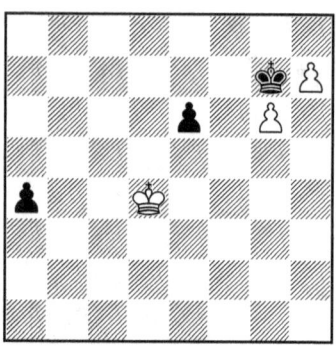

6.♔c4! e5 7.♔d5! a3 8.♔e6 with a win.

In the same **Study 182** (in the B line), the white king moved towards the f7 square in such a way as to prevent the opening of the b1-h7 diagonal. Remember that if the king is afraid of a particular move, it can reach its destination in a roundabout way, which is beautiful as well. Let's look at the next example, **Study 189.**

No. 189. M. Zinar
Start, 1987

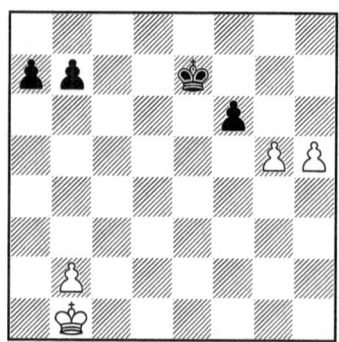

White to play and win

1.g6! Not 1.h6? ♔f7 2.h7 ♔g7 3.g6 a5 4.♔c2 b5 5.♔d3 a4 6.♔e4 b4 7.♔f5

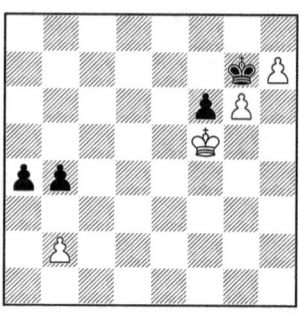

7...a3! 8.bxa3 b3 9.♔e6 b2 10.h8=♕+ ♔xh8 11.♔f7 b1=♕, and there's no checkmate.

With his introductory move, white closes off the b1-h7 diagonal; black loses after 1...a5 2.h6 ♔f8 3.♔c2 b5 4.♔d3 a4 5.♔e4 b4 6.♔f5 a3 7.♔xf6 ♔g8 8.h7+ ♔h8 9.♔f7.

1...f5 2.h6! ♔f6 3.h7 ♔g7 4.♔c2 a5

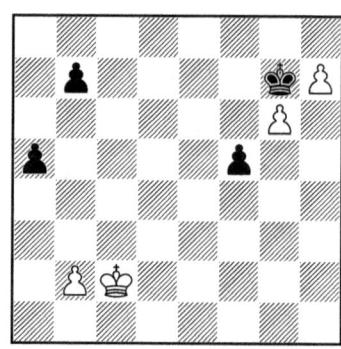

5.♔d3! A double threat! 5.♔c3? or 5.♔d2? are met with 5...f4!, opening the diagonal.

5...b5 6.♔e3! Heading towards f7 in a roundabout way, since 6.♔d4? leads to a draw after 6...f4.

6...a4 7.♔f4 b4 8.♔e5 a3 9.♔e6! axb2 10.h8=♕+ with a win.

So, we have demonstrated several ways to compose endgame studies that use various tactical tricks. But let's suppose that we are not satisfied with the content of our discovery. For instance, we like massive studies with systematic movement. Then let's look at **Study 190**.

No. 190. M. Zinar
USSR State Sports Committee
competition, 1987
1st honorable mention

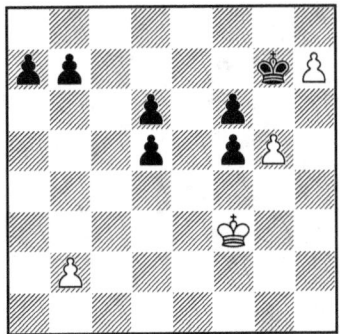

White to play and win

1.g6 d4 2.♔f4! Feint!
2...d3 3.♔e3 d5. If 3...a5, then 4.♔xd3 b5 5.♔d4! f4 6.♔d5 f3 7.♔e6 with checkmate.
4.♔xd3 f4

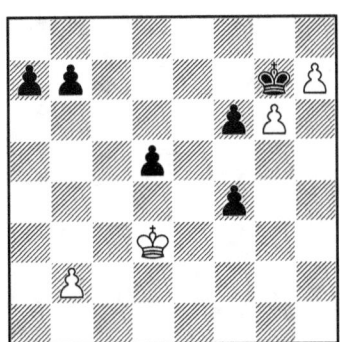

5.♔d4! Another feint!
5...f3 6.♔e3 f5 7.♔xf3 d4 8.♔f4! And the third feint!
8...d3 9.♔e3 a5 10.♔xd3 b5.

That's what black wanted to achieve by stubbornly pushing the pawns: now 11.♔d4? is met with 11...f4!, opening the b1-h7 diagonal, which became possible after the f6 pawn got captured. But it's the same position as in **Study 189** after five moves!
11.♔e3! – going the long way to win.

To conclude this discussion, let's look at some studies where a similar checkmate is achieved more spectacularly – after a queen sacrifice.

No. 191. R. Fontana
Die Tat, 1944

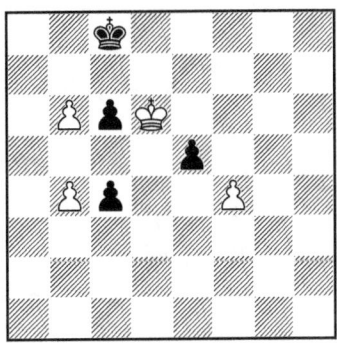

White to play and win

1.f5! We want to close the h2-b8 diagonal.
1...c3 2.f6 c2 3.f7 c1=♕ 4.f8=♕+ ♔b7

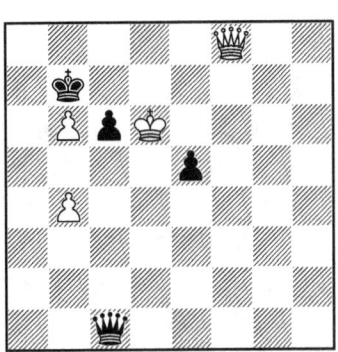

5.♕a8+! ♔xa8 6.♔c7 ♕e3 7.b7+ ♔a7 8.b8=♕+ ♔a6 9.♕b7#.

Unfortunately, it later transpired that it's not necessary to close off the diagonal at all! White can also win with the greedy 1.fxe5! c3 2.e6 c2 3.e7 c1=♕ 4.e8=♕+ ♔b7 5.♕e7+ ♔xb6 6.♕c7+ ♔a6 (6... ♔b5 7.♕a5+ ♔c4 8.♕c5+) 7.♕xc6+ ♕xc6+ 8.♔xc6 ♔a7 9.b5, curtains.

Interestingly, this study had a different form at first — see **Study 192**. The author's desire to get rid of the "unnecessary" h6 pawn made the side solution possible.

No. 192**. R. Fontana
Die Tat, 1944

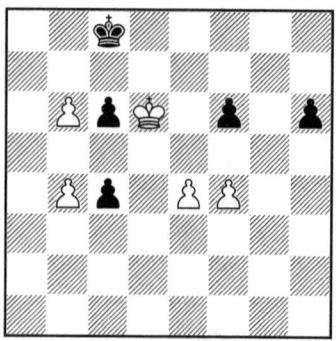

White to play and win

1.e5! fxe5. Black can't save the game with 1...c3 2.exf6 c2 3.f7 c1=♕ 4.f8=♕+ ♔b7

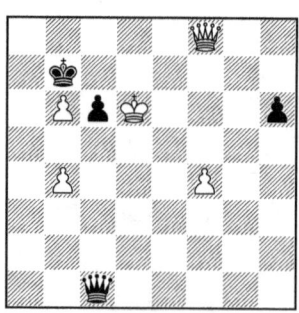

5.♕e7+ (but not 5.♕a8+? ♔xa8 6.♔c7 ♕xf4+) **5...♔xb6 6.♕c7+ ♔b5** (6...♔a6 7.♕xc6+ ♕xc6+ 8.♔xc6 h5 9.b5+ ♔a5 10.b6) **7.♕a5+ ♔c4 8.♕c5+**, losing the queen.

2.f5! 2.fxe5? doesn't win: 2...c3 3.e6 c2 4.e7 c1=♕ 5.e8=♕+ ♔b7 6.♕d7+ ♔xb6 7.♕c7+

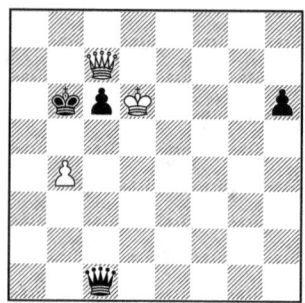

7...♔a6! 8.♕xc6+ ♕xc6+ 9.♔xc6 ♔a7! 10.♔c7 ♔a6 11.♔c6 ♔a7, positional draw.

2...c3 etc., like in **Study 191**.

In **Study 193**, a queen sacrifice is performed twice, and black also replies with a sacrifice.

No. 193. Y. Makletsov and A. Maksimovskikh
Themes 64, 1979

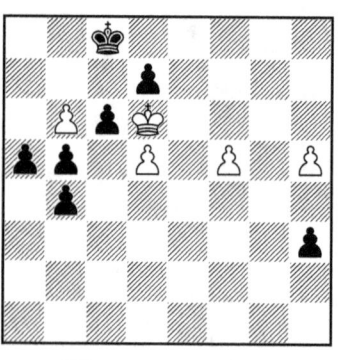

White to play and win

1.f6 h2 2.f7 h1=♕ 3.f8=♕+ ♔b7

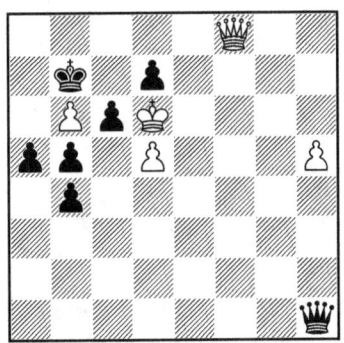

4.♕a8+! ♔xa8 5.♔c7 ♕h2+ 6.d6 ♕xd6+ 7.♔xd6 ♔b7 8.h6 b3 9.h7 b2 10.h8=♕ b1=♕ 11.♕a8+! An echo-sacrifice!

11...♔xa8 12.♔c7 with checkmate.

The mating attack of the newly-promoted queen in **Study 194** crowns white's subtle preparatory play.

No. 194**. M. Minski
Schach, 1993
Special commendation

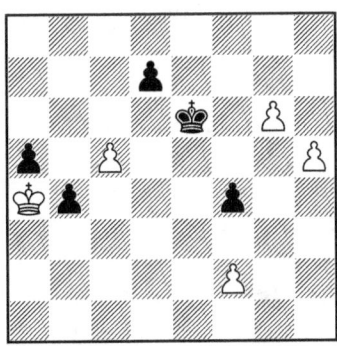

White to play and win

1.h6! The hurried 1.f3? or 1.♔b3? is met with 1...♔f6!, and white can't improve his position. The weak 1.g7? ♔f7 2.h6 f3 3.♔b3 ♔g8 4.♔c4 ♔f7 also leads to equality.

1...♔f6 2.h7 ♔g7 3.f3! Not the rash 3.♔b3? f3!, and, as the finale shows after the players repeat from here the study's solution moves (4.♔c4 ♔h8 5.♔d5 b3 6.c6 dxc6+ 7.♔e6 b2 8.♔f7 b1=♕ 9.g7+ ♔xh7 10.g8=♕+ ♔h6 11.♕g7+ ♔h5 and a draw), the promoted white queen will not have an outpost on g4, unlike in the solution.

3...♔h8 4.♔b3 ♔g7 5.♔c4 ♔h8

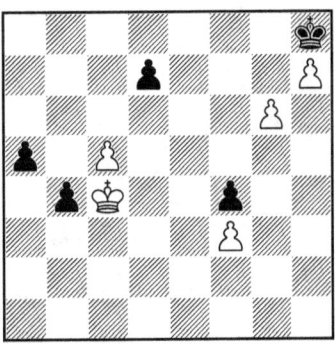

6.♔d5! b3 7.c6! dxc6+ 8.♔e6 b2. Or 8...♔g7 9.h8=♕+ ♔xh8 10.♔f7 b2 11.g7+ ♔h7 12.g8=♕+, mating.
9.♔f7 b1=♕ 10.g7+ ♔xh7 11.g8=♕+ ♔h6 12.♕g7+ ♔h5 13.♕g4+ ♔h6 14.♕h4#.

In **Studies 168–194** we examined various mating ideas. One might have thought that resources of pawn endgames with mating finales are limited. However, ideas for pawn studies with a mating blow delivered by the queen in the finale are far from exhausted. Here are some examples.

In **Study 195**, the author presents an ideal mate with the queen despite absolute material equality in the initial position. The composition is embellished by the choice of the first move and the miniature form – harmony of form and content.

No. 195**. V. Kovalenko
Khatyamov memorial, 2013
Commendation

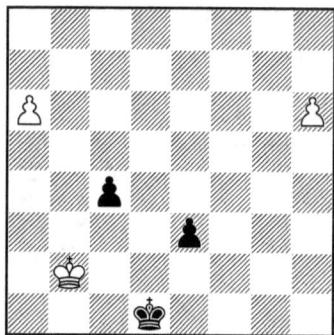

White to play and win

Which pawn should run for glory? Kingside promotion is bad: 1.h7? c3+! (but not 1...e2? 2.h8=♕ e1=♕ 3.♕h5+! ♔d2 4.♕d5+ ♔e3 5.♕e5+) 2.♔b3 c2! 3.h8=♕ c1=♕ 4.♕h1+ ♔d2 5.♕xc1+ ♔xc1 6.a7 e2 7.a8=♕ e1=♕ 8.♕a1+ ♔d2 9.♕c3+ ♔e2, and there's no checkmate.

A push on the other flank, however, is decisive: **1.a7! c3+! 2.♔b3! c2! 3.a8=♕ c1=♕ 4.♕h1+ ♔d2 5.♕xc1+ ♔xc1 6.h7 e2 7.h8=♕ e1=♕ 8.♕b2+ ♔d1 9.♕c2#!**

Look at another elegant miniature, **Study 196**, with a mysterious first move that's made to secure the eventual queen checkmate.

No. 196**. B. Sidorov
MT Grigoriev – 100, 1997
2nd honorable mention

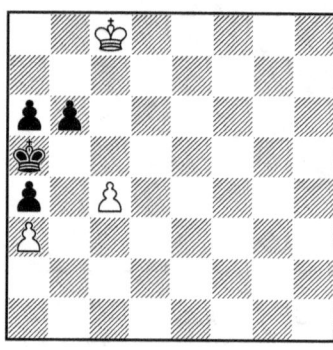

White to play and win

1.♔d8!! b5 2.c5 b4 3.c6 b3. It's the first model mate after 3...bxa3 4.c7 a2 5.c8=♕ a1=♕ 6.♕c5#.

4.c7 b2 5.c8=♕ b1=♕ (without check – that's why white cannot play 1.♔b7?) **6.♕c5+ ♕b5** (without check – and that's why white cannot play 1.♔d7?) **7.♕c3+ ♔b6 8.♕c7#.** The second model mate!

The mating blow in the finale of **Study 197** is prepared by a sacrificial combination!

No. 197**. A. Grin
MT Grigoriev – 100, 1997
Special commendation

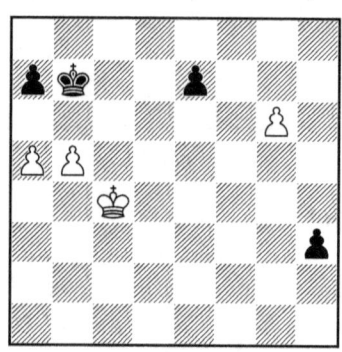

White to play and win

The immediate 1.g7? is a false try: 1...h2 2.a6+ ♔c7! 3.g8=♕ (3.b6+ axb6!) 3...h1=♕, draw.

1.a6+! ♔c7. The first queen mate: 1...♔b6 2.g7 h2 3.g8=♕ h1=♕ 4.♕d8#!

2.b6+! ♔xb6. Or 2...axb6 3.a7 ♔b7 4.a8=♕+ ♔xa8 5.g7 h2 6.g8=♕+ etc.

3.g7 (now it's time) **3...h2 4.g8=♕ h1=♕ 5.♕b8+ ♔xa6** (5...♔c6 6.♕b7+) **6.♕b5#** and a second mate with a promoted queen.

In the two parallel lines of **Study 198** we see a crushing checkmate attack by the promoted queen.

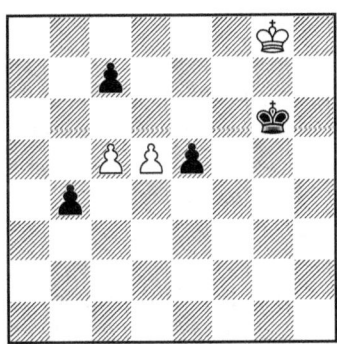

White to play and win

1.d6! Breakthrough! The game branches.

A) **1...b3 2.dxc7! b2 3.c8=♕ b1=♕ 4.♕g4+ ♔f6** (4...♔h6 5.♕h4+ ♔g6 6.♕h7+) **5.♕g7+ ♔e6 6.♕f7#;**

B) **1...cxd6 2.c6!** (2.cxd6?? ♔f6!) **2...b3 3.c7 b2 4.c8=♕ b1=♕ 5.♕g4+ ♔f6** (5...♔h6 6.♕h4+ ♔g6 7.♕h7+) **6.♕g7+ ♔e6 7.♕f7#!** with two model mates.

Two echo-chameleon mates are performed in the finale of **Study 199** from a major Georgian competition.

No. 199**. Y. Bazlov and V. Kovalenko
Mkhedruli, 1975
1st honorable mention

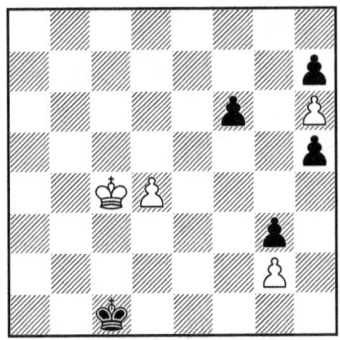

White to play and win

1.♔d3! Taking the sting out of the h-pawn! Not the immediate 1.d5? h4 2.d6 h3 3.gxh3 g2, draw.

1...♔d1 (1...h4 2.♔e2) **2.d5!**

White misses the win with 2.♔e3? h4 3.♔f3 f5 4.d5 h3

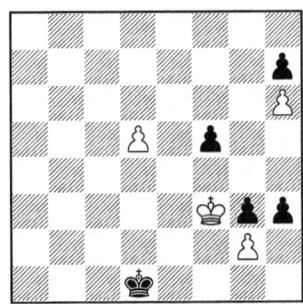

5.gxh3 (5.♔xg3 hxg2 6.♔f2 g1=♕+ 7.♔xg1 ♔e2 8.d6 f4 etc.) 5...f4 6.d6 g2 7.♔xg2 ♔e2 8.d7 f3+ 9.♔g3 f2 10.d8=♕ f1=♕ 11.♕e7+ ♔d2 12.♕xh7 ♕e1+ 13.♔g4 ♕e2+ with perpetual check.

2...h4 3.d6 h3 4.d7. The game branches out.

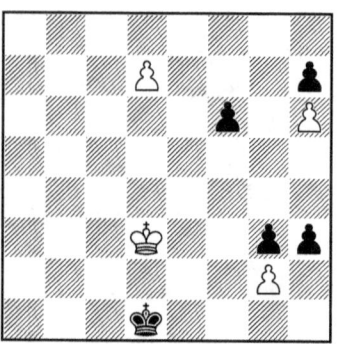

A) **4...hxg2 5.d8=♕ g1=♕ 6.♕xf6 ♔e1 7.♕e5+** (7.♕e6+ or 7.♕e7+ make no difference) **7...♔f2 8.♕e2#.**

B) **4...h2 5.d8=♕ h1=♕ 6.♕d4!** Now 6.♕xf6? doesn't work: 6...♔e1! 7.♕a1+ ♔f2 8.♕xh1, stalemate. **6... ♕f1+ 7.♔c3+ ♔e2 8.♕d2#.**

A well-known problem combination found its way into miniature **Study 200**.

No. 200**. V. Kovalenko
Themes 64, 1985
2nd prize

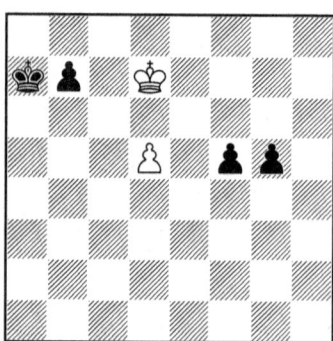

White to play and win

The white king should make way for the pawn — there's no win otherwise.

But if white does that immediately, black saves the game: 1.♔c7? g4! 2.d6 g3 3.d7 g2 4.d8=♕ g1=♕ 5.♕b8+ ♔a6 or 1.♔c8? f4! 2.d6 f3 3.d7 f2 4.d8=♕ f1=♕ 5.♕a5+ ♕a6, with a draw in both cases.

Eureka: black should reveal his hand first!

1.d6!! And two variations.

1) **1...g4 2.♔c8! g3 3.d7 g2 4.d8=♕ g1=♕ 5.♕a5#;**

2) **1...f4 2.♔c7! f3 3.d7 f2 4.d8=♕ f1=♕ 5.♕d4+! ♔a8 6.♕a4+ ♕a6 7.♕e8+ ♔a7 8.♕b8#.**

If we make an algorithm out of the first moves of the false tries and the actual solution, here's what we get: 1.♔c7(A)? g4(a)!, 1.♔c8(B)? f4(b)!, 1.d6(X)! g4(a) 2.♔c8(B)! and 1...f4(b) 2.♔c7(A)! Connoisseurs of chess composition will notice that this is the algorithm of the "Banny theme" in problems. An original idea!

Three different checkmate blows are delivered in the miniature **Study 201**. The third variation, with the quiet play of the promoted queen, is particularly attractive.

No. 201**. B. Ilincic
Zadachi i Etyudy, 2002

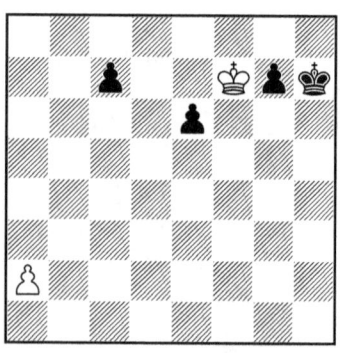

White to play and win

An immediate false try: 1.♔xe6? c5!
2.♔d5 g5! 3.♔xc5 ♚g6 4.a4 ♚f5 5.a5
g4 6.♔d4 g3 7.♔e3 ♚g4 8.a6

8...♚h3! 9.a7 g2 10.♔f2 ♚h2, and
the pawns promote at the same time.

Therefore, white should not delay
the pawn push: **1.a4.** The solution now
branches:

A) **1...c5 2.a5 c4 3.a6 c3 4.a7 c2
5.a8=♕ c1=♕ 6.♕e4+ ♚h8 7.♕h4+
♕h6 8.♕d8+ ♚h7 9.♕g8#;**

B) **1...g5 2.a5 g4 3.a6 g3 4.a7 g2
5.a8=♕ g1=♕ 6.♕e4+ ♚h6 7.♕h4#;**

C) **1...e5 2.a5 e4 3.a6 e3 4.a7 e2
5.a8=♕ e1=♕ 6.♕g2! ♚h6 7.♕g6#.**

The search for the only possible
mating route for the queen is the theme
of the next composition.

No. 202**. A. Babiarz
Polish Chess Federation ty, 2014

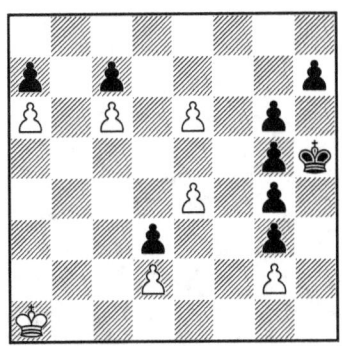

White to play and win

1.e7 ♚h4! 2.e8=♘! (2.e8=♕? h5
3.♕f7, stalemate) **2...h5! 3.♘d6 cxd6
4.c7!** But not 4.e5? due to 4...d5!

4...d5 5.c8=♘! d4! 5...dxe4 is
toothless: 6.♘e7! e3 7.♘xg6#

6.♘b6! axb6 7.a7 b5

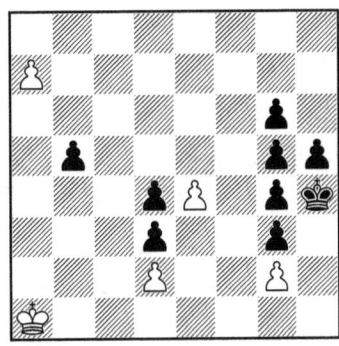

8.a8=♕! But a third underpromotion
misses the win: 8.a8=♘? b4 9.♘c7 b3
10.♘e6 b2+ 11.♔a2 b1=♕+ 12.♔xb1,
stalemate.

**8...b4 9.♕a6! b3 10.♕xd3! b2+
11.♔a2! b1=♕+ 12.♕xb1 d3 13.♕h1#!**
Just in time!

2.6. Stalemate

Stalemate pawn studies obviously
contain many more resources than
checkmate ones. First of all, a stalemate
is the most attractive finale for any
drawing study – just like a checkmate
is for winning studies. Secondly, there's
a clear static final position, which is a
rarity for pawn studies.

What are the drawbacks of pawn
studies in comparison with those with
pieces? In stalemate studies, as well as
in other studies with a fixed finale, the
reasons for this finale's occurrence play
a large role.

The most interesting and unusual final positions are not yet studies. You need to involve as many moving pieces as possible, and the final position should be reached not by simple play, but by some subtle, "study-like" moves.

The slow-moving kings and pawns cannot compete with other pieces in this department. In addition, all the finales have been known long ago, and they are not particularly ingenious. Therefore, you should not try to compete with pieces in terms of dynamism or originality. You need to use other advantages: the clarity of the idea's expression, and the inclusion of other, purely pawn-related ideas. For instance, creating a playing study with the "niche stalemate" theme.

We have divided stalemate studies into three groups: stalemate without pawn promotion, niche stalemate, and stalemate with pawn promotion.

2.6.1. Stalemate without pawn promotion

Let's start with stalemate on the rook file. The following study is a classic example of a stalemate pawn study: a long (if possible) king approach and then a simple, but model stalemate! Sometimes a modest combination is used to deliver the stalemate.

Study 203 was one of the first stalemate pawn studies.

No. 203. A. Selezniev
Deutsches Wochenschach, 1919

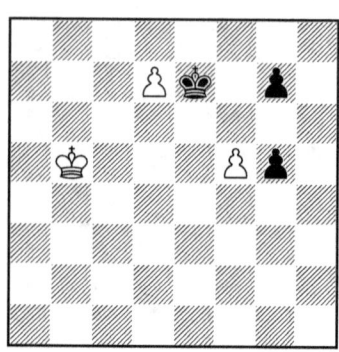

White to play and draw

1.♔c6! ♚d8 2.♔d5! ♚xd7 3.♔e4! ♚d6 4.♔f3! ♚e5 5.♔g4 ♚f6 6.♔h5! ♚xf5, stalemate.

In **Study 204**, the stalemating finale is preceded by the Reti maneuver, which makes the content especially vivid.

No. 204. M. Zinar
Shakhmaty v SSSR, 1982

White to play and draw

1.♔f6! ♚b6 2.♔e5! ♚xc6 3.♔d4(e4) ♚d6 4.♔e3! ♚d5 5.♔f2 ♚e4 6.♔g3 ♚f5 7.♔h4 ♚xf4, stalemate. The stopped pawn stays alive and takes part in stalemating the king. Notice the white king's travel route towards h4!

The position in **Study 205** is almost identical to the previous one.

No. 205. A. Selezniev
Shakhmatny Listok, 1930

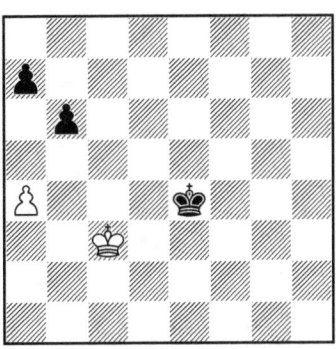

White to play and draw

1.a5! b5! 2.a6! ♚d5 **3.**♔b4 ♚c6 **4.**♔a5 ♚c5, stalemate. The play is even simpler than in **Study 203**.

Study 206 is a twin composition. We will see quite a lot of them when we get to the topic of anti-stalemate studies.

No. 206. M. Zinar
64 – Shakhmatnoe Obozrenie, 1985

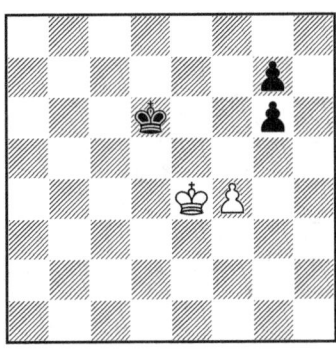

A) diagram;
B) move the g7 pawn to g4.

White to play and draw

A) **1.f5! g5 2.**♔f3 ♚e5 **3.**♔g4 ♚f6 **4.**♔h5 ♚xf5, stalemate.

B)

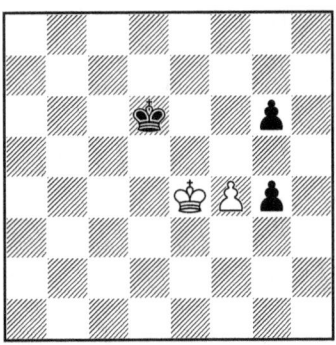

1.♔e3 ♚d5 **2.**♔f2 ♚e4 **3.**♔g3 ♚f5 **4.**♔h4 ♚xf4, stalemate.

Both stalemates and the entire play (except for the first move) are echo-chameleonic. After the first move, the play is the same, but in variation B, the pieces in the finale are all one rank lower.

Study 207 is a famous masterpiece of chess composition, skillfully blending two echo-stalemates. And the introductory play is especially vivid.

No. 207. N. Grigoriev
Shakhmatny Listok, 1929
2nd prize

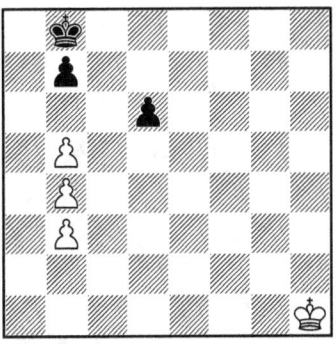

White to play and draw

1.♔g2! ♚c7 2.♔f3! The white king moves closer to the d-pawn and repels the threat to its own pawns. Does black change his plan?

2...♚d7 3.♔f4! Fighting for zugzwang: 3.♔e4? ♚e6 4.♔d4 d5! 5.♔e3 ♚e5, and black wins.

3...♚e6

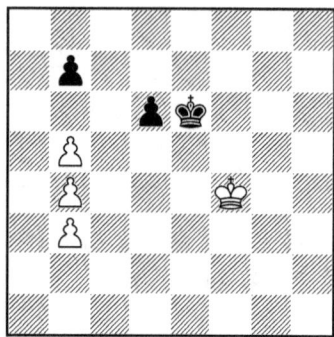

4.♔e4! b6 5.♔d4! d5 6.♔e3(c3). An academic dual that does not diminish the quality of the study.

6...♚e5 7.♔d3 d4 8.♔c4! ♚e4, stalemate.

Or **4...d5+ 5.♔d4! ♚d6! 6.b6! ♚e6 7.b5! ♚d6 8.b4! ♚e6 9.♔c5! ♚e5,** stalemate.

No. 208. A. Davranian
N. Grigoriev memorial, 1985
2nd prize

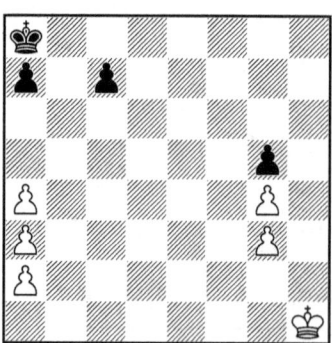

White to play and draw

1.♔g2 ♚b7 2.♔f3 ♚c6. Activating the king is the most logical plan.

3.♔e4 ♚d6

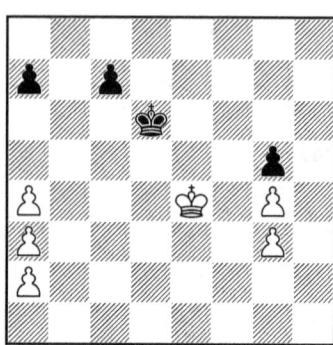

4.♔d4. The continuation 4.♔f5? does not work due to 4...c5 5.♔xg5 ♚e5 6.♔h5 c4 7.g5 c3 8.g6 ♚f6! 9.♔h6 c2 10.g7 c1=♕+, with a decoy into check.

4...c5+ 5.♔c4 ♚c6 6.a5 ♚d6 7.a6 (7.a4 is also possible) **7...♚c6 8.a4 ♚d6 9.a5 ♚c6 10.a4! ♚d6 11.♔b5 ♚d5,** stalemate. However, black knows that there will be a draw if the white king gets to c4, so he chooses another defensive plan.

2...c5 3.♔e4 ♚c6.

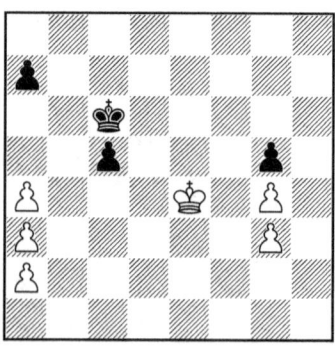

It's clear that the king isn't getting to c4, so the beautiful and unexpected **4.♔e5!!** follows, with branching play:

A) **4...a6 5.♔e4!** The king goes back! Not 5.a5? c4 6.♔e4 (if 6.♔d4, then 6...

♔b5 – zugzwang) 6...♔c5! 7.a4 c3 8.♔e3 ♔c4 – zugzwang again, black wins.

5...♔d6 6.a5! Again very precise, because 6.♔e3? leads to zugzwang after 6...♔e5!

6...♔c6

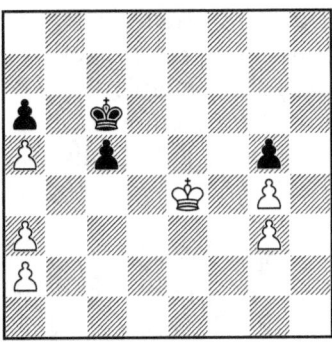

7.a4! But not 7.♔d3? ♔b5! 8.♔c3 ♔xa5 9.♔c4 ♔b6 10.♔d5 ♔b5 11.a4+ ♔b4 12.a5 ♔b5 13.a3 c4 14.♔d4 ♔xa5, and black wins.

7...♔d6 8.a3! And no transpositions – 8.♔e3? ♔e5!

8...♔c6 9.♔d3! ♔d5 10.♔c3 c4 11.♔b4 ♔d4 – an echo-chameleon stalemate! A clear and beautiful variation, but there's another one, too!

B) **4...a5 5.♔e4 ♔d6 6.♔d3.** There's a small fly in the ointment: white can also play 6.♔e3 ♔e5 7.♔d3 etc.

6...♔d5 7.♔c3 c4

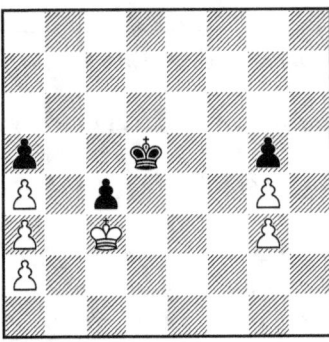

8.♔d2(b2). But not 8.♔c2? ♔d4 9.♔d2 c3+ 10.♔c2 ♔c4 11.♔c1 ♔d3 12.♔d1 ♔e3, and black promotes his g-pawn.

8...♔d4 9.♔c2 c3 10.♔b3 ♔d3 – the third echo-stalemate!

Brilliant development of Grigoriev's classical idea! The author composed this study thanks to a thorough examination of Grigoriev's miniature, which allowed him to find a new variation that made the classic study even more powerful. In Grigoriev's masterpiece **Study 207**, it's also possible to play 2...d5! 3.♔f4! ♔d6 4.♔f5!! b6 5.♔f4! ♔e6 6.♔e3! ♔e5 7.♔d3 d4 8.♔c4! ♔e4 – stalemate. Thus, Davranian has eradicated the dual from **Study 207**!

The initial position of **Study 209** looks intriguing, and the solution only confirms our expectations.

No. 209. A. Botokanov
N. Grigoriev memorial, 1985
4th prize

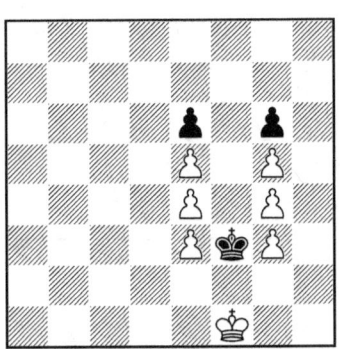

White to play and draw

1.♔e1! Asymmetry! And two continuations:

A) **1...♔xg3 2.♔e2 ♔xg4 3.♔f2 ♔xg5 4.♔g3 ♔h5**

5.♔h3! g5 6.♔g3 g4 7.♔f4 ♚h4 — stalemate.

B) 1...♚xe3 2.♔d1! ♚xe4. 2...♚f3 is met with 3.♔d2! ♚xg3 (if 3...♚xe4, then 4.♔e2! and then like in the main line) 4.♔c3! ♚f3

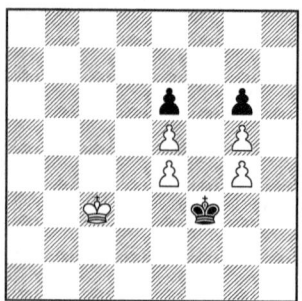

5.♔d3! ♚xg4 6.♔c4! ♚f4 7.♔d4 ♚xg5 8.♔c5 with a draw. Attractive systematic movement!

3.♔e2! But not 3.♔d2? ♚f3! 4.♔d3 ♚xg3, and black wins.

3...♚xe5

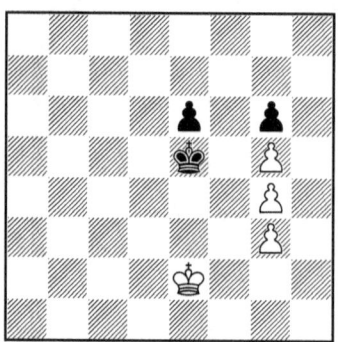

4.♔e3! ♚d5 5.♔d3 e5 6.♔e3 e4 7.♔f4 ♚d4 — an echo-stalemate where the position is turned 180 degrees!

Like a magician's trick! Suddenly, a "wall" of three pawns sticks to the white king! This is also a development of Grigoriev's idea, but while Davranian executed it in a traditional way, so to say, Botokanov, on the other hand, used romantic motifs! Both studies won prizes at a memorial competition marking the 90th anniversary of Grigoriev's birth.

But Grigoriev's idea has not been exhausted yet! The next study received a special prize for task compositions in a strong jubilee competition marking Grandmaster Oleg Pervakov's birthday.

No. 210**. M. Zinar, A. Davranian
JC Pervakov – 60, 2020
Special prize

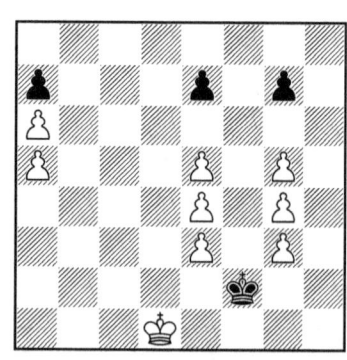

Black to move. White to draw

The study branches at the very start:

A) 1...♚xe3 2.♔c2! Not 2.e6? ♚d3 3.e5 g6 4.♔e1 ♚c3 5.♔e2 ♚b4, curtains.

2...♚xe4 (2...♚d4 3.♔b3 ♚c5 4.♔c3 e6 5.g6 ♚b5 6.♔d4, draw) **3.e6 ♚e5 4.♔d3 ♚xe6 5.♔e4 ♚d6**

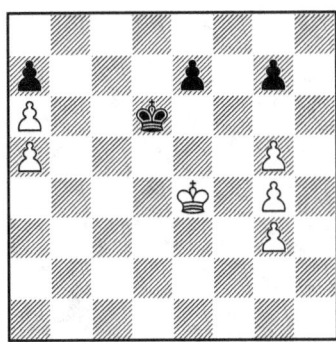

6.♔f5!! A feint! A logical false try: 6.♔d4? e6 7.♔e4 e5 8.g6 ♔e6 9.g5 ♔d6 10.g4 ♔e6, and the mutual zugzwang benefits black.

6...e5 7.♔e4 ♔e6 8.g6 ♔d6 9.g5 ♔e6 10.g4 ♔d6 11.♔f5 ♔d5, stalemate. Or **7...g6 8.♔d3(f3) ♔d5 9.♔e3 e4 10.♔f4 ♔d4,** stalemate.

B) **1...♔xg3 2.♔e2** (a transposition, 2.g6 is also possible) **2...♔xg4 3.g6 ♔g5 4.♔f3 ♔xg6 5.♔g4 ♔h6**

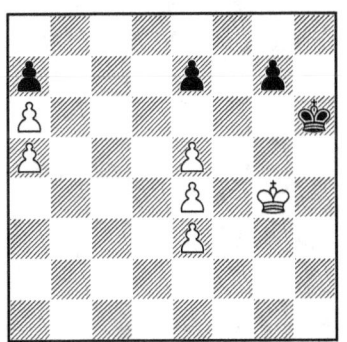

6.♔f5!! A feint! A logical false try: 6.♔h4? g6 7.♔g4 g5 8.e6 ♔g6 9.e5 ♔h6 10.e4 ♔g6, and zugzwang benefits black again.

6...g5 7.♔g4 ♔g6 8.e6 ♔h6 9.e5 ♔g6 10.e4 ♔h6 11.♔f5 ♔h5, stalemate. Or **7...e6 8.♔h3(f3) ♔h5 9.♔g3 g4 10.♔f4 ♔h4** with a new stalemate. Four classical stalemates! I doubt that such a record can be beaten!

Two stalemates in the center of the board are presented in the grotesque **Study 211** by two Georgian authors.

No. 211**. R. and S. Tsurtsumia
Georgian TV (magazine), 1990

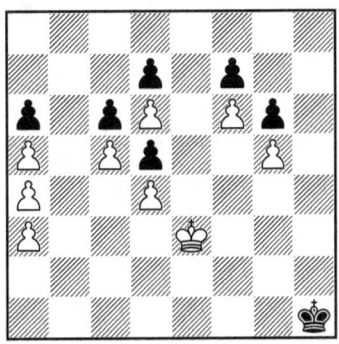

White to play and draw

White must not let the black king get to the white pawns. Therefore, **1.♔f3!!** Not 1.♔f2? ♔h2 2.♔f3 ♔h3 3.♔f4 ♔g2 4.♔g4 ♔f2 5.♔f4 ♔e2, and black wins. The play now branches.

A) **1...♔g1 2.♔g3 ♔f1 3.♔f3 ♔e1 4.♔e3 ♔d1 5.♔d3 ♔c1 6.♔c3 ♔b1 7.♔b3 ♔a1**

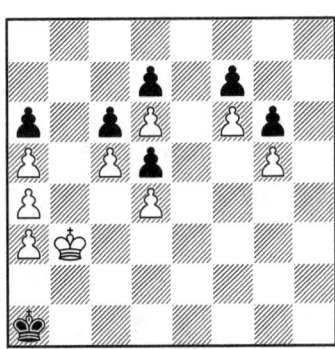

8.♔c3! ♔a2 9.♔b4! ♔b2, stalemate on the queenside;

B) **1...♔h2 2.♔f2 ♔h3 3.♔f3 ♔h4 4.♔f4 ♔h5 5.♔e5 ♔xg5** and stalemate on the kingside.

Study 212 is a classic!

No. 212. V. Halberstadt
Ceskoslovensky Sach, 1929

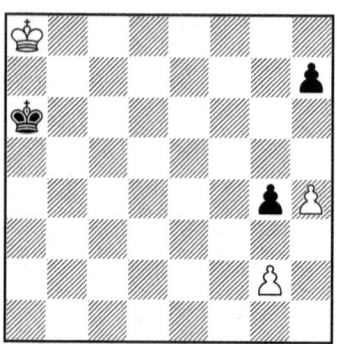

White to play and draw

1.♔b8 ♚b6 2.♔c8 ♚c5. Black is forced to deviate, depriving the white king of its active position.
3.♔d7 ♚d4 4.♔e6 ♚e3 5.♔f5 g3 6.♔g4 ♚f2 7.♔h3 h5, stalemate.

In the next two studies, a similar final stalemate is synthesized with variations on Reti's theme.

In the first part of **Study 213**, the play is similar to **Study 54**.

No. 213. M. Zinar
A. Galitsky memorial, 1987
Commendation

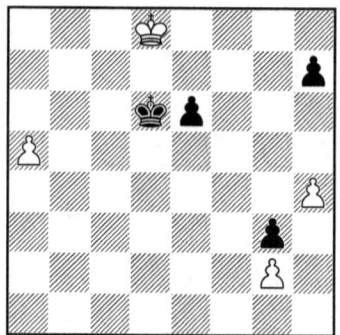

White to play and draw

1.♔c8! ♚c6 2.♔b8! ♚b5

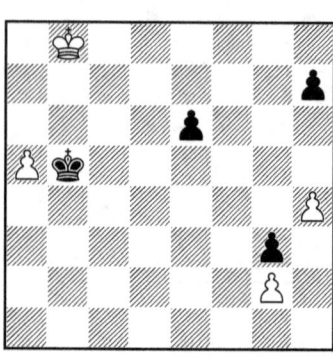

3.♔b7! ♚xa5 4.♔c6 ♚b4 5.♔d6 ♚c4 6.♔xe6 ♚d4 7.♔f5 ♚e3 8.♔g4 ♚f2 9.♔h3 h5, stalemate.

Study 214 is a correction of a famous Soviet-era study composer's work.

No. 214. T. Gorgiev
64, 1932
2nd honorable mention
(correction by M. Zinar, 1986)

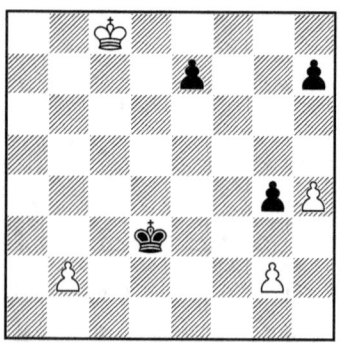

White to play and draw (actually unsolvable)

1.b4! But not 1.♔d7? e5 2.b4 ♚d4!! 3.♔c6 e4! 4.b5 e3 5.b6 e2 6.b7 e1=♕ 7.b8=♕ ♕e6+!, trading queens and winning.

1...♚d4! The black king's desire to get closer to the kingside is refuted by a feint.

2.♔c7! ♔c4. After 3.♔c6? ♔xb4
4.♔d5 ♔c3 5.♔e6 ♔d4 6.♔xe7 ♔e3,
black wins. Therefore, white eschews
the opportunity to capture a pawn and
performs the Reti – Sarychevs feint.

3.♔d7!! e5 4.♔c6 e4 5.b5 e3 6.b6
e2 7.b7 e1=♕ 8.b8=♕ ♕e6+ 9.♕d6
♕xd6+ 10.♔xd6 ♔d4 11.♔e6 g3
12.♔f5 with a stalemate, like in **Studies
212** and **213.**

Unfortunately, time proved that
the correction doesn't work. After
8...♕e4+! 9.♔d7 ♕xg2!, the seven-
piece tablebases show that black wins
in all lines. However, the idea is still
instructive.

We now turn firmly to studies with a
stalemate in the center of the board.

No. 215. H. Rinck
Budapest Chess Club competition, 1911
1st honorable mention

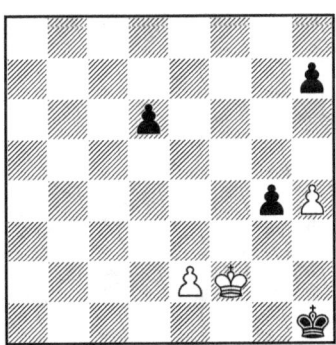

White to play and draw

1.♔g3 h5 2.e4 ♔g1 3.e5! dxe5,
stalemate. Simple and laconic, but isn't
that *too* simple? After shifting the kings
one rank higher and adjusting the pawn
positions, a zugzwang theme becomes
possible, and the solution is therefore
more "study-like":

No. 216. M. Zinar
Shakhmany Bulleten, 1984

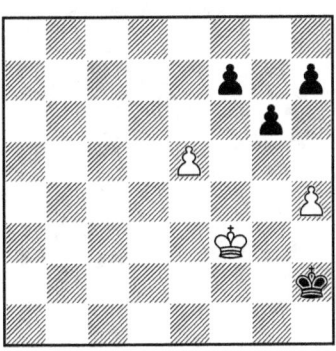

White to play and draw

1.♔f4! h6 2.♔g4! But not 2.h5?
gxh5 3.♔f5 ♔g3 4.♔f6 ♔f4, and wins.
Now black is in zugzwang.

2...♔g2. If 2...♔g1, then 3.h5 g5
4.♔f5 with a draw.

3.h5! g5 4.e6! fxe6, stalemate.

And here's how Rinck's idea was
used in **Study 217**, where both white and
black are stalemated:

No. 217**. V. Kovalenko
Schakend Nederland, 1993
Honorable mention
(correction)

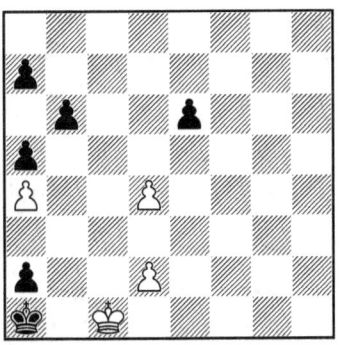

White to play and draw

1.d3! White should not mill about: 1.♔c2? a6 2.d5 (2.d3 b5 3.d5

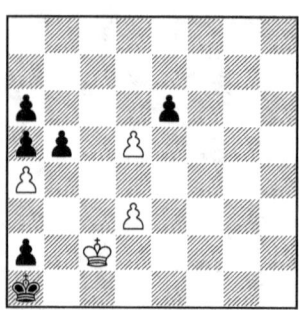

3...e5! 4.d6 b4 5.d7 b3+ 6.♔xb3 ♔b1 7.d8=♕ a1=♕ 8.♕xa5 ♕a2+ 9.♔c3 ♕c2+ 10.♔b4 ♕d2+) 2...exd5 3.d4 b5 4.♔c1 b4 5.♔c2 b3+ 6.♔xb3 ♔b1, and black wins.

1...a6 2.d5! exd5. Or 2...b5

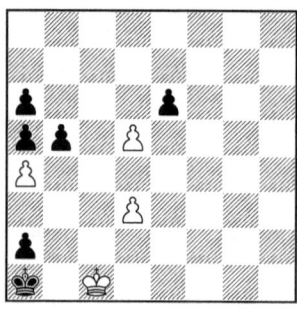

3.dxe6! b4 4.♔c2 b3+ 5.♔xb3 ♔b1 6.e7 a1=♕ 7.e8=♕ ♕a2+ 8.♔c3, draw.

3.d4 b5 4.♔c2 b4. After 4...bxa4 5.♔c1 a3 6.♔c2 a4 7.♔c1 a5 8.♔c2, black is stalemated.

5.♔b3 ♔b1, and now it's white who is stalemated.

Study 218 is truly unique: it's a mirror stalemate (all squares around the white king are unoccupied).

No. 218. V. Halberstadt
64, 1930

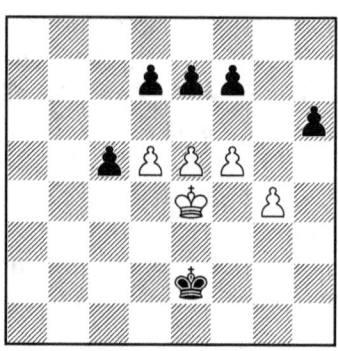

White to play and draw

1.g5! hxg5 2.e6! fxe6 3.dxe6! dxe6 4.f6! exf6, stalemate. Or **2...dxe6 3.fxe6! fxe6 4.d6! exd6,** stalemate.

A mirror stalemate in a pawn study can be constructed with the help of... a promoted black queen. You don't believe us? See **Study 219!**

No. 219**. E. Melnichenko
UAPA, 2015

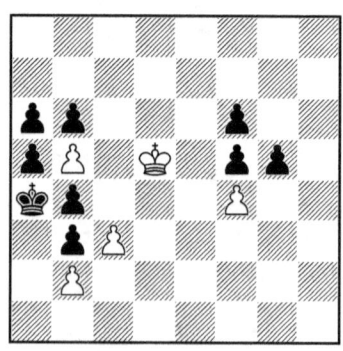

White to play and draw

1.c4! Not 1.bxa6? bxc3 2.a7 cxb2 3.a8=♕ b1=♕, curtains.

1...axb5 (1...gxf4 2.bxa6 f3 3.a7) **2.c5! g4!** After 2...bxc5 3.♔xc5 g4 4.♔d4 g3

5.♔e3 g2 6.♔f2 g1=♕+ 7.♔xg1, black is stalemated in a niche.

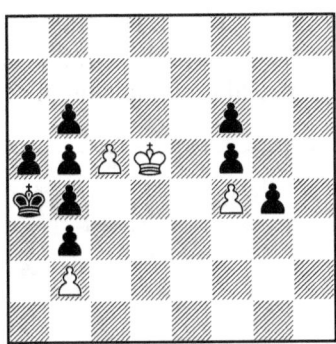

3.c6 g3 4.c7 g2 5.c8=♘! g1=♕ (5... g1=♗ 6.♔c6 ♗d4 7.♘xb6+) **6.♘xb6+ ♕xb6.** Mirror stalemate!

In **Study 220**, white achieves his goal with a tortoise move of the c-pawn and a sacrifice of the f-pawn.

No. 220. F. Lazard
American Chess Bulletin, 1916

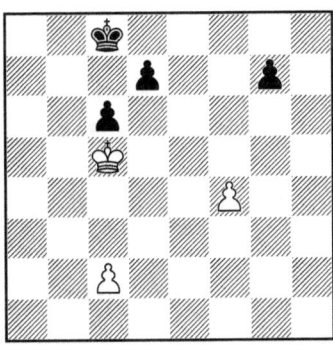

White to play and draw

1.♔d6 ♔d8! 2.f5 ♔e8 3.c3! ♔d8 4.c4 ♔e8 5.c5 ♔d8 6.f6! gxf6, stalemate.

Study 221 is a nice modification of the previous study. The author uses a double threat in the introductory play.

No. 221. S. Zhigis
64, 1930
Commendation
(correction)

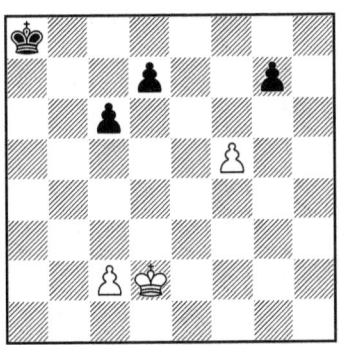

White to play and draw

1.♔e3! ♔b7 2.♔f4! Not 2.♔e4? ♔b6! 3.♔e5 ♔c5, and black wins.

2...♔c7! Now 2...♔b6 is met with 3.♔g5!

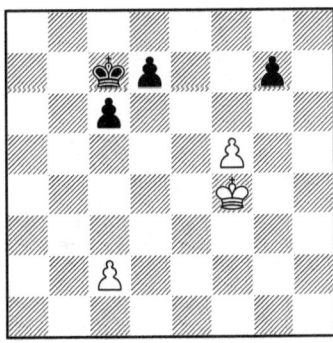

3.♔e5! But now 3.♔g5? is bad: 3... ♔d6! 4.♔g6 ♔e5!, and black wins.

3...♔d8 4.♔d6! ♔e8 5.c3! etc., like on the third move of Lazard's previous study. Not 5.c4? ♔d8 6.c5 ♔e8 7.♔c7 (no stalemate) 7...♔e7 8.♔b6 d6! 9.♔xc6 dxc5 10.♔xc5 ♔f6 with a win.

In **Study 222**, the f-pawn can move to a neighboring file, therefore its square turns into a rectangle: f6-f1-c1-c6. The Reti maneuver is used.

No. 222. T. Gorgiev
Magyar Sakkvilag, 1929
6th honorable mention

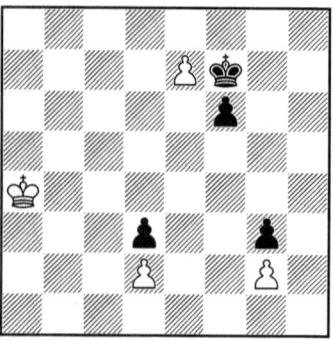

White to play and draw

1.♔b5! f5 2.♔c6! ♚xe7 3.♔d5 ♚f6 4.♔d4 f4!

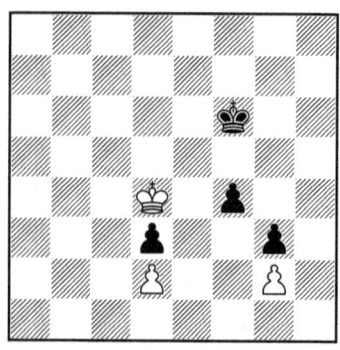

5.♔e4! ♚g5 6.♔f3 ♚f5, stalemate.

In **Study 223**, the stalemating finale is preceded by a subtle battle for the all-important zugzwang (see corresponding squares theory) arising in the author's solution after white's seventh move. In the false try (after the careless 2.♔d5?) the black king demonstrates elegant play along the first rank to pass the

move to its counterparty in the key position.

No. 223**. A. Davranian
Shakhmatnaya Nedelya, 2003
2nd special honorable mention

White to play and draw

1.♔c5! ♚d1! Trying to put white in zugzwang.

2.♔d4! Not 2.♔d5? ♚e1! 3.♔e5 ♚f1! 4.♔f5 ♚g1! 5.♔g4 (5.h4 ♚g2! 6.♔g4 ♚h2 7.♔h5 ♚g3)

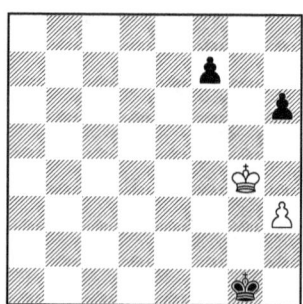

5...♚g2! 6.h4 ♚h2! 7.h5 ♚g2! (key mutual zugzwang) 8.♔f5 ♚g3 9.♔f6 ♚g4, curtains.

2...♚e2! Or 2...♚d2 3.♔e5! ♚e3 4.♔f6 ♚f4 5.♔xf7 h5 6.♔e6! h4 7.♔d5! ♚g3 8.♔e4 ♚xh3 9.♔f3, draw.

3.♔e4! ♚f2 4.♔f4! ♚g2 5.♔g4! ♚h2!

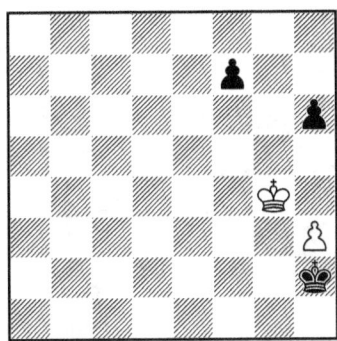

6.h4! ♔g2 **7.h5!** Black is in zugzwang!

7...♔h2 (7...♔f2 8.♔f4) **8.♔h4!** And now, after 8...f6 9.♔g4, it's black who has to scramble for a draw. Retreating to the first rank doesn't help black: 8...♔h1 9.♔h3! ♔g1 10.♔g3 ♔f1 11.♔f3 ♔e1 12.♔e3, each time with zugzwang opposition in favor of white.

After **8...f5,** however, an ideal stalemate is on the board.

Three different stalemates without pawn promotion are found in **Study 224**.

No. 224**. V. Kovalenko
Problem, 1972

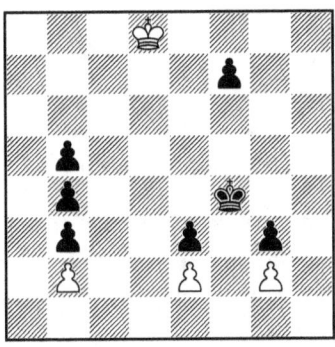

White to play and draw

Black's only chance to win is to play the f4-f3 break. White, of course, is trying to prevent this.

1.♔e7! f5 **2.♔f6!** The play branches:

A) **2...♔g4 3.♔e5 f4 4.♔e4 ♔g5 5.♔f3 ♔f5,** the first stalemate. If 3...♔g5 (instead of 3...f4), then **4.♔d4(d5) f4 5.♔e4 ♔g4 6.♔d4 ♔f5 7.♔d3 ♔e5,** the second stalemate.

B) **2...♔e4 3.♔g5 f4 4.♔g4 ♔e5 5.♔f3 ♔f5,** and the familiar first stalemate is on the board. While 3...♔e5 (instead of 3...f4) is met with **4.♔h4(h5) f4 5.♔g4 ♔e4 6.♔h4 ♔f5 7.♔h3 ♔g5** with a third stalemate. This is a development of an early Henri Rinck study with two stalemating finales.

There are two parallel lines in **Study 225**, with both the white and black king getting stalemated. This is the theme of a **"mutual stalemate"**.

No. 225**. V. Kovalenko
Schach, 2005

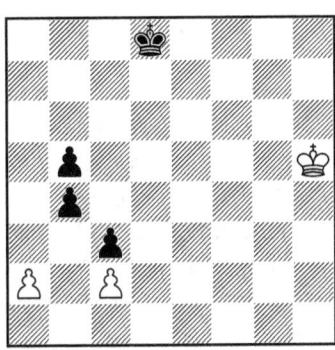

White to play and draw

1.♔g4! The king rushes to help its pawns! Not 1.♔g5? ♔c7 2.♔f4 ♔b6 3.♔e3 ♔a5 4.♔d4 ♔a4 5.♔c5

♔a3 6.♔xb5 ♔xa2 7.♔xb4 ♔b2, curtains.

1...♔c7 2.♔f3 ♔b6 3.♔e2! ♔a5! It's a simple draw after 3...♔c5 4.♔d3 ♔d5 5.♔e3 ♔e5 6.♔d3 etc.

4.♔d1 ♔a4 5.♔c1 b3! (5... ♔a3 6.♔b1) **6.cxb3+.** 6.axb3+? is catastrophic: 6...♔b4 7.♔b1 ♔c5 8.♔c1 ♔d4 9.♔d1 ♔e3 10.♔e1 b4!, and white dies in zugzwang throes.

6...♔a3 7.♔b1

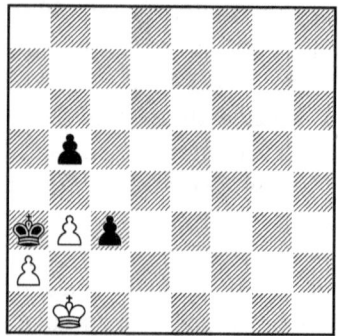

7...b4 8.♔a1! c2 — white is stalemated.

Or **7...c2+ 8.♔xc2 b4** (8...♔xa2 9.b4!) **9.♔b1** – black is stalemated.

2.6.2. Niche stalemate

The theme of "niche stalemate" is a special case in pawn studies. Thanks to its uniqueness, it won the hearts of composers a long time ago, and it's still relevant in modern times. There are two kinds of niches. In the first kind, the king is immured by four pawns of its own color.

Study 226 is a classic example of niche building.

No. 226. J. Berger
Theorie und Praxis der Endspiele, 1890

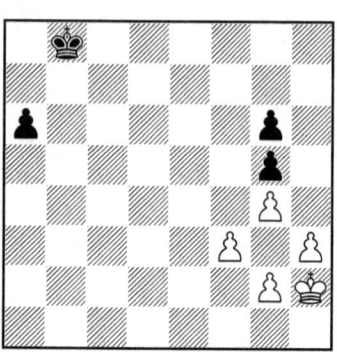

White to play and draw

1.f4! ♔c7! If 1...a5, then 2.h4 gxh4 3.f5 gxf5 4.g5, and the pawn promotes.

2.fxg5! (white's second and third moves are interchangeable: 2.g3 a5 3.fxg5 etc.) **2...a5 3.♔g3 a4 4.♔h4 a3 5.g3** with a stalemate.

No. 227. G. Kasparyan
Shakhmaty v SSSR, 1937

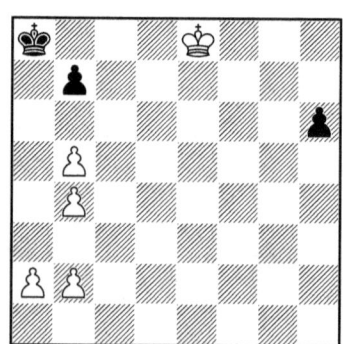

White to play and draw

1.♔d7! A Reti double threat that involves moving away from the black pawn and getting into the niche in time. A rare idea!

1...h5 2.♔c7! h4. Black is forced to allow the king to enter the niche, because after 2...♔a7, white even wins by pushing his pawns.

3.♔b6! h3 4.♔a5

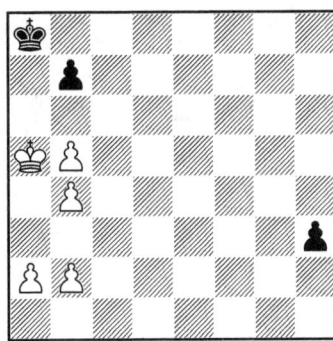

4...b6+ 5.♔a4! h2 6.b3 and **7.a3.** Or vice versa: first 6.a3, then 7.b3 with stalemate.

Or **4...h2 5.b6! h1=♕ 6.b5!** Even a queen cannot stop the self-stalemate.

6...♕b1 7.a4 and **8.b4!** Two echo-chameleon stalemates. A great achievement by the Soviet chess composition grandmaster. Unfortunately, he composed only one pawn study!

No. 228. M. Zinar
Shakhmaty v SSSR, 1978
Special prize

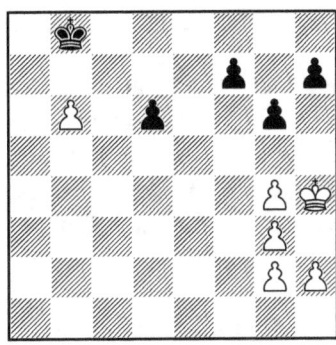

White to play and draw

White wants to lock himself in? Nothing is easier, the four pawns just need to move one square ahead!

1.g5! d5! If 1...♔b7, then 2.g4 ♔xb6 3.g3 ♔c6 4.h3 f5? (black really should accept the stalemate) 5.gxf6 ♔d7 6.g5 with a win.

2.g4! And if 2.h3? then 2...d4 3.g4 d3 4.g3 d2 5.b7 f6, and white is again one tempo short.

2...d4!

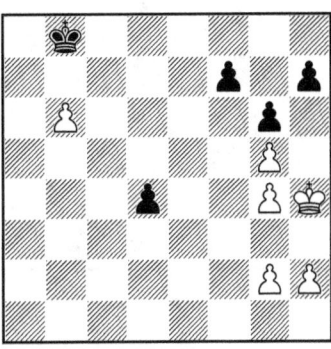

3.♔g3!! The point! White already lacks a tempo, and he voluntarily loses two more by leaving the ready-made niche. An original feint!

3...♔b7 4.h3! Not 4.♔f3? ♔xb6!

4...♔xb6. If 4...d3, then 5.♔f3, winning the pawn.

5.♔h4! And back! Let's review: white did indeed lose some tempi, but after 4.h3! and the elimination of the b-pawn he won them back. Black quickly changes his strategic plan.

5...♔c6 6.g3 f6 7.gxf6 ♔d7. The niche is destroyed, the white pawn is stopped, the black pawn looks unstoppable, but...

8.♔g5! The Reti maneuver!

8...♔e6. If 8...d3, then 9.♔h6! with a draw.

9.♔f4!, and the d-pawn falls! Draw.

Study 230 was considered one of the best pawn studies of the 1970s. First, though, we examine **Study 229**, which was an ultimately failed attempt by this book's author to improve it!

No. 229. N. Kralin and Anatoly Kuznetsov
64, 1975
1st prize
(amended version)

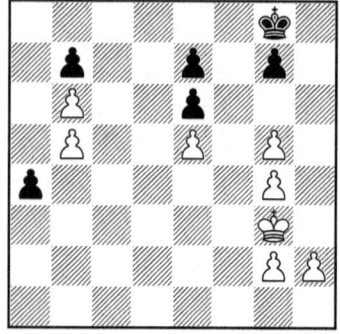

White to play and draw (actually unsolvable)

1.g6! a3 2.g5! a2 3.♔g4! 3.♔h4? a1=♗ 4.♔h5 ♗xe5 5.h4 (white doesn't want to lose a tempo!)

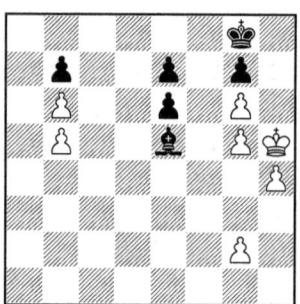

5...♗g3! 6.♔g4 ♗e1 7.♔h5 ♔f8 (but ultimately, he did...) 8.g4 ♗xh4 9.♔xh4 e5 10.♔g3 ♔e8! 11.♔f3 ♔d7 12.♔e4 ♔e6 13.♔e3 ♔d5. Later, in the strong computer era, it transpired that promotion to a queen also wins, which somewhat blemishes the study: 3... a1=♕ 4.♔h5 ♕d4 5.g4

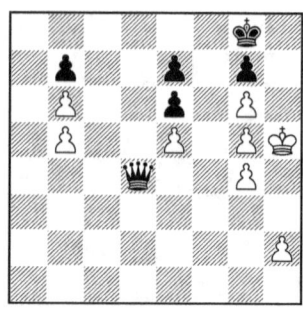

5...♕xb6! 6.h4 ♕f2 7.b6 ♕xh4+ 8.♔xh4 ♔f8 9.♔g3 ♔e8 10.♔f4 ♔d7, curtains.
3...a1=♕. If 3...a1=♗, then 4.♔f4!, and black cannot win.
4.♔h5! ♕xe5 5.h4 ♕e1 6.g4 ♕xh4+ 7.♔xh4 ♔f8. The first part seems to have been no success for white, but in the second part, he will eventually get himself stalemated, albeit to the left of the pawn wall g4-g5-g6.

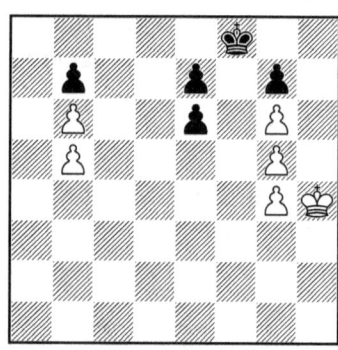

8.♔g3 e5 9.♔f3 e6 10.♔e4 ♔e7 11.♔xe5 ♔d7 12.♔d4(f4). Another blemish: white also saves the game with 12.♔e4! ♔d6 13.♔d4 e5+ 14.♔c4! e4 15.♔d4 e3 16.♔xe3 ♔c5 17.♔e4 ♔d6 18.♔f4 ♔d5 19.♔f5, positional draw.
12...♔d6 13.♔e4 e5 14.♔f5 ♔d5, stalemate. A whole complex of ideas: niche stalemate, Grigoriev stalemate,

and underpromotion with an original motivation. The study is somewhat let down by the technical pawns on the b-file.

As we already know, underpromotion in this study is a mirage, because promotion to a queen also wins. Moreover, in addition to the authors' stalemate idea, the unnoticed continuation 12.♔e4! also saves the game.

But the study has another flaw that kills it completely — it's unsolvable. Instead of 4...♕xe5, black has the quiet 4...♕g1! (or even 4...♕d4!) 5.h4 ♕xb6 6.g4 ♕f2 7.b6 ♕xh4+ 8.♔xh4 ♔f8 etc.

And yet!... all is not as sad as it seems! Both *64* and the *FIDE Album* feature the original version of this study, which lacks all those lethal flaws. Conclusion: not all improvements are beneficial! So here it is:

No. 230**. N. Kralin and Anatoly Kuznetsov
64, 1975
1st prize

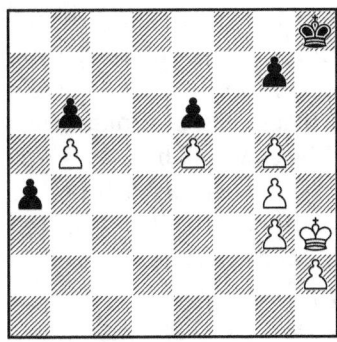

White to play and draw

1.g6! The king should not climb into the niche immediately: 1.♔h4? a3 2.g6 a2 3.g5

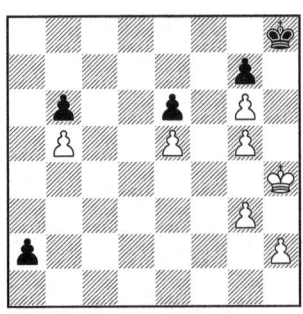

3...a1=♗!! (only this!) 4.g4 ♗xe5 5.h3 ♔g8 6.♔h5 ♗g3! 7.h4 ♗xh4 8.♔xh4 ♔f8 9.♔g3 e5 10.♔f3 ♔e7 11.♔e4 ♔e6!, curtains.

1...a3 2.g5! a2 3.♔g4!! 3.♔h4? is met with the familiar 3...a1=♗!

3...a1=♕ 4.♔h5 ♕xe5

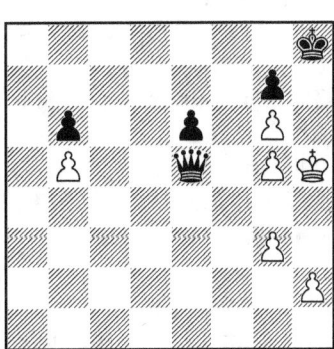

5.h4! **♕e1.** 5...♕xg3 stalemates immediately. 5...♕xb5 6.g4 ♕xg5+ 7.♔xg5 b5 8.♔f4 doesn't work either: the king makes it into the square of the pawn in time.

6.g4 ♕xh4+ 7.♔xh4 ♔g8. The rest is familiar: **8.♔g3 ♔f8 9.♔f4(f3) ♔e7 10.♔e5 ♔d7 11.♔d4(f4) ♔d6 12.♔e4 e5 13.♔f5! ♔d5** with a classical stalemate.

No. 231. S. Tkachenko
N. Grigoriev memorial, 1985
3rd honorable mention

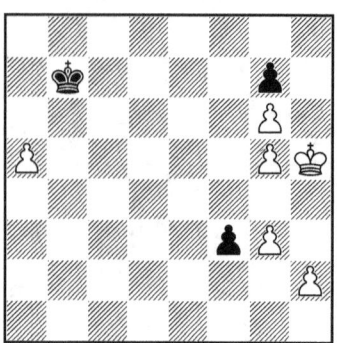

White to play and draw

1.a6+! ♔a7! 1...♔a8 is met with 2.a7 f2 3.h4!, and if 3...f1=♕, then 4.g4. While after 3...f1=♘, there's 4.♔g4!, with a draw in both cases.

2.h3!! Very unexpected! Not the hasty 2.h4? f2 3.g4 (3.♔g4 f1=♕) 3...♔b6! 4.a7 f1=♘! 5.a8=♕ ♘g3#.

2...f2 3.h4! (3.g4? f1=♘!) **3...f1=♕ 4.g4 ♔b6 5.a7 ♕f8 6.a8=♕ ♕xa8,** stalemate.

Note that white's first and second moves are not interchangeable here, because of 1.h3? f2 2.a6 ♔a8!, with a mate in three.

The theme of niche stalemate is solved in a classical way here: white has only one pawn in addition to the necessary "building blocks", but there's also an unexpected zugzwang and a knight in "backstage" lines!

This second kind of niche is built from both black and white pawns. It's very stable – and, therefore, provides great opportunities for new play.

Study 232 is not your usual way of building a niche, but the threat of promoting the h-pawn is used to create a study.

No. 232. T. Kok
Wiener Schachzeitung, 1935

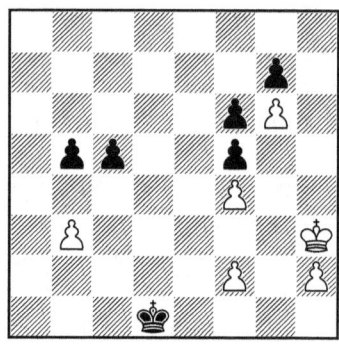

White to play and draw
(actually unsolvable)

1.♔g3! A feint to trade queenside pawns. 1.♔h4? is a mistake due to 1...b4 2.♔h5 ♔e2 3.h4 c4, and black gives checkmate. 1.b4? doesn't help either: 1...cxb4 2.♔h4 b3 3.♔h5 b2 4.h4 b1=♕ 5.f3 ♕e4! etc.

1...c4 2.bxc4 bxc4 (2...b4 3.c5) **3.♔h4** with a stalemate. f2-f3 can be played on any move and white continues with ♔h5 and h4, building the niche.

Unfortunately, this position is unsolvable, too. Instead of the author's 1...c4, black has a stronger reply 1...♔e2! 2.b4 cxb4 3.f3 b3 4.♔h4 b2 5.♔h5 b1=♕ 6.h4 ♕e4 7.fxe4 fxe4 8.♔g4 b4 9.h5 b3 10.h6 gxh6 11.g7 b2 12.g8=♕ b1=♕, and the queen endgame is hopeless for white.

In **Study 233**, white gets stalemated twice in the niche.

No. 233. M. Zinar
Shakhmaty v SSSR, 1986

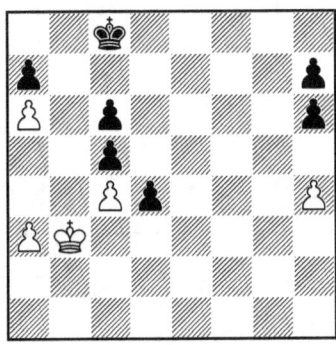

White to play and draw

1.♔a4! But not 1.h5? ♚c7! 2.♔a4 ♚b6, and black wins.

1...d3. With his feint, white forces the black pawn to break away from the group. If 1...♚c7, then 2.♔a5 d3 3.a4 d2 4.h5 d1=♕, stalemate.

2.♔b3! ♚d7 3.♔c3 ♚e6 4.♔xd3 ♚f5 5.♔e3! The king moves further and further away from the niche, but white should not forget about the c4 pawn.

5...♚g4! 5...h5 is met with 6.♔f3, and white holds even without a niche.

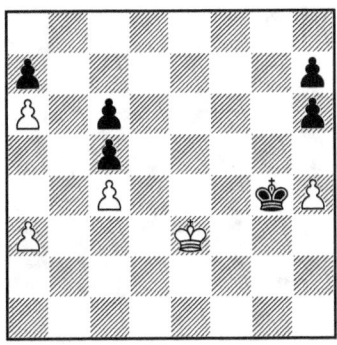

6.h5! Otherwise black wins with h6-h5 — the h-pawn moves closer to the promotion square.

6...♚g5 7.♔e4! ♚xh5. The black king is far enough now, and it's safe to return to the niche.

8.♔d3 ♚g4 9.♔c3(c2) h5 10.♔b3 h4 11.♔a4 h3 12.♔a5 h2 13.a4 h1=♕, stalemate.

Study 234 is a true stalemating masterpiece, which remained underappreciated for a long time because of the wrong evaluation of the h-pawn, which was considered purely technical. But it is not so!

No. 234. V. Chekhover
Sovetskaya Rossiya, 1956

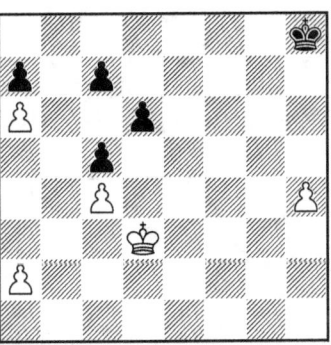

White to play and draw

To begin with, white plays a feint — unexpected but always welcome! He needs to provoke the movement of the black pawns to create a niche.

1.♔e4! c6 2.♔f5! d5 3.♔e5. And now back!

3...d4 4.♔e4 ♚g7 5.♔d3! ♚h6 6.♔c2! If the king simply returned to the niche, it would already be a good study. But the miracles have only just begun!

6...♚g6!

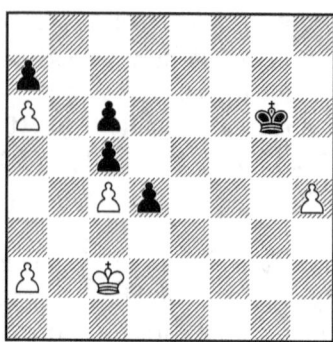

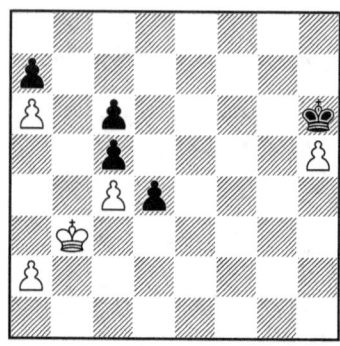

7.♔b2!! Simple and brilliant! Obviously, since the king is not on b3 yet, it's too early to give up the pawn: 7.h5+? ♚xh5 8.♔b3 d3! 9.♔c3 ♚g4 10.♔xd3 ♚f3, winning the c4 pawn and destroying the stalemate position. Nor can white play 7.♔b3? ♚h5! (zugzwang) 8.a3 ♚g6! 9.♔b2 ♚f5 10.♔b3 (the most resilient!) 10...♚f4 11.h5 ♚e3 12.h6 d3 13.h7 d2 14.h8=♕ d1=♕+ 15.♚a2

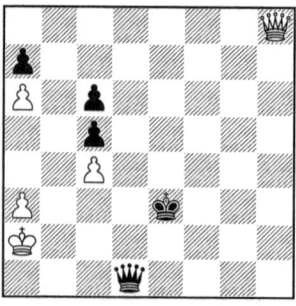

15...♕c2+ 16.♔a1 ♕c1+ 17.♔a2 ♕xc4+ 18.♔b1 ♕b3+ 19.♔c1 ♕xa3+, and black wins. Therefore, white should hang onto the a2-a3 tempo for as long as possible!

7...♚f5! 8.h5! Not 8.a3? ♚g4! 9.♔b3 ♚f3. Both 8.♔b3? ♚f4! and 8.♔a3? ♚f4! 9.h5 d3! etc. are equally bad.

8...♚g5 9.♔b3! But not 9.♔a3? due to 9...d3!

9...♚h6

10.a3!! And now it is time! The h5 pawn is blocked.

10...♚g7   11.♔c2(b2)! Again avoiding getting into the niche in the battle for zugzwang.

11...♚h6   12.♔b3!   ♚g5   13.h6! ♚xh6 **14.♔a4 d3 15.♔a5 d2 16.a4 d1=♕,** stalemate.

Sixteen moves have been made, and what moves! A feint, a tortoise move and an unexpected zugzwang nuance (7.♔b2!!)!

In **Study 235**, the doubled passed e-pawns give white a hint that he should play for stalemate.

No. 235. M. Zinar
Shakhmaty v SSSR, 1986
Special prize

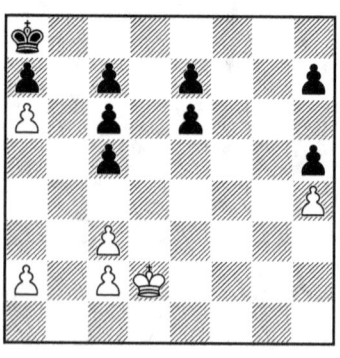

White to play and draw

1.c4! e5 2.c3!! Why should white immediately spend a tempo that can be useful at any time? Because if 2.♔c3?, then 2...♔b8 3.♔b3 e4! 4.c3 e3! and we see that white needs to come back earlier! Now black wins easily: 5.♔c2 ♔c8 6.♔d3 ♔d7 7.♔xe3 e5 8.♔d3 ♔e6 9.♔c2 e4! etc. The attempt to win a pawn doesn't work either: 2.♔d3? ♔b8 3.♔e4 ♔c8 4.♔xe5 ♔d7

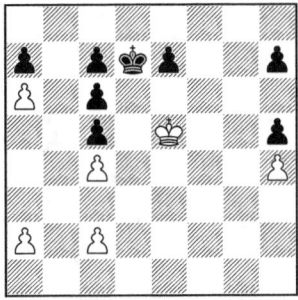

— the white king has wandered too far into the center.

To make it clearer, we should point out that the white king can move into the niche from e4 if and only if the black king is on the seventh rank, and the move c2-c3 has already been made.

In the line above, however, this doesn't work. For instance: 5.♔e4 ♔e6! 6.c3 ♔f6!, and the black king is on the sixth rank. Or 5.c3 e6 6.♔e4 ♔d6! 7.a3! h6! (an unexpected mutual zugzwang) 8.♔f4 ♔e7! 9.♔e5 ♔f7 10.♔e4 ♔f6, and the king is on f6 again. Finally, 5.♔f5 e6+! 6.♔e4 ♔e7!, and if 7.c3, then the king moves to the sixth rank yet again — 7...♔f6!

2...♔b8. The e5 pawn cannot be captured, so white provokes its movement with a feint.

3.♔c2! e4! After 3...♔c8 4.♔b3! e4 5.♔a4 e3 6.♔a5 e2 7.a4 e1=♕, the first stalemate appears.

4.♔d2! The king needs to head back, because 4.♔b3? loses to 4...e3!

4...♔c8 5.♔e3 ♔d7 6.♔xe4 ♔d6! The king is on the sixth rank, and white cannot play 7.♔d3? due to 7...e5!, or 7.♔f4? due to 7...♔e6!

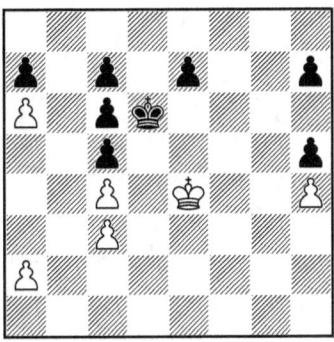

7.♔f5!! And this move is simply beautiful: the white king moves even further from the niche, and black is in zugzwang.

7...♔d7! 8.♔e4! Not 8.♔e5? e6 9.♔e4 ♔d6 10.a3 h6! — and now it's white who is in zugzwang!

8...♔d6 9.♔f5 e6+. Otherwise, there's a positional draw!

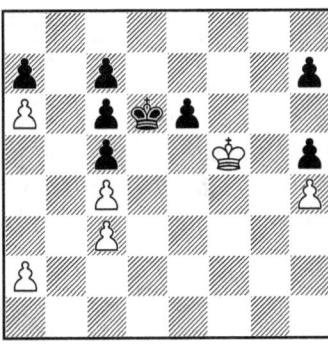

10.♔e4! h6! 11.a3! ♔e7. Black has lost the skirmish, and the white king goes back to take a well-deserved rest!

12.♔d3! e5! 13.♔c2! e4! The pawn cannot be captured, so white plays another feint!

14.♔b3 e3! After 14...♔e6 15.♔a4 e3 16.♔a5 e2 17.a4 e1=♕, there's a second stalemate!

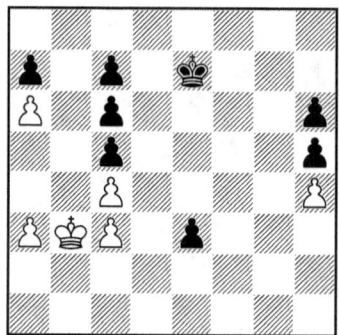

15.♔c2! The king leaves the niche yet again! Interestingly, it got back from c2 the first time, but now, it goes back from b3!

15...♔e6 16.♔d3 ♔f5 17.♔xe3 ♔g4. Black still doesn't lose hope, and white moves into the niche for the third time.

18.♔d2(d3)! ♔xh4 19.♔c2 ♔g3 20.♔b3 h4 21.♔a4 h3 22.♔a5 h2 23.a4 h1=♕, stalemate. Just in time: if black were to move now, he could have played ♕h1–d5!

Twenty-three moves of pure pawn play to achieve stalemate — and to think that all this began with a short, five-move study by Berger!

The previous two examples are rather complicated, but these complications are calculable. And there's no need to make the idea too difficult, because this will turn such an artistic and romantic subgenre as niche stalemate into an analytical one.

It's hard to predict which secrets are hidden in the depths of the niche stalemate theme, where a study composer may find something new. But we are sure that all research is totally worth it!

And research has indeed continued since Zinar's 1990 edition! In **Study 236**, white constructs two separate stalemating niches.

No. 236**. E. Fomichev
Ceskoslovensky Sach, 2015

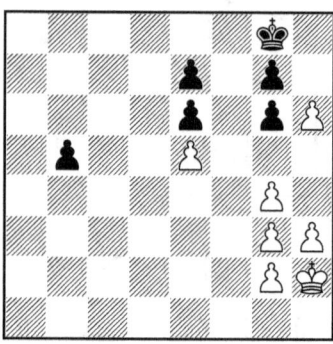

White to play and draw

1.h7+! But not 1.hxg7? g5! or 1.g5? gxh6!, with black winning in both lines.

1...♔xh7 2.g5! b4 3.g4 b3 4.♔g3 b2 5.♔h4 b1=♕ 6.g3 ♕f5! The first niche stalemate occurs after 6...♕b8.

7.gxf5 gxf5!

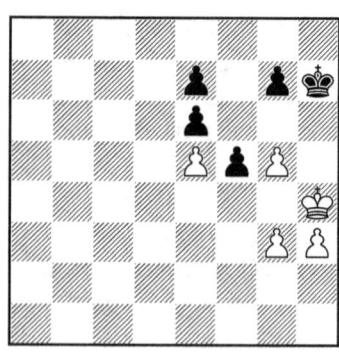

Now white cannot play 8.g4? immediately due to 8...f4 9.g6+ ♔xg6 10.g5 ♔f5, curtains.

A king feint saves white: **8.♔h5!! g6+ 9.♔h4! ♔g7 10.g4! f4** with a second niche stalemate — the missing "building block" on g3 was replaced by a black pawn.

2.6.3. Stalemate with pawn promotion

This category includes studies where black promotes his pawn into a piece that later takes part in creating the stalemate position.

No. 237. L. Kubbel
Shakhmatny Listok, 1922

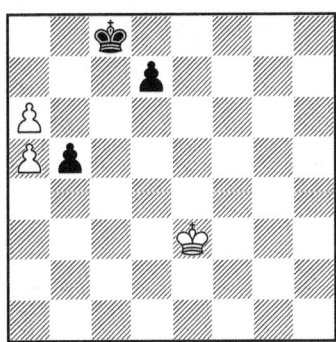

White to play and draw

1.♔d4! d6! 2.♔c3!! This is the first known occurrence of the endgame study trick that was later dubbed "feint" — we can even say that this is the most useful technique in studies! White needs to force the move d6-d5, because after 2.♔d5? ♔c7, white is in zugzwang.

2...d5 3.♔d4! b4! 4.♔xd5! b3

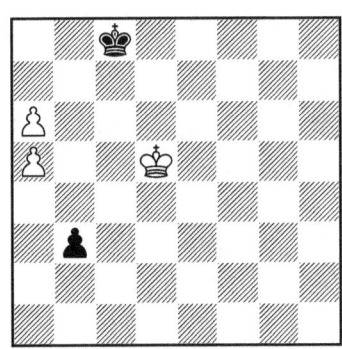

5.♔c6! ♔b8 6.♔b6 b2 7.a7+ ♔a8 8.♔a6 b1=♕, stalemate.

Play in the miniature **Study 238** is beautiful yet complicated.

No. 238. T. Gorgiev
Shakhmaty v SSSR, 1950

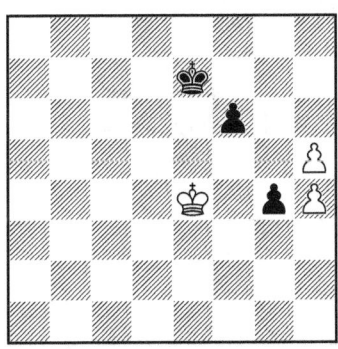

White to play and draw

Here's how fighting for corresponding squares looks: 1.♔f4? f5 2.h6 ♔f6 3.h5 ♔f7! (mutual zugzwang) 4.♔xf5 g3 5.h7 ♔g7, and black wins. So the pawn can only be captured when the king is on the eighth rank!

1.h6! ♔f8! 2.h5! 2.♔f4? is still too early: 2...f5! 3.♔xf5 g3 4.♔f6 ♔g8 5.♔g6 g2, and white doesn't have enough time to self-stalemate.

2...♔f7! 3.♔e3! f5 4.♔f4! White

has won the battle for corresponding squares (f4 and f7). Now black is in zugzwang!

4...♔f6 5.♔g3! (5.♔e3? g3!) **5... ♔f7 6.♔f4 ♔f8**

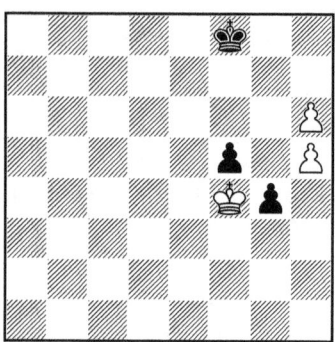

7.♔xf5! It's now time. Otherwise black plays 7...♔g8.

7...g3 8.♔f6! ♔g8 9.♔g6 g2 10.h7+ ♔h8 11.♔h6 g1=♛, stalemate.

No. 239. A. Kovalenko
Shakhmatny Listok, 1927
4th prize

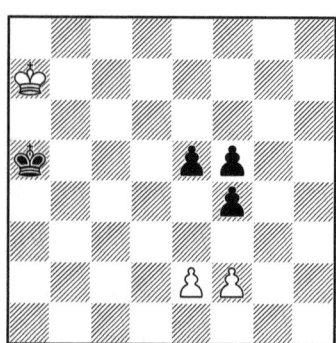

White to play and draw

1.♔b7 e4 2.♔c6! ♔b4 3.♔d5! But not 3.♔d6? e3 4.fxe3 fxe3 5.♔e5 ♔c3, and black wins.

3...♔c3! The black king is forced to move to c3, which leads to stalemate,

because after 3...♔b3 4.♔e5 e3 5.fxe3 fxe3 6.♔f4, it's still a draw.

4.♔e5! e3! 5.♔xf4 exf2 6.♔e3 f1=♛, stalemate. If 6...f1=♘(♗), then the last pawn is traded off.

No. 240. F. Bondarenko and M. Zinar
L'Italia Scacchistica, 1978

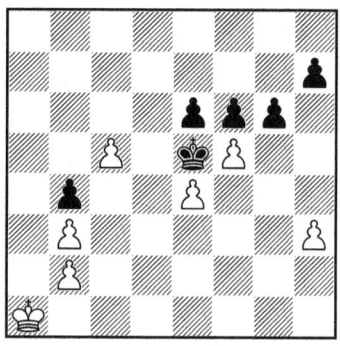

White to play and draw

1.c6! ♔d6 2.e5+! ♔xc6 3.exf6 ♔d7 4.f7 ♔e7 5.fxe6 g5 6.♔b1! A two-move feint that prevents black from capturing the white pawn.

6...h5

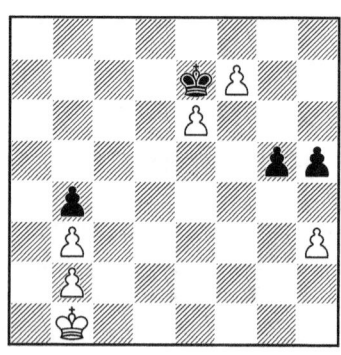

7.♔c2! But not 7.♔c1? g4 8.hxg4 h4 9.g5 h3 10.g6 h2, and black wins — his pawn is promoted with a check.

7...g4 8.hxg4 h4! 9.g5! h3 10.g6! ♔f8 11.♔b1! Back to the hiding place!

11...h2 12.♔a2 with a stalemate.

Alas, this study also failed to withstand the test of time. Instead of the authors' 3.exf6, white can also save the game with **3.fxg6! hxg6 4.exf6 ♚d6 5.♔b1 e5 6.♔c2 ♚e6 7.♔d3 ♚xf6 8.♔c4 ♚f5 9.♔xb4 ♚f4 10.♔c3! ♚f3 11.♔d2 ♚f2 12.♔d3**, positional draw.

In addition to 4.f7, the move 4.fxg6! also saves white. Even on the next move, the same trick is possible: **5.fxg6! hxg6 6.♔b1 ♚xf7 7.♔c2 e5 8.♔d3 ♚f6 9.♔c4** etc..

Study 241 is a miniature with a stalemate caused by pinning a pawn, with a pawn tempo loss for zugzwang.

No. 241. A. Gulyaev
Izvestia, 1930
Commendation

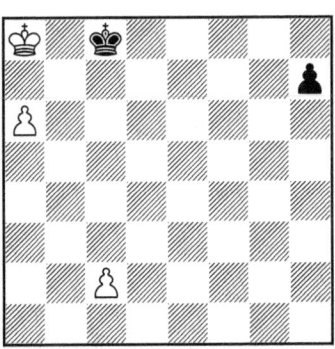

White to play and draw

1.a7! Prompting black to play a committal move.

1...h5 2.c3! An energetic move is met with a slow one. The slow 1...h6, on the other hand, is met with 2.c4!, also drawing.

2...h4 3.c4 h3 4.c5 h2 5.c6 h1=♕, stalemate. Promoting to a rook doesn't help.

In a similar position, the author of **Study 242** demonstrates parallel synthesis of diverse ideas.

No. 242. T. Gorgiev
Ceskoslovensky Sach, 1930
6th honorable mention

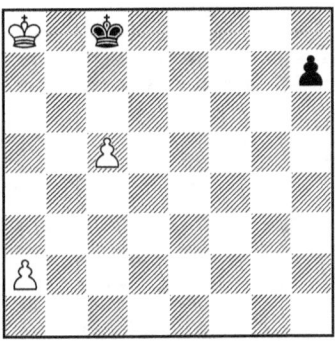

White to play and draw

1.c6! h6! 2.a3! Here, on the contrary, slow moves are met with slow replies!

2...h5 3.a4 h4 4.a5 h3 5.a6 h2 6.a7 h1=♕, stalemate with a pinned pawn.

In the second variation, a Reti maneuver is involved: **2...♚c7 3.a4 ♚xc6**

4.a5! Not 4.♔a7? h5 5.a5 h4 6.a6 ♚b5!! 7.♔b7 h3 8.a7 h2 9.a8=♕ h1=♕+ with a theoretical win for black.

4...♚b5 5.♔b7!, draw.

As we approach the completion of our review of this genre, we would like to express our confidence that stalemate studies with a black pawn promotion haven't exhausted themselves. The main sphere for development is creating interesting play that precedes the stalemate.

To support these prophecies, we show several newer studies on the theme of stalemate after pawn promotion.

In the finale of **Study 243**, a minimal stalemate occurs (only three pieces on the board!). Not immediately, but several moves after the black pawn's promotion.

No. 243**. A. Hadari
Variantim, 1994

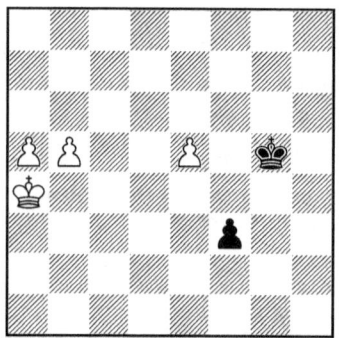

White to play and draw

The white pawns cannot immediately run towards the promotion squares: 1.b6? f2 2.b7 f1=♕ 3.b8=♕ ♕a1+ 4.♔b3 ♕b1+ or 1.a6? f2 2.a7 f1=♕ 3.a8=♕ ♕a1+, skewering the newborn queen.

Preliminary play in the center saves white: **1.e6! ♔f6 2.b6!** The pawns move as a pair! But not 2.e7? ♔xe7 3.b6 ♔d7, curtains.

2...f2 3.e7! ♔xe7 4.b7 f1=♕ 5.b8=♕ ♕a1+ 6.♔b5 ♕b2+ 7.♔a6! ♕xb8. Stalemate.

A lovely model stalemate crowns the subtle **Study 244**; its contours should be foreseen at the very beginning of play.

No. 244**. V. Kovalenko and A. Skripnik
JC Sochnev − 50, 2014
Commendation

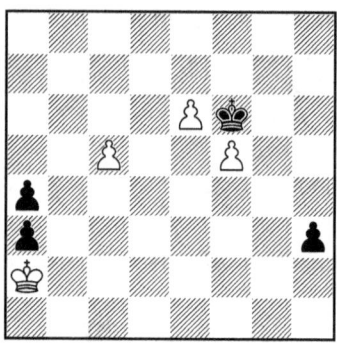

White to play and draw

1.e7!! A false try: 1.c6? h2 2.c7 h1=♕ 3.c8=♕ ♕d5+ 4.♔b1 ♕d1+ 5.♕c1 a2+, curtains.

1...♔xe7 2.c6 (2.f6+? ♔xf6 3.c6 ♔e7) **2...h2.** Not 2...♔d6 3.f6 h2 4.f7 h1=♕ 5.f8=♕+, draw.

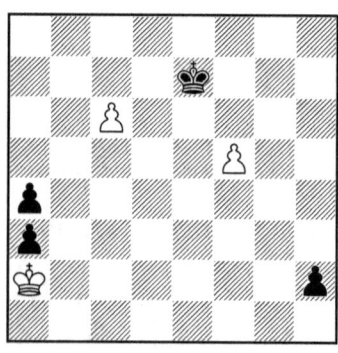

3.f6+! But not the immediate 3.c7? h1=♕ 4.c8=♕ ♕d5+ 5.♔b1 ♕d1+ 6.♔a2 (6.♕c1 a2+ 7.♔xa2 ♕xc1) 6... ♕b3+ 7.♔a1 ♕b2#.

3...♔xf6 4.c7 h1=♕ 5.c8=♕ ♕d5+ 6.♔b1! ♕d1+ 7.♕c1! a2+ 8.♔xa2! ♕xc1. Stalemate.

In **Study 245**, on the other hand, one needs to see the stalemating patterns at the point where the pawn endgame turns into a queen one.

No. 245**. Y. Bazlov and V. Kovalenko
64, 1970

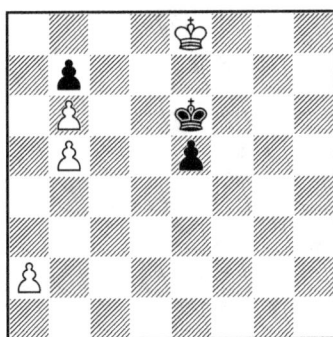

White to play and draw

1.a4 e4 2.a5 e3 3.a6 e2 4.a7! False try: 4.axb7? e1=♕ 5.b8=♕ ♕c3! 6.♔d8 ♕d4+ 7.♔c7 ♕d7#.
4...e1=♕   5.a8=♕   ♕e5! Domination.

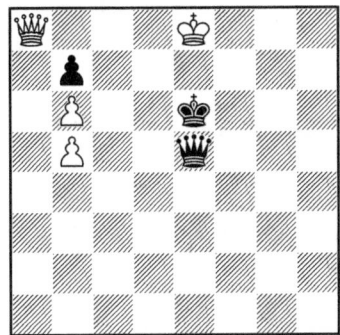

6.♔d8! 6.♕a2+? is hopeless: 6... ♔d6+! 7.♔f8 ♕e7+ 8.♔g8 ♕e6+

9.♕xe6+ ♔xe6 10.♔f8 ♔d6 11.♔e8 ♔c5 12.♔d7 ♔xb5 13.♔c7 ♔a6, and black wins.
6...♕h8+ 7.♔c7! ♕xa8. Stalemate.

Two echo-stalemates by a promoted queen are shown in **Study 246**.

No. 246**. V. Kovalenko
Magadansky Komsomolets, 1988
Commendation

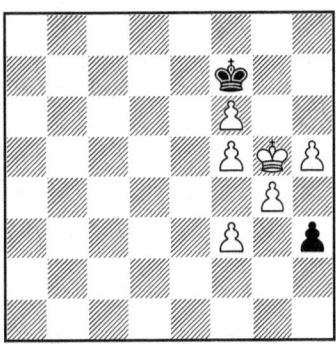

White to play and draw

1.h6 h2 2.h7! It's too early to close off the "house": 2.f4? ♔g8 3.♔g6 h1=♕ 4.f7+ ♔f8 5.h7 ♕c6+ 6.f6 ♕e4+, curtains.
2...h1=♕ 3.f4!

3...♕h2 4.h8=♕ ♕xh8, stalemate. Or **3...♔f8! 4.♔g6 ♕h4 5.g5 ♕h2**

6.f7 ♕h1 7.f6 ♕e4+ 8.f5 ♕h4 9.h8=♕+ ♕xh8 with an echo-stalemate.

Unfortunately, the play in the study is rather mechanical...

2.7. Anti-stalemate

To create a wholesome study, you need to both prevent the opponent's idea and execute your own. This counter-idea must be superior to the idea of the defending side – or at least be equal to it!

A stalemate is a spectacular idea, and it's hard to outdo it without underpromotion. Let's look at the tactical tricks that can help prevent stalemate.

No. 247. V. Archakov and M. Zinar
Nauka i Zhizn, 1986

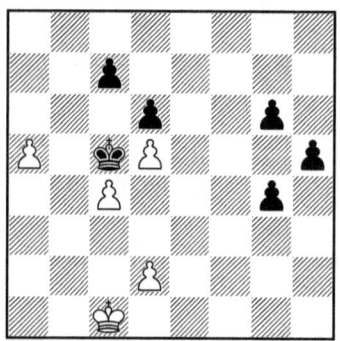

White to play and win

First things first: the menacing black pawns should be stopped.

1.♔d1! h4! 2.♔e2! Not 2.♔e1? g3!, and white is helpless against the opponent's three pawns, especially if he manages to push one to g2.

2...h3! After 2...g3 3.♔f3 c6 4.d4+!, the a-pawn queens.

3.♔f2! But not 3.♔f1? due to 3... g3. Even 4.d4+! does not help now: 4... ♔xd4! 5.a6 h2 6.♔g2 ♔e3 7.a7

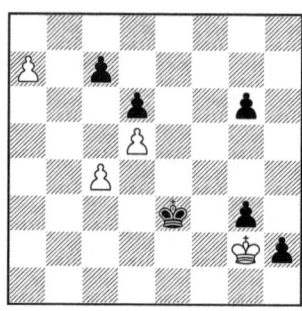

7...h1=♕+! 8.♔xh1 ♔f2 9.a8=♕ g2+ 10.♔h2 g1=♕+ with the white king getting checkmated.

3...h2 4.♔g2 g3

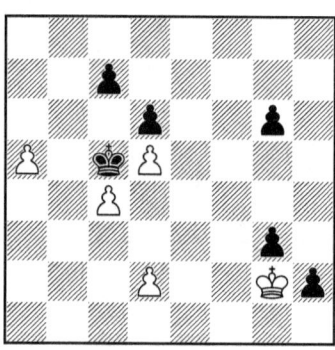

5.♔h1! Black has failed to get a good pawn position, but white has to be careful. 5.d4+? ♔xd4 6.a6 ♔e3, and black delivers checkmate. Black is now in zugzwang, and when he tries to extricate himself, white executes a breakthrough.

5...c6 6.a6! ♔b6

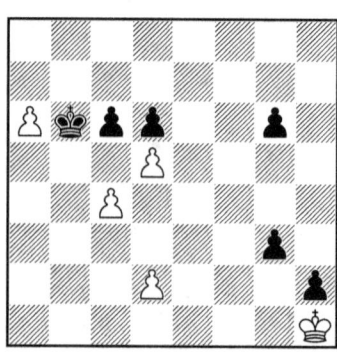

7.c5+! ♚xa6 8.cxd6 ♚b7 9.d7! White creates a strike group out of three pawns.

9...♚c7 10.dxc6 g5. A 1913 Rinck study is now on the board.

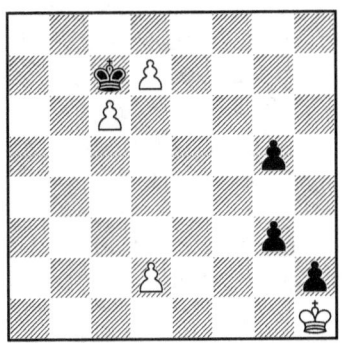

11.d3! ♚d8 12.d4 ♚c7 13.d5 ♚d8 14.d6 g4 15.♚g2 h1=♕+ 16.♚xh1 g2+ 17.♚g1. 17.♚xg2 is also possible.

17...g3 18.c7+ ♚xd7 19.♚xg2 with a win. After 11.d4? white would have been in zugzwang, while after 15.♚h1 g2+ the pawns mutually destroy themselves with stalemate.

No. 248. M. Zinar
Magadanskaya Pravda, 1986

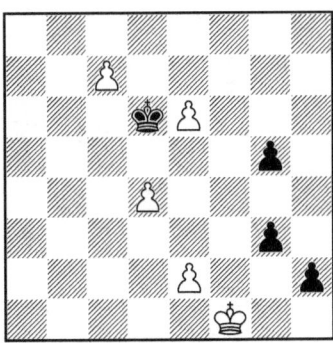

White to play and win

1.c8=♘+! The underpromotion to a knight with check forces the black king to retreat to the eighth rank. Not 1.♚g2? ♚xc7 2.d5 ♚d6 with stalemate;

black avoids zugzwang. For example: 3.e4 ♚e7 4.e5 g4 5.♚h1 ♚e8 6.d6 ♚d8 7.e7+ ♚e8 8.e6 g2+ 9.♚xg2 g3 10.♚h1 g2+ 11.♚xg2 h1=♕+ 12.♚xh1.

1...♚c7 2.♚g2 ♚xc8 3.d5 ♚c7 4.e7 ♚d7 5.d6 g4 6.e3! – the rest is simple.

The anti-stalemate motifs look distinctive and original in studies with a niche.

No. 249. Albert Belyavsky
USSR Central Chess Club Bulletin, 1981

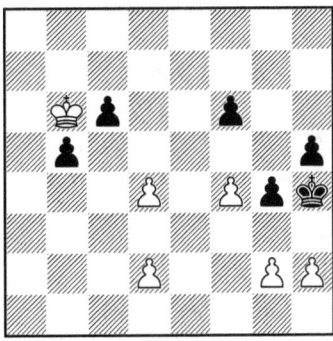

White to play and win

1.♚a5! Imitation of the solution (at least, this is what the author intended – see below): 1.♚c5? g3 2.h3 b4 3.♚c4 b3

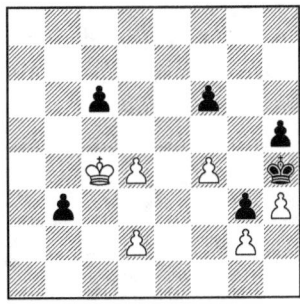

4.♚c3 b2 5.♚c2 f5, and white is in zugzwang: 6.d3 c5 7.d5 c4 8.d6 cxd3+ with a draw or 6.♚b1 c5 7.d5 c4 8.d6 c3 9.d7 c2+ with stalemate.

1...g3 2.h3 b4 3.♚a4! b3

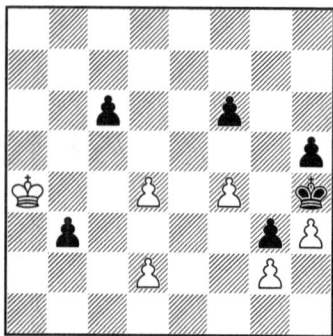

4.♔a3! b2 5.♔a2! Triple capture avoidance!

5...f5 6.d3! Of course, not 6.♔b1? with a draw.

6...c5 7.d5 c4 8.d6 c3 9.d7 b1=♕+ 10.♔xb1 c2+ 11.♔a2! with a win.

Alas, 1.♔c5 is not an imitation of the solution – it's another way to win: 1...g3 2.h3 b4 3.♔c4 b3 4.♔xb3! c5 5.d5 c4+ 6.♔c2! c3 7.d6 cxd2 8.d7, curtains.

Therefore, in the author's own intended solution, white, in addition to 4.♔a3, can win with the capture 4.♔xb3! etc.

Capturing the pawn also works on the next move: as well as 5.♔a2, white can play 5.♔xb2! So this effort fails as a study, but it's nevertheless instructive.

No. 250. V. Balanovsky
N. Grigoriev memorial, 1985
3rd prize

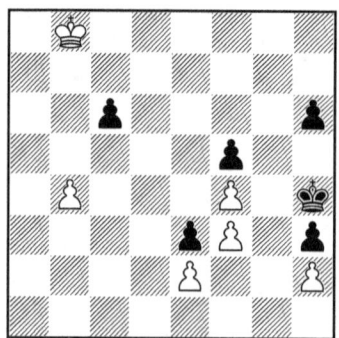

White to play and win (actually unsolvable)

Even at a glance, it's clear that black has prepared a stalemating niche for himself, and he will complete his mission with a couple of precise moves. Of course, the white king should move to the a-file. But where? 1.♔c7? doesn't work due to 1...c5! 2.b5 c4 3.b6 c3 4.b7 c2 5.b8=♕ c1=♕+ 6.♔d7 ♕d2+ 7.♔e6 h5, with a desperado queen. Then, 1.♔a7? h5 2.♔a6, and that's all?!

But what if we don't hurry? 1...♔h5! It turns out that it's not that simple! Let's continue: 2.♔a6 ♔h4! 3.♔a5 ♔h5! 4.♔a4 ♔h4! 5.♔b3 (after 5.♔a3 c5 6.b5 c4, the pawn is promoted with a check) 5...c5! 6.b5 c4+ with a check and draw. But...

1.♔a8!! A beautiful move!

1...♔h5! 2.♔a7! ♔h4 3.♔a6 ♔h5 4.♔a5 ♔h4 5.♔a4. Black is essentially inside the niche already, but he cannot self-stalemate: 5....h5 6.♔a5, and black is in zugzwang.

5...♔h5

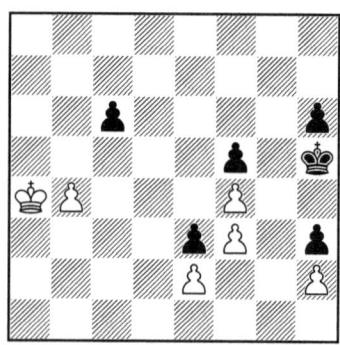

6.♔b3! ♔h4. If 6...c5, then 7.b5 c4+ 8.♔c3 ♔h4 9.b6 h5 10.♔d4 c3 11.b7 with a win.

7.♔c3 h5 8.♔d3(d4) c5 9.♔xe3 c4 10.♔d2! c3+ 11.♔c1 c2 12.e4, and the niche is destroyed. Probably the most distinctive composition of the Grigoriev memorial.

Alas, this brilliant study didn't withstand the test of time either! Instead of the author's solution 2...♔h4?, black can save the game with a spectacular move out of the niche – 2...♔g6!! 3.♔a6 c5! 4.bxc5 (4.b5 c4) 4...♔h5! 5.c6 ♔h4 6.c7 h5 7.c8=♕, and black is stalemated after all.

Now take a look at the interesting **Study 251**, which was composed after the first edition of this work. In this opus, white sidesteps black's stalemate counterplay with a subtle king triangulation.

No. 251**. A. Koranyi
Hungary 1100 JT, 1997
3rd prize

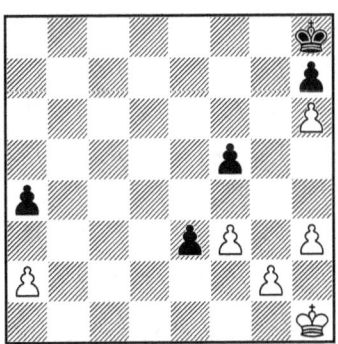

White to play and win

The introductory play isn't hard:
1.♔g1 f4 2.♔f1 ♔g8 3.♔e2 ♔f7 4.g3!
The game cannot be won without this break.
4...fxg3 5.♔xe3 ♔g6

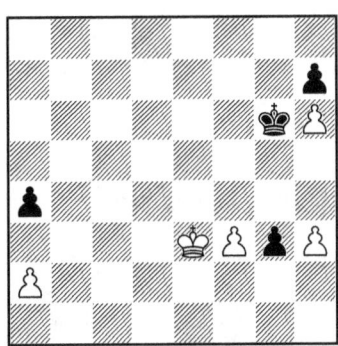

6.♔e2! And back! Not the hasty 6.f4? ♔f5 7.♔f3 g2 8.♔xg2 ♔xf4, draw.

6...♔xh6 7.f4! And now, it's too hasty to move the king: 7.♔f1? ♔g5 8.♔g2 ♔f4 (the simplest) 9.a3 h6 10.h4 h5 11.♔h3 ♔xf3, and white is stalemated.

7...♔h5 8.♔f1!! The point! False try: 8.♔f3? ♔h4 9.♔g2 h5 10.♔g1 a3 11.♔g2 with black stalemated. 11.♔h1?? even loses: 11...♔xh3 12.f5 g2+ 13.♔g1 ♔g3 14.f6 h4 15.f7 h3 16.f8=♕ h2#.

8...♔h4 9.♔g1! h6! 10.♔h1!! The white king returns to the initial square! But not 10.a3? h5! with white in zugzwang.

10...a3 11.♔g2! h5 12.♔g1! Black is in zugzwang!

12...g2 13.♔h2! (13.♔xg2?), and there's no stalemate. White wins. An original idea!

2.8. Underpromotions

2.8.1. One-time underpromotion (except knight)

There are many positions where victory is achieved after an underpromotion, but studies of such a type are too simple because it's hard to construct any interesting play that precedes the pawn promotion. A single example is enough to show this idea.

No. 252. V. Bron
Schach Echo, 1958
2nd honorable mention

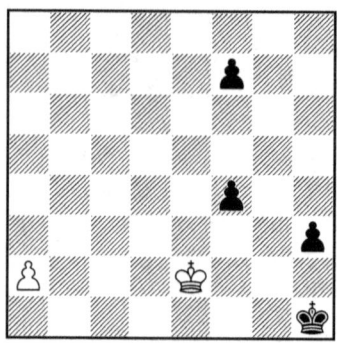

White to play and win

1.♔f1! But not 1.♔f2? h2 2.a4 f3 3.a5 f5 4.a6 f4 5.♔f1 f2 6.a7 f3, draw.

1...h2. If 1...♔h2, then 2.♔f2 with a win.

2.a4. The slow 2.a3? is met with the fast 2...f5 with a draw.

2...f3 3.a5 f6! Like white in **Study 241**, black loses a tempo and plays for stalemate with the pinned pawn.

4.a6 f5 5.a7 f4 6.a8=♖! f2 7.♔xf2 (or 7.♖a1) **7...f3 8.♖a1#** (or 8.♔xf2#).

Therefore, the authors are convinced that the most promising direction for studies with one underpromotion is the synthesis of anti-stalemate ideas with others. In **Studies 144** and **164**, we have seen serial synthesis.

Study 253 demonstrates more possibilities for synthesis.

No. 253. T. Gorgiev
64, 1935

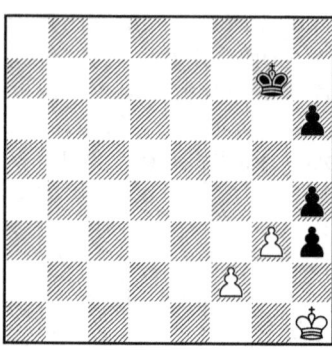

White to play and win

1.g4! After 1.gxh4? ♔g6 2.♔h2 ♔f5 3.♔xh3 ♔f4 4.♔g2 ♔g4, there's only a draw.

1...h5! 2.g5 ♔g6 3.f4 ♔f5.

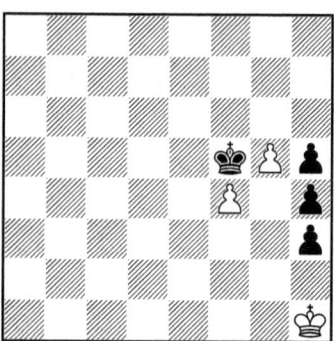

It seems that black is doomed, but here, two studies occur at once: the principled false try 4.♔g1? ♔xf4 5.g6 ♔g3 6.g7 h2+ 7.♔h1 ♔h3 8.g8=♕ – Jaenisch's stalemate! See also **Studies 237** and **238**.

And **4.♔h2! ♔xf4! 5.g6 ♔g5 6.g7 ♔h6 7.g8=♖!** with a win. A great study that synthesizes similar ideas through a false try!

Study 254 features a parallel synthesis of dissimilar ideas.

No. 254. E. Pogosyants
Udmurtskaya Pravda, 1976

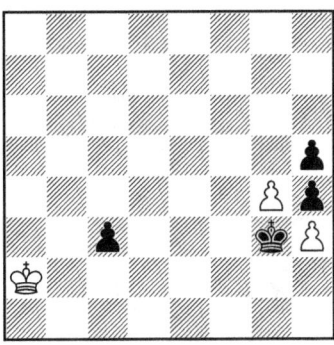

White to play and win

1.g5! It's a theoretical draw after 1.gxh5? ♔xh3.

1...♔f3 2.♔b1! But not 2.♔b3? ♔e4! – the Reti maneuver, with a draw.

2...♔f4! 3.g6 ♔g5 4.g7 ♔h6 5.g8=♖! Or **1...♔f4! 2.g6 ♔e3 3.g7 c2 4.g8=♕ c1=♕ 5.♕g5+** with a win.

Study 255 features a serial synthesis of dissimilar ideas with an underpromotion to a bishop in the finale.

No. 255. M. Zinar
Shakhmaty i Shashki v BSSR, 1989

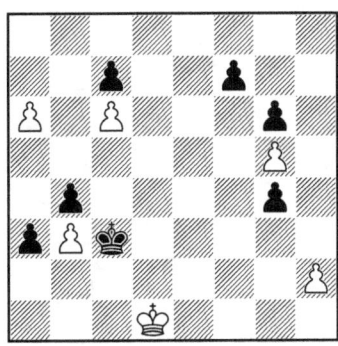

White to play and win

1.a7 a2 2.a8=♕ ♔b2 3.♕h8+ ♔b1

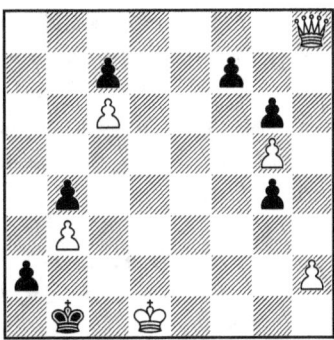

4.♕a1+! A spectacular queen sacrifice! It was performed twice in **Study 158**. Now the black king is trapped.

4...♔xa1 5.♔c2! The king is targeting the d3 square!

5...g3 6.hxg3 f6 7.gxf6 g5 8.f7 g4

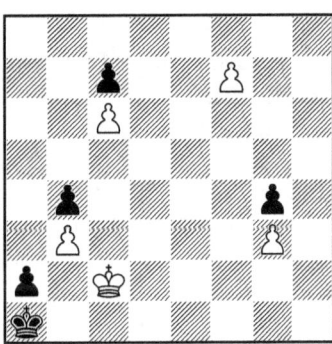

9.♔d3! Otherwise white will lose the pawn endgame after a queen trade; now, however, black gets a stalemating chance.

9...♔b2 10.f8=♗!, and white wins. But not 10.f8=♕? a1=♕ 11.♕f6+ ♔xb3 12.♕xa1, stalemate.

2.8.2. Underpromotion to knight

The knight is a unique piece. It has two differences from other pieces: the L-shaped movement trajectory and the ability to jump over pieces and pawns.

This allows you to use the knight both as an anti-stalemate tool and as a checking piece, as we have seen in **Studies 104, 105** and **248**. The piece can also be sacrificed or checkmate the king in a stalemating niche.

No. 256. D. Petrov
All-Union competition, 1938
Commendation

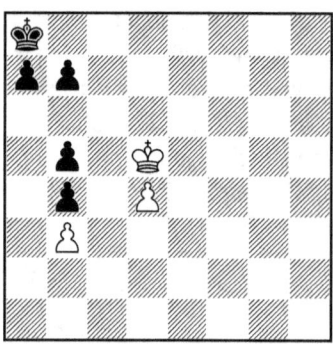

White to play and win

Black is planning to entomb his king. After 1.♔e6 a6! 2.d5 ♚a7 3.d6 ♚b6 4.d7 ♚a5, black either self-stalemates or, after 5.d8=♘ ♚b6!, trades the last pawn.

1.♔d6! ♚b8! 2.d5! b6! 2...a6 is met with 3.♔d7! ♚a7 4.♔c7! Both sides play very inventively!

3.♔e7 ♚b7 4.d6 ♚a6 5.d7 ♚a5 6.d8=♘!, and wins. For instance: 6...♚a6 7.♔d7 (the simplest) 7...♚a5 8.♔c6 ♚a6 9.♔c7 ♚a5 10.♔b7 a6 11.♘c6#. Compare it with **Study 231**.

Note that the Heijden study megabase considers **Study 256** to be flawed, stating that after 1.♔e6 a6 2.♔d7! ♚b8 3.d5, white wins. But this is cooperative play! The correct reply is 1...♚b8!! 2.d5 ♚c7 3.♔e7 a6 4.d6+ ♚b6 5.d7 ♚a5, and black saves the draw.

The knight constantly offers to sacrifice itself in the next example; the stalemate there is different, but still familiar.

No. 257. A. Kazantsev
Shakhmaty v SSSR, 1951
1st honorable mention

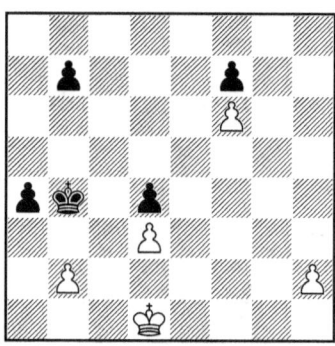

White to play and win

1.h4! ♚b3 2.♔c1 ♚a2! 3.h5 b5 4.h6 b4 5.h7 a3! Black gradually and subtly creates a stalemate position.

6.b3 ♚a1!

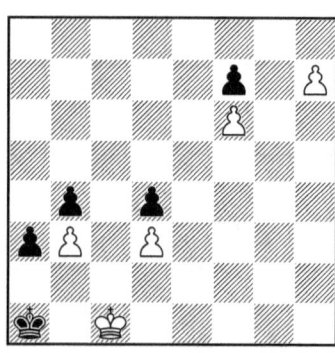

7.h8=♘! Unexpected! But after 7.h8=♕? a2 8.♔d2 ♚b2 9.♕d8 a1=♕ 10.♕xd4+ ♚xb3 11.♕xa1 it's stalemate.

7...♚a2 8.♔c2 ♚a1 9.♘g6! ♚a2 10.♘f4(f8) ♚a1 11.♘e6! ♚a2

12.♘xd4 with a win. The move 9.♘g6! shows that such sacrifices can be made repeatedly.

In **Study 258**, white underpromotes a pawn to a knight twice. There had been studies with three knights before it, but here black builds two separate niches. There's also a line with trapping of the black king.

No. 258. N. Grigoriev
Shakhmaty v SSSR, 1945

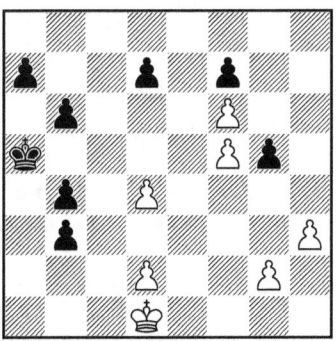

White to play and win

1.♔c1! ♔a4 2.♔b2 b5! Or 2...♔b5 3.d3! ♔c6 4.g3 ♔d5 5.h4 gxh4 6.gxh4 ♔xd4 7.h5 ♔e5 8.h6 ♔xf6 – the king is trapped, and white wins.

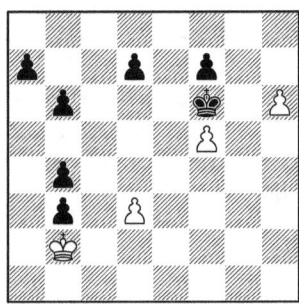

For example: 9.♔xb3 a5 10.♔a4 b5+ 11.♔b3 d6 12.d4 d5 13.♔b2 a4

14.♔a2 b3+ 15.♔a3 b4+ 16.♔b2 a3+ 17.♔xb3, curtains.

3.g3 a5 4.h4 gxh4 5.gxh4 d5

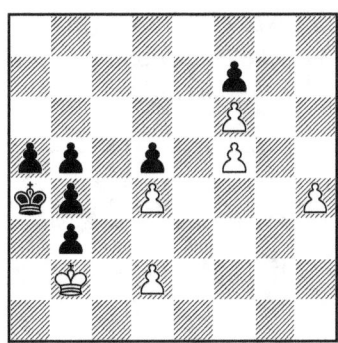

6.♔b1! White is forced to let the black king out of the trap. Not 6.♔a1? because of mate.

6...♔a3 7.h5 b2 8.h6 a4 9.h7 b3 10.h8=♘! **b4.** The entire "stalemate pavilion" on the queenside has moved one rank lower.

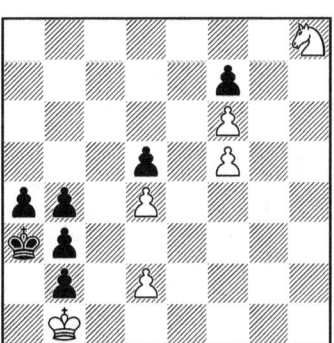

11.♘g6! fxg6 12.f7 gxf5 13.f8=♘! with checkmate.

In his last years, Nikolai Grigoriev leaned more and more towards artistic studies. This endgame study, published after the author's death, is good proof of this.

In **Study 259**, the author easily and casually (and way ahead of his time!) promoted three pawns into knights.

No. 259. H. Geiger
Deutsche Schachzeitung, 1920
(correction)

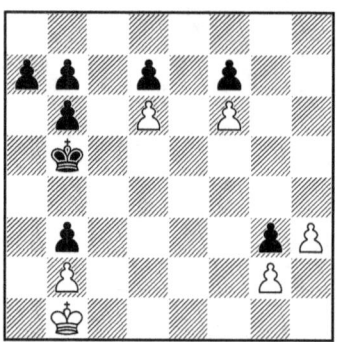

White to play and win

1.h4 a5 2.h5 ♚a4! 3.h6 b5 4.h7 b4 5.h8=♘! b5

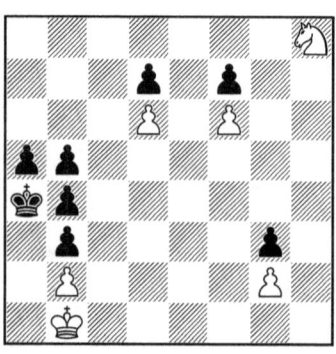

6.♘g6! fxg6 7.f7 g5 8.f8=♘! g4 9.♘e6! dxe6 10.d7 e5 11.d8=♘! with checkmate to come. Systematic movement!

The next study develops the same theme. After the three knights, a queen also appears, but it plays an auxiliary, rather than artistic, role. The scheme

allowed the composition of **Study 261** with four knights!

No. 260. V. Karhia
Suomen Shakki, 1943
1ˢᵗ prize

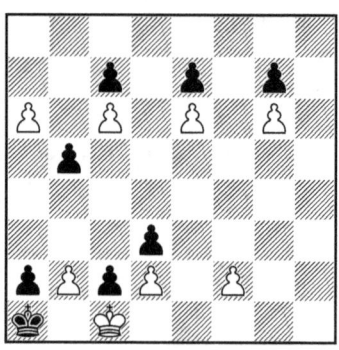

White to play and win

1.a7 b4 2.a8=♘! b3 3.♘b6! cxb6 4.c7 b5 5.c8=♘! b4 6.♘d6 exd6 7.e7 d5

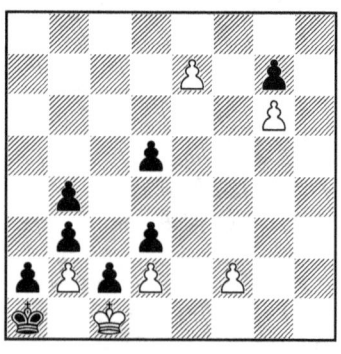

8.e8=♘! d4 9.♘f6! gxf6 10.g7 f5 11.g8=♕ f4 12.♕xb3 f3 13.♕xd3 b3 14.♕xb3 d3 15.♕xa2+! ♚xa2 16.b4 with a win.

No. 261. M. Zinar
USSR Central Chess Club Bulletin, 1983

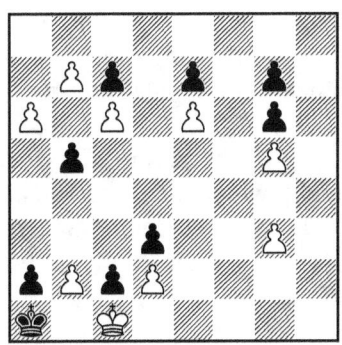

White to play and win

All sixteen pawns are on the board — a rarity for a pawn study! The hand automatically reaches for the b7 pawn, but do not hurry — it will turn into a knight only on move 10! 1.b8=♕? is bad due to 1...b4 2.♕xc7 b3 3.♕d6 exd6 4.e7 d5 5.e8=♘ d4 6.♘f6 gxf6 7.a7 fxg5 with stalemate.

The correct move is **1.a7! b4 2.a8=♘!** Again, 2.b8=♕? b3 3.♕b6 is bad: at the end of the solution, the a7 pawn will come one tempo short to deliver checkmate. Therefore, the last pawn should be promoted on a dark square!

2...b3 3.♘b6! cxb6

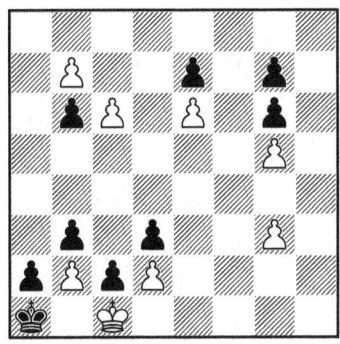

4.c7! (Note that the study is marred by the fact that 4.b8=♕ also wins after

4...b5 5.♕d6 b4 6.c7 exd6 7.c8=♕ d5 8.e7 d4 9.♕f5 gxf5 10.e8=♘!

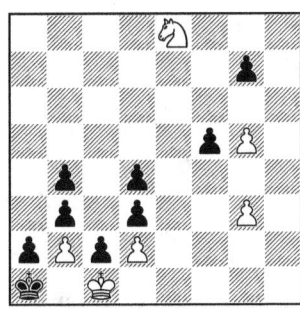

10...f4 (10...g6 11.♘c7 f4 12.♘e6 fxg3 13.♘xd4 g2 14.♘xb3#) 11.gxf4 g6 12.f5 gxf5 13.♘d6 f4 14.♘f5 f3 15.♘xd4 f2 16.♘xb3#.)

4...b5 5.c8=♘! b4 6.♘d6! exd6 7.e7 d5 8.e8=♘! d4 9.♘f6 gxf6

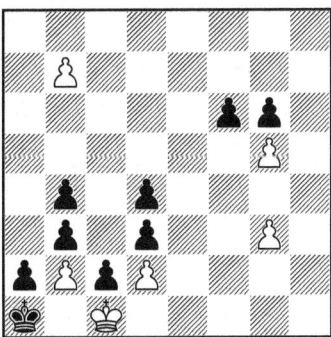

10.b8=♘! But not 10.b8=♕? f5! 11.♕xb4 f4 12.♕xb3 fxg3 13.♕xd3 g2 etc.

10...fxg5 11.♘a6 g4 12.♘c5 g5 13.♘xb3#.

The author did not intentionally want to complicate the theme with the opportunity of a premature b-pawn promotion. This was more or less forced, and we would have gladly eschewed that effect, even though it does have a certain aesthetic quality: the pawn stands on the verge of "coronation" for ten moves and then promotes to a knight!

But the price is too steep: long technical lines. And hyperbolization of the theme leads to increased analytical component.

The single knight underpromotion looks beautiful in conjunction with other ideas, as in the next study.

No. 262. N. Kralin
Shakhmaty v SSSR, 1981
Honorable mention

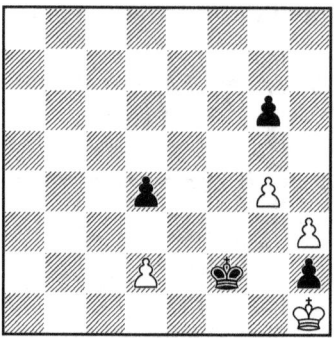

White to play and win

1.h4! d3! 2.h5 gxh5 3.g5! There's also an imitation of the solution: 3.gxh5? ♔e2 4.h6 ♔xd2 5.h7 ♔e1! 6.h8=♕ d2 7.♕h4+

7...♔f1! 8.♕h3+ ♔e1! 9.♕e3+ ♔f1! 10.♕xd2 – a Troitsky stalemate.

3...♔g3 4.g6 ♔h3 5.g7 h4 6.g8=♘! with a win – the Jaenisch stalemate is prevented by underpromoting to a knight. We see the synthesis of a stalemate in the imitation and in the main line of the actual solution.

Study 263 features mutual promotion to a knight, which, however, had already occurred in checkmate **Study 168**. Alas, the computer found a brilliant refutation!

No. 263**. V. Kovalenko
JC Topko – 50, 1994
1st prize

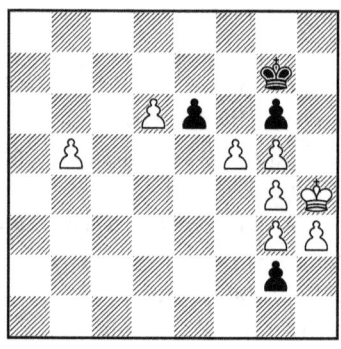

White to play and win (actually unsolvable)

1.f6+! The move order cannot be changed: 1.d7? g1=♘ 2.f6+ ♔h7!, and white is doomed.

1...♔f7 2.d7 g1=♘!

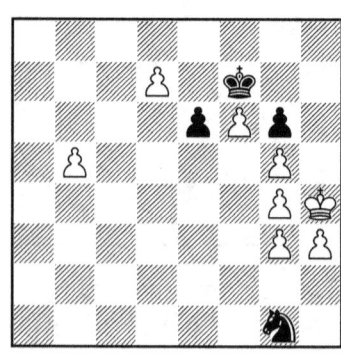

3.d8=♘+! **♚e8** **4.f7+** **♚f8** (4...
♚e7 5.♘c6+ ♚xf7 6.♘e5+ ♚g7 7.b6)
5.♘xe6+ **♚xf7** **6.♘d4** **♚e7** **7.b6** **♚d7**
8.b7 **♚c7** **9.b8=♕+** **♚xb8** **10.♘c6+**
♚c7 **11.♘e5!** The black pawn falls, and
the white king is freed from its prison.
White wins...

Except he doesn't. The computer
found the brilliant 11...♘f3+ 12.♘xf3
♚d6 and it's a draw! We can fix the
study by adding a white pawn, e.g. to d3.

The original idea of underpromotion
in **Study 264** is embellished by the
tortoise move at the very beginning.

No. 264**. V. Kovalenko
Uralsky Problemist, 2003
Special honorable mention

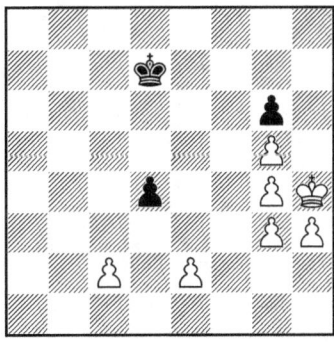

White to play and draw

1.c3!! Forcing black to capture the
pawn! Not 1.c4? ♚d6 (the simplest)
2.c5+ ♚xc5 3.e4 d3 4.e5 d2 5.e6 d1=♕
(or 5...d1=♘ 6.e7 ♘e3 with checkmate)
6.e7 ♕d7! 7.e8=♕ ♕h7#. 1.e4? is also
a mistake: 1...dxe3 2.c4 e2 3.c5 e1=♘!
4.c6+ ♚d6 5.c7 ♘f3(g2)#.
1...dxc3 **2.e4** **c2** **3.e5** **c1=♕** (3...
c1=♘ 4.e6+ ♚d6 5.e7) **4.e6+** **♚d6!**
5.e7 **♕c7!** Hoping for 6.e8=♕? ♕h7#.
Suddenly, **6.e8=♘+!** with a fork. Draw.

2.8.3. Parallel underpromotions

All pawn promotions in this group are
of an obviously anti-stalemate nature:
the pawn promotes to a weaker piece
because a queen would take the squares
away from the enemy king, which
leads to checkmate. Here we shall see
parallel synthesis of similar ideas. The
study only gets better if a similar idea is
repeated in one or more variations. We
are also going to see some twin studies –
"failed" parallel synthesis, so to say.

No. 265. V. Kovalenko
N. Grigoriev memorial, 1985
Commendation

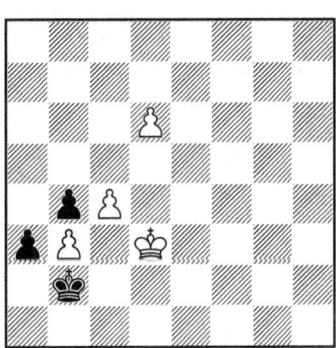

White to play and win

After the obvious **1.d7,** there are two
continuations:
A) **1...a2** **2.d8=♗!** with a win. There
might follow: 2...♚xb3 3.♗f6 ♚a3
4.♗a1! b3 5.♚c3, curtains.
B) **1...♚xb3** **2.d8=♖!**, also with a
win, but not 2.d8=♗? due to 2...♚a2!,
only drawing. For instance: 2...a2 3.♖a8
♚b2 4.c5 b3 5.♚c4! etc.
It's probably the most successful
variation on the theme of parallel
rook+bishop synthesis since the first
one – the 1915 study by the French
composer F. Lazard.

No. 266. L. Zalkind
La Strategie, 1916

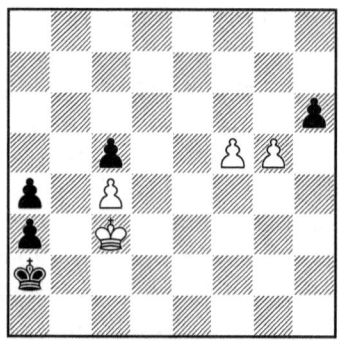

White to play and win

1.♔c2 hxg5 2.f6 g4 3.f7 g3

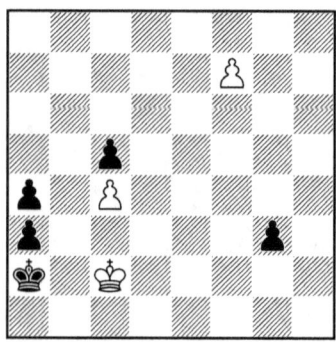

4.f8=♗! But not **4.f8=♕?** g2 5.♕xc5 g1=♕ 6.♕xg1, stalemate.

4...g2 5.♗xc5, and wins.

Or **1...h5 2.g6! h4 3.g7 h3**

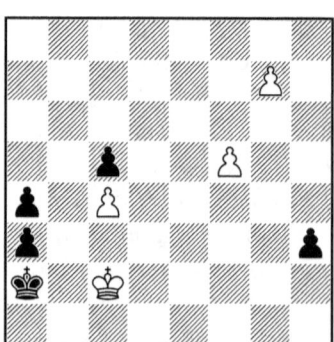

4.g8=♗! There's a familiar stalemate after 4.g8=♕? h2 5.♕d5 h1=♕ 6.♕xh1.

4...h2 5.♗d5 ♔a1 6.f6 a2 7.f7 h1=♕ 8.♗xh1 a3 9.♔b3! ♔b1 10.f8=♕ with checkmate. So in this study we find new stalemating positions and the appearance of two different bishops.

Soviet composer Lazar Zalkind suffered a tragic fate. You can read about him, and admire more of his extensive works, in the seminal book *The Lubyanka Gambit* by Sergei Grodzensky (Elk and Ruby, 2022).

In **Study 267**, there are two stalemates and two knights.

No. 267. J. Selman
Revista de Romana de Sah, 1939

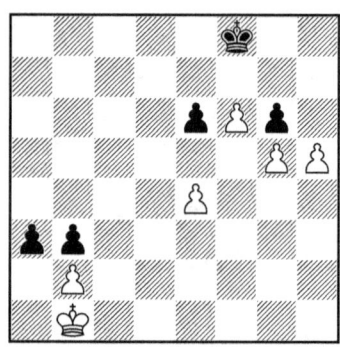

White to play and win

1.h6! a2+ 2.♔a1 ♔g8 3.e5. Black is in zugzwang.

3...♔h8 4.f7 ♔h7 5.f8=♘+! or **3...♔f8 4.h7 ♔f7 5.h8=♘+!**

70 years later, Mikhail Zinar executed the Selman mechanism in two parallel variations **(Study 268)**, with four knight underpromotions!

No. 268**. M. Zinar
Gulyaev and Kofman memorial, 2009
Special prize

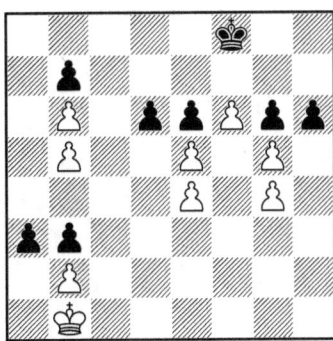

Black to move. White wins

1...a2+ 2.♔a1. The play branches.
A) **2...dxe5 3.gxh6 ♔g8 4.g5 ♔h8 5.f7 ♔h7 6.f8=♘+!** (6.f8=♕?, stalemate) or **4...♔f8 5.h7 ♔f7 6.h8=♘+!**
B) **2...hxg5 3.exd6 ♔e8 4.e5 ♔f8 5.d7 ♔f7 6.d8=♘+!** or **4...♔d8 5.f7 ♔d7 6.f8=♘+!**, every time with a win.

In **Study 269**, there are two rooks and two stalemates – similar to those in **Studies 144** and **265**.

No. 269. M. Zinar
64 – Shakhmatnoe Obozrenie, 1985

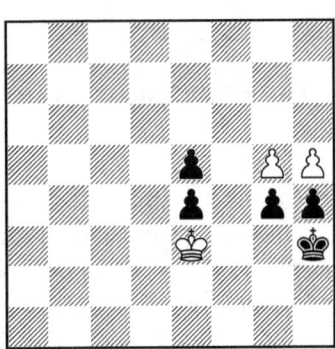

White to play and win

1.g6 g3 2.g7 g2 3.g8=♖! or 1...♔g3 2.h6! h3 3.h7 h2 4.h8=♖! with a win.

Interestingly, this position (in a mirrored version) was discovered back in 1965 by the Romanian study composer Paul Joita – see **Study 270**. So nobody is immune to repeating the past!

No. 270**. P. Joita
Revista de Romana de Sah, 1965

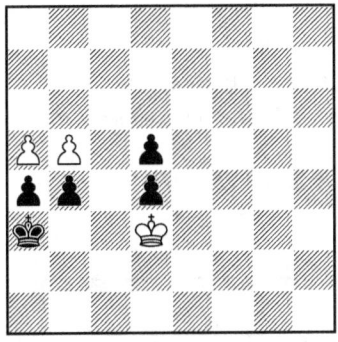

White to play and win

White wins with **1.b6!** etc.

We have not encountered any studies with parallel rook+knight or bishop+knight underpromotions, even though there are some twin studies with such piece combinations.

Underpromotions look good in twin studies where the anti-stalemate idea is flashy, but easy. The lines are similar and equal in value. We should point out that there is no reason to favor the form of twin studies if it is possible to synthesize the two lines without increasing the material too much. For instance, in **Study 269** you can remove the e5 pawn and put the black king on g3, getting a twin study. Although such a method is not recommended.

No. 269a.

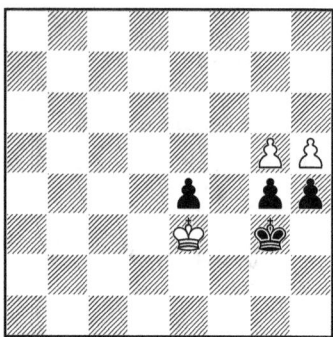

A) diagram;
B) move the king from g3 to h3
White to play and win

A) **1.h6 h3 2.h7 h2 3.h8=♖!**
B)

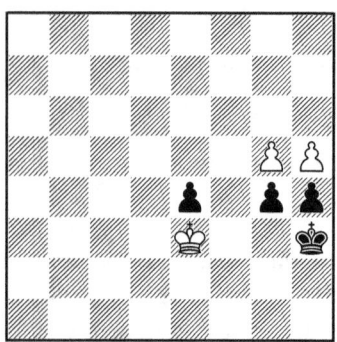

1.g6 g3 2.g7 g2 3.g8=♖!

The changes in twins' positions should be as small as possible. In pawn studies, only the oldest and most classical type of twins is usually used — with only a single piece replaced.

After the publication of **Study 265**, the value of **Study 271** decreased.

No. 271. P. Joita
Revista de Romana de Sah, 1965
3rd honorable mention

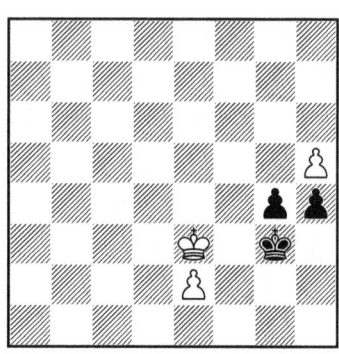

A) diagram
B) move the h5 pawn to a5
White to play and win

A) **1.h6 h3 2.h7 h2 3.h8=♖!** and
B)

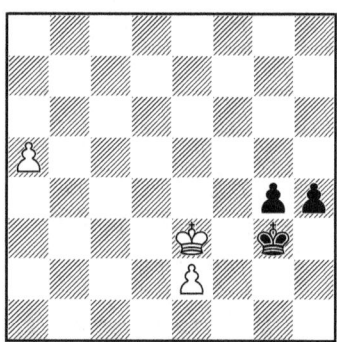

1.a6 h3 2.a7 h2 3.a8=♗!, winning in both lines.

Both in this and in the next example where the twins are created by shifting a single piece, the piece is moved to a faraway square but the positions still remain similar: the piece remains on the same rank and on the rook file.

No. 272. M. Zinar
64 – Shakhmatnoe Obozrenie, 1985

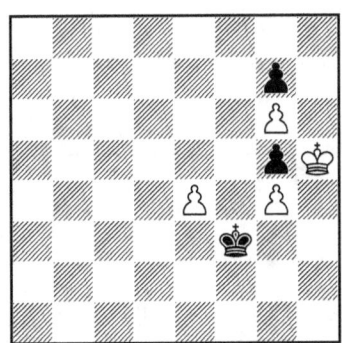

A) diagram
B) move the king from h5 to a5
White to play and win

A) **1.e5 ♚e4 2.e6 ♚e5 3.e7 ♚f6**
4.e8=♘+!;
B)

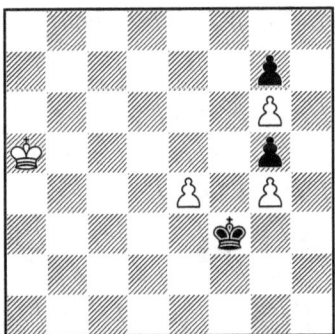

1.e5 ♚e4 2.e6 ♚e5 3.e7 ♚f6
4.e8=♖!. After 4.e8=♘? the pawns die:
4...♚xg6 5.♚b5 ♚f7 6.♘c7 ♚f6 7.♚c5
♚e5 8.♘d5 ♚e4 etc. New stalemating
positions in the finale.

In **Study 273**, Jaenisch's stalemate is
used in black's counterplay.

No. 273. M. Zinar
64 – Shakhmatnoe Obozrenie, 1985

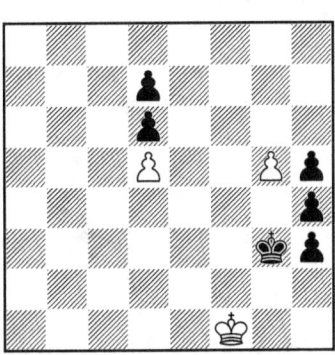

A) diagram
B) move the d5 pawn to d4
White to play and win

A) **1.♚g1 h2+ 2.♚h1 ♚h3 3.g6**
♚g3 4.g7 ♚h3 5.g8=♗!;
B)

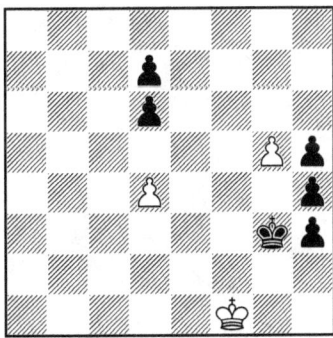

1.♚g1 h2+ 2.♚h1 d5 3.g6 d6 4.g7
♚h3 5.g8=♘! with a win.

2.8.4. Series of underpromotions

This group includes two studies
where both underpromoted pieces stay
on the board.

Study 274 is very good. Systematic movement of four (!) pawns ends with two promotions to a rook!

No. 274. V. Kovalenko
Vecherny Novosibirsk, 1980

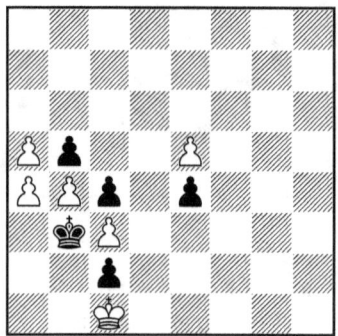

White to play and win

1.e6! bxa4 2.a6! e3. The first cycle! **3.e7! a3 4.a7! e2.** The second cycle!

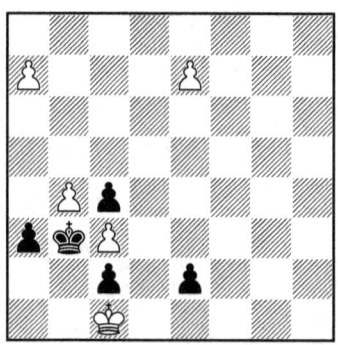

5.e8=♖! a2 6.a8=♖! e1=♕+ 7.♖xe1 a1=♕+ 8.♖xa1 with a win. A beautiful synthesis of ideas!

Alas, this study was also proven to be flawed. In addition to the author's intended 5.e8=♖, the queen promotion also wins: 5.e8=♕ a2 6.♕a4+! ♔xa4 7.♔xc2 e1=♘+ 8.♔b2, curtains.

The author himself later removed

this flaw in **Study 275**, adding two more pawns.

No. 275**. V. Kovalenko
Vecherny Novosibirsk, 1980
(correction, 1987)

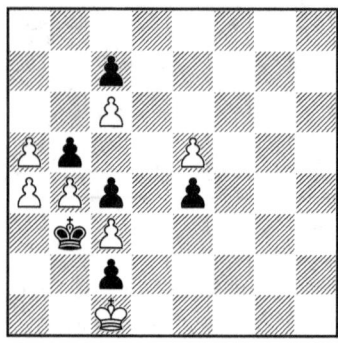

White to play and win

The solution is the same as in the previous study.

The bishops come in pairs in **Study 276**!

No. 276. M. Zinar
64 – Shakhmatnoe Obozrenie, 1983
Commendation

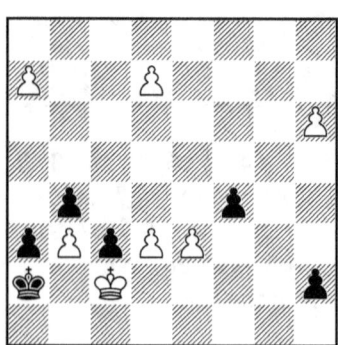

White to play and win

1.a8=♗! But not 1.a8=♕? f3 with a draw.

1...fxe3 2.d8=♗! e2 3.♗h4.

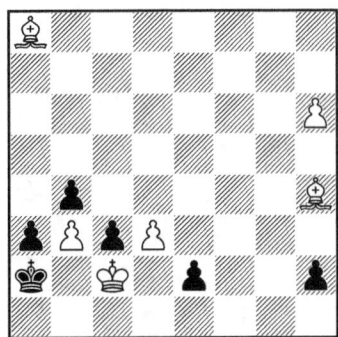

There are now two white bishops of different colors on the board. See also **Study 266** — the promotions are made in parallel there!

There might follow: 3...♚a1 4.h7 h1=♕ 5.♗xh1 a2 6.♔c1! e1=♕+ 7.♗xe1 c2 8.h8=♕(♗)#.

2.9. Studies with two or more phases

Established traditions pose less strict requirements on similarity and connectedness of component ideas for serial synthesis than for other types of synthesis. But still, a truly thematic relationship between the two ideas is desirable — not simply a technical one that becomes possible because of some move.

This relationship is obvious in a two-phase study with underpromotions. Let's start with an "almost pawn study".

In **Study 277**, black has a queen on g4. This position actually occurred after two introductory moves. Moreover, the queen arrived on g4 through normal play.

No. 277. V. Bron
Vechernaya Moskva, 1930
4th prize

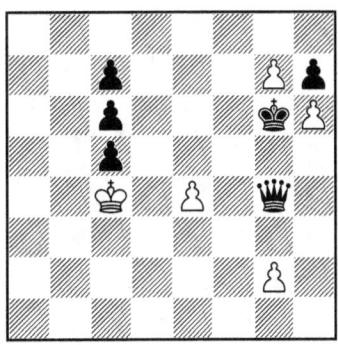

White to play and win

1.g8=♖+! ♔h5 2.♖xg4 ♔xg4

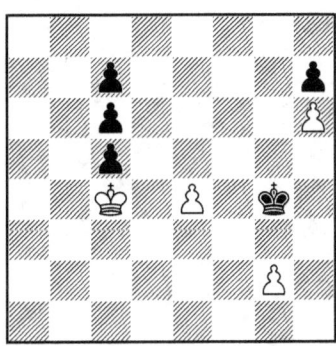

3.g3! ♔xg3! 4.e5 ♔f4 5.e6 ♔e5 6.e7 ♔d6 7.e8=♖!, with a win.

When the author composed **Study 278**, he didn't know about the above example, but his study turned out to be more valuable. Not simply because the second study is a "pure" pawn study, while the first is not. What's more important is that, in **Study 278**, the stalemates are removed further from each other, and the play is longer, even though its "plot" looks similar to the previous example.

No. 278. M. Zinar
USSR Central Chess Club Bulletin, 1978
3rd prize

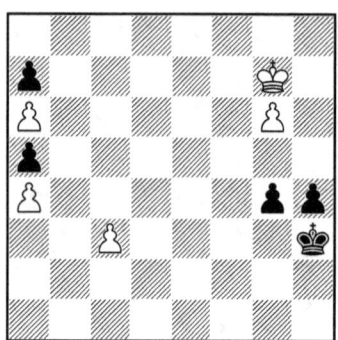

White to play and win

1.♔h6! g3 2.g7 g2 3.g8=♖! ♔h2
4.♔h5! h3 5.♔h4 g1=♕ 6.♖xg1 ♔xg1
7.♔xh3.

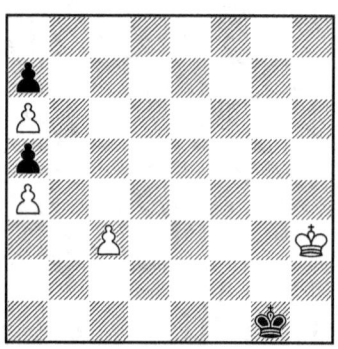

And now the second act of the drama
begins: the seemingly hopeless pursuit of
the pawn.

7...♔f2 8.c4 ♔e3 9.c5 ♔d4 10.c6
♔c5 11.c7 ♔b6 12.c8=♖! with a win.

Interestingly, the start of the solution
of the next study is exactly the same as
in this one, but the second phase of the
solution is entirely different!

No. 279. M. Zinar
Magadanskaya Pravda, 1986
Honorable mention

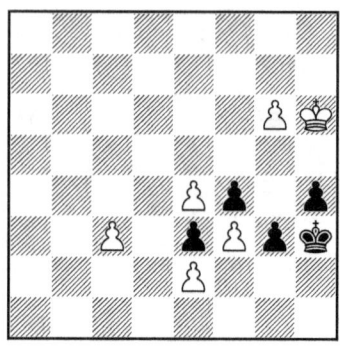

White to play and win

1.g7 g2 2.g8=♖! ♔h2 3.♔h5 h3!

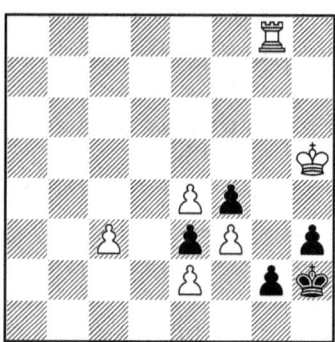

4.♔h4! g1=♕ 5.♖xg1 ♔xg1
6.♔xh3 ♔f2 7.e5 ♔xe2 8.e6 ♔xf3 9.e7
e2 10.e8=♖! with a win.

Study 280 is a great achievement by
the author! The phases with the rook
and bishop are connected smoothly
and simply – no technical pawns are
involved.

No. 280. V. Prygunov

64 – Shakhmatnoe Obozrenie, 1984

1st honorable mention

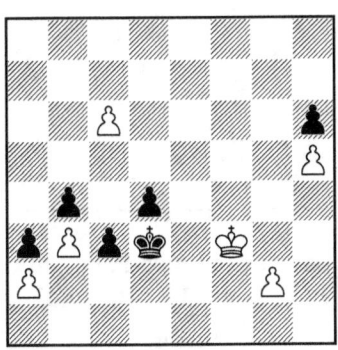

White to play and win

1.c7 c2 2.c8=♖! ♔d2 3.♔e4 c1=♕ 4.♖xc1 ♔xc1 5.♔xd4 ♔b2 6.♔d3 ♔xa2 7.♔c2 ♔a1

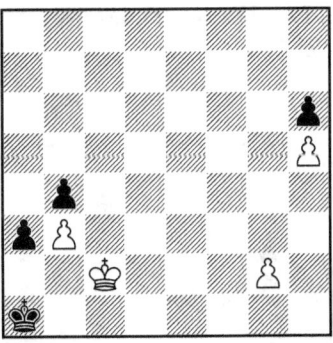

8.g4! ♔a2! 9.g5 hxg5 10.h6 g4 11.h7 g3 12.h8=♗! – we have already seen this promotion in **Study 265**, but here it occurs unexpectedly in an ordinary-looking pawn endgame and leaves a great impression!

The same material combination occurs in the next study as well, but the stalemates are delivered on d3 and b3, not on d3 and a2, as above. So it's a new variation on the bishop+rook theme.

No. 281. M. Zinar

64 – Shakhmatnoe Obozrenie, 1987

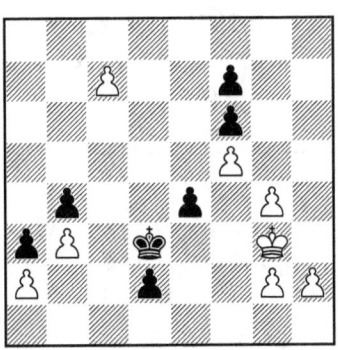

White to play and win (actually unsolvable)

1.c8=♖! There's a classical stalemate after 1.c8=♕? d1=♕ 2.♕d7+ ♔e3 3.♕xd1.

1...d1=♕ 2.♖d8+ ♔e2 3.♖xd1 ♔xd1 4.♔f4 ♔c2 5.♔xe4 ♔b2 6.♔d3 ♔xa2 7.♔c2 ♔a1

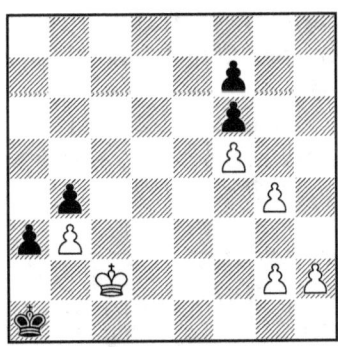

8.h4! a2 9.g5! fxg5 10.h5! g4 11.h6 g3 12.h7 f6 13.♔d3! ♔b2 14.h8=♗! with a win. The final play is already known from **Study 265**. The study would be somewhat less valuable than the previous one because of technical pawns.

Alas, the study is unsolvable. After 1...e3! 2.♖d8+ ♔e4, black saves the game. Thankfully, this can be corrected by moving the white c7-pawn to a different square – **Study 282**.

No. 282**. M. Zinar
64 – Shakhmatnoe Obozrenie, 1987
(correction)

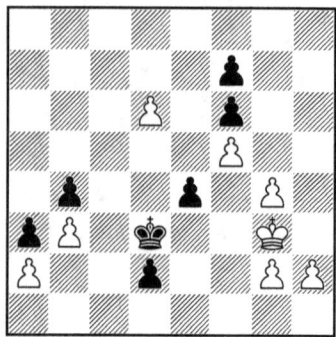

White to play and win

1.d7 d1=♕ 2.d8=♖+! ♔e2 3.♖xd1, and then following the previous solution.

Study 283 features a second phase with another underpromotion to a bishop.

No. 283. M. Zinar
Shakhmaty v SSSR, 1988
Commendation

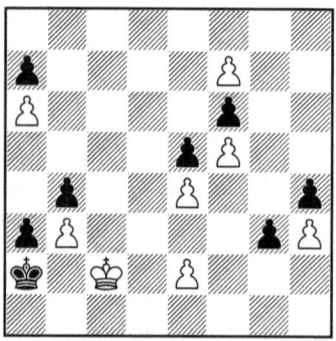

White to play and win

1.f8=♗! g2 2.♗c5 ♔a1! 3.♗e3! g1=♕ 4.♗xg1 a2

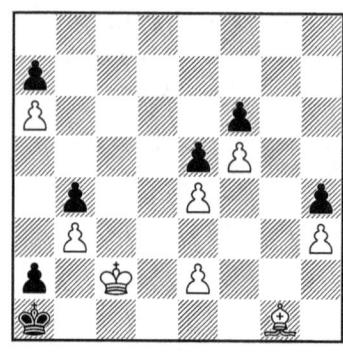

5.♗d4+! exd4 6.e5 fxe5 7.f6 e4 8.f7 d3+ 9.exd3 exd3+ 10.♔xd3! ♔b2! 11.f8=♗! with a win.

The initial position of **Study 284** suggests that some romantic play is involved; you expect something unusual. And the author does not disappoint!

No. 284. G. Nadareishvili
Shakhmatnaya Moskva, 1970
1ˢᵗ prize

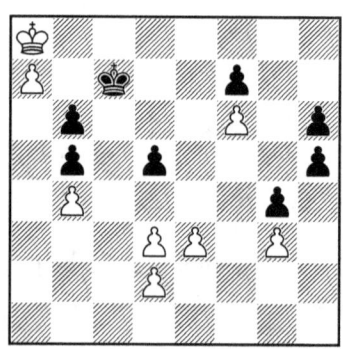

White to play and draw

1.e4! d4! 2.e5 h4 3.e6! h3 4.e7! h2

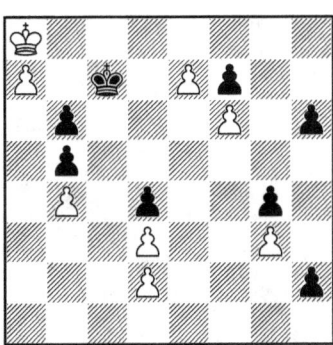

5.e8=♖!! Not 5.e8=♕? h1=♕+
6.♕e4 ♕f3! 7.♕xf3 gxf3 with a win.
    5...h1=♕+ 6.♖e4! ♕xe4+ 7.dxe4.
Another pawn study! And the pawns are
again promoted on the same squares.
    7...h5 8.e5 h4 9.e6 h3 10.e7 h2

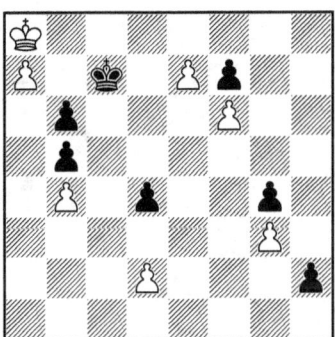

**11.e8=♘+! ♔c8 12.♘d6+! ♔c7
13.♘e8+** with perpetual check. An
outstanding composition! Of course,
one can complain about the technical
pawns on the b- and f-files, but when
you implement complicated ideas
you usually can't avoid a fly in the
ointment. The highlight of this study is
the underpromotion to a rook. In the
next study, the pawns are promoted to
knights twice.

No. 285. M. Zinar
Shakhmaty v SSSR, 1987

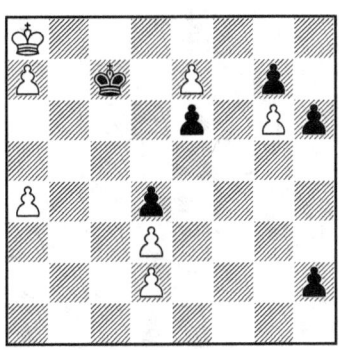

White to play and draw

**1.e8=♘+! ♔c8 2.♘d6+ ♔d7
3.♔b8 h1=♕ 4.a8=♕ ♕xa8+ 5.♔xa8
♔xd6**

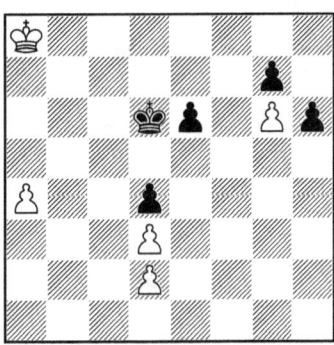

6.a5! But not 6.♔b8? due to 6...
♔c6, and black wins.
    6...♔c7! But not 6...h5? because of
7.♔b8!, and now white wins.
    **7.a6 e5 8.a7 e4 9.dxe4 h5 10.e5
h4 11.e6 h3 12.e7 h2.** The situation
suddenly repeats!
    13.e8=♘+! ♔c8 14.♘d6+! Draw.

In **Studies 286 and 287**, knight
underpromotion is used in black's
play.

No. 286. M. Zinar
Vecherny Leningrad, 1982

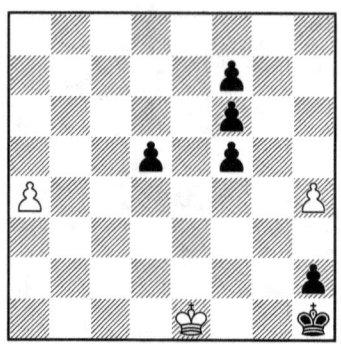

White to play and win

1.♔f2! d4 2.a5 d3 3.a6 d2 4.a7 d1=♘+! 5.♔f1! ♘e3+ 6.♔e2 ♔g1 7.a8=♕ h1=♕ 8.♕xh1+ ♔xh1 9.♔xe3.

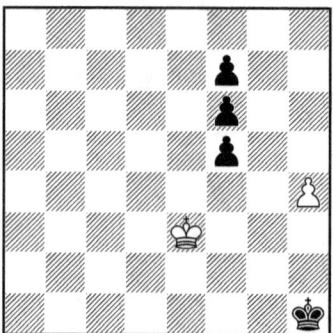

In the second phase (black's new intended stalemating position), white promotes his pawn to a rook.

9...♔g2 10.♔f4 ♔h3 11.h5 ♔h4 12.h6 ♔h5 13.h7 ♔g6 14.h8=♖! and wins.

No. 287. M. Zinar
64 – Shakhmatnoe Obozrenie, 1987

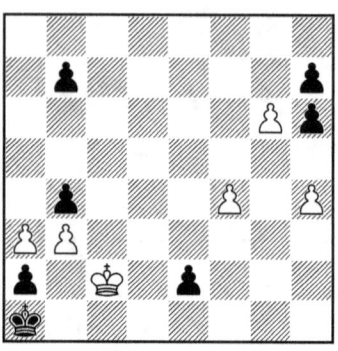

White to play and win

1.gxh7 e1=♘+! 2.♔c1 ♘d3+ 3.♔d2 ♔b1 4.h8=♕ a1=♕ 5.♕xa1+ ♔xa1 6.♔xd3 bxa3. But not 6...♔b2 due to 7.axb4 with a win.

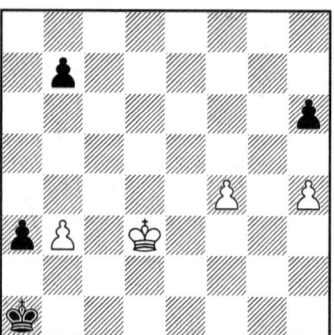

7.♔c2. The subsequent play is familiar: **7...a2 8.f5 b5 9.f6 b4 10.f7 h5 11.♔d3! ♔b2! 12.f8=♗!** with a win.

However, the next study really takes the cake among two-phase compositions.

No. 288. N. Kralin
Shakhmaty v SSSR, 1980
2ⁿᵈ prize

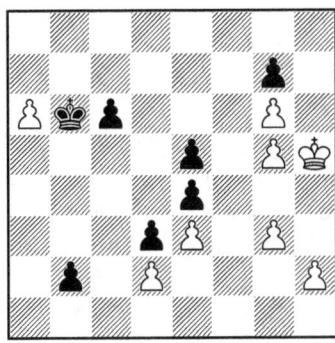

White to play and draw

1.a7! Getting rid of extra material is not easy – some precision is required. If 1.g4?, then 1...b1=♕ 2.a7 ♕h1! 3.h4 ♕xh4+! 4.♔xh4 ♔xa7, and black wins. While 1.h4?, hoping for 1...b1=♕ loses to 1...b1=♘! 2.a7 ♔xa7 3.g4 ♘c3!, and the weakness of the first move will only manifest itself on the 12ᵗʰ move (!!) in a most unexpected way (try playing through this yourself, basing play on the subsequent solution as far as possible)!

1...♔xa7 2.g4! Waiting for the black pawn to promote. If 2...b1=♕ then 3.h4 with stalemate.

2...b1=♘!

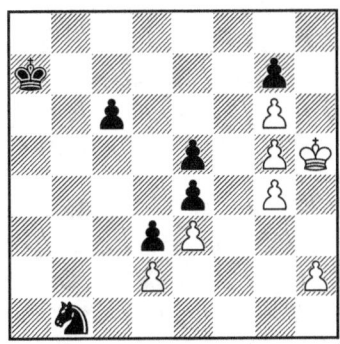

3.h3!! The black king is completely free to move, but still, black is in zugzwang!

3...♘c3 4.h4! ♔b7! 5.dxc3. A pawn endgame again.

5...d2 6.c4 d1=♕ 7.c5 ♕d4 8.exd4 e3 9.d5 e2

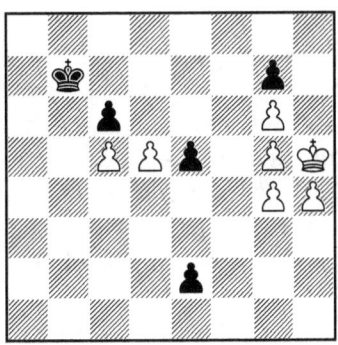

10.d6! But not the natural-looking 10.dxc6+? ♔c8! 11.c7 e1=♕ 12.c6 ♕xh4+!, and black wins.

10...e1=♘! The second knight!

11.d7 ♘d3! 12.d8=♘+! That's why the b7 square was bad.

12...♔a6 13.♘e6! ♘f4+ 14.♘xf4 exf4, stalemate.

A brilliant, masterful study: a long, 12-move zugzwang, three knights, niche stalemate, no technical variations, and no technical pawns!

A laconic study in conclusion.

No. 289. M. Zinar
Volgogradskaya Pravda, 1987

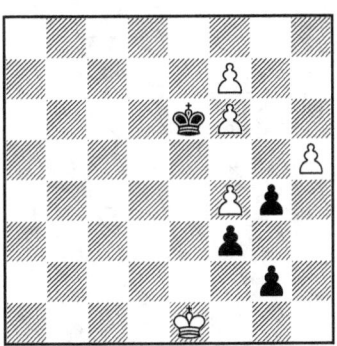

White to play and win

1.f8=♘+! ♚f7 2.♚f2 g3+ 3.♚g1 ♚xf8! 4.h6 ♚g8 5.f5. Black is in zugzwang, but the battle is not over yet!

5...♚f8 6.h7 ♚f7 7.h8=♖! with a win.

In a two-phase study with the pawn's breakthrough towards the promotion square (phase one), the subsequent play of the promoted piece should be interesting as well. In such a case, we are talking about the seamless transition of one phase to another. Here's a worthy example.

No. 290**. M. Dore
Chess Star, 2013
Commendation

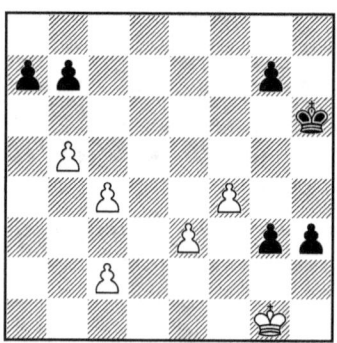

White to play and win

The pawn runs towards the promotion square: **1.c5! ♚h5! 2.c6 ♚g4!**

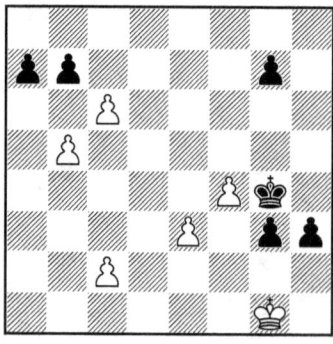

3.c7!! The capture spoils everything: 3.cxb7? ♚f3 4.b8=♕ h2+ 5.♚h1 g2+ 6.♚xh2 ♚f2! 7.f5 g1=♕+ 8.♚h3 ♕h1+ 9.♚g4 ♕g1+, and white cannot win.

3...♚f3 4.c8=♕! Starting the new phase: the black pawns should be stopped.

4...h2+ 5.♚h1 g2+! 6.♚xh2 ♚f2. And now, in comparison with the false try, the new queen is able to stop the pawn: **7.♕g4!** White wins. But not 7.♚h3? g1=♕ 8.♚h4 ♕g3+ 9.♚h5 ♚xe3! 10.♕xb7 ♚xf4 11.♕c7+ ♚f3! with equality.

Serial synthesis of two well-known ideas is found in miniature form in the next composition.

No. 291**. V. Kovalenko
Shakhmaty v SSSR, 1977

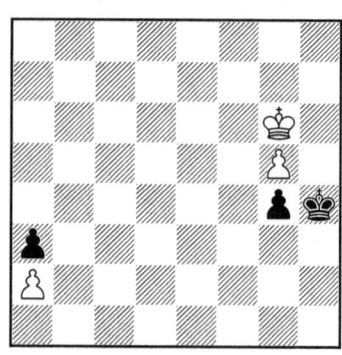

White to play and draw

The first phase involves promoting the pawns...

1.♚h6! g3 2.g6 g2 3.g7 g1=♖! Sidestepping the classical stalemate trap: 3...g1=♕ 4.g8=♕ ♕xg8.

4.♚h7 ♚h5 5.g8=♕ ♖xg8 6.♚xg8. In the second phase, the sides compete for the best possible route towards the remaining pawns...

6...♔g6!

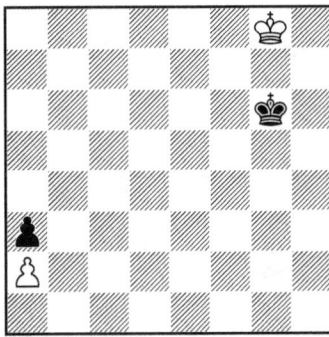

And we have reached a well-known 1924 F. Sackmann study.

7.♔h8!! ♔f6 8.♔h7! ♔e5 9.♔g6 ♔d4 10.♔f5 ♔c3 11.♔e4 ♔b2 12.♔d3 ♔xa2 13.♔c2. Draw.

It's not too hard to find a focus area for your work — just see how many combinations have still not been tried! But if they have already been used, this does not mean that you should not research them further. For instance, studies with rook+bishop promotions. First the pawn is promoted to a rook and then another is promoted to a bishop (in studies parlance we can call this sequence a first "variation" of the study). But what if you try to do it in reverse: a pawn promotes to a bishop in the first phase and to a rook in the second phase (a second variation)? It's possible that you might compose an original study with some special features.

Today, admittedly, you can't surprise anyone with a two-phase pawn study. **Study 292** features three distinct phases.

No. 292**. S. Didukh
Problemist Ukrainy, 2008
1ˢᵗ–2ⁿᵈ prize

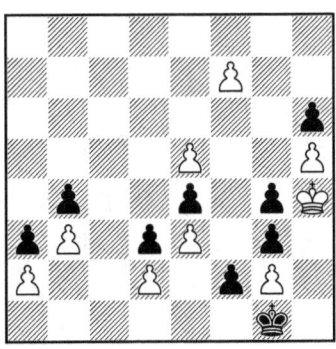

White to play and win

Both sides have a full set of pawns! The first phase is familiar: **1.f8=♖!** But not 1.f8=♕? ♔h2 2.e6 f1=♕ 3.♕xf1, stalemate.

1...f1=♕ 2.♖xf1+ ♔xf1. In the second phase, a stalemating combination in the center of the board is planned.

3.♔xg3. Not 3.♔xg4? ♔g2 4.e6 ♔f2 5.e7 g2 6.e8=♕ g1=♕+, and white cannot win.

3...♔e2! 4.e6 ♔xd2 5.e7 ♔xe3

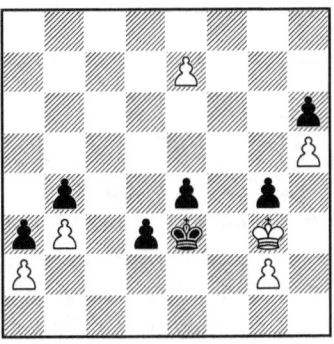

6.e8=♖! A pitfall: 6.e8=♕? d2 7.♕d7 d1=♕ 8.♕xd1, stalemate. **6... d2 7.♖d8 ♔e2 8.♔xg4 d1=♕ 9.♖xd1**

♔xd1. And now the third phase, with a new stalemating trap.

10.♔f4 ♔c2

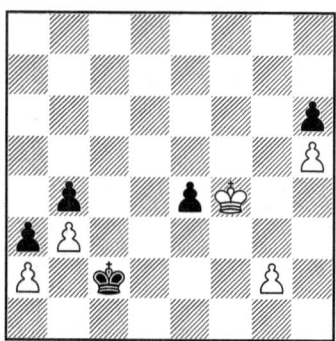

11.♔xe4 (11.g4? ♔d3 12.g5 hxg5+ 13.♔xg5 e3) **11...♔b2 12.♔d3 ♔xa2 13.♔c2** (13.g4? ♔xb3) **13...♔a1 14.g4 ♔a2** (14...a2 15.g5) **15.g5 hxg5 16.h6 g4 17.h7 g3**

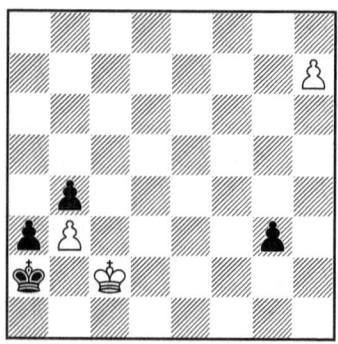

18.h8=♗! Not 18.h8=♕? g2 19.♕d4 g1=♕ 20.♕xg1 with a third stalemate.

18...g2 19.♗d4. White wins.

From the judge's report: "A masterful work! Yes, after three moves, an almost exact copy of the 1984 V. Prygunov study. But Didukh's study doesn't just have an extra rook. Two-phase and three-phase studies should be compared in geometric progression: it's not just 'one more', it's several times more!" (M. Zinar)

The next composition features four phases!

No. 293. D. Gurgenidze**
Problemist Ukrainy, 2008
1st–2nd prize

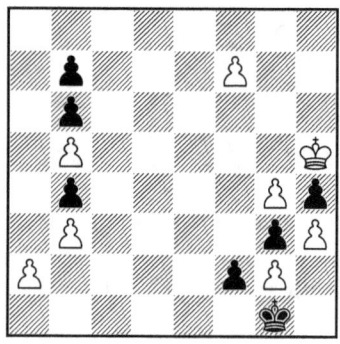

White to play and win

The first phase starts with a rook promotion: **1.f8=♖!** Not 1.f8=♕? ♔h2 2.g5 f1=♕ 3.♕xf1, the first stalemate.

1...f1=♕   2.♖xf1+   ♔xf1. The second phase begins...

3.g5 ♔xg2 4.g6 ♔xh3 5.g7 g2

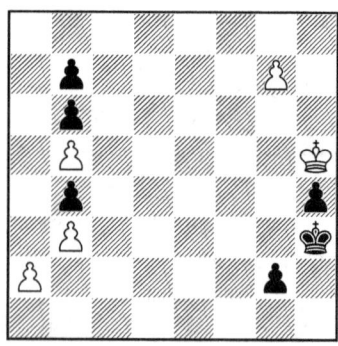

6.g8=♖! But not 6.g8=♕? g1=♕ 7.♕xg1, the second stalemate.

6...♔h2   7.♔xh4   g1=♕   8.♖xg1 ♔xg1. In the third phase, the opponents fight over the most promising version of the mutual zugzwang ♔d6-♚d4 or ♔e6-♚e4.

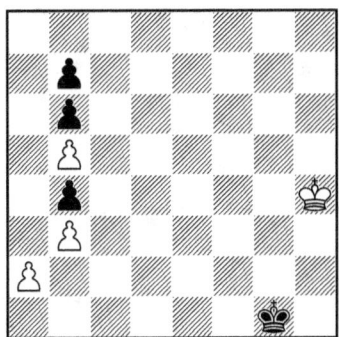

9.♔g5!! Both 9.♔g4? ♚f2 10.♔f4 ♚e2 11.♔e4 ♚d2 12.♔d4 ♚c2 13.♔c4 ♚b2 and 9.♔g3? ♚f1 10.♔f3 ♚e1 11.♔e3 ♚d1 12.♔d3 ♚c1 13.♔c4 ♚b2 spoil the win — black draws in both variations.

9...♚f2 10.♔f6! (10.♔f4? ♚e2) **10...♚e3 11.♔e7!** Not 11.♔e6? ♚e4 12.♔d6 ♚d4 13.♔c7 ♚c5; 11.♔e5? ♚d3 12.♔d5 (12.♔d6 ♚d4) 12...♚c3, draw.

11...♚e4 (11...♚d4 12.♔d6 ♚c3 13.♔c7) **12.♔e6!** The first zugzwang opposition!

12...♚d3 13.♔d7! ♚d4 14.♔d6! And the second! But not 14.♔c7? ♚c5, draw.

14...♚c3

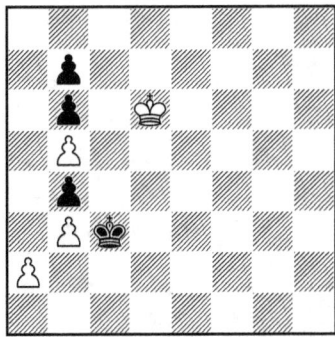

15.♔c7. The fourth phase: getting the pawn to the promotion square.

15...♚b2 16.♔xb7 (16.♔xb6? ♚xa2) **16...♚xa2 17.♔xb6 ♚xb3 18.♔c5!** The symmetrical 18.♔a5? misses the win: 18...♚a3! 19.b6 b3 20.b7 b2 21.b8=♕ b1=♕ 22.♕xb1, with a third stalemate.

18...♚c3 19.b6. White wins.

From the judge's report: "Yes, two rook promotions and systematic movements have already occurred in Davranian and Zinar, 1988. But the author found one more study after three phases!.." (M. Zinar.)

The phase transitions in **Study 294** are spectacular.

No. 294**. I. Aliev
MT Grigoriev – 120, 2016
2nd prize

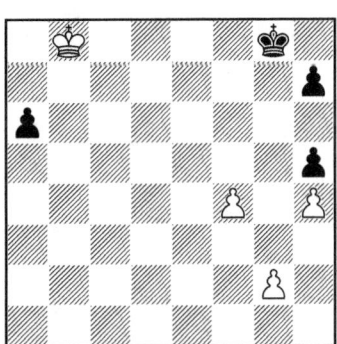

White to play and win

First, there's a Reti chase: **1.♔c7! a5 2.♔d6 a4.** After 2...♚f7, the white monarch catches up with the runaway pawn — 3.♔c5 and a simple win.

3.♔e7 a3 4.f5 a2 5.f6 a1=♕ 6.f7+ ♚g7 7.f8=♕+ ♚g6. The pawn endgame has transposed into a queen one (the second phase). Now white needs to find a good way to trade queens...

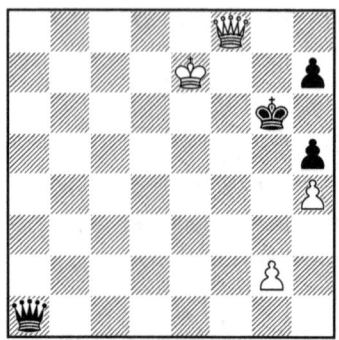

8.♛f7+! But not 8.♛g8+? ♛g7+ 9.♛xg7+ ♔xg7, draw.

8...♔h6 9.♛f4+! It's stalemate after 9.♛f6+? ♛xf6+ 10.♔xf6.

9...♔g7 10.♛g5+ ♔h8 11.♛f6+! ♛xf6+ **12.♔xf6 ♔g8.** And another pawn endgame (the third phase)!

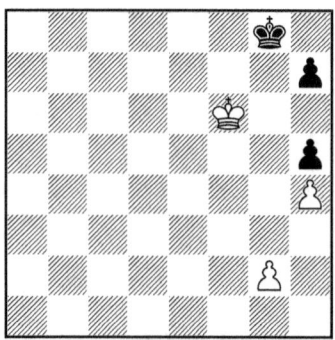

13.♔g5 ♔g7 14.♔xh5 ♔g8 15.♔h6 ♔h8 16.h5. An organic transposition: the move h4-h5 can be made at any time between the 16th and 19th moves...

16...♔g8

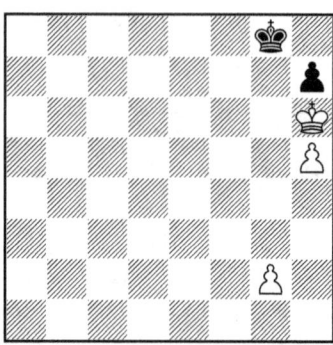

17.g3!! A tortoise move that ensures an advantageous version of mutual zugzwang (the fourth phase).

17...♔h8 18.g4 ♔g8 19.g5 ♔h8 20.g6 hxg6 (20...♔g8 21.g7) **21.hxg6 ♔g8 22.g7.** White wins.

If someone says that the theme of multi-phase pawn studies has been exhausted, and no more original ideas can be found, do not believe them! There are still some brilliant discoveries to be made! The next study serves as good proof.

No. 295**. A. Botokanov
64 – Shakhmatnoe Obozrenie, 2004
2nd prize

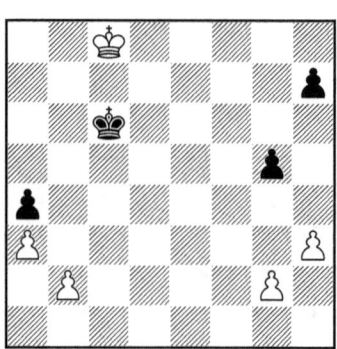

White to play and win

It's too early to run towards the kingside: 1.♔d8? ♔d6 2.g4 (2.♔e8 ♔e5

3.♔f7 ♚f4 4.♔g7 h5 5.♔g6 h4 6.♔h5 ♚f5 7.♔h6 ♚f6) 2...♚e5! 3.♔e7 ♚e4! 4.♔e6!

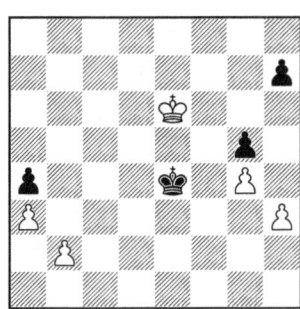

4...h6! 5.♔f6 ♚d3 6.♔g6 ♚c2 7.♔xh6 ♚xb2 8.♔xg5 ♚xa3 9.♔h5 ♚b4 10.g5 a3 11.g6 a2 12.g7 a1=♕ 13.g8=♕ ♕e5+ 14.♕g5 ♕h8+, and the queen endgame is not winnable.

Eureka: white should give up the right to move! **1.g4!!** ♔c5! After 1...♔d6 2.♔b7 ♚c5 3.♔a6 ♚c4 4.♔a5 ♚b3 5.♔b5, it's curtains.

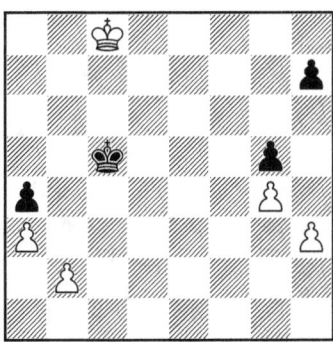

2.♔c7! Turning right is still a mistake: 2.♔d7? ♚d5 3.♔e7 ♚e4! 4.♔e6 h6! 5.♔f6 ♚d3 6.♔g6 ♚c2 etc., with a draw.

2...h6! Black has seized the opposition, so has he now secured the draw?

Suddenly: **3.♔b7!! ♚b5 4.♔a7! ♚a5**

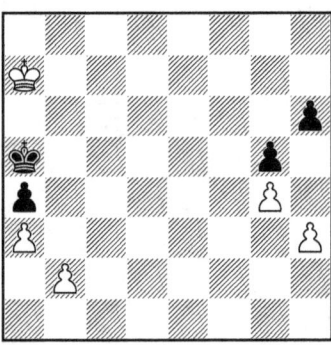

5.♔b8!! That's the trick: the black king had been pulled to a square which is three moves away from the b2 pawn! The battle for opposition continues on the last rank (the second phase).

5...♚b6 (5...♚b5 6.♔b7 ♚c4 7.♔b6) **6.♔c8! ♚c6 7.♔d8 ♚d6 8.♔e8 ♚e6** (8...♚c5 9.♔e7! ♚d5 10.♔d7) **9.♔f8 ♚f6 10.♔g8 ♚g6**

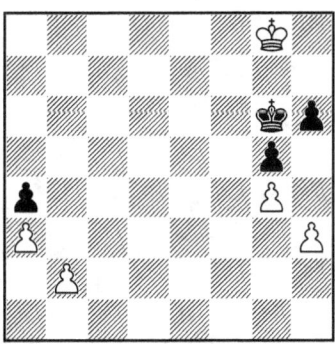

11.♔h8! It turns out that the black pawn blocks his own king from maintaining the opposition:

11...♚f6. Or 11...h5 12.gxh5+ ♚xh5 13.♔g7(h7), curtains.

12.♔h7 ♚f7 13.♔xh6 ♚f6 14.♔h5! White wins. Amazing white king play — from one flank to the other!

The task **Study 296** demonstrates five queen trades. Five phases in total!

No. 296**. V. Kovalenko
Moscow championship, 2006
2nd prize

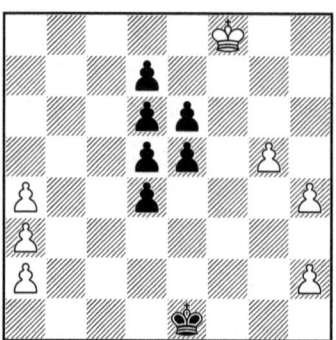

White to play and win

1.g6 d3 2.g7 d2 3.g8=♕ d1=♕
4.♕g1+ ♔d2

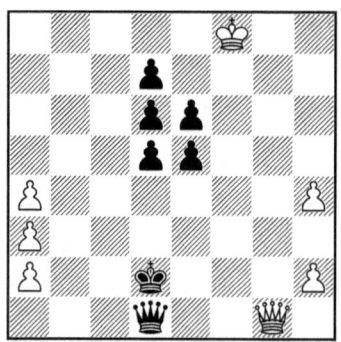

5.♕xd1+ ♔xd1. The first trade!
6.h5 e4 7.h6 e3 8.h7 e2 9.h8=♕
e1=♕ 10.♕a1+ ♔e2

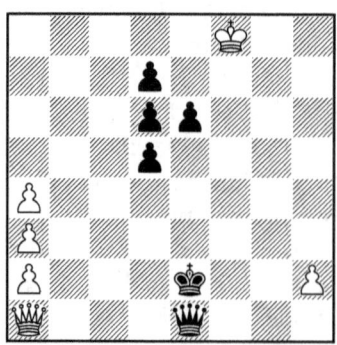

11.♕xe1+ ♔xe1. The second!
12.a5 d4 13.a6 d3 14.a7 d2 15.a8=♕
d1=♕ 16.♕h1+ ♔d2

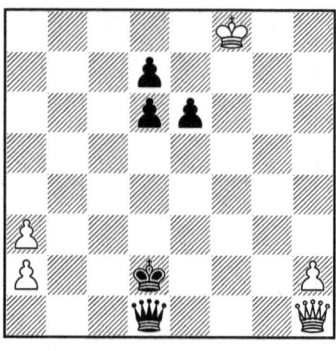

17.♕xd1+ ♔xd1. The third!
18.h4 e5 19.h5 e4 20.h6 e3 21.h7 e2
22.h8=♕ e1=♕ 23.♕a1+ ♔e2

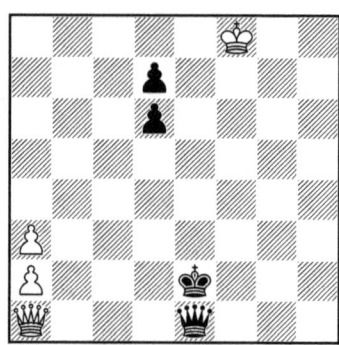

24.♕xe1+ ♔xe1. The fourth!
25.a4 d5 26.a5 d4 27.a6 d3 28.a7 d2
29.a8=♕ d1=♕ 30.♕h1+ ♔d2

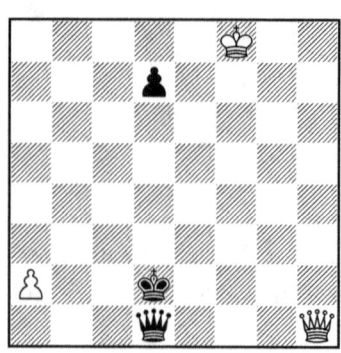

31.♕xd1+ ♔xd1. The fifth!
**32.a4 d5 33.a5 d4 34.a6 d3 35.a7 d2
36.a8=♕.** White wins.

2.10. Domination

This group consists of studies where winning the queen plays an important part. This is often achieved by winning several queens in sequence. Strictly speaking, if we define "domination" as complete reign over the board, then winning two queens, let alone just one, can hardly be classified as domination. However, composers may define that term as simply winning or trapping the queen, even though they do accept that true reign over the board is only felt if three or even more queens are won.

Winning one queen has no aesthetic value – it's simply a good embellishment for a study. We have seen such studies repeatedly – winning the queen was only a secondary idea for them. First, go back and take another look at Henri Rinck's **Study 56**.

The idea of Rinck's study was significantly improved in the next one.

No. 297. N. Grigoriev
64, 1937

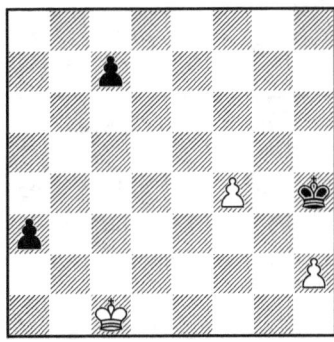

White to play and win

1.h3 c5 2.♔b1! c4 3.♔a2 c3!

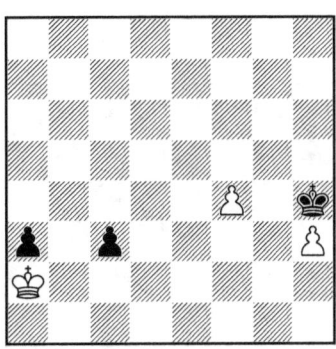

4.♔b3! If 4.♔xa3?, then 4...♔g3!! (leaving the square of the f-pawn) 5.f5 ♔f4 6.f6 ♔e3 7.f7 c2 8.f8=♕ c1=♕+, and black saves the game with the Reti maneuver. 4.♔b3!, on the other hand, is a feint that allows white to capture the pawn on a2.

4...a2 5.♔xa2 ♔g3! 6.f5 ♔f4. But not 6...♔f3 due to 7.♔b1!, with a win.

7.f6 ♔e3 8.f7 c2 9.f8=♕ c1=♕ 10.♕h6+, winning the queen.

No. 298. N. Grigoriev
Shakhmaty, 1929

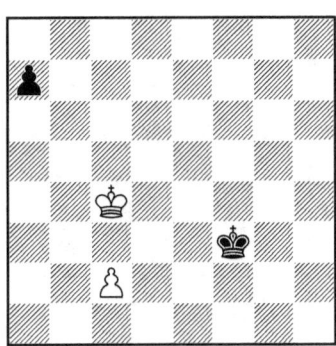

White to play and win

1.♔d4! Shouldering the king.
1...♔f4! 2.c4 ♔f5. If 2...a5 3.c5 a4, then the white king will stop the pawn.

3.♔d5 ♚f6. If 3...a5, then the white pawn promotes with a check: 4.c5 etc.

4.♔d6 a5. Now the pawn promotes without check. If 4...♚f7, then 5.c5 ♔e8 6.♔c7!, again promoting with a check.

5.c5 a4 6.c6 a3 7.c7 a2 8.c8=♕ a1=♕ 9.♕h8+ etc.

No. 299. H. Rinck
Deutsche Schachzeitung, 1929
(correction by M. Zinar, 1990)

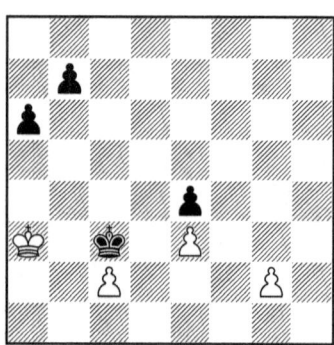

White to play and win

1.g4! ♔c4 2.g5! ♔d5 3.c4+ ♔e6 4.c5. White fixes the hole on b6.

4...♔f5 5.♔a4(b4) ♔xg5 6.♔a5 ♔f6. The king will be checked on the h3-c8 diagonal, but it's important to get

closer, because otherwise after 7.♔b6 a5 white will simply play 8.♔xa5 etc.

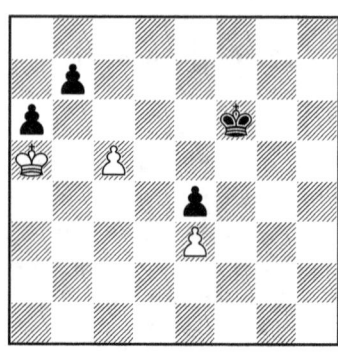

7.♔b6 a5 8.♔xb7 a4 9.c6 a3 10.c7 a2 11.c8=♕ a1=♕ 12.♕h8+ with a win.

In the first part of **Study 300**, there's a race between passed pawns. Black performs a Reti double threat.

No. 300. M. Zinar
Novaya Zhizn, 1988

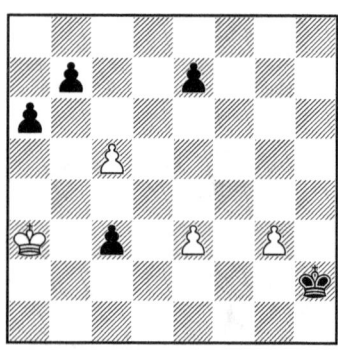

White to play and win

1.g4! ♔g3 2.g5 ♔f3! 3.♔b3 ♔e4! 4.♔xc3 ♔f5 5.♔b4 ♔xg5 6.♔a5 etc., like in the previous study.

When two queens are won, or only one queen is won, but in two different ways, then the idea of winning the queen becomes the main one. There are a lot of these studies. Here we show what we consider to be the best ones, where the queens are won after some interesting play.

No. 301. A. Mandler
Prace, 1955

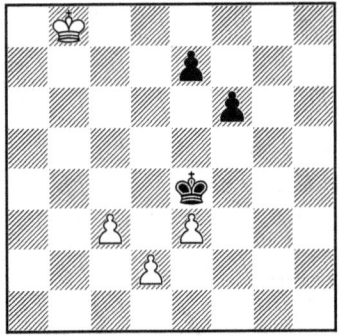

White to play and win

1.c4 f5 2.♔a7!! A great and original move! The c-pawn's advance must be prepared, but without blocking the pawn's promotion square. Regrettably, the study has a side solution that doesn't reflect the main idea. White can also play 2.c5! ♔d5 3.d4 e5 4.♔b7 f4 5.exf4 exf4 (5...e4 6.c6 e3 7.c7 e2 8.c8=♕ e1=♕ 9.♕c5+) 6.c6 f3 7.c7 f2 8.c8=♕ f1=♕ 9.♕d7+ ♔c4 10.d5, and white will win.

2...e5 3.c5 f4 4.c6 f3 5.c7 f2 6.c8=♕ f1=♕ 7.♕b7+! ♔f5 8.♕f7+, skewering the queen vertically. While after 7...♔d3 8.♕a6(b5)+, the queen falls due to the diagonal skewer.

No. 302. A. Selezniev
Pravda, 1927
4th honorable mention
(correction by N. Grigoriev, 1931)

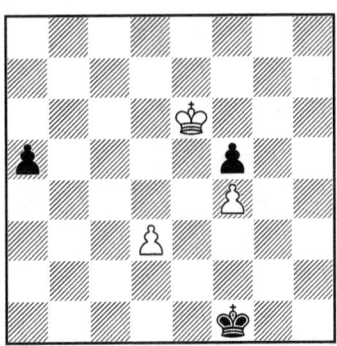

White to play and win

1.♔d5 ♔e2 2.♔c4! But not 2.d4? ♔d3 and a draw or 2.♔d4? a4 3.♔c4 a3 and black wins.

2...♔e3 3.d4 ♔xf4 4.d5 ♔e5 5.♔c5

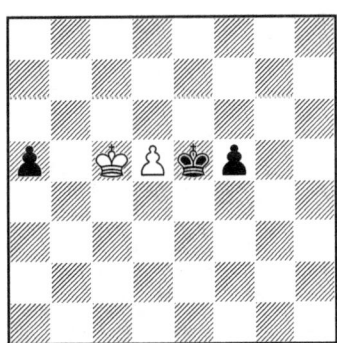

5...f4 6.d6 ♔e6 7.♔c6 f3 8.d7 f2 9.d8=♕ f1=♕ 10.♕e8+ ♔f6 11.♕f8+, winning the queen with a vertical skewer.

Alternatively, 5...a4 6.d6 ♔e6 7.♔c6 a3 8.d7 a2 9.d8=♕ a1=♕ 10.♕e8+ ♔f6 11.♕h8+, winning the queen with a diagonal skewer.

A pawn is sacrificed to open the diagonal in the next study.

No. 303. R. Rey Ardid
De Schaakwereld, 1944

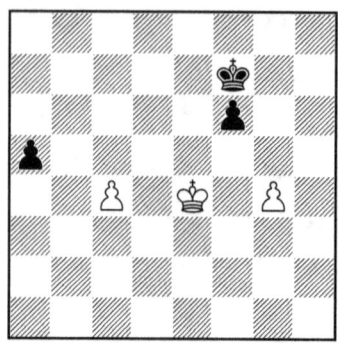

White to play and win

1.♔d4! But not 1.♔d5? due to 1...a4 with a draw.

1...♔e6 2.♔c5 ♔e5 3.♔b5 ♔d4. Black has repelled the threat to the a-pawn, but the king winds up on a poor square.

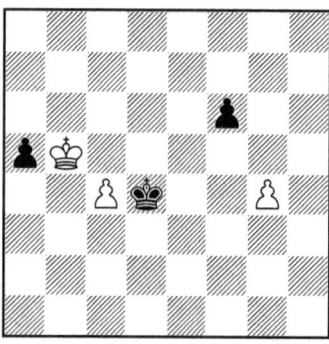

4.g5! Regrettably, it's not necessary to sacrifice the pawn: white can also play the prosaic 4.c5 a4 5.g5! (only now) 5...a3 (after 5...fxg5 6.c6 a3 7.c7 a2 8.c8=♕ a1=♕ 9.♕h8+ the black queen is skewered, like in the author's solution) 6.gxf6 a2 7.f7 a1=♕ 8.f8=♕, and white wins.

4...fxg5 5.c5, winning the queen with diagonal skewers:

5...a4 6.c6 a3 7.c7 a2 8.c8=♕ a1=♕ 9.♕h8+ or 5...g4 6.c6 g3 7.c7 g2 8.c8=♕ g1=♕ 9.♕c5+.

Study 304 also features two skewers, diagonal and vertical, but it has interesting introductory play, and the d5 pawn plays a unique role. In the first line, white wins because it is on the board, while in the second, he wins because... it isn't! To achieve the goal, white uses the well-known, but still valuable roundabout way technique.

No. 304. V. Tacu
Revista de Romana de Sah, 1951
1st–2nd prize

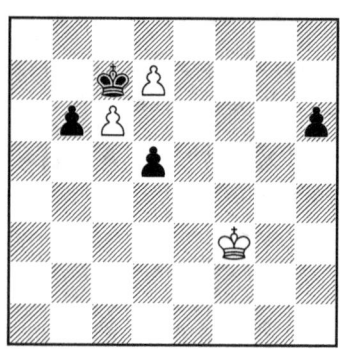

White to play and win

1.♔e3! But not 1.♔f4? d4! 2.♔e4 b5! 3.♔xd4 b4! with a draw.

1...h5 2.♔d4 h4 3.♔xd5! h3 4.♔e6 h2 5.♔e7 h1=♕ 6.d8=♕+ ♔xc6 7.♕a8+

Or **1...b5 2.♔d4! b4 3.♔e5! b3 4.♔e6(f6) b2 5.♔e7 b1=♕ 6.d8=♕+ ♔xc6 7.♕c8+ ♔b6 8.♕b8+,** winning the queen in both cases.

Study 305 is a classic miniature. One of the founders of the artistic study genre, Vasily Platov, wrote about it thus: "Winning three different queens in such a subtle and classical way with such limited pawn material is something that only a true master in this sphere can achieve."

No. 305. N. Grigoriev
Shakhmaty, 1927
3rd prize

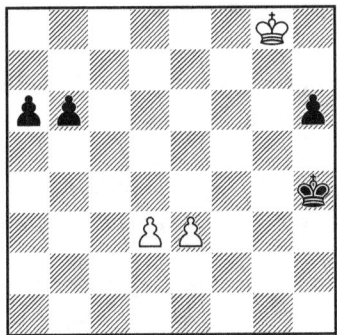

White to play and win

1.d4! But not 1.e4? ♔g5 2.d4 ♔f6 with a draw.

1...♔g5! 2.♔f7! Not 2.d5? ♔f6! 3.e4 h5, drawing.

2...♔f5 3.d5 ♔e5 4.e4

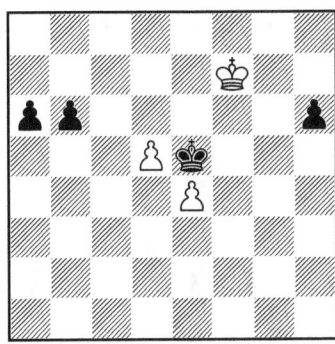

And there are three equally attractive lines with diagonal skewers:

A) **4...a5 5.♔e7 a4 6.d6 a3 7.d7 a2 8.d8=♕ a1=♕ 9.♕h8+;**

B) **4...b5 5.♔e7 b4 6.d6 b3 7.d7 b2 8.d8=♕ b1=♕ 9.♕d6+ ♔xe4 10.♕g6+;**

C) **4...h5 5.♔e7 h4 6.d6 h3 7.d7 h2 8.d8=♕ h1=♕ 9.♕d6+ ♔xe4 10.♕c6+ etc.**

White's domination is now felt more clearly. But the more queens there are, the more forced is the win and the stronger is the pattern.

Study 306 is a task: winning six (!) queens with skewers!

No. 306. M. Zinar
Chervony Girnik, 1977
2nd–3rd prize

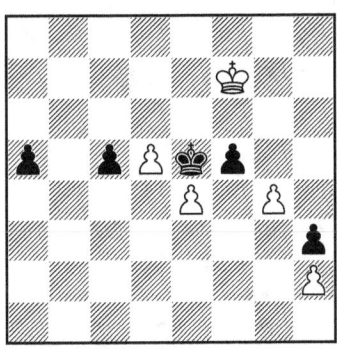

White to play and win

1.♔e7! But not 1.g5? f4! with a draw. And now, there are six variations!

1) **1...a4 2.d6 a3 3.d7 a2 4.d8=♕ a1=♕ 5.♕h8+;**

2) **1...c4 2.d6 c3 3.d7 c2 4.d8=♕ c1=♕ 5.♕d5+ ♔f4 6.♕xf5+ ♔e3 7.♕g5+;**

3) **1...fxe4 2.d6 e3 3.d7 e2 4.d8=♕ e1=♕ 5.♕d6+ ♔e4 6.♕e6+;**

4) **1...f4 2.d6 f3 3.d7 f2 4.d8=♕ f1=♕ 5.♕d5+ ♔f4 6.♕f5(f7)+;**

5) **1...fxg4 2.d6 g3 3.d7 gxh2 4.d8=♕ h1=♕ 5.♕d6+ ♔xe4 6.♕c6+;**

6) **1...fxg4 2.d6 g3 3.d7 g2 4.d8=♕ g1=♕ 5.♕d5+ ♔f4 6.♕f5+ ♔e3 7.♕xc5+.**

Thus, four queens are won by diagonal skewers, and two more by vertical ones.

No. 307. M. Zinar
L'Italia Scacchistica, 1982
Special prize
(correction)

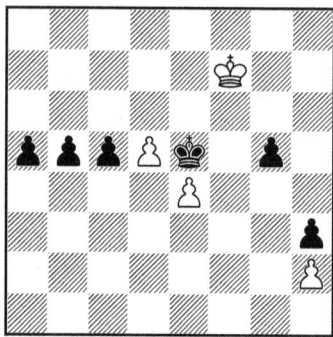

White to play and win

1.♔e7, and there are "only" five lines:

1) **1...a4 2.d6 a3 3.d7 a2 4.d8=♕ a1=♕ 5.♕h8+;**

2) **1...b4 2.d6 b3 3.d7 b2 4.d8=♕ b1=♕ 5.♕d6+ ♔xe4 6.♕g6+;**

3) **1...g4 2.d6 g3 3.d7! gxh2 4.d8=♕ h1=♕ 5.♕d6+ ♔xe4 6.♕c6+;**

4) **1...g4 2.d6 g3 3.d7! g2 4.d8=♕ g1=♕ 5.♕d5+ ♔f4 6.♕f5+ ♔e3 7.♕xc5+;**

5) **1...c4 2.d6 c3 3.d7 c2 4.d8=♕ c1=♕ 5.♕d5+ ♔f4 6.♕f5+ ♔e3 7.♕xg5+.**

Domination is obvious! The second and third lines, as well as the fourth and fifth, are absolutely symmetrical. Two pairs of echo-chameleon checkmates with an "addition" – the first line.

All five skewers are diagonal, although

the total number is one less than in the previous study. However, the author considers this study to be more artistic because the lines are more similar. The studies were composed at the same time, but published with a big delay. A composer should always be willing to wait!

Study 308 is another classic. We already know the discovered attack technique. In the studies coming next, such an attack (the second-most important way of winning the queen) is the main idea.

No. 308. L. Kubbel
Leningradskaya Pravda, 1927

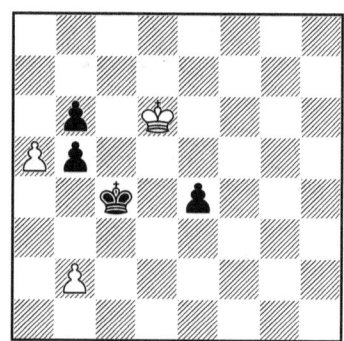

White to play and win

1.a6! e3 2.a7 e2 3.a8=♕ e1=♕ 4.♕d5+ ♔b4

5.♕d3! A "quiet" move that leads to "loud" echo variations.

5...♕c1 6.♕a3+! ♔c4 7.b3+ or **5...♕a1 6.♕c3+! ♔a4 7.b3+** with a win.

Study 309 features obvious domination by white. This is again a task: winning different queens with a discovered attack.

No. 309. M. Zinar
Chervony Hirnik, 1981
Honorable mention

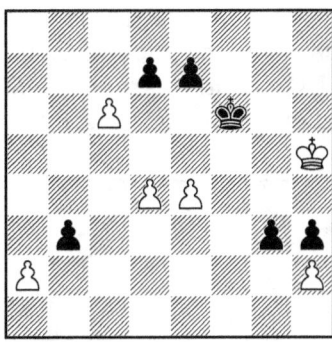

White to play and win

1.c7!, with the following branches:

1) **1...b2 2.c8=♕ b1=♕ 3.♕f8+ ♔e6 4.♕f5+ ♔d6 5.e5+;**

2) **1...bxa2 2.c8=♕ a1=♕ 3.♕f8+ ♔e6 4.♕f5+ ♔d6 5.♕e5+ ♔c6 6.d5+;**

3) **1...g2 2.c8=♕ g1=♕ 3.♕f8+ ♔e6 4.♕f5+ ♔d6 5.♕c5+ ♔e6 6.d5+;**

4) **1...gxh2 2.c8=♕ h1=♕ 3.♕f8+ ♔e6 4.♕f5+ ♔d6 5.♕c5+ ♔e6 6.♕d5+ ♔f6 7.e5+.**

Two pairs of echo variations!

As we analyze the available information, we come to the conclusion that it's probably impossible to develop the idea quantitatively. Even if you manage to win seven queens, such a study will not have great artistic value. We think that it's advisable to try to keep the number of won queens smaller and emphasize creating interesting play that precedes the domination.

To conclude this section, we shall show you two miniatures that were published after the first edition of this book. In the pretty **Study 310**, the final capture of the queen is preceded by a small but neat and logical combination.

No. 310**. V. Shkril
JC Yamalo-Nenetsky District, 1992
Special honorable mention

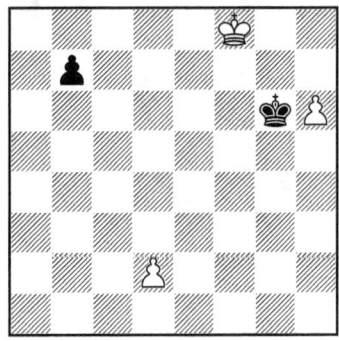

White to play and win

1.d4! Not the hasty 1.♔g8? ♔xh6 2.d4 ♔g6 3.d5 ♔f6, curtains.

1...b5 2.d5 b4

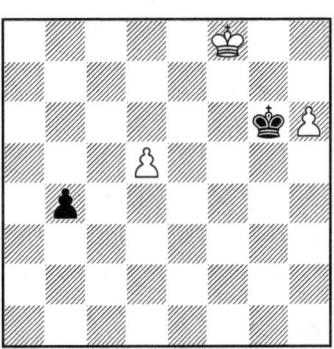

3.♔g8!! And now, the pawn should not hurry: 3.d6? b3 4.d7 b2 5.d8=♕ b1=♕, draw.

3...♔xh6 4.d6 b3 5.d7 b2 6.d8=♕ b1=♕ 7.♕h4+! ♔g6 8.♕h7+, with a skewer.

In the miniature **Study 311**, the theme of winning the black queen is presented in the form of twin studies.

No. 311**. D. Antonioni
Solidarity competition, 2003
Special prize

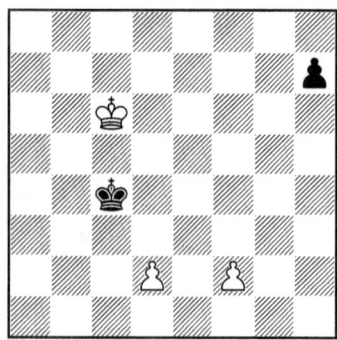

A) diagram;
B) move the position one file to the left.
White to play and win

A) The winning move in the diagram position is **1.♔d6!** Not the immediate 1.f4? h5 2.f5 h4, and the black queen promotes with a check.

1...♔d4 2.♔e6! ♔e4 3.♔f6! Not 3.f3+? ♔xf3 (or even 3...♔f4) 4.d4 h5 5.d5 h4 6.d6 h3 7.d7 h2 8.d8=♕ ♔g2, with a draw.

3...♔f4 4.d4! ♔e4. The pawn race doesn't save black: 4...h5 5.d5 h4 6.d6 h3 7.d7 h2 8.d8=♕ h1=♕ 9.♕d6+ ♔g4 (9...♔f3 10.♕d5+) 10.♕g3+ ♔h5 11.♕g5#.

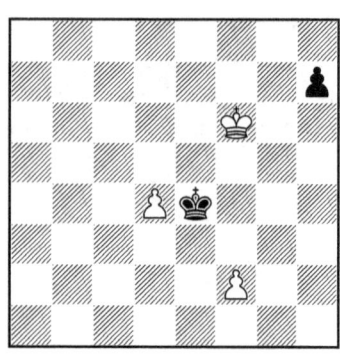

5.f3+! (5.f4? h5! 6.♔g5 h4) **5...♔xd4 6.f4 h5 7.♔g5 ♔e4 8.f5 h4.** Or 8...♔e5 9.f6 ♔e6 10.♔g6 etc.

9.f6 h3 10.f7 h2 11.f8=♕ h1=♕ 12.♕a8+, and the black queen falls.

B) If the position is shifted to the left, the first two moves are the same:

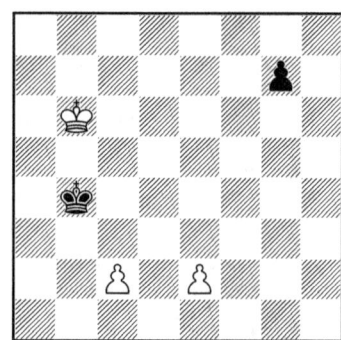

1.♔c6 ♔c4 2.♔d6 ♔d4

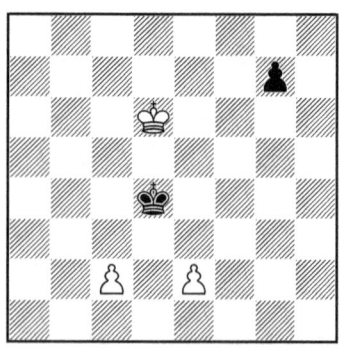

3.e3+!! The point! The familiar 3.♔e6? has a flaw: 3...♔e4 4.c4 ♔d4 5.e3+ ♔xc4 6.e4 g5 7.♔f5 ♔d4 8.e5 g4 9.e6 g3, and the white queen won't have a corner square to skewer the black queen.

3...♔xe3 4.c4 g5 5.c5 g4 6.c6 g3 7.c7 g2 8.c8=♕ g1=♕. 8...♔f2 doesn't help now.

9.♕c5+ with another diagonal skewer.

2.11. Anti-domination

This group features several studies where white prevents black from winning the queen with a skewer. As of now, only the familiar theme of "mined" squares has been actively developed – or, as we also refer to it below, the theme of "square choice". The pawn promotion itself usually doesn't require much effort in such studies.

No. 312. M. Zinar
64, 1979

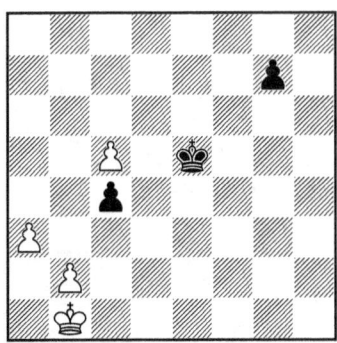

White to play and draw

1.♔c2! g5! 2.♔c3! A feint to force the pawn advance. White can't immediately play 2.♔d2? due to 2... ♔d5 3.♔e3 ♔xc5 4.♔f3 ♔b5 5.♔g4 ♔a4 6.♔xg5 ♔b3, and black wins.

2...g4! 3.♔d2! ♔d5 4.♔e3 ♔xc5 5.♔f4 ♔b5 6.♔xg4 ♔a4. We have now reached a key position from a study by Selezniev.

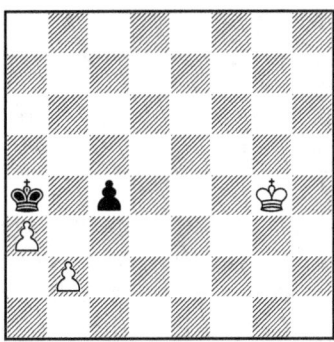

7.♔f5! After 7.♔f4? the pawn promotes with check, while after 7.♔f3? the queen is lost after a skewer from h1.

7...♔b3 8.a4! with a draw. Compare with the domination **Studies 299** and **300**.

The Selezniev position is reached in a different way in **Study 313**, involving the Reti maneuver.

No. 313. M. Zinar
Shakhmaty v SSSR, 1982
Special commendation

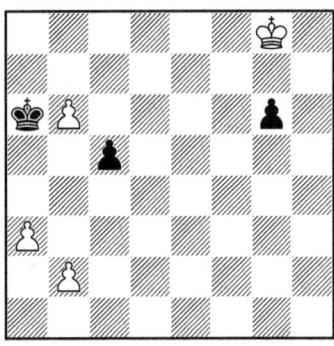

White to play and draw

1.♔f7! g5 2.♔e6! g4

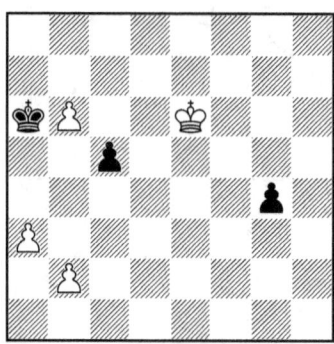

3.♔d5! The Reti double threat in conjunction with the roundabout way.

3...♔xb6 4.♔e4 c4 5.♔f4 ♔b5 6.♔xg4 ♔a4 7.♔f5! with a draw.

The same square choice with only two pawns on the board is featured in **Study 314**.

No. 314. M. Zinar
All-Russian competition, 1987
Commendation

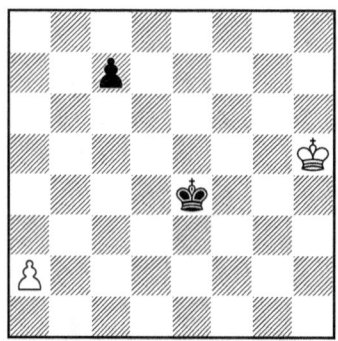

White to play and draw

1.♔g4! Not 1.♔g5? c5 2.a4 c4 3.a5 c3! 4.a6 c2 5.a7 c1=♕+ or 1.♔g6? c5! 2.a4 c4 3.a5 ♔d5! with a win.

1...♔d3! 2.♔f5! But not 2.♔f3(f4)? c5 3.a4 c4 4.a5, and the black pawn either promotes with check or skewers the new white queen.

2...c5 3.a4 ♔c4 4.♔e4! Not 4.♔e5? ♔b4 5.♔d5 c4 6.a5 c3, losing the queen once again.

4...♔b4 5.♔d3! with a draw.

Study 315 features the same combination of themes as the previous one, plus the Reti – Sarychevs feint on the first move. Many spectacular playing themes are demonstrated in this miniature.

No. 315. M. Zinar
64 – Shakhmatnoe Obozrenie, 1982
1st prize

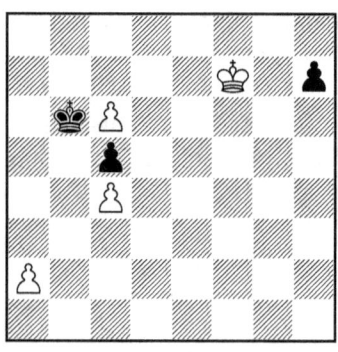

White to play and draw

1.♔g7! Again, like in **Study 73**, this paradoxical maneuver leads to the goal.

1...h5 2.♔f6! h4 3.♔e5! ♔xc6 4.♔f4 ♔b6 5.♔g4 ♔a5 6.♔xh4 ♔b4

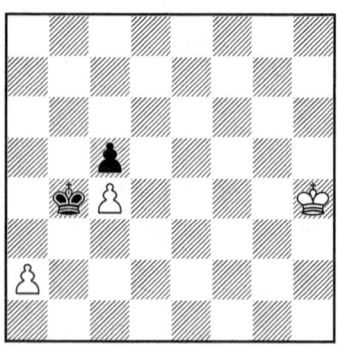

7.♔g3! ♛xc4 8.♔f2! Again, after 8.♔f4? or 8.♔f3?, the black queen either promotes with check or skewers the white queen.

8...♔c3

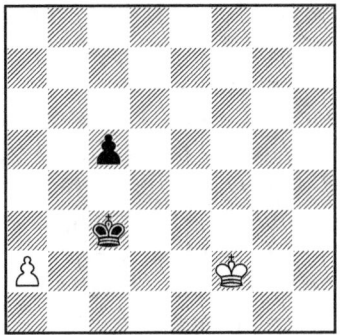

9.♔e2! Again avoiding the check on e1 or e3.

9...c4 10.a4! with a draw.

In **Study 316**, white has to choose one of the three squares on the sixth rank to bring the king closer.

No. 316. M. Zinar
Krymskaya Pravda, 1988

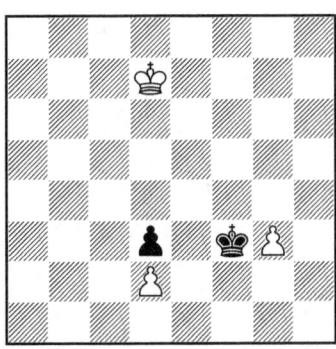

White to play and draw

As in the previous example, white cannot play either 1.♔d6? because the pawn will promote with a check: 1...

♕e2 2.g4 ♔xd2 3.g5 ♔e3 4.g6 d2 5.g7 d1=♕+, or 1.♔e6? ♕e2 2.g4 ♔xd2 3.g5 ♔e3 4.g6 d2 5.g7 d1=♕ 6.g8=♕ because the queen will be skewered after 6...♕b3+. 1.♔c7? loses to 1...♔xg3, as the white king is too far from the pawns.

The only solution is **1.♔c6! ♔e2 2.g4 ♔xd2 3.g5 ♔e3 4.g6 d2 5.g7 d1=♕ 6.g8=♕** and a draw.

Interestingly enough, if we move the g3 pawn to e3, then *all* three squares on the sixth rank will be bad.

No. 316a.

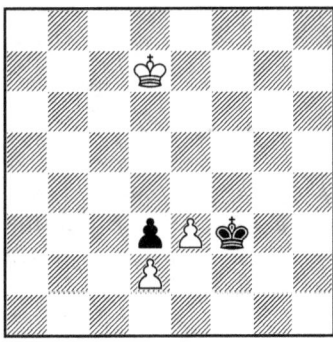

White to play and draw

The king hinders its own pawn if it moves to e6: 1.♔e6? ♔e2 2.e4 ♔xd2 3.e5 ♔c3 4.♔f7 d2, curtains.

The pawn promotes with a check if the king moves to d6: 1.♔d6? ♔e2 2.e4 ♔xd2 3.e5 ♔c3 4.e6 d2 5.e7 d1=♕+.

And the queen gets skewered if the king moves to c6. 1.♔c6? ♔e2 2.e4 ♔xd2 3.e5 ♔c3 4.e6 d2 5.e7 d1=♕ 6.e8=♕ ♕a4+.

On the other hand, the pawn itself is not in any danger on e3, and **1.♔c7 (c8)!** makes a draw: it's not necessary to get closer at all. **1...♔e2 2.e4 ♔xd2 3.e5 ♔c3 4.e6 d2 5.e7 d1=♕ 6.e8=♕.**

If not for the dual, it would be a spectacular pair of twins.

We have saved the older **Study 317** for last as it contains an "optical illusion".

No. 317. J. Moravec
28 Rijen, 1925

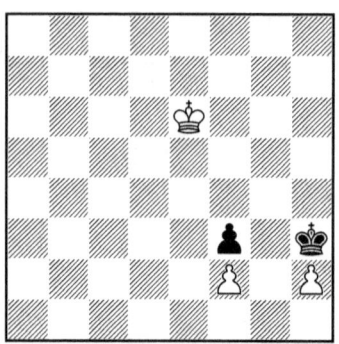

White to play and draw

The solution is **1.♔d5!,** and this is why it compares favorably with the previous one. From the chessboard point of view, both ways (♔e6–d5–e4xf3 and ♔e6–f5–f4xf3) are equal. Geometrically, however, the diagonal way is the longest: ♔e6–d5–e4xf3. To win, white should choose the longest way.

Not either 1.♔e5? ♔g2 2.h4 ♔xf2 3.h5 ♔g2 4.h6 f2 5.h7 f1=♕ 6.h8=♕ ♕a1+ 7.♔e4 ♕xh8 or 1.♔f5? ♔g2 2.h4 ♔xf2 3.h5 ♔g2 4.h6 f2 5.h7 f1=♕+!

1...♔g2. But not 1...♔xh2? 2.♔e4 ♔g2 3.♔e3 and now white even wins.

2.h4 ♔xf2 3.h5 ♔g2 4.h6 f2 5.h7 f1=♕ 6.h8=♕, and a draw.

It can be probably said that the anti-domination genre is still in its infancy, and the main discoveries still lie ahead.

2.12. Logical studies

In the last few decades, "logical studies" have grown in popularity.

The authors of the study section of the *Dictionary of Chess Composition Terms* (Kyiv 2004), Oleg Pervakov and Sergei Tkachenko, described a logical study in the following way:

"A logical study is a study where the execution of the main plan (idea) is hindered by certain obstacles. With introductory play (a preliminary plan or plans), white eliminates the obstacle (or obstacles), and then initiates the main plan. Introductory play may include a Zwischenschach, a waiting move, the sacrifice of a piece that hinders subsequent play, etc."

The modern logical study has accumulated a lot of theoretical trends and branches. Currently, those studies that offer a choice between two or more moves or branches that look equivalent at first glance are also classified as logical...

Note that a logical false try is a very important element of a logical study. This false try should be thematically intertwined with the main solution. The play in the logical false try should strictly consist of only moves. In other words, the requirements for a logical false try are the same as for the author's solution! However, two refutations of an author's logical false try destroy the value of a logical study. Only one refutation of each logical false try is acceptable.

The logical genre has, of course, made inroads into pawn studies as well. However, as it turns out, the old pawn studies also had logic! Here's what Mikhail Zinar wrote in his article "Logic in Nikolai Grigoriev's pawn studies"

(*Shakhmatnaya Kompozitsiya* magazine, No. 126, 2015):

"For many years, logical studies have been dominating study composition. Modern authors do not bother with studying the classical legacy and think that they are composing highly original studies. Nevertheless, they are often reinventing the wheel, with their 'novelties' actually having a long history.

A pawn study has fewer logical resources than a piece endgame. Yet even there, many elements were discovered long ago, but the term 'logical study' didn't exist back then, and nobody awarded prizes simply because the study was 'logical'. A false try was just perceived as one of the forms of expression of the study idea, the same as, for instance, parallel or serial synthesis." Then, Zinar showed ten studies by Grigoriev that all have the features of logical studies...

What can the modern study composer say in this regard? Let's start the "logical show" with original **Study 318**, containing logic pervading the entire solution, from the first move to the last!

No. 318**. N. Ryabinin
Problemist Ukrainy, 2008
3rd–4th prize

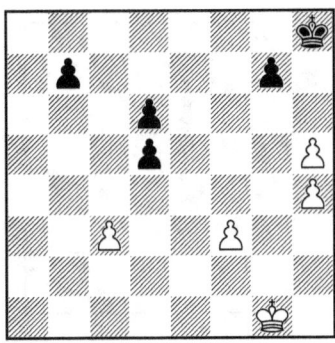

White to play and draw

The natural-looking main plan is 1.♔f2?, counting on 1...♔h7?! 2.♔e3 ♔h6 3.♔d4 ♔xh5 4.♔xd5 ♔xh4 5.♔xd6 ♔g3 6.♔c7 ♔xf3 7.♔xb7 ♔e4

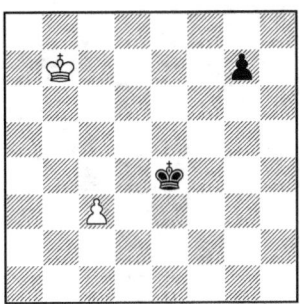

8.♔c6 (but not 8.c4? ♔d4 9.♔c6 ♔xc4) 8...g5 9.c4 g4 10.c5 g3 11.♔b7 g2 12.c6 g1=♕ 13.c7 with a classical draw.

But black has a much stronger reply: 1...d4!! 2.c4, and only now 2...♔h7 3.♔e2 ♔h6 4.♔d3 ♔xh5 5.♔xd4 ♔xh4 6.♔d5 ♔g3 7.♔xd6 ♔xf3

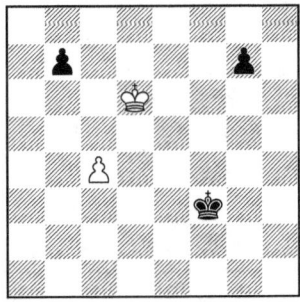

8.♔c7 ♔e4 9.♔xb7 ♔d4! 10.♔c6 ♔xc4 11.♔d6 ♔d4 12.♔e6 ♔e4 13.♔f7 g5, and black wins.

Therefore, white executes a preparatory plan first:

1.h6!! g6! Capture avoidance!

2.♔f2 d4! A return sacrifice...

3.c4! And avoiding capture in return!

3...♔h7 4.♔e2 ♔xh6 5.♔d3 ♔h5 6.♔xd4 ♔xh4 7.♔d5 ♔g3 8.♔xd6 ♔xf3

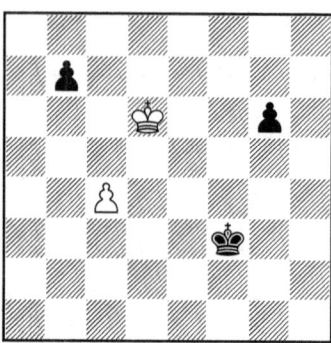

A familiar position, but with the black g-pawn one square lower. And this changes the evaluation in a big way! You will encounter many examples of almost similar diagrams in logical studies, in the solution and false try.

9.♔c7 ♔e4 10.♔xb7 ♔d4

11.♔c6! (11.♔c7? ♔c5!) **11...♔xc4 12.♔d6 ♔d4 13.♔e6 ♔e4 14.♔f6**, draw.

An original logical study. I think that this is one of the best pawn spectacles of recent times!

Of course, Mikhail Zinar is right when he says that there are many more "logical" resources in piece endgame studies than in pawn ones. But even the "logic" of pawn studies can captivate strict judges. The next study won a bronze medal in the traditionally strong FIDE Cup.

No. 319**. M. Zinar
3rd FIDE Cup, 2013
3rd prize

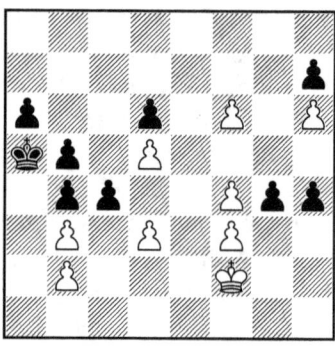

Black to move. White wins

Eight white pawns against eight black — wall to wall!

1...g3+ 2.♔g2! The first rank is "mined": 2.♔g1? cxd3 3.f7 d2 4.f8=♕ d1=♕+ 5.♔g2 ♕e2+ 6.♔h3 ♕h2+ 7.♔g4 ♕f2, curtains.

2...h3+ 3.♔xg3!! Capturing the other pawn is a logical false try ("LFT"): 3.♔xh3? cxb3 4.f7 g2! (4...♔a4 5.f8=♕ g2 6.♕a8 a5 7.♕xa5+! ♔xa5 8.♔xg2) 5.♔xg2 ♔a4

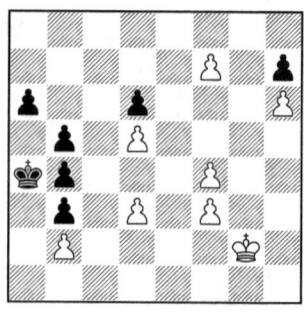

6.f8=♘! a5 7.♘g6 hxg6 8.h7 g5

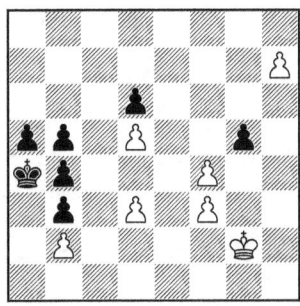

9.h8=♕ gxf4 10.♕e5! dxe5 11.d6 e4 12.d7 e3 (not 12...exf3+ 13.♔f1 f2 14.d8=♕ f3 15.♕xa5+ ♔xa5 16.♔xf2 ♔b6 17.♔xf3 ♔c5 18.♔e4, curtains) 13.d8=♘! e2, and white has to settle for a draw with 14.♔f2, because 14.♘b7?? even loses: 14...e1=♘+ 15.♔h3 ♘xd3 16.♔g4 ♘xb2 etc.

3...cxb3! 4.f7 h2 5.♔xh2 ♔a4 6.f8=♘ a5 7.♘g6 hxg6 8.h7 g5

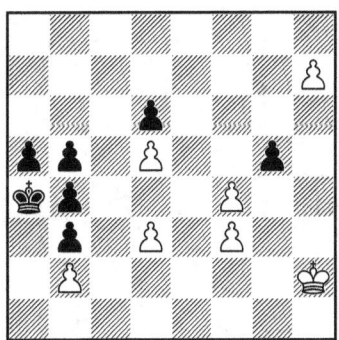

9.h8=♕! No liberties with promotion here: 9.h8=♗? g4 10.♗d4 g3+ 11.♔g1 g2 12.♗c5 dxc5 13.d6 c4 14.dxc4 bxc4 15.d7 c3 16.d8=♕ cxb2 17.♕d3 ♔a3 18.♕b1 a4 19.f5, stalemate with the niche moved one rank lower.

9.f5? is also bad: 9...g4 10.h8=♕ g3+ 11.♔g1 g2 12.♕e5 dxe5 13.d6 e4 14.d7 exf3 15.d8=♕ f2+, draw.

9...gxf4 (9...g4 10.♔g3 gxf3 11.♕h1 f2 12.♕a1#) **10.♕e5! dxe5 11.d6 e4**

12.d7 e3 13.d8=♘! e2 14.♘b7(e6) e1=♘ (without check!) 15.♘c5#.

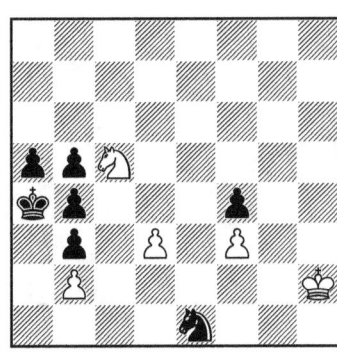

A strong three-phase logical study! The solution features two promotions to a knight, a queen sacrifice and three stalemate traps.

Later, in the next study, Zinar showed how to decrease the number of pawns in the initial position, even though some of the content also had to be cut.

No. 320**. M. Zinar

Published online, 2017 (the entry for Mikhail Zinar in the Russian-language Wikipedia contains a link to the archived version of this study in pdf format as of this book's publication date).

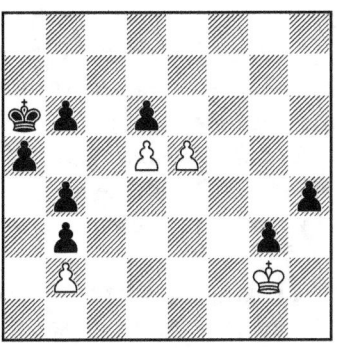

White to play and win

1.e6 h3+ 2.♔xg3!! A logical false try: 2.♔xh3? g2 3.♔xg2 ♔b5 4.e7 ♔a4

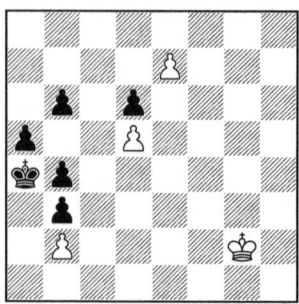

5.e8=♕+ b5 6.♕e5 dxe5 7.d6 e4 8.d7 e3 9.d8=♘ e2, and white can't play 10.♘b7? due to 10...e1=♘+! 11.♔f1 ♘d3 with a draw.

2...h2 3.♔xh2 ♔b5 4.e7 ♔a4

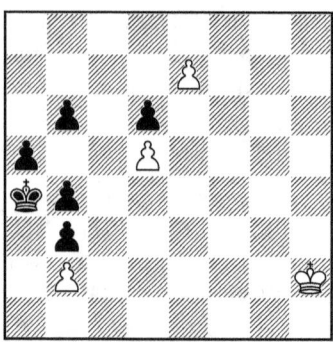

5.e8=♕+! There is no dual in the promotion: 5.e8=♖? ♔b5! 6.♔g3 a4 7.♖e3 ♔c4, and now it's white who has to scramble for a draw with precise moves. Again, just one move different from the previous diagram.

5...b5 6.♕e5! dxe5 7.d6 e4 8.d7 e3 9.d8=♘! e2 10.♘e6(b7) e1=♘ (without check) **11.♘c5#.**

In the next study, white again should make a precise choice of squares for his king. On his way to victory, white

prevents black from building two stalemate niches.

No. 321**. M. Zinar
Kalyagin memorial, 2013
Honorable mention

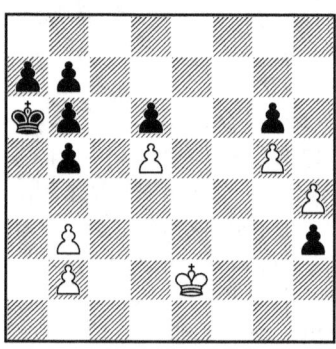

White to play and win

1.♔f1!! LFT: 1.♔f2?! b4 2.♔g3 (or 2.h5 ♔a5 3.h6 b5 4.h7 a6

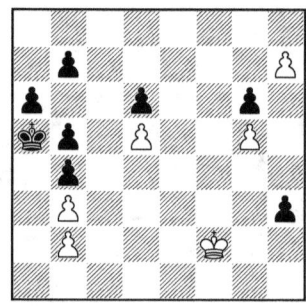

5.h8=♕ b6 6.♕e5 dxe5 7.d6 e4 8.d7 e3+ 9.♔xe3 h2, and white can't play 10.d8=♘?? due to 10...h1=♕, and the queen protects the mating square) 2...b5 3.♔xh3 ♔a5 4.♔g4 a6 5.♔f4 ♔b6 6.h5 ♔a5 7.♔e3 ♔b6, positional draw.

1...♔a5 2.h5! The check is not dangerous: 2.b4+? ♔a6! 3.h5 gxh5 4.g6 h2 5.♔g2 h4 6.g7 h3+ 7.♔xh2, and the king is stalemated on a6.

2...b4 3.h6! But not 3.hxg6? h2 4.♔g2

b5 5.g7 a6 6.g8=♕ b6 7.♕h7 h1=♕+ 8.♕xh1 with an echo-chameleon stalemate on a5.

3...b5 4.h7 a6

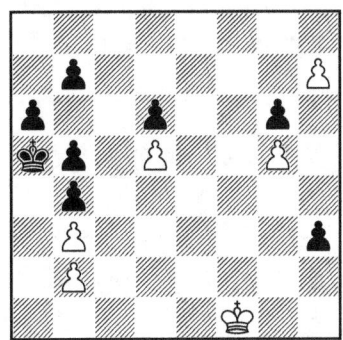

5.h8=♕! The bishop promotion does not work: 5.h8=♗? ♔b6! 6.♗d4+ ♔c7! 7.♔g1 a5 8.♔h2 b6 with a drawing fortress. Again, one move difference with the previous diagram.

5...b6 6.♕e5! dxe5 7.d6 e4 8.d7 e3 9.d8=♘! with inevitable mate.

The pawn study competition in honor of Grigoriev's 120th birth anniversary featured interesting logical compositions. The winner, **Study 322**, delighted the judge.

No. 322**. L. Katsnelson
MT Grigoriev – 120, 2016
1st prize

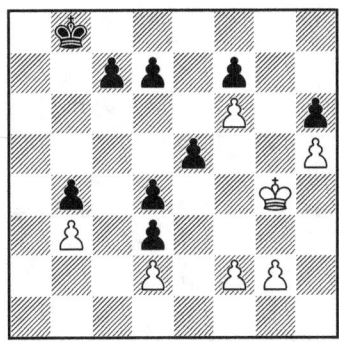

White to play and win

1.♔f5 c5! If black tries to defend the pawn, he loses quickly: 1...d6 2.g4 c5 3.g5 hxg5 4.h6 etc.

2.♔xe5 c4

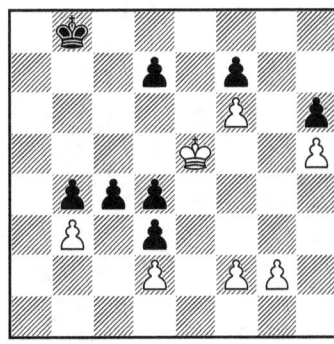

3.♔e4!! Avoiding the capture! LFT: 3.♔xd4? cxb3 4.♔xd3 ♔c7 5.g4 ♔d6 6.g5 ♔e5 7.gxh6 ♔xf6 8.f3 d6 9.f4 d5 10.f5 d4, and black wins because of zugzwang.

3...cxb3 4.♔xd3 ♔c7 5.g4 ♔d6 6.g5 ♔e5 7.gxh6 ♔xf6

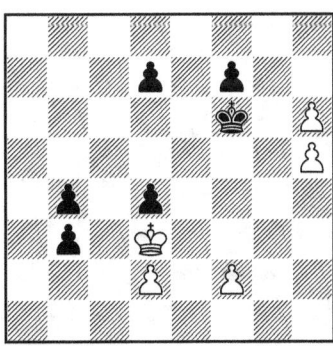

8.f3! A tortoise move in action!

8...d6 9.f4 d5 10.f5. Black is in zugzwang (he cannot play 10...d4). White wins.

From Mikhail Zinar's judge's report: "A romantic black/white trap in a modern logical package!"

The following year, the author published a slightly different version of the winning study.

No. 323**. L. Katsnelson
MT Grigoriev – 120, 2016
1ˢᵗ prize (version)

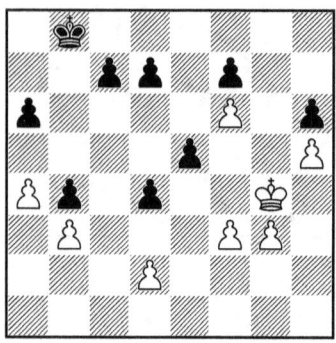

White to play and win

1.♔f5 c5 2.♔xe5. A false try: 2.♔e4? c4 3.bxc4 b3 4.♔d3 ♔c7 5.g4 ♔d6 6.g5 ♔e6 7.gxh6 ♔xf6 8.a5 d6, and white is in zugzwang.
2...c4

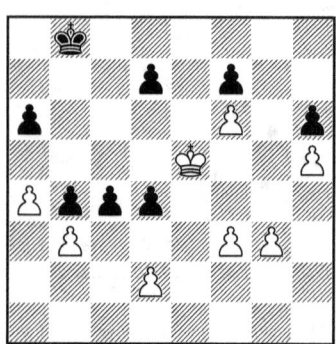

3.♔e4!! Logical false try: 3.♔xd4? cxb3 4.♔d3 ♔c7 etc.

3...cxb3 4.♔d3 ♔c7 5.g4 ♔d6 6.g5 ♔e6 7.gxh6 ♔xf6 8.a5 d6 9.f4 d5 10.f5 with a zugzwang for black.

The next study is a natural continuation of this work.

No. 324**. L. Katsnelson and M. Zinar
3ʳᵈ UAPA internet ty, 2016
Special honorable mention

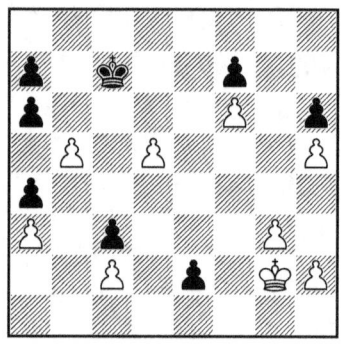

White to play and win

1.b6+!! LFT: white cannot immediately play 1.♔f2? due to 1... axb5 (1...♔d6? 2.g4 axb5 3.g5) 2.♔xe2 b4! 3.♔d3 bxa3 4.♔xc3 ♔d6 5.g4 ♔xd5

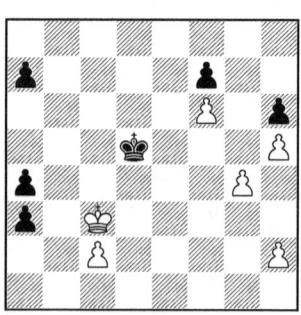

6.g5 ♔e5 7.gxh6 ♔xf6 8.h3 a6! 9.h4 a5, and white is ground down by zugzwang.
1...axb6 2.♔f2 b5 3.♔xe2 b4 4.♔d3. Not 4.g4? bxa3 5.g5 a2 6.g6 a1=♛ 7.d6+ ♔c6 8.gxf7 ♛c1 9.f8=♛ ♛xc2+, and only black can win.
4...bxa3 5.♔xc3 ♔d6 6.g4 ♔xd5

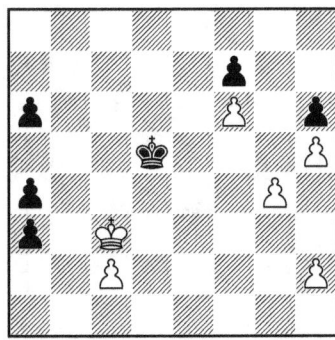

Again, one square difference from the previous diagram changes the result.

7.g5 ♔e5 8.gxh6 ♔xf6 9.h3! A tortoise move that prepares the final zugzwang.

9...a5 10.h4. White wins.

Two false tries at once are featured in another prizewinning study from the same Grigoriev memorial competition.

No. 325**. L. Katsnelson
MT Grigoriev – 120, 2016
4th prize

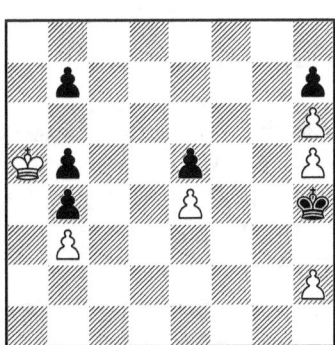

White to play and win

The white king is surrounded by black pawns – take any one, it's free! But suddenly: **1.♔b6!!** Capture avoidance! Logical false try: 1.♔xb5? ♔g4 2.♔c5 ♔f3 3.♔d5 ♔f4 4.h3 b6 5.h4 b5 (white

is in zugzwang) 6.♔e6 ♔xe4 7.♔f6 ♔d5! 8.♔g7 ♔e6 9.♔xh7 ♔f7, and black wins.

Another logical false try: 1.♔xb4? ♔g4 2.♔c5 ♔f4! 3.♔d5 b4 4.h3 b6 5.h4 b5, and zugzwang again benefits black.

1...♔g4 2.♔c5 ♔f3 3.♔d5 ♔f4 4.h3! b6 5.h4 (mutual zugzwang), and black has no pawn tempo. White wins. For instance: 5...♔e3 6.♔xe5 ♔d3 7.♔f4 ♔c3 8.e5 ♔xb3 9.e6 ♔c2 10.e7 b3 11.e8=♕ etc.

From the judge's report: "The tactical trick of capture avoidance to cause zugzwang is executed very clearly and laconically."

The next logical study from the same competition features familiar ideas – shouldering and the Reti maneuver.

No. 326**. V. Kalashnikov
MT Grigoriev – 120, 2016
Commendation

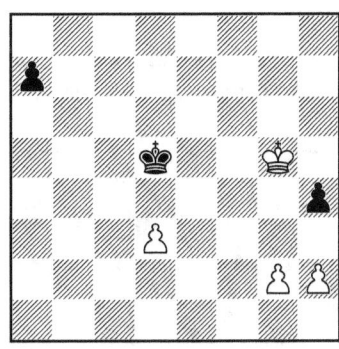

White to play and draw

The attempt to clear the way for the pawns 1.♔xh4? is doomed: 1... a5, and the black pawn is unstoppable. Therefore, the white king runs towards the enemy pawn:

1.♔f4! ♔d4! Shouldering his

counterpart! After 1...a5 2.♔e3 a4 3.♔d2 a3 4.♔c2, the pawn is stopped.

2.♔f3‼ White insists! Logical false try: 2.g4? hxg3 3.hxg3 (3.♔xg3 a5 4.h4 a4 5.h5 ♔e5 6.d4+ ♔f6 7.d5 a3 8.h6 a2 9.h7 ♔g7) 3...a5 4.g4 a4 5.g5 a3 6.g6 a2 7.g7 a1=♛ 8.g8=♛ ♛f1+ 9.♔g3 ♛g1+, curtains.

2...♔xd3. Or 2...a5 3.♔e2 ♔c3 4.d4! ♔xd4 5.♔d2 with equality.

3.g4! Now it's time!

3...hxg3 4.h4‼ ♔d4 5.♔xg3 a5 6.♔f4! A Reti double threat: 6.♔f3? a4 or 6.♔g4? ♔e5 7.♔g5 ♔e6, and black triumphs.

As a result of these maneuvers, the kings have got back to d4 and f4, but now the h-pawn moves forward. Draw, for instance: 6...♔d5 (the only move!) 7.♔e3 etc.

A nice logical study with a preliminary king maneuver.

In **Study 327**, the result depends on which pawn to push on the second move.

No. 327**. B. Gelfand and M. Zinar**
64 – Shakhmatnoe Obozrenie, 2016

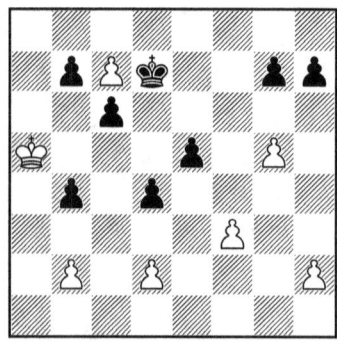

White to play and win

1.♔b6 ♔c8 2.d3‼ Thematic false try: 2.b3? d3

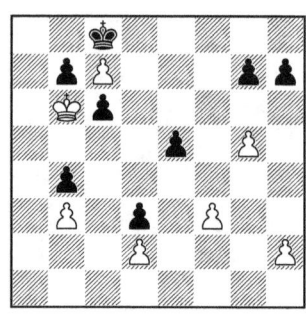

And white cannot play 3.g6?! hxg6 4.h4 g5 5.h5 e4 6.fxe4 g4 7.e5 g3 8.e6 g2 9.e7 g1=♛+, because the pawn promotes with check.

Instead of 3.g6?!, white will have to scramble for a draw: 3.h3 h5! 4.gxh6 gxh6 5.♔c5 ♔xc7 6.♔xb4 ♔d6 7.♔c3 ♔e6 9.♔xd3

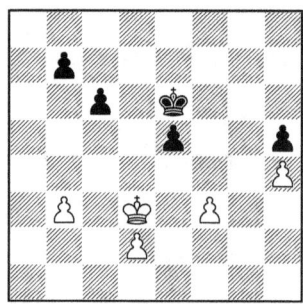

For lovers of concrete lines, we will show an interesting variation: 9...♔f5 10.♔e3 c5 11.♔d3 ♔f4 12.♔c4 ♔g3 (12...♔xf3 13.♔xc5 ♔g4 14.♔d5) 13.♔d5 b6

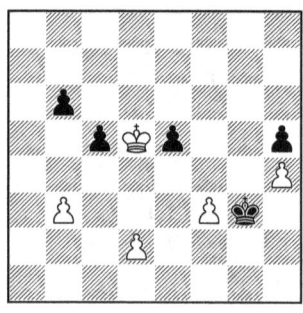

14.♔e4!! ♔f2 15.d3 ♔g3 16.♔xe5 ♔xf3 17.♔f5 ♔e3 18.♔g5 ♔xd3 19.♔xh5 ♔c3 20.♔g4 ♔xb3 21.h5, and, according to the computer evaluation, white saves the queen endgame.

2...b3 3.g6!! The point! After 3.h3? h5! 4.gxh6 gxh6 5.h4 h5, white is in zugzwang.

3...hxg6 (3...h6 4.h3) **4.h4 g5**

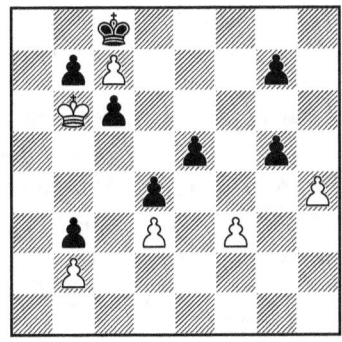

5.h5 e4. Neither 5...g4 6.fxg4 e4 7.g5 nor 5...c5 6.♔xc5 e4 7.fxe4 g4 8.♔xd4 g3 9.♔e3 etc. help black save the game.

6.fxe4 g4 7.e5 g3 8.e6 g2 9.e7 and white wins, since the a7-g1 diagonal is blocked, and so the black pawn promotes without a check.

In **Study 328**, we see the characteristic systematic movement of black and white pawns. But the main merit of the composition is the logical false try!

No. 328**. V. Kovalenko
Diagrammes, 1996
2nd honorable mention

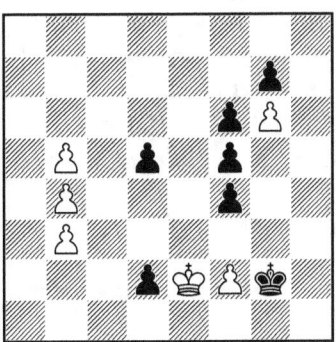

White to play and win

There's a natural-looking pawn march: 1.b6?! f3+! 2.♔xd2 ♔xf2 3.b7 ♔g2 4.b8=♕ f2 5.♕f4 f1=♕

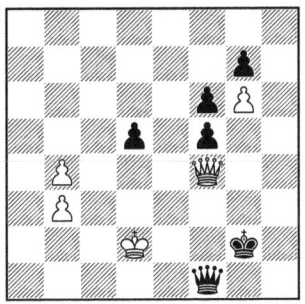

6.♕xf1+ ♔xf1 7.b5 (7.♔e3 f4+ 8.♔xf4 ♔e2 9.b5 d4 10.b6 d3 11.b7 d2 12.b8=♕ d1=♕ 13.♕e8+ ♔f1!) 7...f4 8.b6 f3 9.b7 f2 10.b8=♕ ♔g2

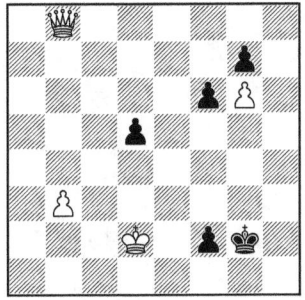

11.♕f4 f1=♕ 12.♕xf1+ ♔xf1 13.b4 f5 14.b5 f4 15.b6 f3 16.b7 f2 17.b8=♕ ♔g2, and white cannot improve his position: 18.♕f4 f1=♕ 19.♕f7 ♕f2+, draw. This is the logical false try!

The correct line is **1.f3!! d1=♕+ 2.♔xd1 ♔xf3 3.b6 ♔g2 4.b7 f3 5.b8=♕ f2 6.♕f4.** But not 6.♕b5? f4! 7.♕xd5+ f3 8.♕d2 ♔g3 9.♕e3 ♔g2, draw.

6...f1=♕+

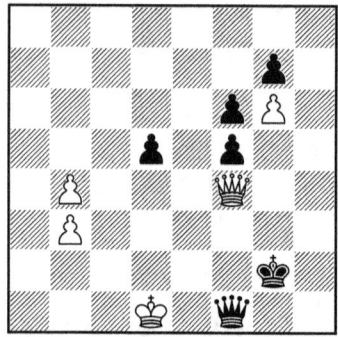

In this and the next diagram, we again see one move difference compared with the logical false try.

7.♕xf1+ ♔xf1 8.b5 f4 9.b6 f3 10.b7 f2 11.b8=♕ ♔g2

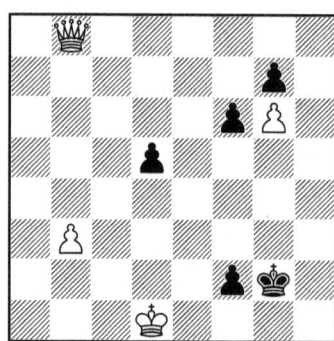

12.♕f4(b5) f1=♕+ 13.♕xf1+ ♔xf1 14.b4 f5 15.b5 f4 16.b6 f3 17.b7 f2 18.b8=♕ ♔g2

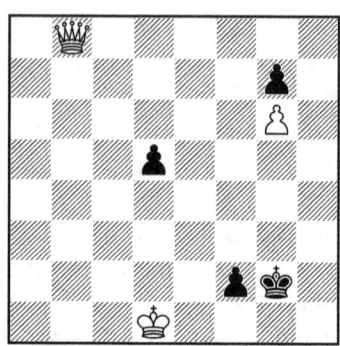

19.♕b2! Now, in contrast with the false try, the second rank is not blocked by the king.

19...♔g1 20.♕d4. White wins.

In **Study 329**, the phases are smoothly and organically strung together, like pieces of kebab on a spit: pawn endgame − queen endgame − pawn endgame − queen endgame.

No. 329**. S. Didukh
Shakhmatnaya Kompozitsiya, 2005
2nd prize

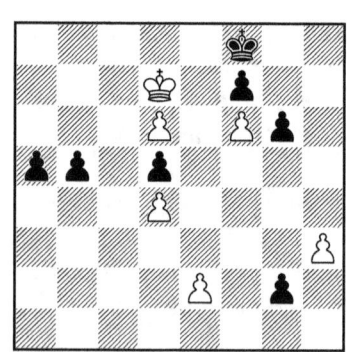

White to play and win

1.♔c8! LFT: 1.♔c6? g1=♕ 2.d7 ♕e3! 3.d8=♕+ ♕e8+ 4.♕xe8+ ♔xe8 5.♔c7 (5.♔xb5 ♔d7)

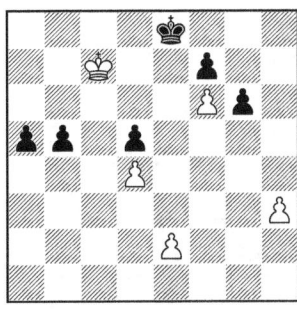

5...♔f8! 6.e4 dxe4 7.d5 e3 8.d6 e2
9.d7 e1=♕ 10.d8=♕+ ♕e8 11.♕d6+
♔g8, and the g6 pawn blocks the mating
maneuver ♕g3-g7#. 1.♔c7? g1=♕
2.d7 ♕g3+ is also bad: black wins.

1...g1=♕ 2.d7 ♕c1+! But not the
immediate 2...♕e3 3.d8=♕+ ♕e8
4.♕xe8+ ♔xe8 5.e4 dxe4 6.d5, and
white wins.

3.♔b7 ♕e3 4.h4!! The point!
Impulsive promotion spoils the win:
4.d8=♕+? ♕e8 5.♕d6+! ♔g8 6.♕e7
♕f8 7.e4 b4 8.exd5 b3 9.d6 b2 10.♕xf8+
♔xf8

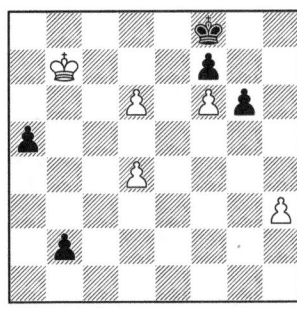

11.d7 b1=♕+ 12.♔a7 ♕b5
13.d8=♕+ ♕e8 14.♕d6+ ♔g8 15.d5
a4 16.♕e7 ♕b5 17.d6 a3 18.d7 ♕a5+
with perpetual check.

4...♕e8. Or 4...b4 5.h5! b3 6.h6! b2
7.d8=♕+ ♕e8 8.h7! b1=♕+ 9.♔a7
♕h1 10.♕d6+, mating.

5.dxe8=♕+ ♔xe8 6.h5!

6...gxh5. Black can't avoid the
capture: 6...♔f8 7.e4! b4 (7...dxe4 8.d5
e3 9.d6 e2 10.d7 e1=♕ 11.d8=♕+ ♕e8
12.♕xe8+ ♔xe8 13.h6) 8.exd5 b3 9.d6
b2 10.d7 b1=♕+

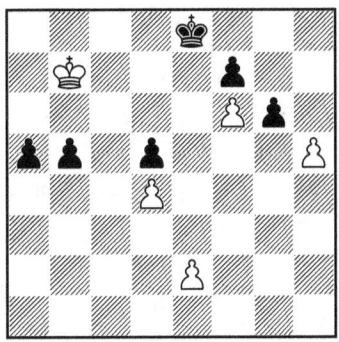

11.♔a7! with a win.

7.♔c7! Why not 7.♔c8? This will be
clear later. 7.e4? is too early due to 7...♔d7.

**7...♔f8 8.e4! dxe4 9.d5 e3 10.d6 e2
11.d7 e1=♕ 12.d8=♕+ ♕e8.**

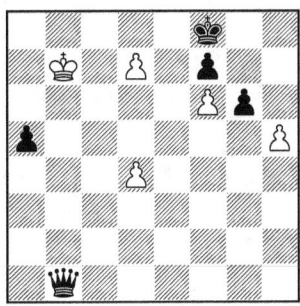

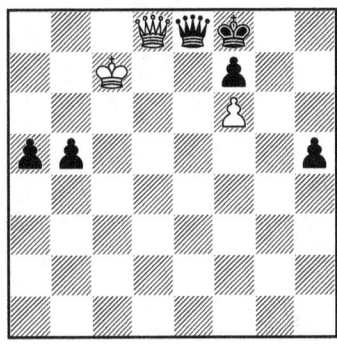

The g-file is free, and white executes a mating attack:

13.♕d6+. Had white played 7.♔c8?, the queen would now have been pinned.

13...♔g8 14.♕g3+ ♔h7 15.♕g7#!

In the next six studies, the fate of the game is also decided in a queen endgame.

No. 330**. A. Chernov
Chess Life & Review, 2006

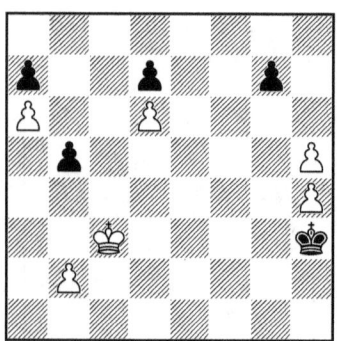

White to play and win

Logical false try: **1.♔b4? ♔xh4 2.♔xb5 ♔xh5 3.♔c4 g5 4.b4 g4**

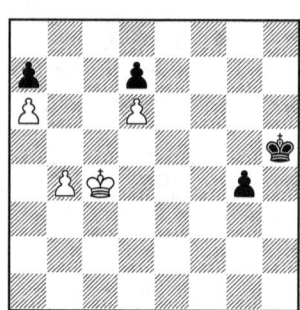

5.♔d3 ♔h4 6.b5 g3 7.♔e2 ♔h3 8.b6 g2 9.bxa7 g1=♕ 10.a8=♕ ♕h2+ 11.♔e3 ♕g1+, and white can't avoid perpetual check.

1.h6!! gxh6 2.h5! ♔g4 3.♔b4! The black pawn is now located one rank to the right, and the main plan can be implemented!

3...♔xh5 4.♔xb5 ♔g4

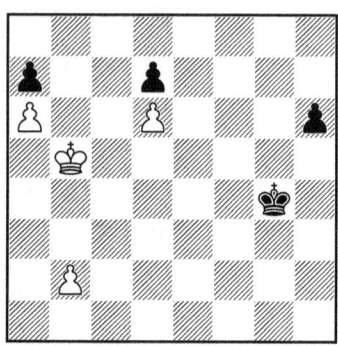

5.♔c4! h5 6.♔d3 ♔g3. Both 6... h4 7.♔e2 ♔g3 8.♔f1 and 6...♔f5 7.b4 ♔e6 8.b5 ♔xd6 9.b6 are hopeless, white wins.

7.♔e2 ♔g2 8.b4 h4 9.b5 h3 10.b6 h2 11.bxa7 h1=♕ 12.a8=♕+ (check!). White wins.

No. 331**. A. Bill
Chess Life and Review, 2004

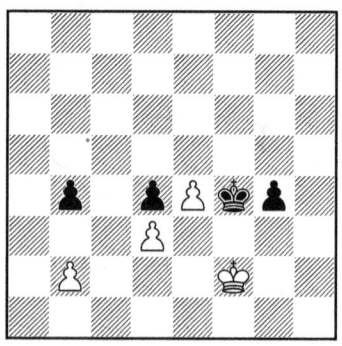

White to play and win

Logical false tries: **1.♔g2? g3 2.b3 ♔e3! 3.e5 ♔xd3 4.e6 ♔c2 5.e7 d3 6.e8=♕ d2 7.♕e4+ ♔c1 8.♕f4 ♔c2** or

1.♔g1? ♔e3 2.e5 ♔xd3 3.e6 ♔c2 4.e7 d3 5.e8=♕ d2 6.♕e4+ ♔c1 7.♕f4 ♔c2 8.♕xb4 d1=♕+ (check!), with a draw every time.

The correct line is **1.♔f1!! ♔g3! 2.♔g1!** Not 2.e5? ♔h2! 3.e6 g3 4.e7 g2+ etc.

2...♔f4 3.♔f2! White gives black the right to move with triangulation.

3...g3+ 4.♔g2! ♔e3. Or 4...♔g4 5.e5 ♔f5 6.♔xg3 ♔xe5 7.♔g4 with a technical win.

5.e5 ♔xd3 6.e6 ♔c2 7.e7 d3 8.e8=♕ d2.

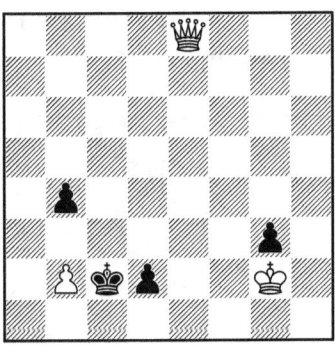

Almost a position from the false tries has occurred, but with one small difference each time (compare with the positions after black plays d2 in those lines).

9.♕e4+. Other queen moves artificially prolong play.

9...♔c1 10.♕f4 ♔c2 11.♕xb4 d1=♕ 12.♕a4+ with a queen trade and win.

No. 332**. E. Bonazzi
Scacchi & Dintorni, 2006
Commendation

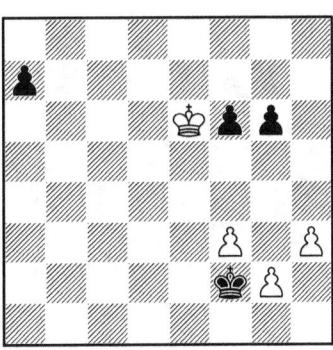

White to play and draw

1.h4! Hoping for a breakthrough! After 1.♔xf6? a5, the march of the black pawn decides matters. 1.f4? f5 2.g4 a5 3.♔d5 ♔g3 4.gxf5 gxf5 etc. also loses

1...♔g3! Not 1...a5 2.g4 a4 3.h5 gxh5 4.gxh5 a3 5.h6, with a draw.

2.f4! ♔xf4. 2...a5 is met with 3.f5! gxf5 4.h5!, breaking through.

3.♔f7!! Logical false try: 3.♔xf6? a5 4.♔xg6 a4 5.h5 a3 6.h6 a2 7.h7 a1=♕, and the promotion square is under control.

3...a5. Or 3...♔f5 4.g4+ ♔xg4 5.♔xg6 ♔xh4 6.♔xf6 a5 7.♔e5, catching up with the pawn.

4.♔xg6 a4 5.h5 a3 6.h6 a2 7.h7 a1=♕ 8.h8=♕. Promotion becomes possible because the long diagonal is blocked. A small study but still logic!

Study 333 with its subtle logic was one of the highlights of the memorial tournament honoring one of the strongest study composers of the 20th century, Genrikh Moiseevich Kasparyan.

No. 333**. E. Martorosian
Kasparyan memorial, 2006
2nd–4th prize

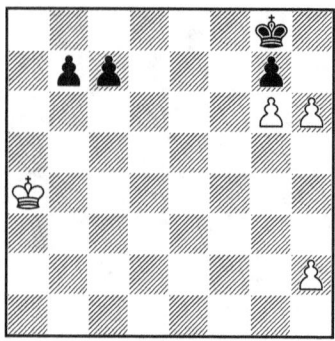

White to play and win

1.h7+ ♔h8 2.h4!! Logical false try: 2.♔b3? c5! 3.h4 c4+! 4.♔b4 b6!! 5.h5 b5! (mutual zugzwang) 6.♔c3 b4+ 7.♔c2

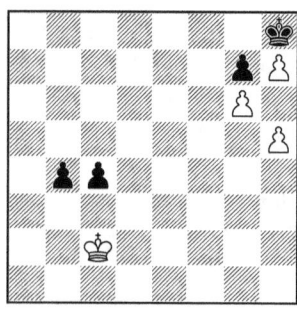

7...c3! 8.♔b3 c2 9.♔xc2 b3+ 10.♔b1 b2 11.♔xb2, stalemate. 11.h6? even loses: 11...gxh6 12.♔xb2 h5 13.♔c3 h4 14.♔d4 h3 15.♔e5 h2 16.♔f6 h1=♕ etc.

2...c5 (or 2...b5+ 3.♔b3! c5 4.h5 c4+ 5.♔b4 etc., like in the main line) **3.h5 c4**

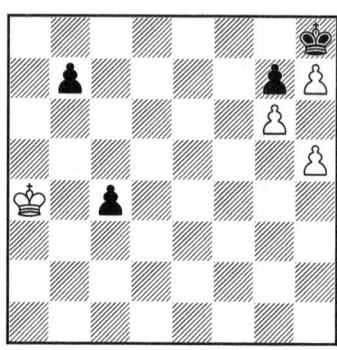

4.♔a3!! Not 4.♔b4? b5! 5.♔c3 b4+ 6.♔c2 c3 etc., like in the false try.

4...b6! 5.♔a4! b5+ 6.♔b4! Mutual zugzwang favors white.

6...c3 7.♔xc3 b4+ 8.♔b2! b3 9.h6 gxh6 10.♔xb3 h5

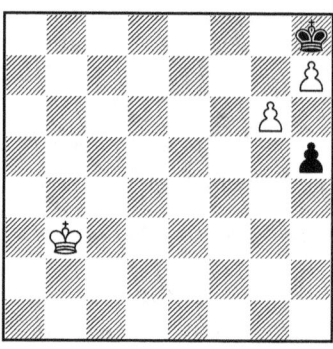

11.♔c4! In contrast with the false try, this diagonal brings white success.

11...h4 12.♔d5 h3 13.♔e6 h2 14.♔f7 h1=♕ 15.g7+ ♔xh7 16.g8=♕+. White wins.

In **Study 334**, white leaves a black pawn intact to deprive the opponent of stalemate opportunities at the right moment.

No. 334**. S. Didukh
Problemaz, 2007
1st prize

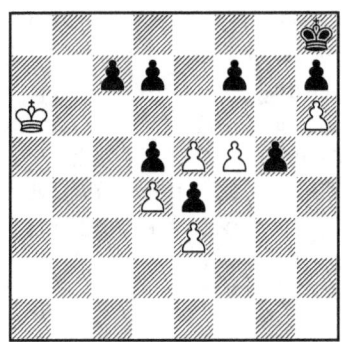

White to play and win

1.♔b7 g4 2.♔c8!! The consequences of the greedy 2.♔xc7? will become clear eleven moves later!

2...g3 3.♔xd7 g2 4.e6 fxe6

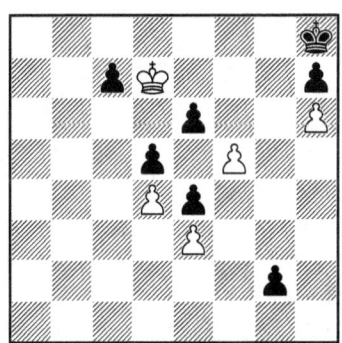

5.f6! g1=♕ 6.f7 ♕f1! Not 6...♕g8 7.fxg8=♕+ ♔xg8 8.♔xe6, curtains.

7.♔e7 e5! 8.dxe5 d4 9.e6. The organic transition 9.f8=♕+ is also possible.

9...d3 10.f8=♕+ ♕xf8+ 11.♔xf8 d2 12.e7 d1=♕ 13.e8=♕ ♕d5. If the c7 pawn were not on the board, black could have saved the game with 13...♕d8! 14.♔f7+ (14.♕xd8, stalemate) 14...♕xe8+ 15.♔xe8 ♔g8

16.♔e7 ♔h8 17.♔e6 ♔g8 18.♔e5 ♔f7 19.♔xe4 ♔e6 with a drawing opposition.

14.♔e7+ ♕g8

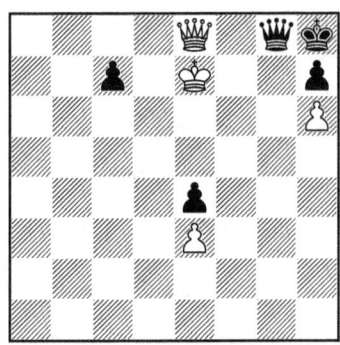

15.♕b5! But not 15.♕h5? ♕g3 16.♕c5 because of the trade 16...♕d6+!

15...c5 16.♕b2+ with checkmate.

No. 335**. S. Didukh and S. Hornecker
Z. Birnov memorial, 2010
2nd prize

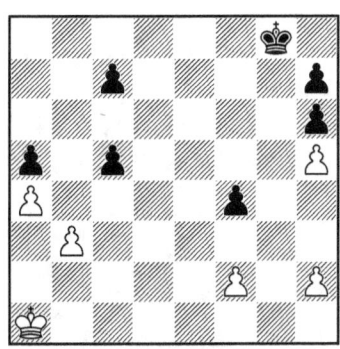

White to play and win

Black has an extra pawn, but his queenside is very weak...

1.♔b2 ♔f7 2.♔c3 ♔e6 3.♔c4 ♔d6

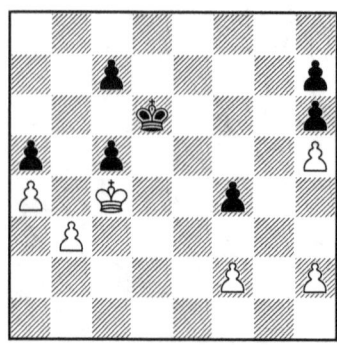

4.f3!! To stop the enemy king! Logical false try: 4.♔b5? ♔d5 5.♔xa5 c4 6.♔b4 c5+ 7.♔c3 cxb3 8.♔xb3 ♔d4

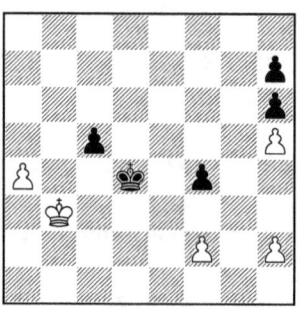

9.a5 ♔d3 10.a6 c4+ 11.♔b4 c3 12.a7 c2 13.a8=♕ c1=♕, draw. The tortoise move 4.h3? doesn't help either due to 4...f3! 5.♔b5 ♔d5 6.♔xa5 c4 7.♔b4 c5+ 8.♔c3 cxb3 9.♔xb3 ♔d4

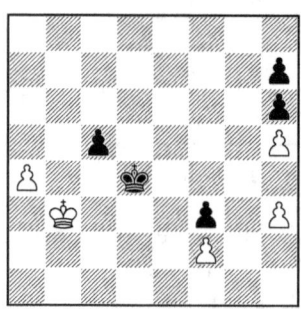

10.a5 ♔d3 11.a6 c4+ 12.♔b4 c3 13.a7 c2 14.a8=♕ c1=♕ 15.♕xf3+

♔d4 16.♕f6+ ♔d5, and the queen endgame cannot be won.

4...♔c6 5.h3!! And now the tortoise move wins! Not 5.h4? ♔d6 6.♔b5 ♔d5 7.♔xa5 c4 8.♔b4 cxb3 9.♔xb3 ♔d4 10.a5 ♔c5, and white is in zugzwang.

5...♔d6 6.♔b5 ♔d5 7.♔xa5 c4 8.♔b4 c5+. After 8...cxb3 9.♔xb3 ♔d4 10.a5 ♔c5 11.♔a4 c6, white has an extra tempo 12.h4!, and black is in zugzwang.

9.♔c3 cxb3 10.♔xb3 ♔d4

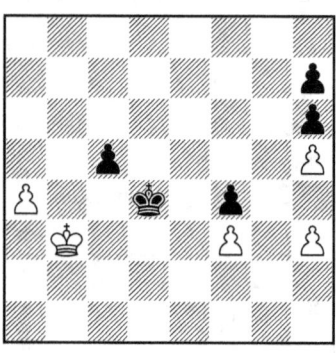

11.a5 ♔d3 12.a6 c4+ 13.♔b4 c3 14.a7 c2 15.a8=♕ c1=♕ 16.♕e4+! The white queen, in contrast to the false try, has a protected square to give a check from!

16...♔d2 17.♕xf4+. White wins.

The foresight at the very first move of **Study 336** will manifest itself at the very end of the solution!

No. 336**. S. Didukh and S. Hornecker
Olimpiya Dunyasi, 2010
1ˢᵗ honorable mention

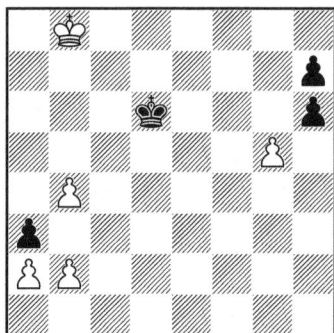

White to play and draw

Logical false try: 1.bxa3? hxg5 2.a4 g4 3.a5 g3 4.a6 g2 5.a7 g1=♕ 6.a8=♕ ♕g8+ 7.♔b7 ♕xa8+ 8.♔xa8 ♔c6 9.♔a7 ♔b5 10.a4+ ♔xa4 11.♔b6 ♔xb4

12.♔c6 ♔c4 13.♔d6 ♔d4 14.♔e6 ♔e4 15.♔f6 ♔f4 16.♔g7 h5, and the pawn runs away.

Eureka: **1.g6!! hxg6 2.bxa3 g5 3.a4 g4 4.a5 g3 5.a6 g2 6.a7 g1=♕ 7.a8=♕ ♕g8+ 8.♔b7!** (8.♔a7? ♕xa2+) **8... ♕xa8+ 9.♔xa8 ♔c6.** Or 9...h5 10.♔a7 h4 11.b5, and the pawns queen at the same time.

10.♔a7! The immediate 10.a4? doesn't work: 10...♔b6 11.a5+ ♔a6 12.♔b8 h5 13.♔c7 h4 14.♔c6 h3

15.b5+ ♔xa5 16.b6 h2 17.b7 h1=♕+, and the white king is in check.
   10...♔b5 11.a4+! ♔xa4 (11...♔xb4 12.♔b6 ♔xa4 13.♔c5) **12.♔b6! ♔xb4.**

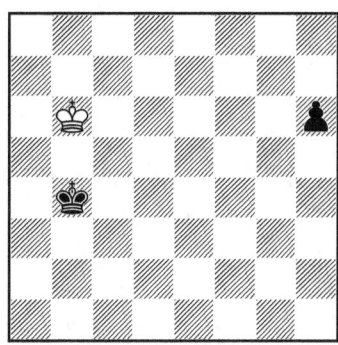

In contrast to the false try, the black pawn is one square ahead...
   13.♔c6! ♔c4 14.♔d6 ♔d4 15.♔e6 ♔e4 16.♔f6 ♔f4 17.♔g6 ♔g4 18.♔xh6. Until the bare kings!

The fight for an advantageous opposition is the main idea of logical **Study 337**.

No. 337**. I. Akobia
Hornecker–25 JT, 2011
2ⁿᵈ prize

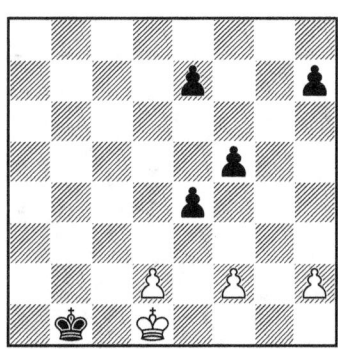

White to play and draw

1.d3! Not 1.d4? e6! (en passant capture is not obligatory!) 2.♔d2 ♔b2 3.♔e3 ♔c3, and black wins.

1...exd3 2.♔d2 h5 3.h4! But not in the center: 3.f4? e6! 4.♔xd3 ♔c1 5.h4 ♔d1, and white is in zugzwang. Nor can he play 3.♔xd3? ♔c1 4.♔d4 ♔d2 5.♔e5

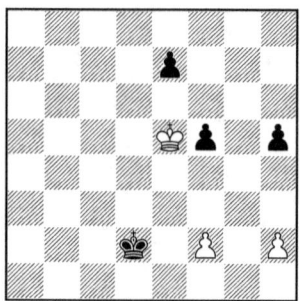

5...e6! 6.♔xe6 f4 7.♔f5 f3 8.♔f4 ♔e2 9.♔g3 h4+!, and black triumphs.

3...e6 4.♔c3!! Capture avoidance! Logical false try: 4.♔xd3? ♔c1! 5.f4 ♔d1! (the zugzwang benefits black) 6.♔e3 ♔c2 7.♔d4 ♔d2 8.♔e5 ♔e3, and black wins.

4...♔c1. If 4...e5, then it's possible to play 5.♔xd3 ♔c1 6.♔c4 ♔d2 7.♔d5 e4 8.♔e5 ♔e2 9.♔xf5 ♔f3 10.♔e5, draw.

5.♔xd3 ♔d1

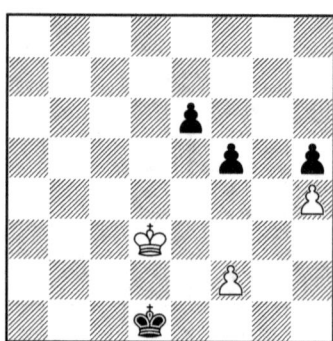

6.f4! Black is in zugzwang. Both 6.♔e3? e5 7.f4 e4 and 6.f3? e5 7.♔c4 ♔e2 etc. lose.

6...♔c1 7.♔c3 ♔d1 8.♔d3 ♔e1 9.♔e3 ♔f1 10.♔f3 ♔g1 11.♔g3 ♔h1 12.♔h3. Positional draw.

Capture avoidance, feint and decoying the black king into check are the main contents of the logical **Study 338**.

No. 338**. G. Costeff
EG, 2012
Special honorable mention

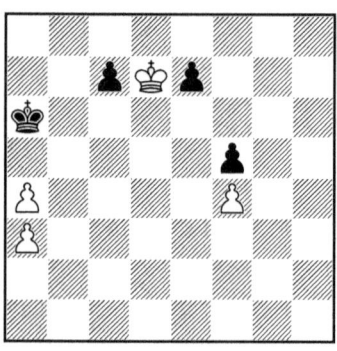

White to play and win

1.♔c6!! The pawn is poisoned: 1.♔xc7? ♔a5 2.♔d7 e5 3.fxe5 f4 4.e6 f3 5.e7 f2 6.e8=♕ f1=♕, and white cannot win. For instance: 7.♕a8+ ♕a6 8.♕d5+ ♔xa4 9.♕d4+ ♔b3 etc.

1...♔a5! 2.♔xc7! ♔xa4. The breakthrough will not work: 2...e5 3.fxe5 f4 4.e6 f3 5.e7 f2 6.e8=♕ f1=♕

7.♕a8+! ♕a6 8.♕d5+ ♔xa4
9.♕d1+ ♔b5 10.♕d3+ ♔a5 11.♕c3+
♔b5 12.♕b4#.

3.♔d8!! Leaving the square!
3...e6!

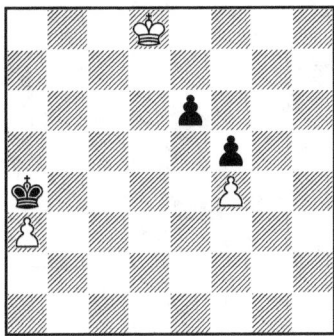

4.♔c7! And now giving chase!
4...e5. If 4...♔xa3, then 5.♔d6,
catching up with the pawn.
5.fxe5 f4 6.e6 f3 7.e7 f2 8.e8=♕+.
White wins.

Even the Reti maneuver, loved by
many composers, can serve as the basis
for a logical study!

No. 339**. M. Zinar
Moscow competition, 2014
Special honorable mention

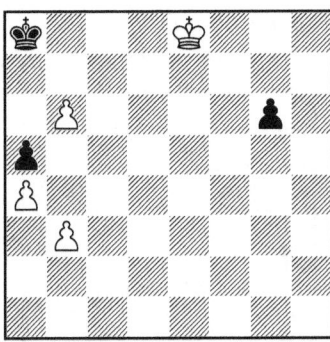

White to play and draw

The main plan with the Reti maneuver
does not work because of shouldering in
the finale of the variation: 1.♔d7? ♔b7
2.♔e6 ♔xb6 3.♔f6 ♔c5 4.♔xg6 ♔b4
5.♔f5 ♔xb3 6.♔e4 ♔xa4 7.♔d3 ♔b3!
8.♔d2 ♔b2, and black wins.

White is saved by the preliminary
feint **1.♔e7!! g5 2.♔d6!** Now the Reti
maneuver works one rank lower!

**2...♔b7 3.♔e5 ♔xb6 4.♔f5 ♔c5
5.♔xg5 ♔b4**

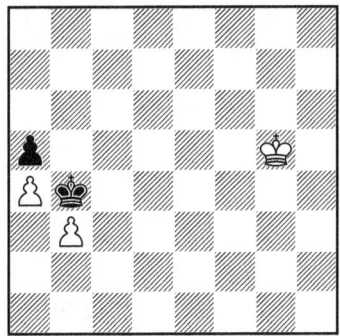

**6.♔f4! ♔xb3 7.♔e3 ♔xa4 8.♔d2
♔b3 9.♔c1.** Draw.

Even the familiar multiple knight
promotion can be embellished with logic!

No. 340**. M. Zinar
Shakhmatnaya Kompozitsiya, 2014
Commendation

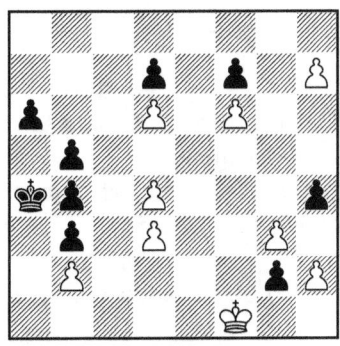

White to play and win

The white king is in check, and the outcome of the game depends on its next move!..

Logical false try: 1.♔f2? h3 2.h8=♘ a5 3.♘g6 fxg6 4.f7 g5

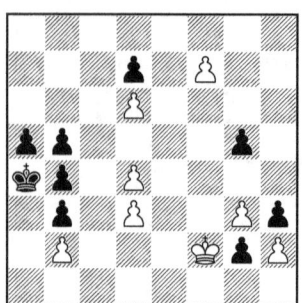

5.f8=♘ g4 6.♘e6 dxe6 7.d7 e5 8.d5 (8.d8=♘ exd4) 8...e4 9.dxe4 (9.d8=♘? e3+ 10.♔g1 e2 even loses) 9...g1=♕+ 10.♔xg1, draw.

Eureka: **1.♔g1!! h3 2.h8=♘! a5 3.♘g6 fxg6 4.f7 g5**

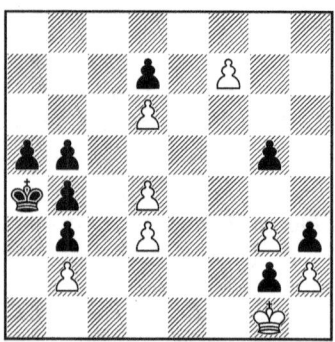

5.f8=♘! g4 6.♘e6 dxe6 7.d7 e5 8.d5! But not the immediate 8.d8=♘? exd4 9.♘b7, stalemate.

8...e4 9.d8=♘! e3 (without check!) **10.♘e6(b7) e2 11.♘c5#.**

Three Reti maneuvers are met with an anti-Reti in the subtle logical miniature **Study 341**.

No. 341**. M. Zinar
JC Sochnev − 50, 2014
Special honorable mention

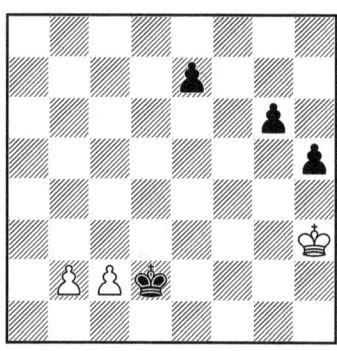

White to play and win

Logical false try: 1.b4? e5 2.b5 e4 3.b6 e3 4.b7 e2 5.b8=♕ e1=♕ 6.♕b4+ ♔e2 7.♕xe1+ ♔xe1

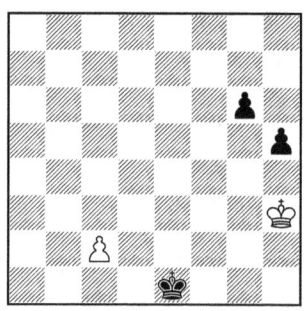

8.♔h4 ♔f2 9.c4 g5+ 10.♔xh5 (10. ♔xg5 ♔g3! Reti-1)

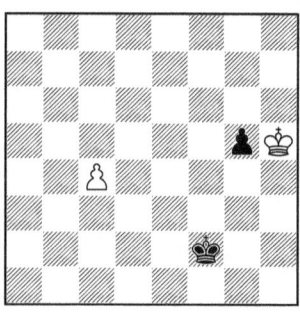

10...♔f3! (Reti-2) with equality.

The winning move is **1.c4!! e5 2.c5 e4 3.c6 e3 4.c7 e2 5.c8=♕ e1=♕ 6.♕c3+ ♔e2 7.♕xe1+ ♔xe1**

8.♔h4. Not 8.b4? g5 9.b5 ♔f2 10.b6 g4+ or 8.♔g2? g5 9.b4 h4 10.b5 g4 11.b6 h3+, with a draw in both cases.

8...♔f2 9.b4 g5+ 10.♔xg5! But not 10.♔xh5? ♔f3! – Reti-3!

10...♔g3 11.b5 h4 12.b6 h3 13.b7 h2 14.b8=♕+. The anti-Reti trick worked! White wins.

To take or not to take black's rook pawn? In **Study 342**, the answer will only become apparent after many more moves!

No. 342**. V. Kovalenko
Shakhmatnaya Kompozitsiya, 2006
Commendation

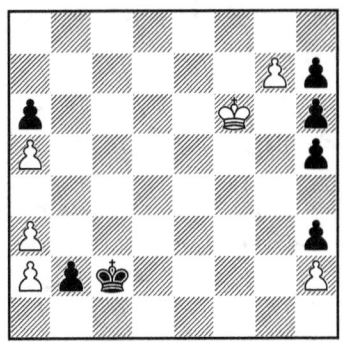

White to play and win

1.g8=♕ b1=♕ 2.♕c4+!! Why not the "logical" 2.♕xh7+? This will only become clear 23 moves later!

2...♔b2 (2...♔d2 3.♕b4+) **3.♕b3+ ♔a1 4.♕xb1+ ♔xb1**

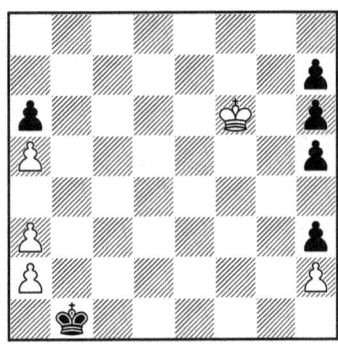

5.♔e5! The king must shoulder its opponent!

5...♔c2 6.♔d4! ♔d2 7.♔c5 ♔e2 8.♔b6 ♔f2 9.♔xa6 ♔g2 10.♔b6 ♔xh2

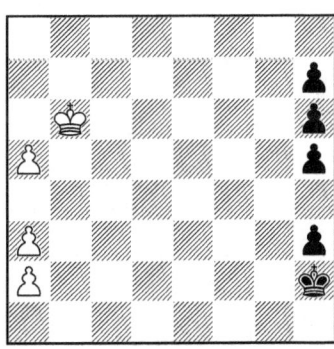

11.a6! The start of a systematic pawn march!

11...♔g1 12.a7 h2 13.a8=♕ h1=♕ 14.♕xh1+ ♔xh1 15.a4 h4 16.a5 h3 17.a6 h2 18.a7 ♔g1

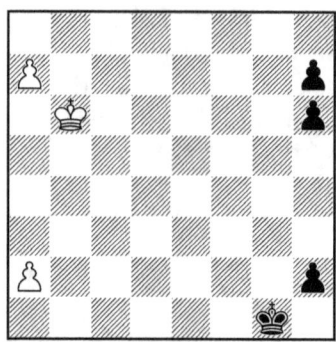

19.a8=♕ h1=♕ 20.♕xh1+ ♔xh1 21.a4 h5 22.a5 h4 23.a6 h3 24.a7 h2 25.a8=♕+. White wins. Only now, the importance of the prescient second move becomes clear. After 2.♕xh7+?, this would have been a draw − if you've managed this far then you can figure out the moves of the logical false try by yourself based on the solution!

The fate of the h5 pawn in the next study hinges on white's "logical" play.

No. 343**. V. Kovalenko**
Shakhmatnaya Kompozitsiya, 2005
2nd−3rd honorable mention

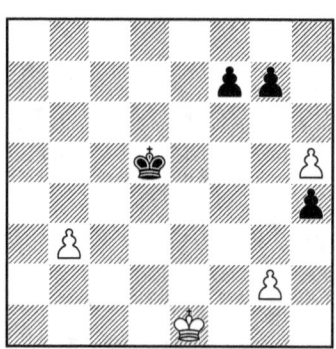

White to play and win

White needs to capture black's rook pawn and organize the breakthrough of his own infantrymen...

1.♔f2! But not 1.♔e2? h3! 2.gxh3 ♔d4 (the simplest) 3.♔f3 ♔c3, draw. 1.♔f1? ♔c5 2.♔g1 ♔b4 3.♔h2 ♔xb3 is also bad: white loses an important tempo for the breakthrough.

1...♔e4 (1...♔c5 2.♔f3 ♔b4 3.♔g4 ♔xb3 4.♔xh4; 1...h3 2.g4!) **2.♔g1!**

Logical false try: 2.b4? ♔d4 3.♔f3 ♔c4 4.♔g4 ♔xb4 5.♔xh4 ♔c5!

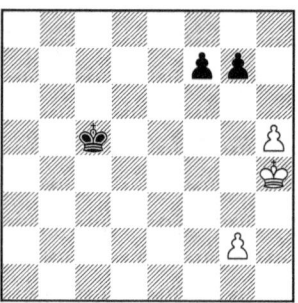

6.g4 ♔d6 7.g5 ♔e7 8.h6 gxh6 9.gxh6 ♔f8!, and the black king makes it to the key square.

Now, however, it stands on the wrong diagonal: **2...♔d4 3.♔h2 ♔c3 4.♔h3 ♔xb3 5.♔xh4 ♔c4**

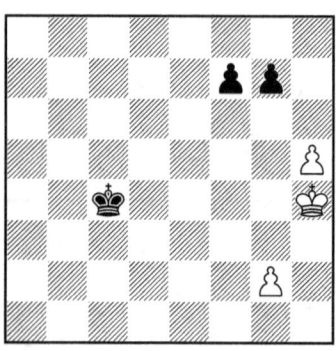

6.g4 ♔d5 7.g5 ♔e6 8.h6 gxh6 9.gxh6 ♔f6 10.♔h5! Mutual zugzwang and wins. Subtle work by the white monarch!

The elegant logical **Study 344** was a highlight of a prestigious memorial competition honoring the founding father of modern chess studies.

No. 344**. V. Tarasiuk
MT Troitsky — 150, 2017
2ⁿᵈ prize

White to play and win

1.♔b2! Logical false try: 1.c4? ♔b6 2.♔b2 ♔c5 3.♔c3 b2 4.♔xb2 ♔d4

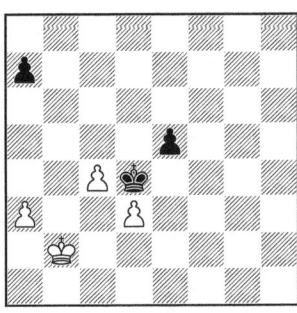

5.♔b3 (5.♔c2 e4 6.dxe4 ♔xc4) 5...♔xd3 6.c5 e4 7.c6 e3 8.c7 e2 9.c8=♕ e1=♕, and white cannot win.

1...♔a4 2.c4 a6! (2...a5 3.♔b1 ♔xa3 4.c5) **3.♔a1!!** Back to the initial square! After the "obvious" 3.♔b1? a5 4.♔b2 e4 5.dxe4, there's stalemate on the board.

3...♔a5 4.♔b1 ♔b6! (4...♔a4

5.♔b2 ♔a5 6.♔xb3) **5.♔b2 ♔c5 6.♔c3!!** Capture avoidance! After the greedy 6.♔xb3? ♔d4 (mutual zugzwang)

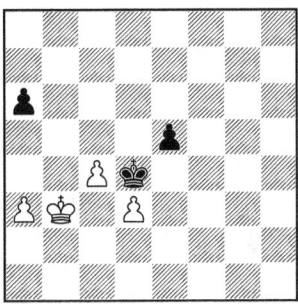

7.♔a4 ♔xd3 8.c5 e4 9.c6 e3 10.c7 e2 11.c8=♕ e1=♕ 12.♕xa6+ ♔c2!, white cannot outplay his opponent. Another false try!

6...b2 7.♔xb2 ♔d4

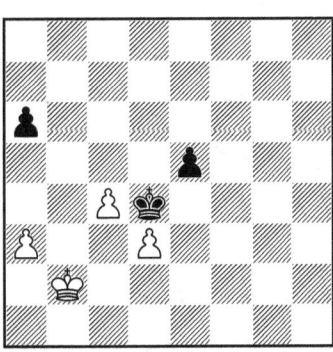

8.♔b3! The zugzwang benefits white.

8...♔xd3 9.c5 e4 10.c6 e3 11.c7 e2 12.c8=♕ e1=♕ 13.♕xa6+ ♔d4 14.♕d6+, and white wins by trading queens and pushing the rook pawn. With inventive play, white forced black to move the a7 pawn to a6 to capture it with check in the finale.

In the opinion of Yuri Bazlov, chief judge of the competition, this was one of the best pawn studies of recent years.

Logical studies have given new life to many well-known ideas! Look how hackneyed ideas (stalemating niche + underpromotions) have been executed in the following composition.

No. 345**. M. Zinar
Zadachi i etyudy, 2017
2nd honorable mention

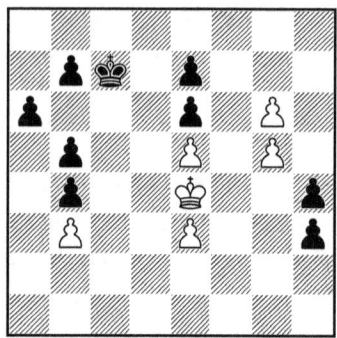

White to play and win

1.♔f3 h2 2.♔g2 h3+! 3.♔xh2. After 3.♔h1?, as later events show, white won't be able to escape the stalemate trap.

3...♔b6! Quick, into the stalemate shelter!

4.g7 ♔a5 5.g8=♘! b6

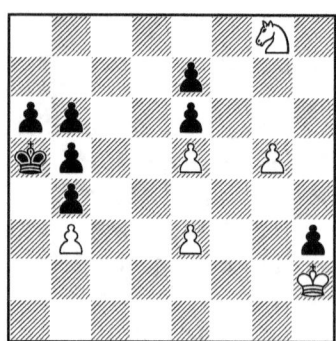

6.♘f6! Logical false try: 6.♔g3? h2 7.♘xe7 h1=♕ 8.♘c6+ ♕xc6, and there's no checkmate.

6...exf6 7.g6! fxe5 8.g7 e4 9.g8=♘! **e5 10.♔g3!** Now that the long diagonal is blocked, white can revert to the main plan.

10...h2 11.♘e7 h1=♕ 12.♘c6#. Nice logic!

Another logical spectacle with a stalemate niche and knight underpromotion is presented in the next study.

No. 346**. M. Zinar
EG-50, 2016
Special honorable mention

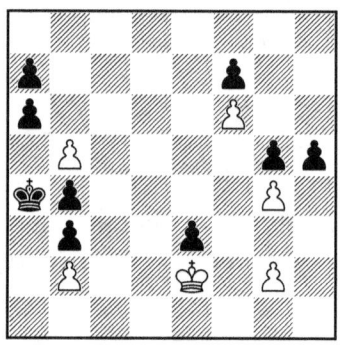

White to play and win

1.b6!! Logical false try: 1.gxh5? axb5 2.h6 g4! 3.h7 g3! (3...a5? 4.h8=♘! or 3... a6? 4.h8=♕!)

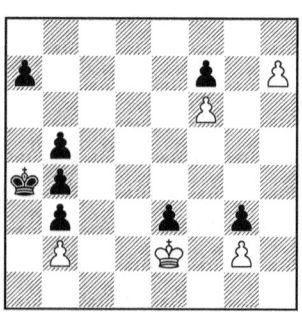

4.h8=♘ a6!! 5.♘g6 a5 6.♔e1 e2! (6...fxg6? 7.f7 g5 8.f8=♘) **7.♔xe2 fxg6 8.f7 g5 9.f8=♘ g4 10.♘d7,** stalemate.

1...axb6 2.gxh5 b5. Or the prosaic bind: 2...g4 3.h6 g3 4.h7 a5 5.h8=♘ ♔b5 6.♘xf7 a4 7.♘d6+ ♔c6 8.f7 a3 9.f8=♕ etc.

3.h6 g4 4.h7 g3

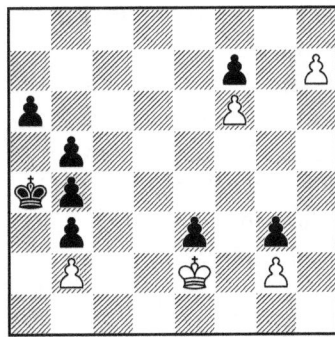

5.h8=♘! a5 6.♘g6 fxg6 7.f7 g5 8.f8=♘! g4

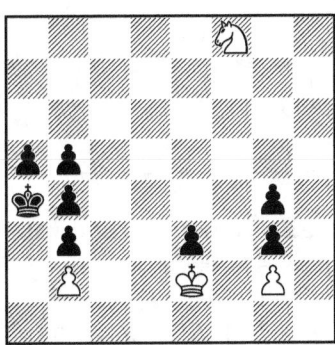

9.♔d3! The "traitor" black pawn is still alive!

9...e2 10.♘d7! But not 10.♘e6? e1=♘+ 11.♔e2 ♘d3 12.♔xd3, stalemate.

10...e1=♕. Or 10...e1=♘+ 11.♔e2 ♘d3 12.♘b6#.

11.♘b6(c5)#.

Even the promotions themselves, or, to be more precise, their order, can serve as a "plot" for a logical

study! An example is shown in **Study 347.**

No. 347**. M. Zinar
Shakhmatnaya Kompozitsiya, 2017
Special honorable mention

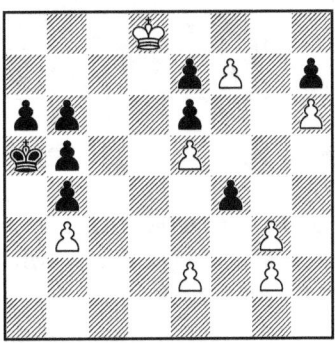

White to play and win

Which promotion order to choose? 1.f8=♘? is a false try: 1...fxg3! 2.♘g6 hxg6 3.h7 g5 4.h8=♕ g4 5.♕f6 exf6 6.exf6 e5 7.f7 e4

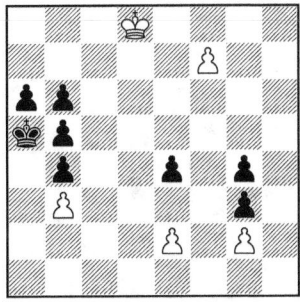

8.f8=♘ e3 and stalemate to come. 1.f8=♖? f3! 2.e4 f2! doesn't work either, stalemate is inevitable.

The correct move is **1.f8=♕! fxg3.** Or 1...f3 2.♕f4 fxg2 3.♕d2 g1=♕ 4.♕a2#.

2.♕f6! exf6 3.exf6 e5 4.f7 e4

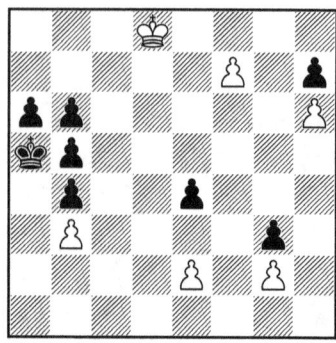

5.f8=♘! But not 5.f8=♕? e3 with stalemate.

5...e3 6.♘g6! hxg6 7.h7 g5 8.h8=♕ g4 9.♕a1#!, checkmating with the longest possible move.

In the next logical study, white's success depends on correct interpretation of the mutual zugzwang position.

No. 348**. O. Pervakov and K. Sumbatian
MT Manvelian − 70, 2017
2nd−3rd prize

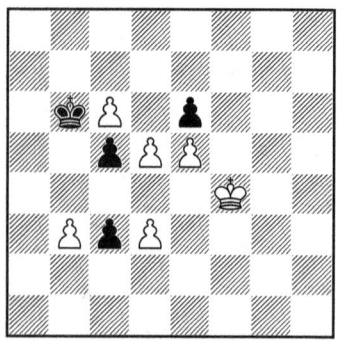

White to play and win

Immediate LFT: 1.♔e3? exd5 2.d4 cxd4+ 3.♔d3 ♔c7!! 4.b4 ♔xc6 (mutual zugzwang) 5.♔c2 d3+! 6.♔xc3 d4+ 7.♔xd3 ♔d5 8.e6 ♔xe6 9.♔xd4 ♔d6, draw.

Therefore, **1.c7!! ♔b7!** Not 1...♔xc7 2.d6+ ♔c6 3.♔e3 etc. The mutual queen promotion doesn't help either: 1...c2 2.c8=♕ c1=♕+ 3.♔g4 ♕g1+ 4.♔h5 ♕h1+ 5.♔g6 ♕xd5 6.♕b8+ ♔a5 7.♕d6 ♕f3 8.♕xc5+ ♔a6 9.b4 ♕xd3+ 10.♔f6 with a technical win.

2.♔e3! White shouldn't sacrifice the queen − it's dangerous: 2.c8=♕+? ♔xc8 3.♔e3 exd5 4.d4 cxd4+ 5.♔e2 ♔d7! 6.b4 ♔e6 7.b5 ♔xe5, and now it's black who wins.

2...exd5 3.d4 cxd4+

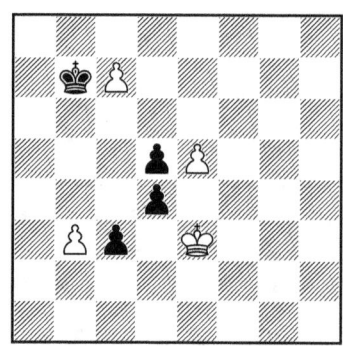

4.♔e2!! Another point! After the "obvious" 4.♔d3? ♔xc7 5.b4 ♔c6!, white is in zugzwang.

4...♔xc7 (4...♔c8 5.b4 ♔xc7 6.b5) **5.b4! ♔c6 6.♔d3!** Mutual zugzwang now benefits white!

6...♔b5 (6...♔d7 7.b5) **7.e6 ♔c6 8.b5+ ♔d6 9.b6.** White wins.

To promote the pawn to a knight with decisive effect in **Study 349**, white has to block an important diagonal first.

No. 349**. A. Oganesian
Gravyura, 2016
3rd commendation

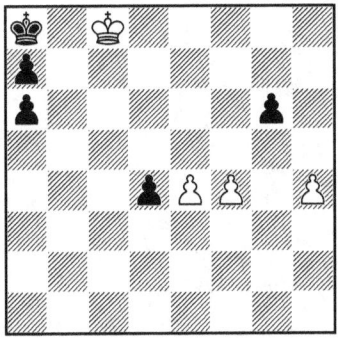

White to play and win

The rush towards the promotion square looks logical: 1.e5?! d3 2.e6 d2 3.e7 d1=♕ 4.e8=♕ (not 4.e8=♘? due to 4...♕g4+) 4...♕c2+! (but not 4...♕c1+? 5.♔d7+ ♔b7 6.♕e4+! ♔b8 7.♕c6) 5.♔d7+ ♔b7 6.♕e5 ♕c6+, and black is safe.

Eureka: **1.f5! gxf5 2.e5!** Not 2.exf5? d3 3.f6 d2 4.f7 d1=♕ 5.f8=♕ ♕c2+! (5...♕c1+? 6.♔d7+ ♔b7 7.♕b4+! ♔a8 8.♕e4+ ♔b8 9.♕c6) 6.♔d7+ ♔b7, draw.
2...d3 3.e6 d2 4.e7 d1=♕

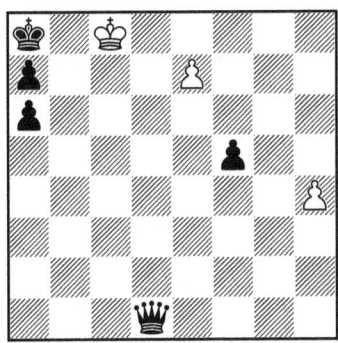

5.e8=♘! And now the knight promotion works because the h3-c8 diagonal is blocked.

5...♕c1+ 6.♘c7+ ♕xc7+ 7.♔xc7 f4 8.h5 f3 9.h6 f2 10.h7 f1=♕ 11.h8=♕(♖)+ with checkmate. Solvers love such studies!

The well-known zugzwang opposition in the finale of **Study 350** was presented in a logical way.

No. 350**. M. Zinar
MT Wotawa – 120, 2016
2nd prize

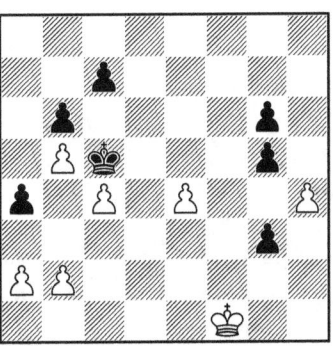

White to play and win

Logical false try: 1.e5? (1.hxg5? ♔xc4 2.♔g2 ♔d4) 1...gxh4 2.♔g2 c6 3.e6 ♔d6 4.c5+ ♔xe6 5.cxb6 ♔d6 6.b7 ♔c7 7.bxc6 g5

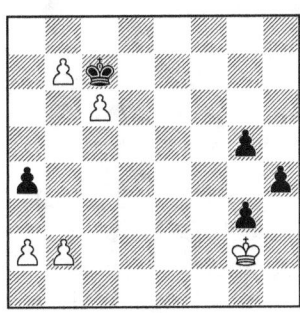

8.b3! axb3! 9.axb3 g4 10.b4 ♔b8 11.b5 ♔c7 12.b6+ ♔b8 (mutual zugzwang) 13.♔h1

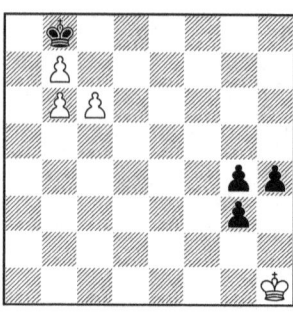

13...h3! 14.♔g1 g2 15.♔h2 g3+ 16.♔g1 h2+ 17.♔xg2 h1=♕+ 18.♔xh1 g2+ 19.♔h2 g1=♕+ 20.♔xg1, stalemate.

The winning move is **1.h5!! gxh5 2.e5 h4 3.♔g2!** 3.b4+? loses to 3...axb3 4.axb3 h3 5.b4+ ♔d4 6.e6 h2 7.♔g2 ♔e3 8.e7 h1=♕+ 9.♔xh1 ♔f2, curtains.

3...c6! Or 3...g4 4.b4+ axb3 5.axb3 c6 (5...♔d4 6.e6) 6.b4+!, winning.

4.e6 ♔d6 5.c5+ ♔xe6 6.cxb6 ♔d6 7.b7 ♔c7 8.bxc6 g4

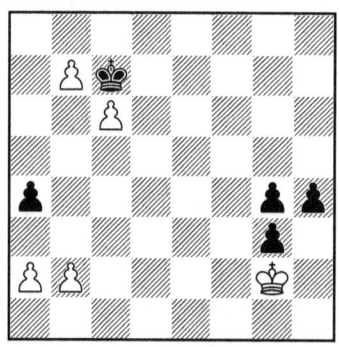

9.b4! (9.b3? a3) **9...axb3 10.axb3 ♔b8 11.b4 ♔c7 12.b5 ♔b8 13.b6.** Mutual zugzwang benefits white.

13...h3+ 14.♔xg3. White wins.

In **Study 351**, white cannot win without a queenside breakthrough. But this plan must be skillfully prepared!

No. 351**. M. Zinar
M. Dvoretsky memorial, 2017
6th honorable mention

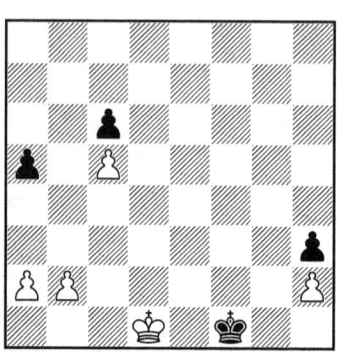

White to play and win

A logical false try at first: 1.b3? ♔g2 (or 1...♔f2 2.♔d2 ♔g2 3.♔e2 etc.) 2.♔e2 ♔xh2 3.♔f2 ♔h1 4.♔f1 (4.♔g3 ♔g1! 5.♔xh3 ♔f2 6.a3 ♔e3) 4...♔h2 5.♔f2 (5.a3 ♔g3! 6.♔g1 ♔f4) 5...♔h1! (mutual zugzwang) 6.a3 h2 7.♔f1 a4 8.bxa4, stalemate.

1.♔d2! ♔f2! 2.♔d3! But not 2.a4? ♔g2 3.b4 axb4 4.a5 ♔xh2, and the pawns promote at the same time.

2...♔f3 3.♔d4! ♔f2. 3...♔f4 is met with 4.a4 ♔f3 5.b4 axb4 6.a5, and wins.

4.♔e4! ♔g2 (4...♔e2 5.b3 ♔f2 6.a3) **5.♔e3! ♔h1!**

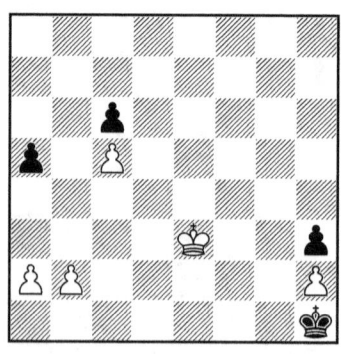

6.♔f3!! After 6.♔f2? ♔xh2 7.b3 ♔h1! there's a familiar zugzwang from the false try on the board! 6.♔e2? ♚g2 7.♔e3 ♚h1 etc. also gives nothing. Now, however, black is forced to take the pawn, because 6...♚g1 is met with 7.♔g3.

6...♚xh2 7.♔f2 ♚h1 (7...a4 8.b4)

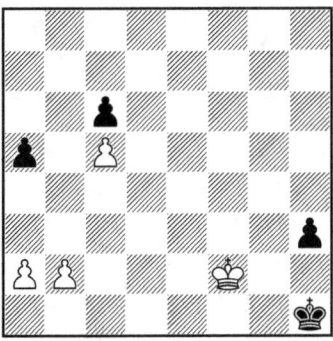

8.b3! It's time to execute the main plan! A mutual zugzwang is on the board.

8...h2 9.♔f1! a4 10.b4! a3 11.b5. White wins.

The stalemate **Study 352**, featuring a zugzwang in the finale, is embellished with logical light.

No. 352**. M. Zinar
JC Masimov, 2017
3rd prize

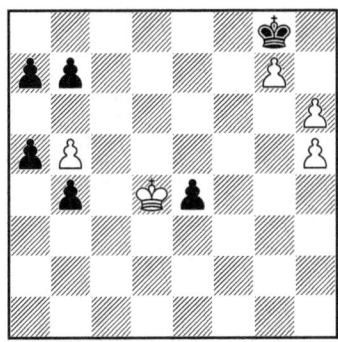

White to play and draw

The capture looks natural: 1.♔xe4? a4 2.♔d3 a3 3.♔c2 a2 4.♔b2 b3 5.♔a1 a5! (5...a6? 6.b6)

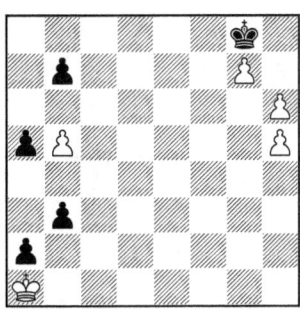

6.bxa6 bxa6 7.♔b2 a5 8.♔a1 a4 9.♔b2 a3+ 10.♔a1 ♔h7 (mutual zugzwang) 11.g8=♕+ ♔xg8 12.h7+ ♔xh7 13.h6 b2+, and black wins. This is a logical false try!

White is saved by the spectacular capture avoidance: **1.♔e5!! ♔f7** (1... e3? 2.♔f6 e2 3.♔g6 e1=♕ 4.h7#) **2.♔xe4 a4 3.♔d3 a3 4.♔c2 a2 5.♔b2 b3 6.♔a1 a6!**

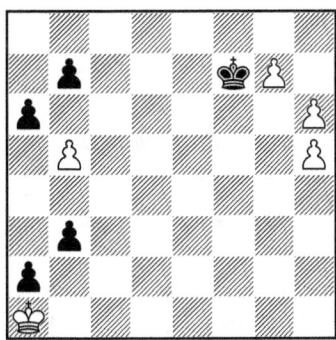

7.bxa6! bxa6 8.♔b2 a5 9.♔a1 a4 10.♔b2 a3+ 11.♔a1. And now it's black who is in zugzwang!

11...♔g8 12.h7+ ♔xg7 13.h6+ ♔xh7. Stalemate.

The logical motif of a false try with an en passant capture in the next composition is quite original.

No. 353**. O. Comay and G. Costeff
Zadachi i Etyudy, 2017
3rd honorable mention

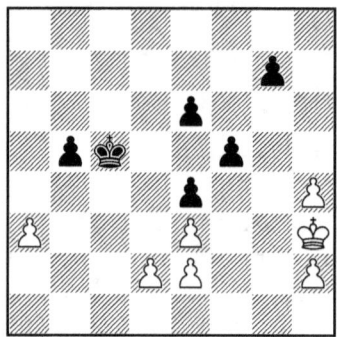

White to play and draw

Logical false try: **1.h5? ♔c4 2.♔h4 ♔b3 3.♔g5 ♔xa3**

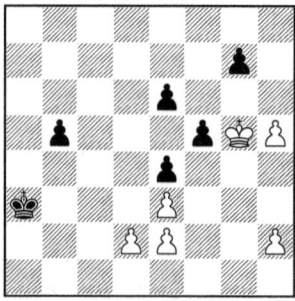

4.♔g6 b4 5.♔xg7 b3 6.h6 b2 7.h7 b1=♕ 8.h8=♕ ♕a1+ 9.d4 (9.♔h7 ♕xh8+ 10.♔xh8 e5) 9...exd3+, en passant!

Eureka: **1.d3!! ♔b6 2.h5 ♔a5 3.♔h4 ♔a4 4.♔g5 ♔xa3**

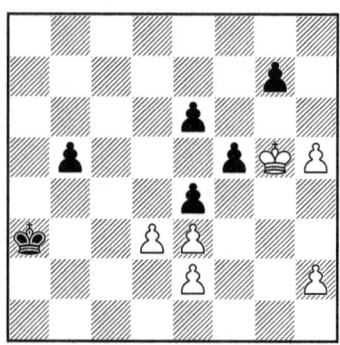

5.♔g6 b4 6.♔xg7 b3 7.h6 b2 8.h7 b1=♕ 9.h8=♕ ♕a1+ 10.d4!, and there is no en passant! Draw.

The early pawn sacrifice prepares a checkmate combination in the finale of **Study 354**, in a classical mutual zugzwang.

No. 354** M. Zinar
Gravyura, 2018
3rd commendation

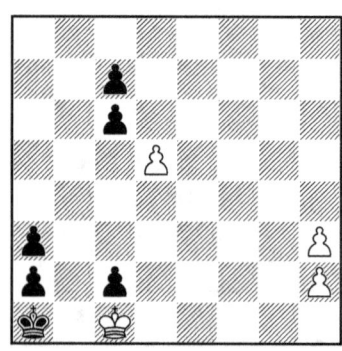

White to play and win

Logical false try: **1.h4? cxd5 2.h5 d4 3.h6 d3 4.h7 d2+ 5.♔xc2 d1=♕+ 6.♔xd1 ♔b1 7.h8=♕ a1=♕ 8.♕xa1+ ♔xa1 9.♔c1! a2! 10.h4**

10...c6!! (a tortoise move!) 11.h5 c5 12.h6 c4 13.h7 c3 (white is in zugzwang) 14.h8=♕ with a classical stalemate.

A preliminary pawn sacrifice helps white: **1.d6! cxd6 2.h4 d5 3.h5 d4 4.h6 d3 5.h7 d2+ 6.♔xc2 d1=♕+ 7.♔xd1 ♔b1**

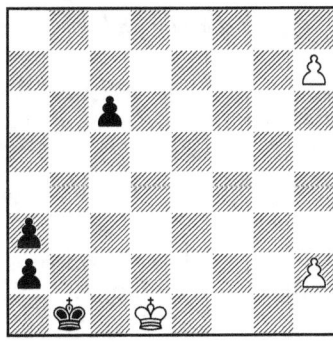

8.h8=♕! But not 8.h8=♗? c5! 9.h4 c4 10.h5 c3 11.♗xc3 a1=♕ 12.♗xa1 ♔xa1, draw.

8...a1=♕ 9.♕xa1+ ♔xa1 10.♔c1! a2 11.h4 c5 12.h5 c4 13.h6 c3 14.h7! Now black is in zugzwang, and he is forced to open the diagonal for checkmate.

14...c2 15.h8=♕(♗)#.

At first, Mikhail Zinar was quite skeptical about logical studies. But then he got a taste for them and composed a series of beautiful studies in the logical genre. We have already seen several of his creations. Here, at the end of this chapter, I present three more logical studies of the Master, composed a few years before his untimely death.

No. 355**. M. Zinar
Memorial I. Akobia – 80, 2017
Honorable mention

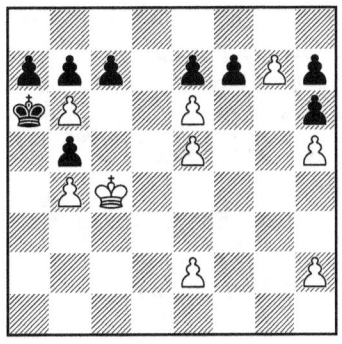

White to play and win

The white king is in check...

Retreating to the d-file is bad: 1.♔d3? cxb6 2.g8=♘ fxe6 3.♘f6 exf6 4.exf6 e5 5.f7 e4+ (check!) 6.♔d4 e3, and black is stalemated.

Logical false try: 1.♔b3? cxb6 2.g8=♘! fxe6 3.♘f6 exf6 4.exf6 e5 5.f7 e4 6.f8=♘! e3 7.♘g6 hxg6 8.hxg6 h5 9.g7 h4 10.g8=♕ h3, and white has to settle for stalemate.

The correct move is **1.♔c3!! cxb6 2.g8=♘!** A second logical false try: 2.g8=♕? fxe6 3.♕g6 hxg6 4.hxg6 h5 5.g7 h4 6.g8=♘ h3 7.♘f6 exf6 8.exf6 e5 9.f7 e4 10.f8=♕ e3, and black again reaches his stalemating oasis.

2...fxe6 3.♘f6 exf6 4.exf6 e5 5.f7 e4

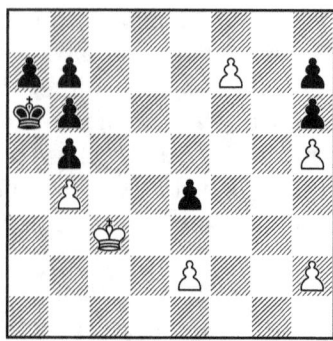

6.f8=♘! e3 7.♘g6 hxg6 8.hxg6 h5 9.g7 h4 10.g8=♕ h3 11.♕a2#! The checkmate became possible because of the opened a2-g8 diagonal (see the first false try) and the new queen appearing on g8 (see the second false try).

No. 356**. M. Zinar
Cirtdan, 2018
1st honorable mention

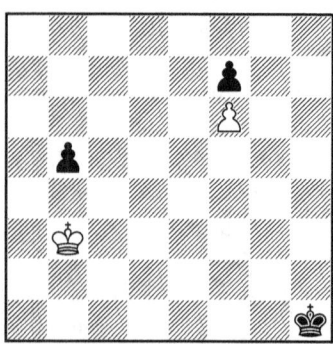

White to play and draw

White has to deal with the black passed pawn and then run to the kingside...

1.♔b4 ♔g2 2.♔c5!! Capture avoidance! After the "obvious" 2.♔xb5? ♔f3! 3.♔c4 ♔e4!, black shoulders the white king.

4.♔c3 ♔e5 5.♔d3 ♔xf6 6.♔e4 ♔g5, and the opposition doesn't work.

2...b4. After 2...♔f3 3.♔d6!, white saves the game.

3.♔xb4 ♔f3 4.♔c3! ♔e4 5.♔d2! ♔f5 6.♔e3 ♔xf6 7.♔f4 with drawing opposition.

No. 357**. M. Zinar
Problemist Ukrainy, 2019

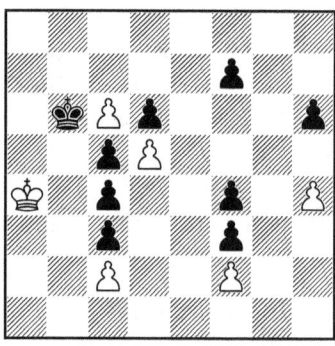

White to play and win

After **1.h5!** and the tortoise move **1... f6!**, there's a natural-looking logical false try: 2.c7? ♔xc7 3.♔a5 ♔b7 4.♔b5. But after 4...f5!, white cannot win because of zugzwang.

Therefore, he has to force black to lose another pawn tempo: **2.♔a3!! ♔a6 3.♔a2 ♔a7 4.♔b1 ♔a6 5.♔c1 ♔a7 6.♔d1 ♔a6 7.♔e1 ♔a7 8.♔f1 ♔a6 9.♔g1 ♔a7 10.♔h2 ♔a6 11.♔h3 f5.** Otherwise, the white king breaks into black's camp.

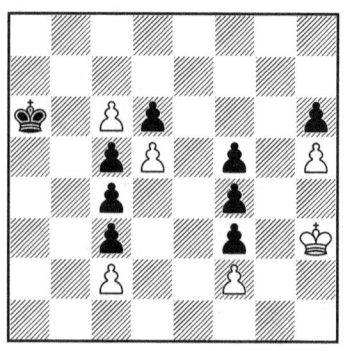

12.♔h2! And back!

12...♚a7 13.♔g1 ♚a6 14.♔f1 ♚a7 15.♔e1 ♚a6 16.♔d1 ♚a7 17.♔c1 ♚a6 18.♔b1 ♚a7 19.♔a2 ♚a6 20.♔a3 ♚a7

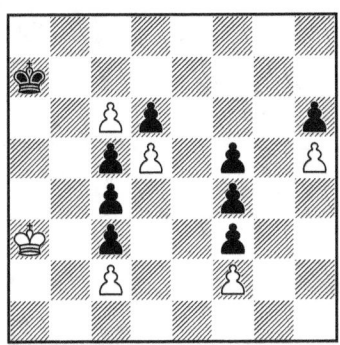

21.♔a4! ♚b6. The position is familiar, but black has no pawn tempi anymore...

22.c7! ♚xc7 23.♔a5 ♚b7 24.♔b5 ♚c7 25.♔a6. White wins.

And here's a fresh logical study from a recent composition tournament. The collective **Study 358** even won the annual competition of a famous chess magazine!

No. 358**. N. Ryabinin and K. Sumbatian
64 – Shakhmatnoe Obozrenie, 2021
1ˢᵗ prize

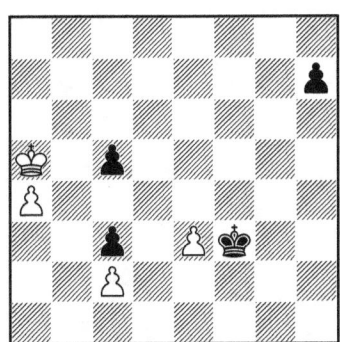

White to play and win

The main plan is flawed: 1.♔b6? ♚e2 2.a5 ♚d2 3.a6 ♚xc2 4.a7

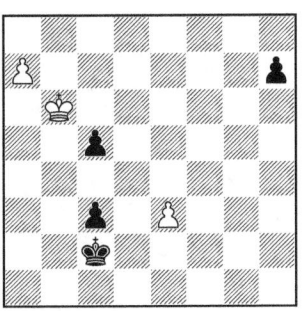

4...♚b1!! (but not 4...♚b2? 5.a8=♕ c2 6.♕h8+ ♚b1 7.♕xh7 ♚b2 8.♕g7+ ♚b1 9.♕g1+, curtains) 5.a8=♕ c2 6.♕e4 ♚b2 7.♕e5+ ♚b1 8.♕xc5 c1=♕ 9.♕xc1+ ♚xc1 10.e4 h5, and the pawns promote at the same time.

1.e4!! ♚xe4. The pawn race doesn't save black: 1...h5 2.e5 h4 3.e6 h3 4.e7 h2 5.e8=♕ h1=♕ 6.♕c6+, skewering the queen.

2.♔b6!! Another false try: 2.♔b5? ♚e3 3.a5 ♚d2 4.a6 ♚xc2 5.a7 ♚b1 6.a8=♕ c2 7.♕e4 ♚b2 8.♕e2 ♚b1, and white cannot win.

2...♚e3 3.a5 ♚d2 4.a6 ♚xc2 5.a7 ♚b2! 6.a8=♕ c2

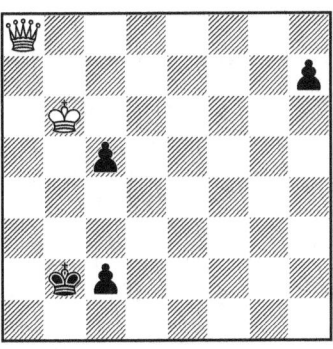

7.♕g2! But not 7.♕h8+? ♚b1 8.♕xh7 ♚b2 with a theoretical draw.

7...♔b1 8.♕e4 ♔b2 9.♕e2 ♔b1 10.♕b5+! – the b5 square is free. White wins.

The interweaving of diverse ideas in this logical composition is solid proof that there are many more brilliant spectacles created in this genre to come!

Chapter III

ARTISTIC REQUIREMENTS FOR ENDGAME STUDIES

The key artistic requirements for endgame studies are driven by the principles of (1) unity of form and content and (2) harmonic alignment of the main idea and the means used to execute that idea.

Artistic requirements have changed over time in the course of artistic development of chess composition. Violation of these requirements is not punished as severely as violation of the formal requirements we discussed at the start of the book (legality, solvability, and uniqueness of solution). That is to say, studies with a low artistic level still have a right to exist, unlike those that violate the formal requirements. However, neglecting the main historical artistic requirements hinders both creative achievements and success in competitions.

Naturally, as in any other art form, every endgame study artist has his or her own views, principles and unique creative style. A uniform approach to artistic requirements is not possible. Some authors are stricter and more dogmatic in their evaluation of studies, while others are less so. Which of the numerous artistic requirements should be considered the key ones?

1. Expressiveness of the idea — the clear identification of the main line, which explains the very purpose of the given endgame study. The secondary technical lines should not obscure the main play.

This requirement is fulfilled in the following way: the idea should not be ordinary and uninteresting, but it should be prominent and immediately obvious. In the vast majority of studies, this criterion is fulfilled. But let's look at a different type of example.

No. 359. H. Cohn
Maestros Latinoamericanos, 1940

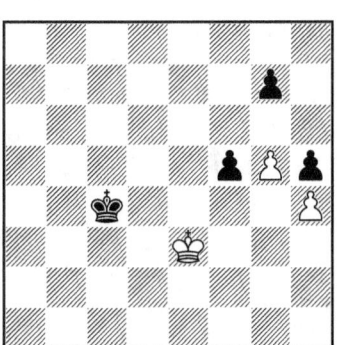

White to play and draw

White is a pawn down. The first move is obvious — otherwise black creates a protected passed pawn.

1.g6! ♔d5 2.♔f4 ♔e6 3.♔g5, and after **3...f4 4.♔xf4** or **3...♔e5 4.♔xh5 f4 5.♔g4 ♔e4 6.h5,** it's a draw.

What did the author like here? It's hard to tell! White easily wins a pawn with a guaranteed draw.

And now compare this with **Study 145**, despite its hole. White also has to regain a pawn there, but the solution is much more expressive. White uses the same technique three times – the echo principle!

Therefore, expressiveness is achieved above all through applying the principle of repetition: serial, parallel, in a false try, in the play of both sides, etc.

We have seen repetitions numerous times. Let's remember all its types again, expressed in the "cowardly maneuver" of **Studies 91–95**. These are all diverse types of synthesis. As you study synthesis, you will notice that dissimilar ideas can also be synthesized, but then all these ideas should be interesting by themselves and approximately equal in value, otherwise the harmony of the study is violated.

And, finally, expressiveness can be achieved by other means. For instance, spectacular points, such as 3.♔e5!! in **Study 47**, 1.♔g7! in **Study 73**, 3.♔a7!! in **Study 125**, 2.♔h5!! in **Study 127**, 1.♔g7!! in **Study 134**, etc. Or other techniques: avoidance of capture, sacrifice, unusual path towards the goal, systematic movement, underpromotion, a pretty picture painted by the solution, special study techniques such as the stalemate niche, a record expression of the idea or other methods.

2. Efficiency. *Efficiency of the form.* This artistic requirement means that the author's idea should be executed with the minimal possible means. The initial position is efficient if all pieces take part in the solution. The main group of pieces required to express the idea constitutes the scheme of the composition. In addition, technical pieces (or pawns) are used to eliminate side solutions, unsolvability or duals.

It's preferable to avoid using technical pawns, but it's not always possible. For instance, in **Study 18**, the g2 and g3 pawns are required for the queen to be promoted on h1 without check. Side solutions are eliminated by the e6 pawn in **Study 82** and h2 pawn in **Study 86**, the g3 pawn in **Study 208** eliminates insolvability, etc. The more complicated and wide-ranging the idea, the more technical pawns become necessary.

Efficiency of play in studies means that you should avoid unnecessary trades and eliminate technical variations, which improves the expressiveness of the main line. Sometimes technical pawns are necessary to ensure the efficiency of play. For instance, in **Study 276**, the technical d3 pawn allows us to avoid long lines after 1.a8=♕? f3 2.d8=♕?! These lines are hence "weeded out"!

Efficiency of the final position means that all remaining pieces should be involved in it if possible. This is preferable, but you should not strive for this all the time – sometimes, inefficiency cannot be avoided.

All pieces take part in the mating picture of **Study 167**, but compare it with **Study 169**: the h-pawns do not "take part" in the finale, but how much more impressive the latter study is! The echo-chameleon checkmate became possible exactly because of these pawns. However, it's less attractive when the pawn "remnants" of previous play survive until the finale.

For instance, in **Study 283**, the a6 and a7 pawns are needed solely to force black to trap his king in the corner. They are not needed for the finale. Efficiency should not be pursued at the expense of expressiveness. Otherwise, you'll be getting efficient but uninteresting studies with bland play.

3. Beauty of the solution. The hardest requirement to explain! As we know, there's no accounting for taste. But still, let us try to dissect this requirement. Of course, no beauty is possible without observing the principles of expressiveness and efficiency. In addition, the initial position must look natural. Nobody is stopping you from constructing unwieldy, obviously artificial structures, and if an unusual position is won by unusual moves, then so be it. However, when "miracles" start to happen in a simple-looking position, it looks much more spectacular!

In pawn studies in particular, vertical "pawn walls" and horizontal "pawn lines" with many pawns on the same rank or file are not that attractive. But, on the other hand, Grigoriev's masterpiece **Study 207** would have been impossible without tripled pawns.

And, as in all other forms of art, grotesque is an acceptable form of chess composition. For instance, the authors of **Studies 209** and **260** deliberately constructed exaggerated initial positions.

As we know, an endgame study usually consists of three parts: the introduction, thematic play and the finale. We have stated numerous times that some studies

lack a finale, or that it is overly simple. There are also some studies without an introduction, for instance, **Study 317**. 1.♗d5! is played immediately – the entire study is expressed in a single move, even though we added the lines for clarity.

For the solution to be beautiful, it's preferable that these three parts of the study be organically united; this requirement is fulfilled in the vast majority of the studies we have reviewed in this book. The introductory play should, if possible, be performed by the same pieces that will take part in the subsequent thematic play.

A large number of captures and trades in the play is considered unattractive – both in the main and the introductory part. Let's look at a good example of how not to compose endgame studies.

No. 360. J. Cumpe
Ceskoslovensky Sach, 1936

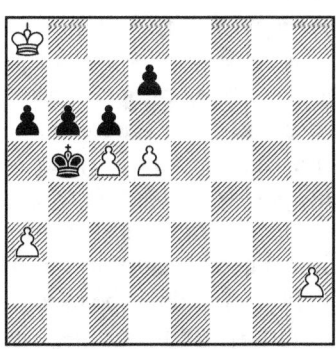

White to play and win

1.dxc6 dxc6 2.cxb6 ♚xb6. This play is not clever in any way; the literary and theater critic and famous study composer Gurvich wittily referred to it as a "brawl": half of all the pawns are taken off the board! And all this is done to get to a simple finale:

3.h4 c5 4.h5 c4 5.h6 c3 6.h7 c2 7.h8=♕ c1=♕ 8.♕b8+ with a win.

How long should the introductory play be, if you can extend it without adding new pieces? The majority of study composers add as many moves as possible in this case.

Let's return to **Study 15**. The main play starts with 3.♔d4!, while the first two moves are forced and do not contain anything new or interesting. Still, Grigoriev added them.

Let's now look at **Study 127**. 1.a4 ♔d4 is an introduction that does not help express the main idea. Later, a question arose: what if black plays 1...d4 and tries to win the queen endgame? It was proved that white still made a draw, but the desire to prolong the play at all cost gave rise to a technical variation. In this case, it would have been better to start the study from the position after the first move.

In **Study 279**, the f3 pawn could have been placed on its initial square f2 and the black king on g4, and then the solution could have started with 1.f3+ ♔h3 etc. But the unsightly position of the white pawn on f2 (under two attacks) and technical variations that arise after 1.g7? convinced the author that such an introduction should not be used.

In contrast to problems, the first move of a study is not subject to strict requirements. Still, if the first move is beautiful, this improves the study. You should avoid captures on the first move. In all the studies examined above, only one – **Study 287** – featured a capture on the first move.

In such situations, another technique is used: the solution starts with black's

move. While in the past it was considered a weakness to begin with black's move, in recent times solutions where black is to move are now perfectly acceptable, especially if introductory play with white to move is impossible. Moreover, there are even some studies where the white or the black king is in check in the initial position.

A solution is considered beautiful if it features dynamic, subtle play, interesting false tries and equal play from both sides. Ultimately, though, there is no limit to what is considered beauty in a study.

4. Precision of the solution – the study should not have duals or move transpositions.

The term "dual" has different meanings in problem and study composition. In pawn endgame studies, a dual is normally when there are two possible king moves that do not violate the author's idea.

A dual usually lowers the quality of a study, but not always. There are weak duals that are organically inherent to the idea. These are either impossible to eliminate or require adding a lot of material. In this case, the treatment is worse than the disease! Examples of such duals: 2.♔f2(f1) in **Study 95**, 3.♔e5(f6) in **Study 122** 5.♔f3(f2) in **Study 127**, 3.♔e7(e8) in **Study 134**, etc.

Let's look at **Study 312**. You can move the black king to e8 and remove the c5 pawn. But this allows for unpleasant duals: 3.♔d2(d4) and 4.♔e3(e4). It was possible to eliminate them, which was done by the author.

We think that the author of **Study 153** could also have eliminated or, at least, decreased the number of duals, shortening the solution. But let's call the artistic requirements there a different approach. Still, most prominent authors are tolerant towards duals, but eliminate them whenever possible.

We have also seen some move transpositions. If such transpositions do not happen during a climactic moment of the study and do not violate the author's idea, they are acceptable, albeit undesirable.

Some move transpositions, such as in **Studies 130** and **208**, may be impossible to eliminate. But if there are opportunities, transpositions should be eliminated — through changing the scheme, adding material, shortening the solution, etc. For instance, why didn't the author of **Study 205** put the kings on a1 and g2? Because that allowed for transpositions: white could then play 1.a5 or 1.♔b2 and then play either 2.a5 or 2.♔c3.

This is probably all there is to say about the key artistic requirements. There are many more principles of endgame study composition — you will encounter them during your own work. Some of them will become a part of your creative style, some you will reject, but we should warn you against categorical judgments, because the process of learning, evaluation and re-evaluation of creative style is truly endless.

Chapter IV

THE PRACTICE OF STUDY COMPOSITION

It's hard to explain exactly how the idea of a particular endgame study arises. It's easier to trace the path from the idea's appearance to its implementation in a concrete position. These paths are always different, but we think that by letting budding composers take a look into an expert's creative laboratory, we might help them develop their own methods and techniques of composition.

An attentive reader has likely already digested quite a lot of information about composition methods while studying this book. We have deliberately increased the number of studies on certain themes to show both what was already done and how the study ideas were developed.

Let's now analyze the composition process further. For instance, how was **Study 278** composed?

No. 361. N. Grigoriev
64, 1929

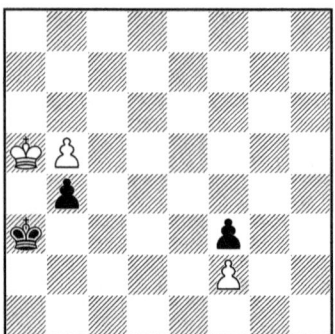

White to play and win

The author of **Study 278** looked at the diagram of **Study 361** many times and eventually noticed that after **1.b6 b3 2.b7 b2 3.b8=♖! ♚a2 4.♚a4! b1=♛ 5.♖xb1 ♚xb1**, another pawn endgame occurs. However, the play was very simple: **6.♚b3!**, winning. But can this second pawn endgame be made more interesting, for instance, by introducing a second underpromotion? And so, the

author decided to use the idea of **Study 362** as the second phase...

No. 362. A. Herbstman
L'Echiquier, 1928

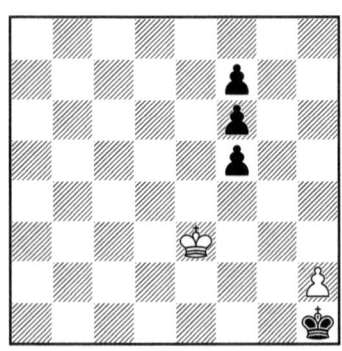

White to play and win

1.h4 ♚g2! 2.♚f4 ♚h3 3.h5 ♚h4 4.h6 ♚h5 5.h7 ♚g6 6.h8=♖! with a win.

To stop the pawn from moving forward too early, another black pawn was added in the first phase.

The following sketch resulted:

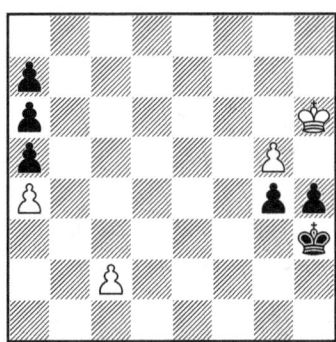

Solution: **1.g6 g3 2.g7 g2 3.g8=♖!**
♔h2 **4.**♔h5 **h3 5.**♔h4 **g1=♕ 6.**♖xg1
♔xg1 **7.**♔xh3.

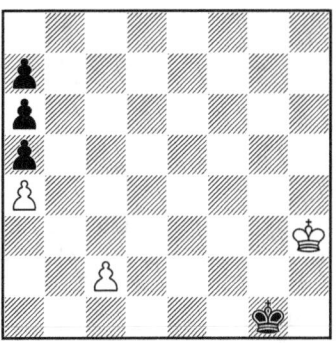

However, simple verification showed
that after **7...**♔f2 **8.c4** ♔e3 **9.c5** ♔d4
10.c6 ♔c5 **11.c7** ♔b6, the pawn could be
promoted to a bishop, not only to a rook.

To eliminate this flaw, the black a6
pawn was replaced with a white pawn.

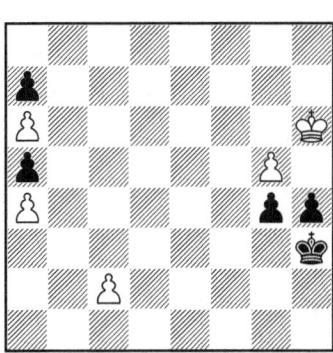

Now **12.c8=♖!** is indeed the only
winning move, but another verification
showed that a new side solution had
appeared: instead of 8.c4, white can play
8.♔g4! and wins after taking on a7. This
solution was also easy to eliminate: the
c2 pawn was moved to c3. The study was
ready, only with one final refinement:
instead of 1.g6, it would be better to put
the white king on g7, the white pawn on
g6 and start the solution with 1.♔h6!
And voila, we get **Study 278**.

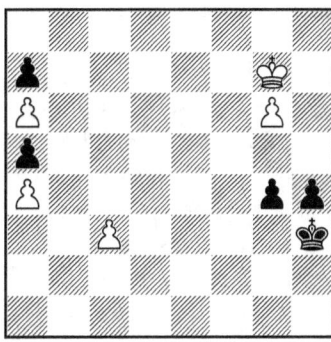

Years later, the author noticed that
the kingside pawns could be blocked,
which he did. Let's look at the next
composition.

No. 363. M. Zinar
USSR Central Chess Club Bulletin, 1978
(reworked, 1986)

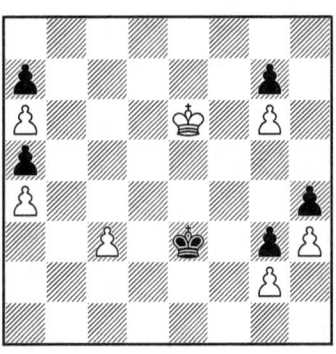

White to play and win

1.♔f7 ♚f2 2.♚xg7 ♚xg2 3.♚h6! ♚xh3 4.g7 g2

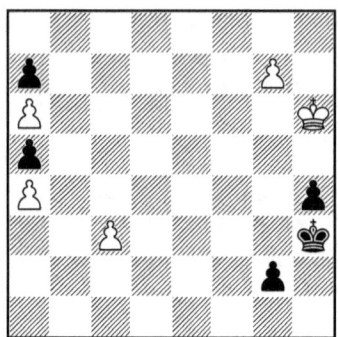

5.g8=♖! etc.

The rework itself probably didn't deserve much attention. The dynamics of the study did improve, but at the cost of capturing three pawns. However, the new stable position became a starting point for further creative investigation. An idea arose: if the kingside pawns can remain in their place for as long as I want, why not try to create a study where this play occurs in the second part, not the first? But what should I do in the first phase? I looked exhaustively through studies with lots of trades and chanced upon **Study 271**.

So, we leave the kingside pawns as in **Study 363**, and then place the remaining pieces on the queenside similarly to **Study 271**: white – ♔d3, pawn a6 (2), black – ♚b3, pawns a3, b4 (3). Looks good at first glance: after **1.a7 a2 2.a8=♖! ♚b2 3.♚c4 a1=♕ 4.♖xa1 ♚xa1 5.♚xb4 ♚b2 6.♚c4** etc. the kings will traverse the entire board, and then the second rook will be promoted.

But another pair of pawns should be put somewhere – otherwise, there

is no win. And here, I faced the first disappointment: there's no good place for them! I only managed to construct a winning position after adding four more pawns – **Study 364**.

No. 364. M. Zinar
Nove Zhittya (Brovary), 1988

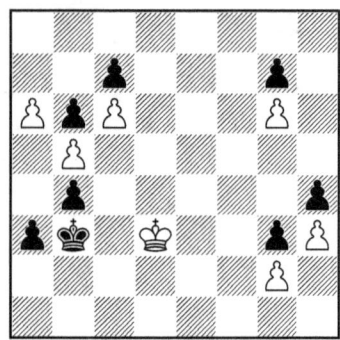

White to play and win

1.a7 a2 2.a8=♖! There's the first rook! But not 2.a8=♕? a1=♕ 3.♕xa1, stalemate.

2...♚b2 3.♚c4 a1=♕ 4.♖xa1 ♚xa1 5.♚xb4 ♚b2 6.♚c4 ♚c2 7.♚d5 ♚d2 8.♚e6 ♚e2 9.♚f7 ♚f2 10.♚xg7 ♚xg2 11.♚h6! ♚xh3 12.g7 g2

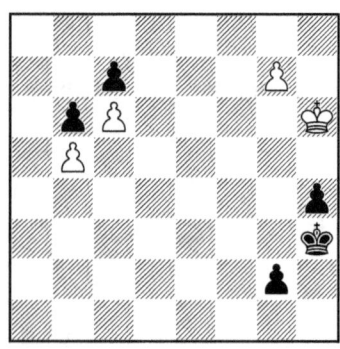

13.g8=♖! And the second rook has materialized! Not 13.g8=♕? g1=♕ 14.♕xg1, stalemate.

13...♔h2 14.♔h5! h3 15.♔h4! g1=♕ 16.♖xg1 ♔xg1 17.♔xh3.

And the joint march to the pawn island is to white's advantage: 17...♔f2 18.♔g4 (or you can extend the solution with the move 18.♔h4, to reach the d7 square on move 22) 18...♔e3 19.♔f5 ♔d4 20.♔e6 ♔c5 21.♔d7 ♔xb5 22.♔xc7, curtains.

This obviously didn't satisfy me: **Study 278** featured just 10 pieces, but this one has fifteen, almost half of an entire chess set...

The search continued. I finally found a way to eliminate one pawn – see **Study 365**.

No. 365. M. Zinar
Nove Zhittya (Brovary), 1988

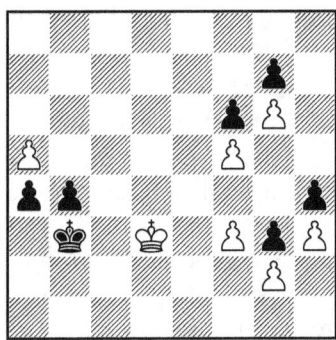

White to play and win

1.a6 a3 2.a7 a2 3.a8=♖! (3.a8=♕? a1=♕ 4.♕xa1) **3...♔b2 4.♔c4 a1=♕ 5.♖xa1 ♔xa1 6.♔xb4 ♔b2 7.♔c4** (or 7.♔c5) **7...♔c2 8.♔d5 ♔d2 9.♔e6 ♔e2 10.♔f7 ♔f2 11.♔xg7 ♔xg2**

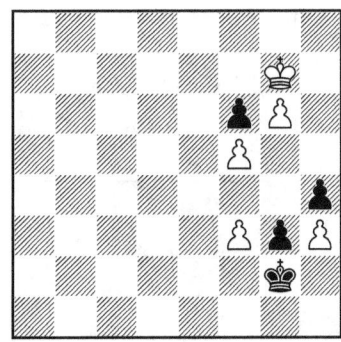

12.♔h6! ♔xh3 13.g7 g2 14.g8=♖! (14.g8=♕? g1=♕ 15.♕xg1) **14...♔h2 15.♔h5 h3 16.♔h4 g1=♕ 17.♖xg1 ♔xg1 18.♔xh3 ♔f2**

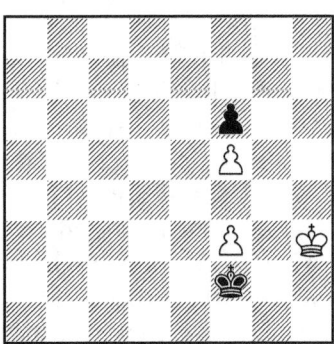

And the final battle over the pawn island without duals by the king:
19.♔g4 ♔e3 20.♔h5 ♔f4 21.♔g6 ♔e5 22.f4+! White wins.

But again, this was not exactly what I wanted: there were too many pawns on the kingside, for a start, in addition to the duals after 6.♔xb4 ♔b2 7.♔c4(c5) – 8.♔d5(d6) – 9.♔e6(e7) – 10.♔f7(f8).

And if black plays 4...b3 instead of 4...a1=♕, then white can play both 5.♔b4 and a move with his rook on the a-file – again, an unsatisfactory composition.

Then I got another idea: move all the queenside pieces in **Study 365** one file to the right.

No. 365a. M. Zinar
Nove Zhittya (Brovary), 1988

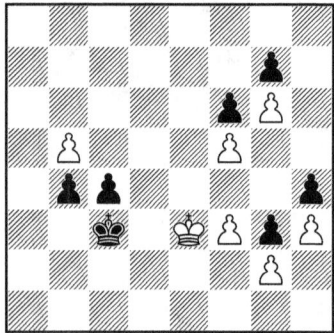

White to play and win (actually unsolvable)

Now, after 1.b6 b3 2.b7 b2 3.b8=♖ ♔c2 4.♔d4 b1=♕ 5.♖xb1 ♔xb1 6.♔xc4 ♔c2 7.♔d5, there are no duals, but it turns out that black can play 4...c3! instead of 4...b1=♕, and white cannot win. Another thought crossed my mind: if the white king were on h5, rather than on h6, when the second pawn gets promoted to a rook in **Study 364**, then one pawn pair would be enough to ensure the win at the end.

This can be achieved if we move the g6-g7 pawn pair in **Study 364** one rank lower. But now we need the black king to be one step behind the white one after the first phase is over. How to do that?

What if we place a bait pawn on the queenside? After a long ordeal, **Study 366** came to life:

No. 366. M. Zinar
Nove Zhittya (Brovary), 1988

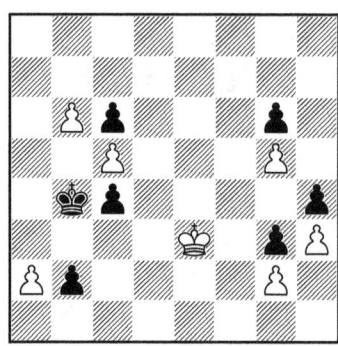

White to play and win

1.b7 ♔c3 2.b8=♖! ♔c2 3.♔e4 b1=♕ 4.♖xb1 ♔xb1 5.♔d4 ♔xa2 6.♔xc4 ♔b2.

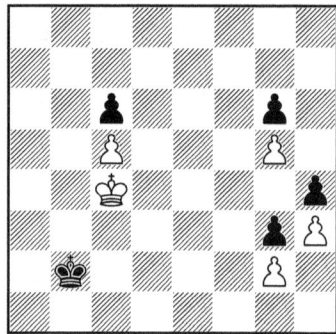

The kings have reached the "starting point" of the second phase. Now, full speed ahead!

7.♔d4 ♔c2 8.♔e5 ♔d3 9.♔f6 ♔e3 10.♔xg6 ♔f2 11.♔h5 ♔xg2 12.g6 ♔xh3 13.g7 g2 14.g8=♖! with a win.

Still, I wasn't fully satisfied: fifteen pieces on the board again, and lots of captures during the phase transition.

These examples showed you how studies are composed. Fortune is not always on the composer's side, as the last three positions show.

What were the main features of this

work? First of all, good knowledge of earlier studies. Secondly, the ability to analyze variations.

Unfortunately, the computer later found that the idea of **Study 366** still doesn't work after 3.♔d4! (or 3.a4) 3...b1=♕ (3...c3 4.a4) 4.♖xb1 ♔xb1 5.a4, and white wins. This flaw is eliminated by adding a black pawn to e4 — **Study 367**.

No. 367**. M. Zinar
Nove Zhittya (Brovary), 1988
(correction)

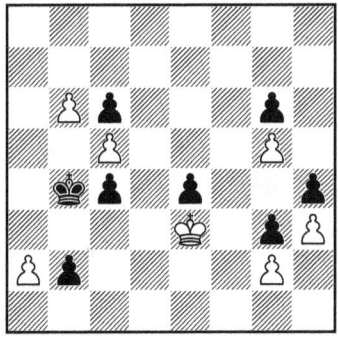

White to play and win

1.b7 ♔c3 2.b8=♖! ♔c2 3.♔xe4 and so on, like in **Study 366**.

The same qualities were necessary during work on the next study.

No. 368. Scheme 1

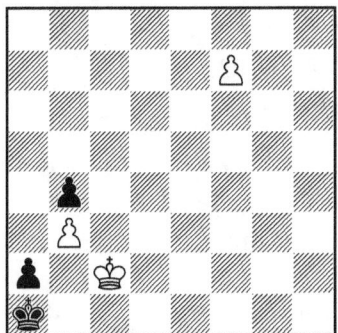

White to play and draw

It has been known for a long time that in **Scheme 368** white should play **1.♔d3!**, because if 1.♔d2?, then 1...♔b2 2.f8=♕ a1=♕ 3.♕f6+ ♔a2 4.♕xa1+? (the correct move is 4.♕a6+ with a draw) 4...♔xa1 5.♔d3 ♔b2 6.♔c4 ♔a3, and black even wins.

Black should meet 1.♔d3 with **1...♔b2!**, because after 1...♔b1 2.f8=♕ a1=♕ 3.♕f1+ ♔a2 4.♕xa1+ ♔xa1 5.♔c4, white wins.

Now, after the precise king moves, there follows: **2.f8=♕ a1=♕ 3.♕f6+ ♔xb3 4.♕xa1,** stalemate.

However, if white had another pawn somewhere, he would have promoted the f-pawn to a bishop instead and won. That other pawn should be blocked, otherwise both 1.♔d3 and 1.♔d2 are possible.

Therefore, a pawn pair should be placed somewhere.

No. 368a

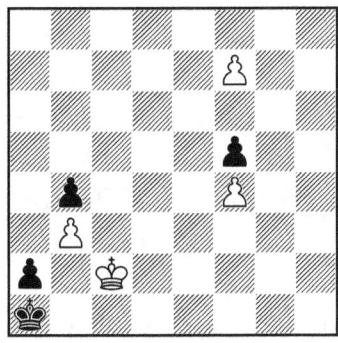

Here, after **1.♔d3 ♔b1! 2.f8=♕ a1=♕** white can play **3.♕xb4!**, with a winning queen ending.

Meanwhile, the pawns cannot be placed on **h2** and **h3**:

No. 368b

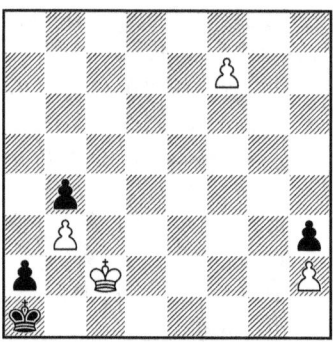

...because of the line 1.♔d3 ♔b2 2.f8=♗ ♔xb3 3.♗g7 a1=♕ 4.♗xa1 ♔a2 5.♗e5 b3 6.♔e4 b2 7.♗xb2 ♔xb2 8.♔f3 ♔c3 9.♔g3 ♔d4 10.♔xh3 ♔e5 with a draw.

This same line spoils the win for white if the pawns are on **h3** and **h4**:

No. 368c

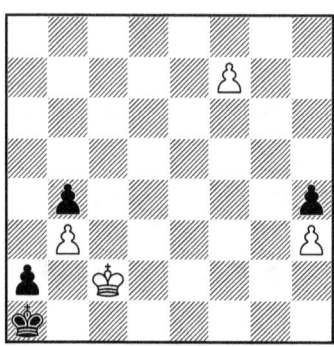

...in addition, black now has yet another way to save the game: 1.♔d3 ♔b2 2.f8=♗ ♔xb3 3.♗g7 ♔a3 4.♗a1 ♔b3 5.♗f6 ♔a3 6.♔c2 b3+ 7.♔c1 ♔b4 8.♔b2 ♔c4 9.♗xh4 ♔d5 10.♗f6 ♔e4 (or 10...♔e6) 11.♔xb3 ♔f5 12.♗d4 ♔g5 13.♔xa2 ♔h4 with a draw.

For the same reason, the pawns cannot be placed on **g2** and **g3**.

No. 368d

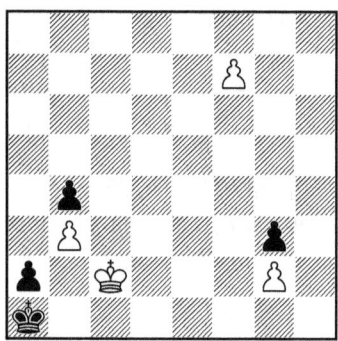

1.♔d3 ♔b2 2.f8=♗ ♔xb3 3.♗g7 ♔a3 4.♗a1 ♔b3 5.♗e5 ♔a3 6.♔c2 b3+ 7.♔c1 ♔b4 8.♔b2 ♔c4 9.♗xg3 ♔d4 10.♗h4 ♔e3 11.♗f6 ♔f4, and the white pawn falls.

A very different calamity awaits white if the pawns are placed on **e2** and **e3**.

No. 368e

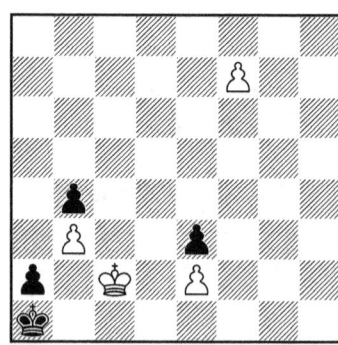

1.♔d3 ♔b2 2.f8=♗ a1=♕ 3.♗g7+ ♔a2 4.♗xa1 ♔xa1 5.♔c4 ♔b2 6.♔xb4 ♔c2 with a draw.

Again, as we see, you cannot compose an endgame study without thorough analysis! We have already seen this bishop underpromotion in the second phase of some two-phase studies (see **Studies 255, 281, 283** and **287**); and here is another bishop-related story.

The author noticed that **Study 257**, where the pawn is promoted to a knight, has a position similar to the one above. Perhaps a two-phase "knight+bishop" study could be composed?

And so, first we follow the Kazantsev study: after the sixth move in **Study 257**, we would like to promote the h-pawn to a knight, sacrifice it on g6 and then play f6-f7. Thus, black should have only one tempo. Therefore, we put pawns on g3 and g4 and remove the d3 and d4 pawns from **Study 257**.

No. 368f

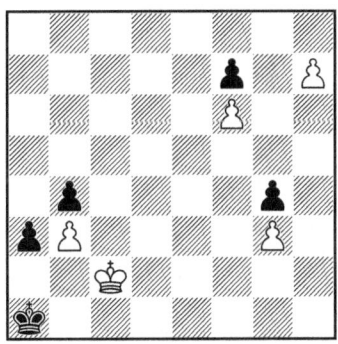

1.h8=♘ a2 2.♘g6 fxg6 3.f7 g5 4.♔d3 ♔b2 5.f8=♗ ♔xb3 6.♗g7 and so on.

Our first verification shows that white can simply promote the pawn to a queen and give checkmate on h1: 1.h8=♕ a2 2.♕h1#. This is because, in our position, the white king stands on c2, rather than on c1 as in **Study 257**, in order to be able to play ♔c2-d3.

So, let's close the h-file with the **h2** and **h3** pawns.

No. 368g

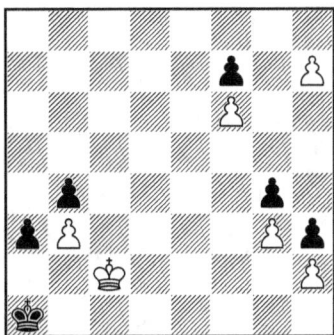

Now is that all right? No! White still can play 1.h8=♕ a2 2.♔d3! ♔b2 3.♕a8, and wins after the queen trade.

So, we block the a-file with the **a6** and **a7** pawns, getting the following position:

No. 369. Scheme 2

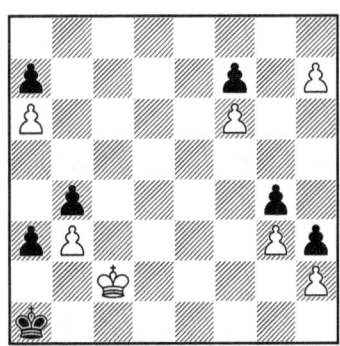

White to play and win

1.h8=♘! a2 2.♘g6 fxg6 3.f7 g5 4.♔d3 ♔b2 5.f8=♗! White wins.

Everything looks correct. Let's try to create some introductory play without adding material. How to do that? We can extend the play backwards, or, in other words, carry out retrograde analysis.

What was black's last move? ♚a2-a1, and so we put the king on a2. What could white have played before that? Obviously, h6-h7 – so, we put the pawn on h6. Black could push the pawn, b5-b4 – so the pawn goes back to b5. White could play h5-h6, and so we put the pawn back on h5. And so on: the black pawn goes back to b6, the white one to h4, the black one from g4 to g5. Finally, the king goes back to d1 from c2. And that's all, there's nowhere to retreat! As a result, I got **Study 370**, which was first published without the d5 and d6 pawns and even won a prize as follows:

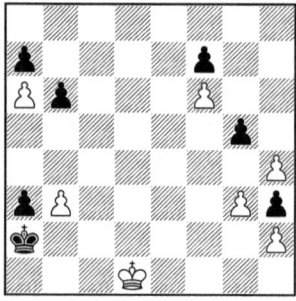

White to play and win (actually unsolvable)

But then I suddenly saw that the study was unsolvable without the d5 and d6 pawns!

After **1.♚c2 g4 2.h5 b5 3.h6 b4 4.h7 ♚a1 5.h8=♘! a2 6.♘g6! fxg6 7.f7 g5 8.♚d3 ♚b2 9.f8=♗**

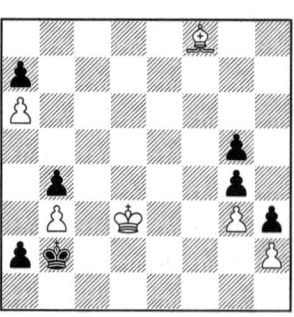

black plays not 9...a1=♕ 10.♗g7+ ♚xb3 11.♗xa1 where there is no stalemate and white wins (as I had originally intended), but 9...♚xb3 10.♗g7 ♚a4 11.♚c4 ♚a5 12.♚b3 ♚xa6 13.♚xb4 ♚b6 14.♚c4 ♚c6! (I overlooked this move, only considering 14...♚a5) 15.♗a1 a5! with a drawn queen endgame. And if white plays 12.♗d4 first, then 12...♚a4! 13.♗a1 ♚a5 14.♚b3 ♚xa6 15.♚xb4 ♚b6 16.♚c4 ♚a5! – also winning a tempo by attacking the bishop.

No. 370. M. Zinar
Z. Birnov memorial, 1987
2nd–3rd prize
(correction)

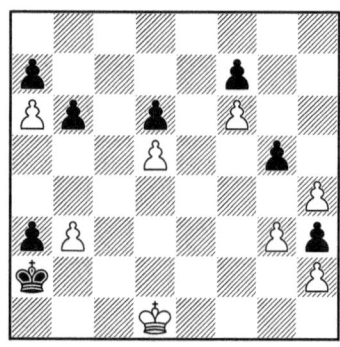

White to play and win

In this case, white does win after **1.♚c2 g4 2.h5 b5 3.h6 b4 4.h7 ♚a1 5.h8=♘! a2 6.♘g6! fxg6 7.f7 g5 8.♚d3 ♚b2 9.f8=♗ a1=♕ 10.♗g7+ ♚xb3 11.♗xa1**

As we see, inadequate analysis led to the publication of an incorrect position. The method of correction in this case is simple: add some material. The study was not too great even before then (four technical pawns), and it gets even worse afterwards.

Let's point out that an idea can usually be expressed in several ways. Some undemanding composers settle for the first position that seems correct for them, without trying to further refine the idea.

The scheme of **Study 370** looks very rigid, but when it turned out that the earlier version of the study was unsolvable, I first found a way to correct it by adding the d5 and d6 pawns.

Moreover, later, other ways were also found. For instance, it is possible to put a white passed pawn on d3 that gives an obvious win after a bishop promotion, while stalemate similar to **Study 257** will be achieved if the king is on d2. Thanks to these considerations, another corrected version appeared, **No. 371**.

No. 371. M. Zinar
Z. Birnov memorial, 1987
2nd–3rd prize
(correction)

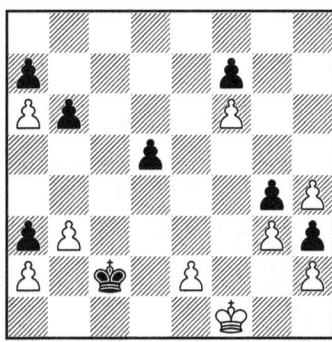

White to play and win

1.♔e1! ♔b2 2.♔d1(d2) ♔xa2 3.♔c2 d4 4.h5 d3+! 5.exd3 Here's the sought position with the pawn on d3!.

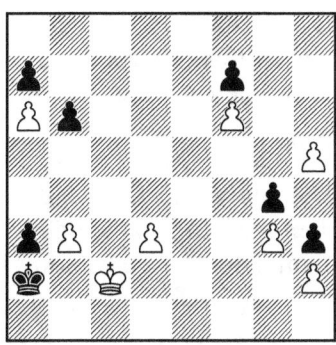

5...♔a1 6.h6 a2 7.h7 b5 8.h8=♘! b4 9.♘g6! fxg6 10.f7 g5 11.♔d2 ♔b2 12.f8=♗! with a win. But it's stalemate after the wrong promotion: **12.f8=♕? a1=♕ 13.♕f6+ ♔xb3 14.♕xa1.**

Let me show you an example of the development of related positions, from the moment the primary idea is found, through the discovery of additional subtleties, and until the final formulation of the composition.

To begin, I once took note of the following study:

No. 372. A. Wotawa
Deutsche Schachzeitung, 1954

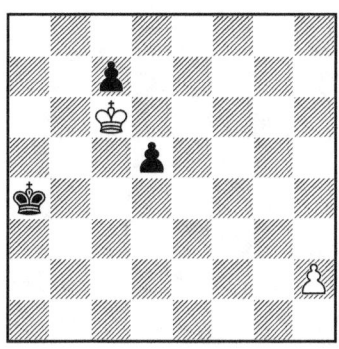

White to play and win

I analyzed the solution: **1.♔c5! d4 2.♔c4 d3 3.♔c3 c5 4.h4 c4 5.h5 ♔a3**

6.h6 d2 7.♔xd2(c2), winning, and got interested in this curious idea. A triple capture avoidance was executed in this miniature.

Everything would have ended here, but I then noticed great similarity with another miniature by the founding father of pawn studies, Nikolai Grigoriev.

No. 373. N. Grigoriev
Shakhmatnoe Tvorchestvo
N. D. Grigorieva, 1952

White to play and win

1.♔d2! ♔b2! If 1...♔b3, then 2.h4 c5 3.♔c1 with a win.

  2.♔d3! ♔b3 3.♔d4! ♔b4 4.h4 c5+

  5.♔e3! An anti-check maneuver!

  5...♔b3. Black cannot win a tempo because he has no checks.

6.h5 c4 7.h6 c3 8.h7 c2 9.♔d2! ♔b2 10.h8=♕+, and black will not promote his pawn.

Therefore, in Wotawa's **Study 372** white can also play 2.♔xd4 ♔b4 3.h4 c5+

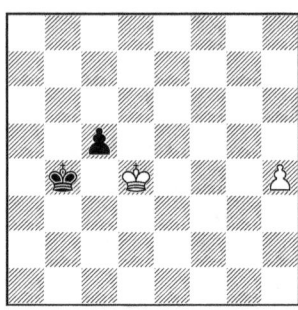

and then continue as in Grigoriev's study: 4.♔e3! ♔b3 5.h5 c4 6.h6 c3 7.h7 c2 8.♔d2 ♔b2 9.h8=♕+ etc.

We can now point out that the third capture avoidance in **Study 372** is not necessary. After 1.♔c5! d4 2.♔c4 d3, in addition to 3.♔c3, white can win with the pragmatic 3.♔xd3 ♔b3! 4.♔d4! ♔b4 5.h4 c5+ 6.♔e3! etc., following the Grigoriev study.

So let's eliminate the side solution by blocking the a1-h8 diagonal with a white f6 pawn and a black f7 pawn:

No. 372a

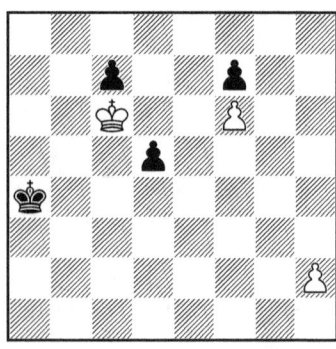

White to play and win

1.♔c5 d4 2.♔c4! d3! 3.♔c3! c5 4.h4 c4 5.h5 ♔a3 6.h6 d2 7.♔xd2 (or 7.♔c2 d1=♕+ 8.♔xd1 ♔b2 9.h7 c3 and then following the solution).

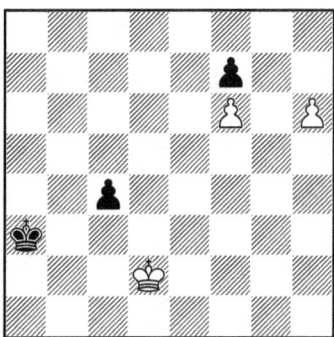

At first the author of this book assumed the resulting position to be drawn, but the 7-piece endgame tablebases demonstrate that this is not the case: **7...♔b2 8.h7 c3+ 9.♔e2** (or 9.♔d3) **9...c2 10.h8=♕ c1=♕ 11.♕b8+! ♔a3 12.♕a7+ ♔b2 13.♕xf7,** and white gradually wins by converting the extra pawn.

However, there is another path to victory: 1.♔xd5! ♔b5 2.h4 c5 3.h5 c4 4.h6 c3 5.h7 c2 6.h8=♕ c1=♕ 7.♕e8+ ♔b4 8.♕e7+ ♔b5 9.♕b7+ ♔a5 10.♕xf7, and the queen endgame is lost for black.

And even if we find a way to erase the 1.♔xd5 side solution, the analytical properties of the arising queen endgame ruin the main theme of the study – the constant avoidance of capturing the black pawn.

In order to avoid the queen endgame in the author's solution, we need to make the a3 square inaccessible for the white king, which is achieved by moving the pieces (except for the h2, f6 and f7 pawns) one file to the right and

adding a white pawn on a2 with a black counterparty on a5:

No. 372b

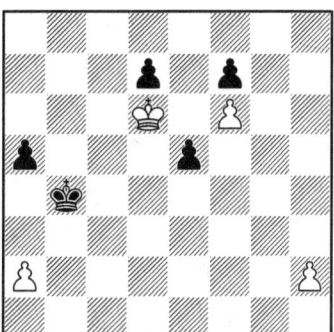

White to play and win

One problem is that because the black king is now on b4, it manages to get into the square of the h-pawn. For example: 1.♔d5 e4 2.♔d4 e3 3.♔d3 e2 (or 3...♔c5) 4.♔xe2 ♔c3 5.♔f3 (5.h4 ♔d4) 5...d5 6.♔e2 ♔d4, and now it's white who needs to think about saving the game.

And that's not all! There is another unthematic solution: 1.♔xe5! ♔c5 2.h4 d5 3.h5 d4 4.h6 d3 5.h7 d2 6.h8=♕ d1=♕ 7.♕f8+ ♔c6 8.♕xf7, and again the 7-piece tablebases call victory for white.

Let's find a different way to close the a1-h8 diagonal: from **No. 372b** we delete the black pawn on f7, move the white pawn to f5 and add black pawns to e7 and f6.

We have to give up the first capture avoidance. Therefore, we delete the first move from the solution and reach the following position:

No. 374. Scheme 3

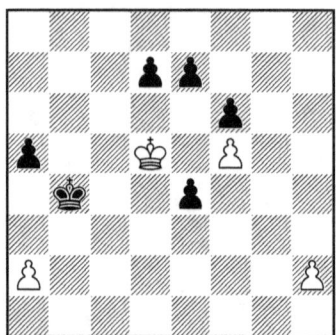

White to play and win

1.♔d4! e3! 2.♔d3! e2 3.♔xe2!
White cannot avoid the capture: 3.♔d2?
e1=♕+! 4.♔xe1 ♔c3 5.h4 ♔c2!! 6.♔e2
d5 7.♔e3 ♔c3 8.♔e2 ♔c2, positional
draw.
3...♔c3 4.h4! After 4.♔d1?, the
black king makes it to the square of the
pawn in time — 4...♔d4.
4...♔c2 5.♔e3! (as in Grigoriev's
study) **5...♔c3**

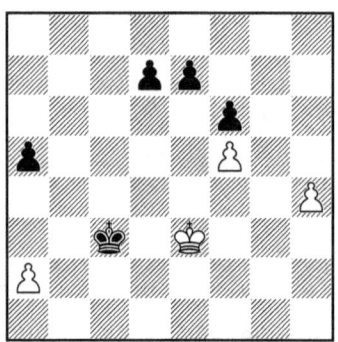

6.♔e4! ♔c4 7.h5 (or 7.♔f3
immediately) **7...d5+ 8.♔f3! d4 9.h6**
(another dual: 9.♔e2 ♔c3 10.♔d1) **9...
d3 10.h7 d2 11.♔e2** with a win.
Thus, as long as we close our eyes to
the duals we have Wotawa's idea without
the beginning plus Grigoriev's idea

without the finale. To combine these
truncated ideas, we had to pay a hefty
price — five technical pawns! Isn't it
better to lengthen the h-pawn's journey
rather than block the diagonal?

No. 375. M. Zinar
Radyanska Ukraina, 1987

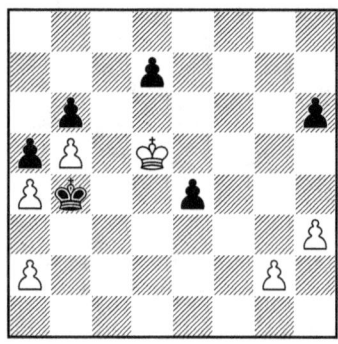

White to play and win (actually unsolvable)

The journey of the h-pawn is
lengthened here. But the price is even
heftier: there are seven whole technical
pawns on the board now, including two
to lengthen the journey and the a4-pawn
to eliminate the counterplay against the
a2-pawn.
What at first seemed to the author
to be the correct solution is **1.♔d4! e3
2.♔d3! e2.** The game ends in checkmate
after 2...d5 3.g4 d4 4.h4 ♔c5 5.g5 hxg5
6.h5 g4 7.h6 e2

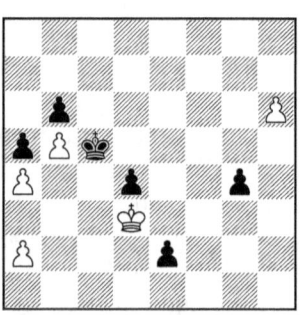

8.♔xe2 g3 9.h7 d3+ 10.♔xd3 g2 11.h8=♕ g1=♕ 12.♕e5+ ♔b4 13.♕c3+ ♔xa4 14.♕b3#

Or 4...♔a3 5.g5 hxg5 6.hxg5 ♔b2 7.g6 e2

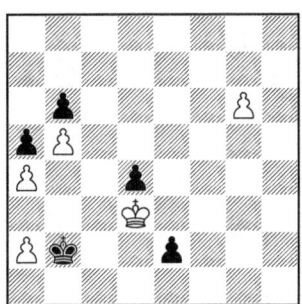

8.♔xe2 ♔c2 9.g7 d3+ 10.♔e3 d2 11.g8=♕ d1=♕ 12.♕b3+ with a win.

3.♔xe2 ♔c3 4.g4. 4.h4 is also possible – another flaw!

4...♔c2. Or 4...♔d4 5.♔f3! ♔e5 6.h4 and wins thanks to the outside passed pawn.

5.♔e3! ♔c3 6.♔e4 ♔c4 7.h4 (organic dual: 7.♔f3) **7...d5+**

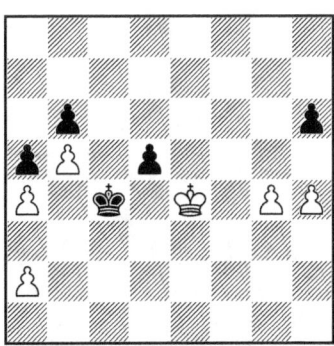

8.♔f3! ♔c3 9.g5 hxg5 10.h5! d4 11.h6 d3 12.h7 d2 13.h8=♕+, and white wins.

This is better. Not as good as in Grigoriev's study, but decoying the king

into check, adding two technical pawns and the deletion of unnecessary lines fully justifies the composer's work on his idea.

Unfortunately, though, years later a hole was discovered in this position by the computer. After 1.♔d4! e3! 2.♔d3! d5! 3.g4

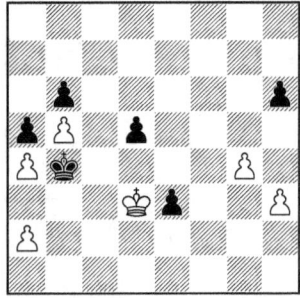

black has the powerful 3...e2!! 4.♔xe2 ♔c3! 5.♔d1 ♔d3 6.h4 ♔e4 7.♔d2 ♔f4 8.♔d3 ♔xg4 9.♔d4 ♔xh4 10.♔xd5 ♔g4 11.♔c6 h5 12.♔xb6.

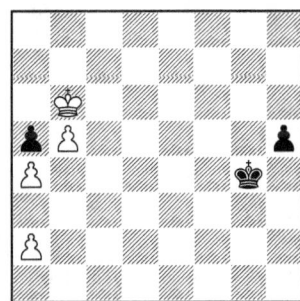

At first glance, the two extra pawns should ensure white a win in the queen endgame, but black can save the day: 12...h4 13.♔xa5 h3 14.b6 h2 15.b7 h1=♕ 16.b8=♕ ♕d5+! 17.♕b5 ♕xa2, and the 7-piece tablebases show that white's extra pawn isn't enough to win.

Yet it can all be fixed! Moreover, we managed to include three avoidances of capturing the black pawn, just like in Wotawa's study. Here it is:

No. 375a. M. Zinar
Radyanska Ukraina, 1987
(corrected by S. Tkachenko, 2022)

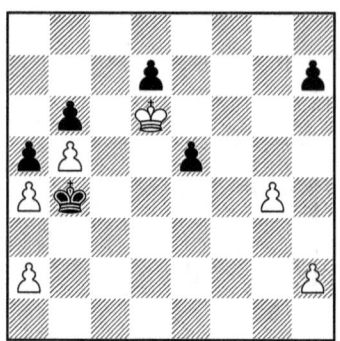

White to play and win

1.♔d5! The first capture avoidance! Not 1.♔xe5? ♔c5! 2.h4 d5 3.g5 d4 4.♔e4 ♔c4 5.h5 d3 6.g6 hxg6 7.hxg6 d2 8.g7 d1=♕ 9.g8=♕+ ♔c5, and a draw.

1...e4! Black has no chance to save the game after 1...d6 2.h4 ♔c3 3.g5 ♔d3 4.h5 e4 5.g6 hxg6 6.hxg6 e3 7.g7 e2 8.g8=♕ e1=♕ 9.♔xd6 ♕f2 10.♔c7, and the black pawns collapse...

2.♔d4! The second capture avoidance! But not 2.♔xe4? ♔c4! 3.h4 d5+ 4.♔f3 ♔c3 5.♔e2 ♔c2 6.♔e3 ♔c3, and a draw.

2...e3! 3.♔d3! And the third! After 3.♔xe3? black is saved with 3...♔c3! 4.♔e4 ♔c4 and so on.

3...e2! Black has no salvation after 3...d5 4.h4 e2! 5.♔xe2 ♔c3 6.♔d1! ♔d3

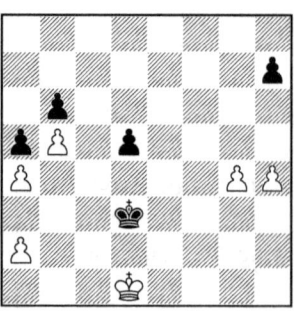

7.g5! ♔e4 8.♔d2 d4 9.♔e2 ♔f4 10.♔d3 ♔g4 11.♔xd4 ♔xh4 12.♔d5 ♔xg5 13.♔c6 h5

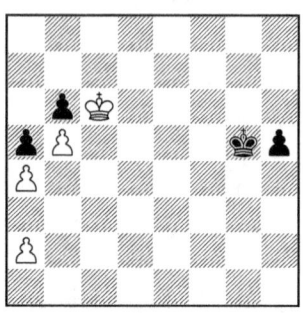

14.♔xb6 h4 15.♔xa5 h3 16.b6 h2 17.b7 h1=♕ 18.b8=♕ ♕e1+ (18...♕d5+ 19.♕b5) 19.♕b4 ♕e5+ 20.♕b5!, with the black king pinned!

4.♔xe2! White cannot avoid the capture for the fourth time: 4.♔d2? e1=♕+ 5.♔xe1 ♔c3! 6.♔d1 ♔d3 7.g5 ♔e3 8.♔c2 ♔f4, and the white king is too slow to catch the d-pawn.

4...♔c3! 5.g5 (or 5.h4) **5...♔c2.** If 5...d5 then white wins with 6.♔d1! ♔d3 7.h4 ♔e4 8.♔d2 and victory in the queen endgame (see above).

6.♔e3! ♔c3

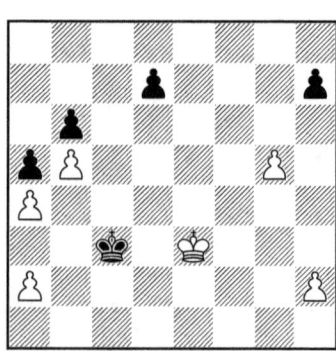

7.♔e4!   ♔c4   8.h4 (8.♔f3 is the organic dual we have already encountered) **8...d5+   9.♔f3!   ♔c3**

10.h5 d4 11.g6 hxg6 12.h6! d3 13.h7 d2 14.h8=♕+, winning.

And so, you have now taken a look into a study composer's creative laboratory. Of course, every study comes to life and is composed in a different way. There are no general rules. Still, we hope that you have got some initial ideas about pawn study composition technique. And so, enriched by this knowledge, a chess composition enthusiast − of course, if they have a creative spark − will try to compose a pawn endgame themselves.

But this does not mean that their first pawn composition will immediately turn out as interesting and shaped as the examples in this book. There are no universal recommendations that can ensure quick improvement for every aspiring study composer.

Throughout their career, a chess study composer encounters a lot of incredible, hard-to-explain phenomena in their creative work: they might spend several years on one composition, just one day on another, and yet another may require a few weeks or months to develop. Of course, this does not mean that the composer works on the study the entire time. The study simply refuses to come together, but the idea still looks very attractive, and so the composer tries again and again to refine it for a time after each failure.

Which factors influence such phenomena? There are many. For instance, you might return to a position you once abandoned, or the idea may be very difficult and require a lot of hard work to refine.

And sometimes there are lucky epiphanies, when the idea occurs immediately as a ready-made composition; in most cases, such positions require only some small time and effort to check for flaws, refine them and turn them into true pawn studies.

We should highlight that it's not easy to teach someone to compose pawn studies. It is, however, possible to bring a chess player who wants to try their hand in composition closer to the knowledge of composing technique, partially revealing the thought processes of a study composer.

Every composer has their own approach. One constructs sketches of studies in their head. Another needs to have a chessboard before them to actually see the pieces. Yet another might use a known composition (their own or someone else's) as a starting point.

Some experienced study composers just randomly place the main pieces on the board before constructing the scheme of the future opus. To put it simply, there are different ways to compose a study.

Chapter V

COMPOSITION TESTS

So you have now had the chance to learn the fundamentals of pawn study composition. These include the formal and artistic requirements of studies, as well as the themes and ideas most often used by leading composers. You also have some understanding of methods available to solve them.

We have already shown you the list of the most popular ways to hone the technical skills of pawn study composition: finding and eliminating flaws in studies, expressing known ideas in a more efficient form, and creating introductory play among others. And now, it's time to test your skills at pawn study creation, as this will help to train you in these techniques. Then look at the last pages of the book with the solutions and compare your own findings with ours. In total there are 21 tests. Oh, and by the way, there may be a trick question along the way...

First, in **Studies 376–380**, find the author's idea and the element making the given study unsolvable — if there is one! Then eliminate the unsolvability as you see fit — in the simplest possible way.

No. 377. A. Wotawa
Deutsche Schachzeitung, 1960

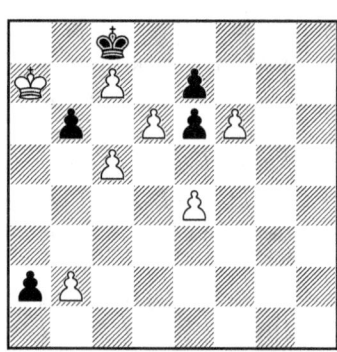

White to play and win

No. 376. T. Kok
Residentiebode, 1935

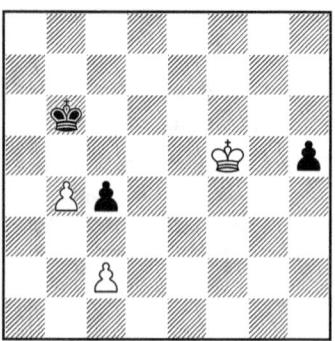

White to play and win

No. 378. A. Troitsky
Shakhmaty v SSSR, 1931

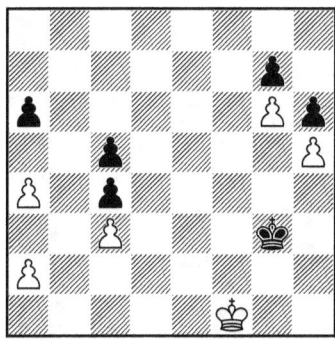

White to play and draw

No. 379. K. Kupchevsky
64, 1931

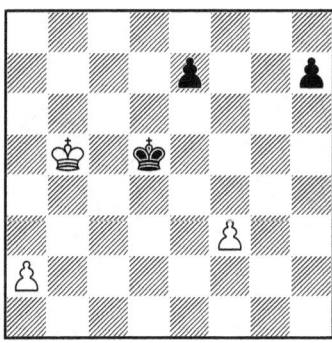

White to play and win

No. 380. A. Troitsky
500 Endspielstudien, 1924

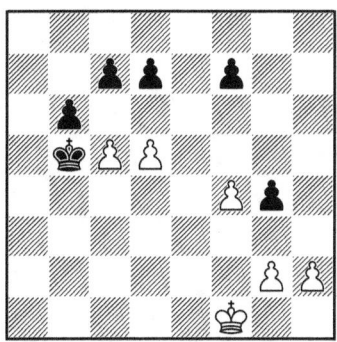

White to play and win

In **Studies 381–386**, find side solutions and try to eliminate them.

No. 381. N. Grigoriev
Izvestia, 1930

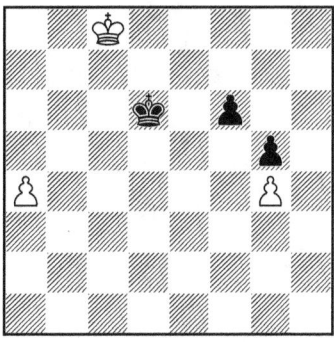

White to play and win

No. 382. H. Geiger
Deutsche Schachzeitung, 1920

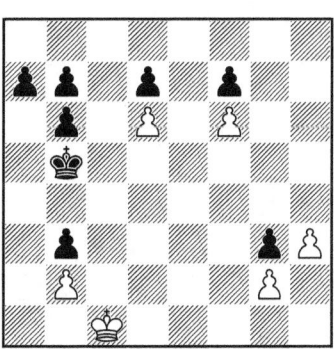

White to play and win

No. 383. S. Zhigis
64, 1930
Commendation

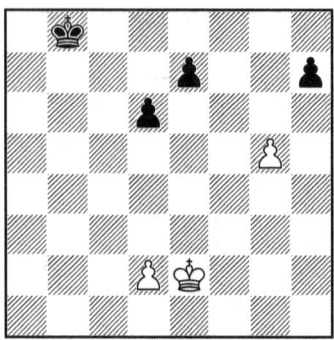

White to play and draw

No. 384. N. Grigoriev
64, 1930
2nd prize

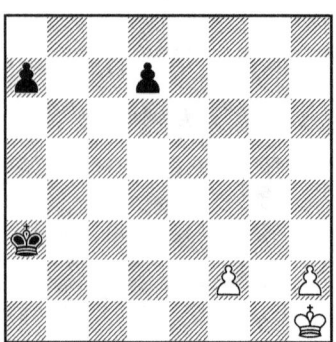

White to play and win

No. 385. A. Wotawa
Deutsche Schachzeitung, 1962

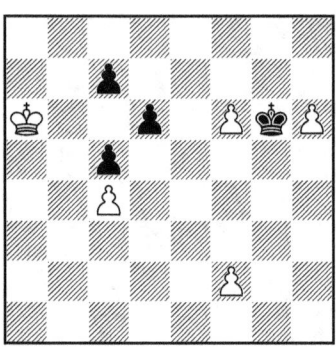

White to play and win

No. 386. A. Wotawa
Deutsche Schachzeitung, 1954

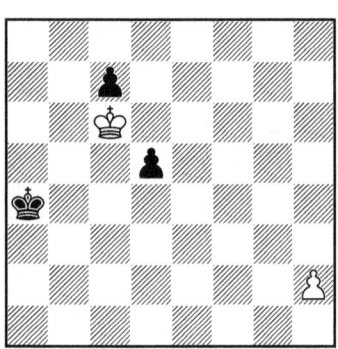

White to play and win

In **Studies 387−388**, find duals in the white king's moves and eliminate them.

No. 387. R. Brown
The Chess Player's Chronicle, 1841

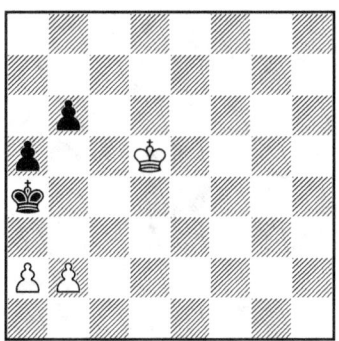

White to play and win

No. 388. N. Grigoriev
Sbornik Etyudov, 1952

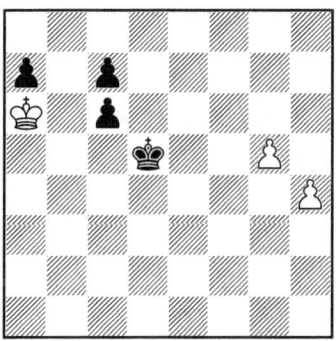

White to play and win

The solution of **Study 389** is simple, but you need to find a transposition and try to eliminate it.

No. 389. A. Van Tets
EG, 1970

White to play and win

After analyzing and solving **Studies 390–391**, try to add introductory play to them, but without adding material. Such exercises will be useful for you to create introductory play in your own compositions.

No. 390. T. Dawson
The Chess Amateur, 1924

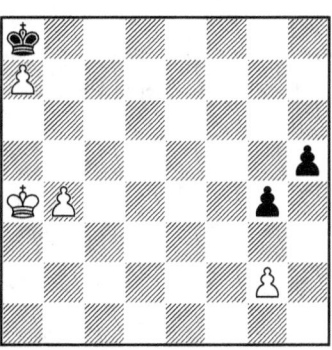

White to play and draw

No. 391. N. Grigoriev
Shakhmatny Listok, 1924

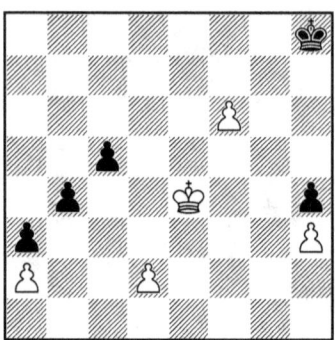

White to play and draw

No. 392. Return to Selezniev's **Study 302**, analyze it thoroughly and add a single move to the introduction.

The final series of exercises will require a special effort. You have to express the same idea, but in a more efficient form – i.e., to use less material. We should point out that in such exercises it's not always possible to fully preserve the idea of the original study, but still, such exercises are useful for budding study composers to improve their skills at creating efficient positions.

First, solve **Study 393** and then try to use one fewer pawn in your new version of the study.

No. 393. A. Troitsky
The Chess Amateur, 1917

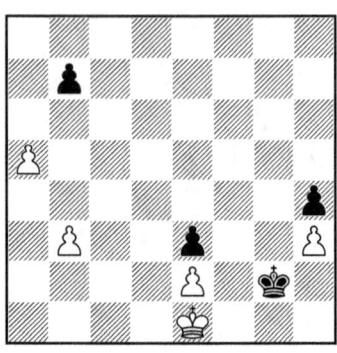

White to play and win

Solve **Study 394** and try to express the same idea, but using two fewer pawns. Think about what you can do to eliminate the duals in Henri Rinck's position.

No. 394. H. Rinck
Deutsche Schachzeitung, 1912

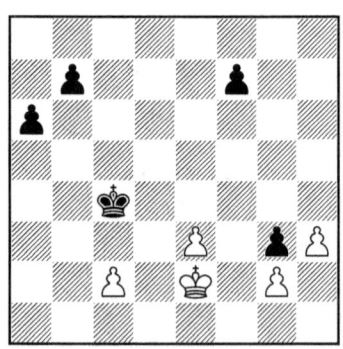

White to play and win

No. 395. Analyze A. Botokanov's **Study 135** again, more deeply. And now answer the following questions: what role do the queenside pawns play? Can we reduce the number of queenside pawns by rearranging the pawn setup?

No. 396. Return to **Study 249**. Fix it, analyze it and identify the author's main idea. Can this idea be expressed in a more refined way?

SOLUTIONS TO TESTS

No. 376. The author's intended solution was **1.c3 ♔b5 2.♔g5 ♔a4 3.♔h4!** etc. – see **Study 123**, where the two introductory moves are removed. At first glance, we want to show that black has a sturdier defense, which is why the study is cooked: 2...♔c6! 3.♔xh5 ♔d5 4.♔g4 ♔e4 5.♔g3 ♔e5 6.♔f3 ♔f5 7.♔g3 ♔e4 8.♔g4 ♔e5 with a theoretical draw.

However, it's not necessary to remove the first two moves to fix it! Instead, we can make a few adjustments on the board that preserve the idea in full while ensuring that white wins: see **Study 376a**. Don't worry about not solving this exercise, the idea is to get you thinking along the right lines!

No. 376a**. T. Kok
Residentiebode, 1935
(correction by S. Tkachenko)

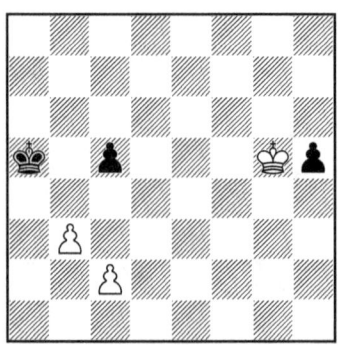

White to play and win

1.c3! c4! Not 1...♔b5 2.♔xh5 ♔c6 3.♔g5 ♔d5 4.♔f5, curtains.
2.b4+ ♔a4! 3.♔h4! etc.

No. 377. The author's solution was: **1.d7+ ♔xc7 2.d8=♕+ ♔xd8 3.f7 a1=♕+ 4.♔b7 ♕f1 5.c6 ♕f4 6.e5! ♕f3 7.b3! b5 8.b4** with a win.

At first glance, it seems that black can play better and that the study is cooked: 3...♔c7 4.cxb6+ ♔c6 5.f8=♕ a1=♕+ 6.♔b8 ♔xb6 with a draw.

The correction in that case would be a bit more complicated: you would need to remove the first two moves, put the white king on b7 and the a2 pawn on f2. The solution would then be: 1.f7 f1=♕ 2.c6 etc.

However, this nice study actually doesn't need correction! The line 3...♔c7 4.cxb6+ ♔c6 5.f8=♕ a1=♕+ 6.♔b8 ♔xb6 does not save black. For instance: 7.♕xe7 ♕a2 8.♕b7+ ♔c5 9.♕a7+, and white wins. So a trick question...

No. 378. The theme of niche stalemate was only starting to develop back then, so this study is rather easy to solve: **1.♔e2!** (to save the c3 pawn)

1...♔g4 2.a5! ♔xh5 3.♔d2(d1) ♔xg6 4.♔c2(c1). As you might see, the founding father of modern artistic endgame study deemed such duals acceptable!

4...h5 5.♔b2 h4 6.♔a3 h3 7.♔a4 h2 8.a3 h1=♕, stalemate.

But black still has a way to win the c3 pawn: 1...♔f4 2.a5 ♔e4! 3.♔d2 ♔f3 4.♔c2 ♔e3 5.♔b2 ♔d3 6.♔a3 ♔xc3 7.♔a4 ♔d2 8.a3 c3, ruining the stalemate construction. This unsolvability was used to compose **Study 233**.

It's easy to correct the study: simply remove the first move of the solution.

No. 379. The author's solution: **1.a4 ♔d6 2.♔b6 ♔d7 3.♔b7 h5 4.a5 h4 5.a6 h3 6.a7 h2 7.a8=♕ h1=♕ 8.♕c8+ ♔d6 9.♕c6+ ♔e5 10.f4+** with a win.

But black has a killer reply 1...♔e6!!, and 2.♔b6 is met with 2...h5 with a draw. While 2.a5 is met with 2...♔d7, also with a draw.

The correction method is familiar: remove the first move of the solution.

No. 380. Here, the "snare" theme is used in conjunction with pawn sacrifices: **1.c6! dxc6 2.d6! cxd6 3.h4 gxh3 4.gxh3 ♔c5 5.h4 ♔d5 6.h5 ♔e6 7.h6 ♔f6 8.f5!** etc., with a theoretical win in the king vs. three pawns endgame.

At first glance, the study is unsolvable on move four: instead of 4...♔c5, black can play 4...♔a4!, and the b-pawn is promoted. To eliminate this flaw, it's enough to move the white king closer to the queenside, for instance, on a1.

However, the study actually becomes unsolvable much earlier: 1...d6! 2.h4 gxh3 3.gxh3 ♔a4! 4.h4 b5 5.h5 b4 6.h6 b3 7.h7 b2 8.h8=♕ b1=♕+ etc. American grandmaster Pal Benko proposed eliminating the flaw by moving all pieces one file to the left.

No. 381. The author's solution: **1.a5 ♔c6 2.♔b8 ♔b5 3.♔b7! ♔xa5** (3...f5 4.a6) **4.♔c6 f5 5.gxf5 g4 6.f6 g3 7.f7 g2 8.f8=♕ g1=♕ 9.♕a3#.** But white can also play **2.a6! ♔b6 3.a7! ♔xa7 4.♔c7!,** with a win.

Here's how the side solution can be removed:

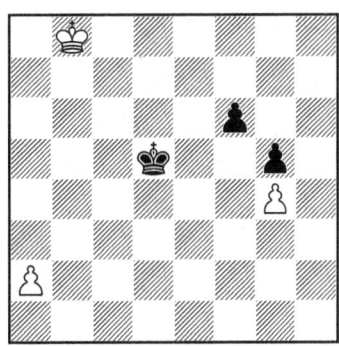

White to play and win

The solution begins as follows: **1.a4! ♔c6 2.a5! ♔b5 3.♔b7!** etc.

No. 382. Look at **Study 259** – this is the corrected version of this composition; the white king was moved to b1.

In the author's version, instead of 11.d8=♘, white could play 11.d8=♕! e4 12.♕d6 e3 13.♕xg3 e2 14.♔d2 e1=♕+ 15.♕xe1 g3 16.♕a1#.

No. 383. The author's idea: **1.♔f3! ♔c7 2.♔g4! ♔d7! 3.♔f5! ♔e8 4.♔e6 ♔f8 5.d3 ♔e8 6.d4 ♔f8 7.d5 ♔e8 8.g6 hxg6,** stalemate.

But there's a side solution: 5.d4 ♔e8 6.d5 ♔f8 7.♔d7 ♔f7 8.♔c6! e6 (or 8...e5 9.♔xd6 e4 10.♔c6! with a draw) 9.♔xd6 exd5 10.♔xd5 ♔g6 11.♔e4 with a draw, because black's remaining pawn is a rook one.

As he worked on an idea of Lazard's (**Study 220**), Belorussian study composer S. Zhigis decided to shift the final position to the right for some reason. The flaw can be eliminated by moving all pieces in the position one file to the left, as was done in **Study 221**.

No. 384. The author's solution: **1.f4! ♔b4! 2.h4! d5 3.f5 ♔c5 4.h5! d4! 5.f6 ♔d6 6.h6 d3 7.f7 ♔e7 8.h7 d2 9.f8=♕+ ♔xf8 10.h8=♕+** with a win.

Side solution: 5.♔g2(g1) ♔c4 6.f6 d3 7.f7 d2 8.f8=♕ d1=♕ 9.♕f1+ with a win.

This study was corrected by the French chess endgame composer Cheron – see **Study 86**.

No. 385. Author's idea: **1.h7! ♔xh7 2.♔b5 ♔g6 3.♔c6 ♔f7 4.f3! ♔g6 5.f4 ♔f7 6.f5 ♔xf6 7.♔xc7** with a win.

Firstly, at the critical moment, white can play more resolutely: 4.f4! ♔g6 5.♔xc7! d5 6.♔d6 d4 7.♔e7, again with a win.

Further, the study has a serious defect at the very beginning of the study: 1.♔b7! d5 2.cxd5 c4 3.♔xc7 c3 4.h7! ♔xh7 5.♔d7! ♔g6 6.♔e6 c2 7.f7 c1=♕ 8.f8=♕ ♕e1+ 9.♔d7 winning.

It's very hard to correct this study while preserving the author's idea in its entirety. But this idea was successfully used to compose **Study 151**.

On the other hand, we can go the other way and effectively try to retain the solution as the only one. To do this, the f2 pawn in the initial flawed position of **Study 385** should be moved one step ahead, to f3.

No. 385a. A. Wotawa
Deutsche Schachzeitung, 1962
(correction by M. Zinar, 1990)

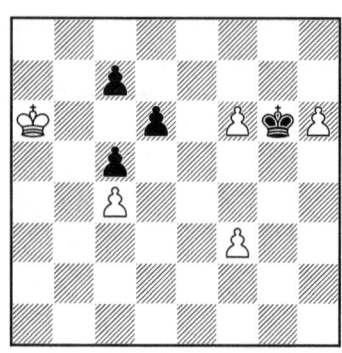

White to play and win

1.h7 But not 1.♔b7? d5 2.cxd5 c4 3.♔xc7 c3 4.h7 ♔xh7 5.♔d7 ♔g6 6.♔e6 c2 7.f7 c1=♕ 8.f8=♕ ♕e3+! 9.♔d7 ♕a7+ 10.♔c6 ♕a6+ 11.♔c7 ♕a7+, and perpetual check.

1...♔xh7 2.♔b5 ♔g6 3.♔c6 ♔f7! 4.f4! ♔g6! 5.♔xc7! d5 6.♔d6! (a Reti maneuver) **6...dxc4 7.♔e7** (or 7.♔e6) winning. For example: 7...c3

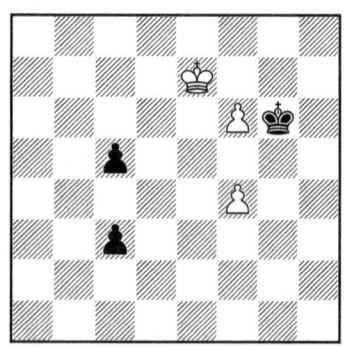

8.f7 (or 8.f5+) 8...c2 9.f8=♕ c1=♕ 10.♕g8+ (the quickest way to win) 10...♔h6 11.♕g5+ ♔h7 12.♔f8, curtains.

While **6...♔xf6** loses to **7.♔xd5** and a victory march by the c4-pawn.

No. 386. Here, the author wanted to express the idea of triple capture avoidance: **1.♔c5 d4! 2.♔c4! d3 3.♔c3 c5 4.h4 c4 5.h5 ♚a3 6.h6** with a win.

To find a side solution, you should remember **Study 84** and play in a similar way: **2.♔xd4 ♚b4 3.h4 c5+ 4.♔e3! ♚b3! 5.h5 c4 6.h6 c3 7.h7 c2 8.♔d2! ♚b2 9.h8=♕+** with a win.

It's impossible to correct this study with simple methods and techniques of study composition. Nevertheless, the Georgian study composer Makhatadze introduced some constructive changes to the position. And even though he only managed to execute a double capture avoidance, his study won the top prize at the all-Union competition of the *Chervony Girnik* (Kryvyi Rih) newspaper.

No. 386a. D. Makhatadze
Chervony Girnik, 1986
1st prize

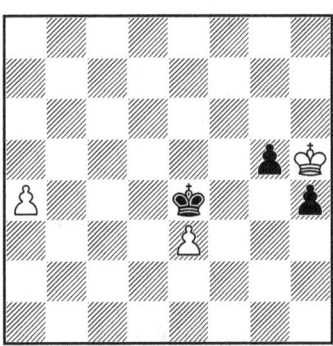

White to play and win

1.♔g4 h3 2.♔g3! g4 3.a5 ♚xe3 4.a6 h2 5.♔g2! with a win.

But this study also had a flaw! **2.♔xh3! ♚f3 3.a5 g4+ 4.♔h4 g3 5.a6 g2 6.a7 g1=♕ 7.a8=♕+ ♚f2 8.♕a2+! ♚f3 9.♕d5+ ♚f2 10.♕f5+ ♚e2 11.e4,**

and white gradually converts his extra pawn.

To eliminate this flaw, Alain Pallier proposed adding a black pawn on g7 – see **Study 386b**.

No. 386b**. D. Makhatadze
Chervony Girnik, 1986
1st prize
(correction)

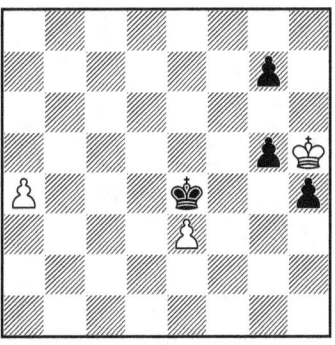

White to play and win

No. 387. Solution: **1.♔c4 b5+ 2.♔c3 b4+ 3.♔c4 b3 4.axb3#.**

Duals are already possible on the very first move, because both 1.♔c4 and 1.♔c6! win. And on the second move, white can play both 2.♔c3 and 2.♔c5!

Thankfully, the correction is easy in this case: simply put the white king on d6 or d7, if the composer wishes to — like in **Study 167**.

No. 388. Author's solution: **1.h5 ♚e6 2.h6! ♚f7 3.h7 ♚g7 4.g6 ♚h8 5.♔a5 ♚g7 6.♔b4 a6 7.♔c5 a5 8.♔c4! ♚h8 9.♔d4 a4 10.♔e5 a3 11.♔f6 a2 12.g7+** with inevitable mate.

Duals: 7.♔c4! a5 8.♔c5 etc. Or 7.♔b3! a5 8.♔c4. To eliminate this flaw, the solution should be shortened, as Grigoriev himself did in **Study 180**.

No. 389. The author's idea: **1.♔e5 ♕b6 2.♔d6! ♔a7 3.♔c7 b5 4.d5 b4 5.d6 b3 6.d7 b2 7.d8=♕ b1=♕ 8.♕d4+ ♔a6 9.♕a4#.** Here, the move transposition looks quite unsightly: white can play 3.d5 and then 4.♔c7. But first, try to solve the following position:

No. 389a. L. Prokes
Rude Pravo, 1950

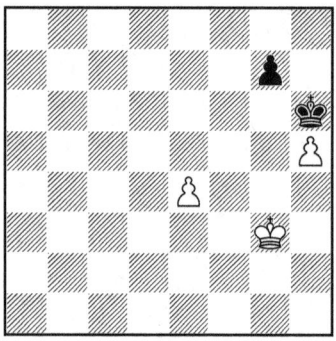

White to play and win

1.♔f4! (1.♔g4? g6!) **1...♔xh5 2.♔f5! ♔h6! 3.e5 ♔h7 4.♔e6! g5 5.♔f7! g4 6.e6 g3 7.e7 g2 8.e8=♕ g1=♕ 9.♕e4+ ♔h6 10.♕h4#.**

So, no move transpositions at all in this version! Van Tets probably just didn't know about Prokes' earlier study.

No. 390. The decisive move is **1.♔b5! ♔xa7.** 1...h4 2.♔a6 h3 3.b5 etc. even loses. Or 1...♔b7 2.a8=♕+ ♔xa8 3.♔c6 h4 (3...♔b8 4.♔d5) 4.♔c7 h3 5.b5 hxg2 6.b6 g1=♕ 7.b7+ ♔a7 8.b8=♕+ ♔a6 9.♕b7+, and black cannot win.

2.♔c6! ♔b8 3.♔d5 h4 4.♔e4, draw.

Here is the improved version:

No. 390a. T. Dawson
The Chess Amateur, 1924
(Version by M. Zinar, 1990)

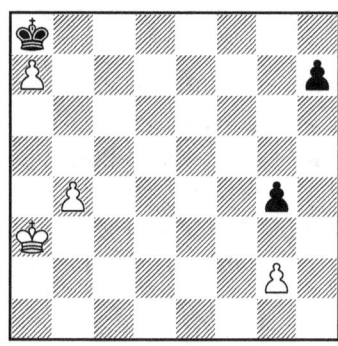

White to play and draw

In this case, the solution begins **1.♔a4! h5,** and then like in the original study. The Reti maneuver is used in conjunction with the roundabout way here.

No. 391. Author's solution: **1.♔d5! ♔g8.** Or 1...b3 2.♔e6 bxa2 3.f7, draw.

2.♔c4 ♔f7 3.d4 cxd4 4.♔xb4 d3! 5.♔c3 ♔xf6 6.♔xd3 ♔f5 7.♔e3 ♔e5 8.♔f3! False try: 8.♔d3? ♔f4 9.♔e2 ♔g3 10.♔e3 ♔xh3 11.♔f3 ♔h2 12.♔f2 h3, curtains.

8...♔d4 9.♔f4 (9.♔f2 is also possible) **9...♔c3 10.♔e3 ♔b2 11.♔d2 ♔xa2 12.♔c2** with a draw.

In this case, two moves can be added to the introduction thanks to the Reti maneuver:

No. 391a. N. Grigoriev
Shakhmatny Listok, 1924
(Version by M. Zinar, 1990)

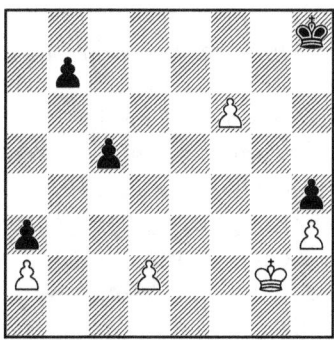

White to play and draw

The introductory play goes like this:
1.♔f3! b5 2.♔e4! b4, and now following the actual play – **3.♔d5! ♚g8 4.♔c4** etc.

No. 392. Unfortunately, the play in this study cannot be significantly extended – the starting position can only be modified in a minor way.

No. 392a. A. Selezniev
Pravda, 1927
(Version by M. Zinar, 1979)

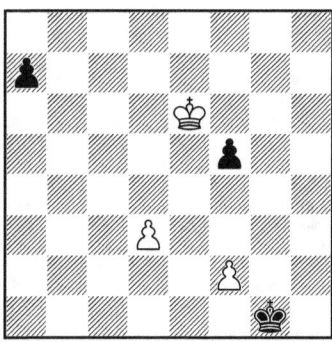

White to play and win

At first we thought that this version would work. The winning move was **1.f4!**

But not 1.♔xf5? a5 2.♔e4 a4 3.♔d4 ♔xf2 with a draw. Or 1.d4? a5 2.♔d5 ♔xf2, again with equality.
1...♔f2! 2.d4! a5 3.♔d5 ♔e3 4.♔c4! etc.

Alas, this version failed to withstand the test of time. White also wins with 2.♔xf5 ♔e3 3.d4!! a5 (3...♔xd4 4.♔e6 a5 5.f5 a4 6.f6 a3 7.f7 a2 8.f8=♕ a1=♕ 9.♕g7+) 4.d5 a4 5.d6 a3 6.d7 a2 7.d8=♕ a1=♕ 8.♕b6+ ♔f3 9.♕b3+ ♔e2 10.♕d5, then slowly pushing the second pawn to promotion.

The solution can be extended by moving the black king to e1.

No. 392b**. A. Selezniev
Pravda, 1927
(Version by S. Tkachenko)

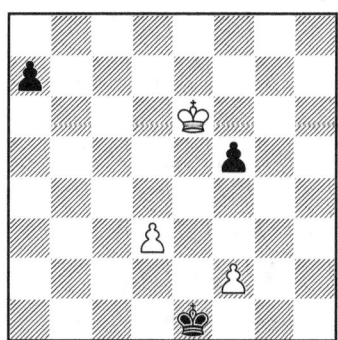

White to play and win

1.f4! a5 2.♔d5 ♔e2 3.♔c4! Not 3.d4? ♔d3!, shouldering the white king.
3...♔e3 4.d4! etc.

No. 393. The solution: **1.b4 ♔xh3 2.♔f1 ♔h2.** Or 2...♔g3 3.b5 h3 4.♔g1 h2+ 5.♔h1 ♔f2 6.a6 bxa6 7.bxa6, curtains.
3.b5 h3 4.a6 ♔h1! 5.a7 h2 6.a8=♖! with a win, because there's no stalemate

with the pinned pawn, while 6...b6 is met with 7.♖a5!

Here's what can be done to eliminate a pawn: put the black king on h3 instead of the pawn, and move the h4 pawn back one rank.

No. 393a. A. Troitsky
The Chess Amateur, 1917
(Version by M. Zinar, 1990)

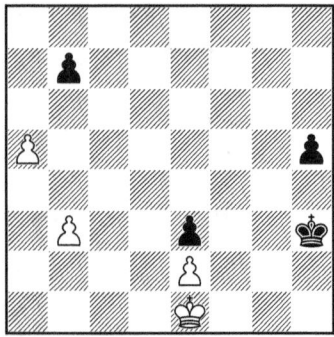

White to play and win

1.♔f1! ♔h2 2.b4 h4 3.b5 etc.

No. 394. Author's solution: **1.h4 ♔d5 2.c4+! ♔e5 3.c5 ♔f5 4.♔d3(d2) ♔g4 5.♔c4(c3) ♔xh4 6.♔b4 ♔g5 7.♔a5 ♔f6**

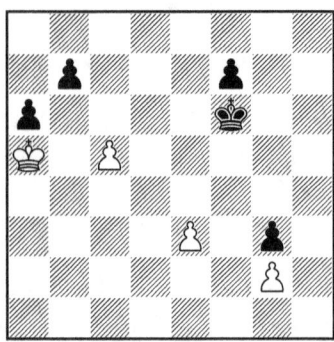

8.♔b6 a5 9.♔xb7 a4 10.c6 a3 11.c7 a2 12.c8=♕ a1=♕ 13.♕h8+ with a win.

The duals can be eliminated rather easily – by putting the white king on e1. And two pawns are eliminated in the same way as was done in **Study 299**.

No. 395. The pawns are necessary, because otherwise there's an obvious, bland draw on the board. The a5 and a6 pawns cannot be simply removed – then black will win even after the most persistent struggle by trading queens.

The exercise is very difficult because it's hard to push the b4-b5 pawns to the back ranks due to white's new resource: 1.♔d6 ♔g3 2.f4 ♔xf4 3.♔c6 with a draw.

The pawns cannot be unblocked because the opposition ♔g8–♔g3 is a mutual zugzwang!

Finally, the a1-h8 and a2-g8 diagonals cannot be blocked. It seems that we have hit a dead end, and the exercise is unsolvable. But no: we can put pawns on b2 and a4!

No. 395a. A. Botokanov
Shakhmaty v SSSR, 1986
Commendation
(Version by M. Zinar, 1990)

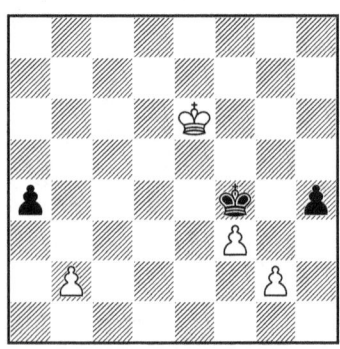

White to play and draw

The solution is the same (see **Study**

135), because 2.♔g7? ♔xg2 3.f4 is met with 3...a3! 4.bxa3 h3 5.f5 h2 6.f6 h1=♕ 7.f7 ♕a1+ 8.♔g8 ♕a2 9.a4 ♔g3, and black wins.

Later, Zinar used the same scheme to compose an interesting logical spectacle, **Study 395b**.

No. 395b**. M. Zinar
Z. Birnov memorial, 2013
Honorable mention

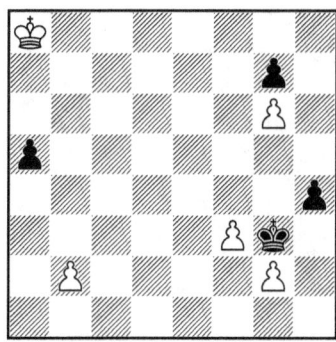

White to play and draw

1.♔b8!! Not the immediate 1.♔a7? a4! 2.♔b6 ♔xg2 3.f4 h3 4.f5 a3 5.bxa3 h2 6.f6 h1=♕ 7.fxg7 ♕b1+, and the black queen easily eliminates the white pawns.

1...a4. Or 1...♔xg2 2.f4 h3 3.f5 h2 4.f6 h1=♕ 5.fxg7 ♕h2+ 6.♔b7, draw.

2.♔a7! Black is in zugzwang!

2...♔xg2 3.f4 h3 4.f5 a3 5.bxa3 h2 6.f6 h1=♕ 7.fxg7 ♕g1+ 8.♔a8!, returning to the initial square. Draw.

Interestingly enough, the mechanism of this idea was actually "patented" back in 1968!

No. 395c**. V. Evreinov
64, 1968
2nd prize

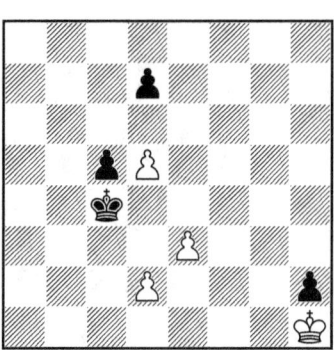

White to play and draw

1.d6! Protecting the pawn doesn't work: 1.e4? ♔d4 2.d3 c4! 3.dxc4 ♔xc4 4.♔xh2 ♔d4 5.♔g3 ♔xe4 6.d6 ♔e5 7.♔f3 ♔xd6 8.♔e4 ♔c5, curtains.

1...♔d3 2.♔g2!! Capture avoidance that ensures a favorable mutual zugzwang position! After 2.♔xh2? c4 3.♔g2 ♔xd2 4.e4 c3 5.e5 c2 6.e6 c1=♕ 7.exd7 ♕c6+!, black wins.

2...c4 (2...h1=♕+ 3.♔xh1 c4 4.♔h2! etc.) **3.♔xh2!** Mutual zugzwang!

3...♔xd2 4.e4 c3 5.e5 c2 6.e6 c1=♕ 7.exd7! Draw.

Evreinov's discovery provided the foundation for **Study 395d**.

No. 395d**. Y. Gordian
Ukrainian team championship, 2011
6th–7th place

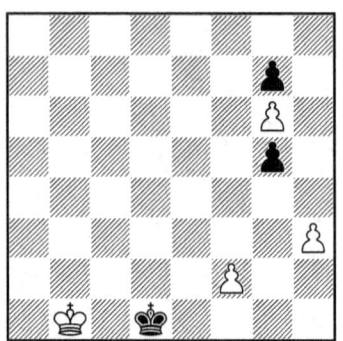

White to play and draw

1.♔a2!! Logical false try: 1.♔b2? ♔e2 2.f4 gxf4 3.h4 f3 4.h5 f2 5.h6 f1=♕ 6.hxg7 ♕f6+, and the pawn island is ruined. 2.♔c3 (instead of 2.f4) doesn't save white either: 2...♔xf2 3.♔d4 ♔g3 4.♔e5 ♔xh3 5.♔e6 g4 6.♔f7 g3 7.♔xg7 g2 8.♔h7 g1=♕ 9.g7 ♕a7, curtains.

1...♔e1! 2.f3!! The tortoise move that lures the black king to the second rank.

2...♔e2! If 2...♔d2, then 3.♔b3! works: 3...♔e3 4.♔c4 ♔xf3 5.♔d5 ♔g3 6.♔e6 ♔xh3 7.♔f7 g4 8.♔xg7 g3 9.♔f7 g2 10.g7 g1=♕ 11.g8=♕, just in time!

3.f4! gxf4 4.h4 f3 5.h5 f2 6.h6 f1=♕ 7.hxg7, and the pawn island is unbreakable. Draw.

No. 396. Yes it can, but the solution becomes somewhat less sharp. Look at this position, for instance. Notice that it features three (!) fewer pawns.

No. 396a. A. Belyavsky
USSR Central Chess Club Bulletin, 1981
(Version by M. Zinar, 1990)

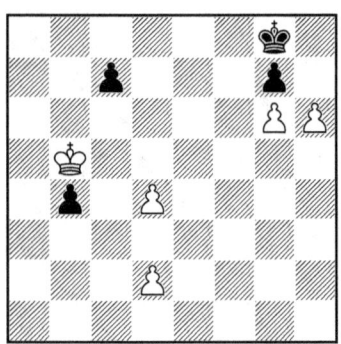

White to play and win

The solution: **1.h7+ ♔h8 2.♔a4!** But not 2.♔c4? due to 2...b3 3.♔c3 b2 4.♔c2 c6! (zugzwang) 5.d3 c5 6.d5 c4 7.d6 cxd3+ 8.♔xb2 d2, draw.

2...b3 3.♔a3! b2 4.♔a2! c6! 5.d3! c5 6.d5 c4 7.d6 c3 8.d7 b1=♕+ 9.♔xb1 c2+ 10.♔a2 c1=♕ 11.d8=♕#.

Afterword — Some Final Tips

Dear reader! Our small set of exercises has brought you into the creative laboratory of a pawn study composer. And now, we offer you some practical advice.

To become a good study composer, you should improve your over-the-board playing skills. The stronger you are as a player, the easier it is to analyze and find defects and hidden resources in the position.

Study the classical legacy closely, follow current study publication trends, analyze them thoroughly and evaluate them objectively. It's advisable to keep a database of your chosen study genres or themes. This will help you to develop your artistic taste and aesthetic views.

Improve your technical skills — to do this, we recommend you to seek and eliminate flaws in endgame studies or rework known ideas.

After you compose an endgame study, do not immediately submit it for publication or competition. Give it some time to "mature", and then analyze it thoroughly again, checking for potential new flaws.

Learn to wait patiently! Do not lose heart after your first setbacks: in chess composition, like in figure skating, it's important to make your name familiar to the judges.

When you evaluate someone else's studies and interact with other composers (most likely by correspondence), be tolerant of their creative views, even if they are the total opposite of yours.

A very simple tip: your submission should be well-designed. First impressions are always important!

The authors hope that this book will help many enthusiasts take their first steps in chess composition — and maybe a future heir of the King of Pawn Endgames, Nikolai Dmitrievich Grigoriev, will be among them.

We wish you many creative successes!

Index of Studies by Author

(Bracketed numbers indicate co-composed studies or endgames
of over-the-board games)